Recent Developments in Cointegration

Special Issue Editor

Katarina Juselius

MDPI • Basel • Beijing • Wuhan • Barcelona • Belgrade

Special Issue Editor
Katarina Juselius
University of Copenhagen
Denmark

Editorial Office
MDPI
St. Alban-Anlage 66
Basel, Switzerland

This edition is a reprint of the Special Issue published online in the open access journal *Econometrics* (ISSN 2225-1146) from 2016–2018 (available at: http://www.mdpi.com/journal/econometrics/special_issues/cointegration).

For citation purposes, cite each article independently as indicated on the article page online and as indicated below:

Lastname, F.M.; Lastname, F.M. Article title. *Journal Name* **Year**, *Article number*, page range.

First Editon 2018

ISBN 978-3-03842-955-5 (Pbk)
ISBN 978-3-03842-956-2 (PDF)

Table of Contents

About the Special Issue Editor

Katarina Juselius, Professor Emerita at the University of Copenhagen, has been a visiting professor at numerous universities around the world, led eight large research projects, and served on the editorial board of several scientific journals. She has published more than one hundred articles in international journals and given several hundred lectures and seminars. She has taught numerous PhD courses and organized a series of summer schools on the Cointegrated VAR model and its methodology. She has been a member of the Danish Research Council for Social Sciences and the chairperson of the EuroCore and Forward Look Programmes of the European Science Foundation. She has also been dubbed a knight by the Queen of Denmark and is a member of the Danish Royal Society of Sciences and Letters. In the period of 1990–2000 she was number eight among the most cited economists in the world.

Preface to "Recent Developments in Cointegration"

As an empirical econometrician, I have always strongly believed in the power of analyzing statistical models as a scientifically viable way of learning from observed data. In the aftermath of the great recession, this seems more important than ever. Most economic and econometric models in macroeconomics and finance did not seem well geared to address features in the data of key importance for this crisis. In particular, the long persistent movements away from long-run equilibrium values typical of the pre-crisis period seem crucial in this respect. Because of this, I hoped that the papers submitted to this Special Issue would use cointegration to address these important issues, for example by applying cointegration to models with self-reinforcing feed-back mechanisms, or by deriving new tests motivated by such empirical applications, or by dealing with near integration in the I(1) and I(2) models. Without a doubt, the outcome has surpassed my most optimistic expectations. This Special Issue contains excellent contributions structured around several interconnected themes, most of them addressing the abovementioned issues in one way or the other. While some of the papers are predominantly theoretical and others are mainly empirical, all of them represent a good mixture of theory and application. The theoretical papers solve problems motivated by empirical work and the empirical papers address problems using valid statistical procedures. In this sense, the collection of articles represents econometric modeling at its best. As the guest editor, I feel both proud and grateful to be presenting an issue containing so many high-quality research papers.

The high quality of the articles is to a significant degree a result of detailed, insightful, and very useful referee reports. I would like to take the opportunity to express a deeply felt gratitude to all the reviewers who have invested their precious time to check and improve the quality of the articles. Your efforts made all the difference.

Katarina Juselius
Special Issue Editor

econometrics

MDPI

Editorial

Recent Developments in Cointegration

Katarina Juselius

Department of Economics, University of Copenhagen, DK-1353 Copenhagen, Denmark; katarina.juselius@econ.ku.dk

Received: 25 December 2017; Accepted: 28 December 2017; Published: 31 December 2017

How to link a theoretical model with empirical evidence in a scientifically valid way is a tremendously difficult task that has been debated as long as economics and econometrics have existed. The dilemma facing an empirical economist/econometrician is that there are many economic models but only one economic reality: which of the models should be chosen? Rather than choosing one economic model and forcing it onto the data, the CVAR model structures the data based on the likelihood principle to obtain broad confidence intervals within which potentially relevant economic models should fall. This is consistent with the basic ideas of Trygve Haavelmo, who, with his Nobel Prize winning monograph "The Probability Approach to Economics", can be seen as the forefather of the modern likelihood-based approach to empirical economics. Juselius (2015) argues that the Cointegrated VAR model, by allowing for unit roots and cointegration, provides a solution to some of the statistical problems that Trygve Haavelmo struggled with. Hoover and Juselius (2015) argue that a theory-consistent CVAR scenario can be interpreted in terms of Haavelmo's notion of an "experimental design for data based on passive observations". A CVAR scenario translates all basic hypotheses of an economic model into a set of testable hypotheses describing empirical regularities in the form of long-run relations and common stochastic trends. A theoretical model that passes the first check of such basic properties is potentially an empirically relevant model. Also, because scenarios also can be formulated for competing models and then checked against data, they can be seen as a scientifically valid way of selecting the most empirically relevant economic model among available candidates. Examples of CVAR scenarios for a variety of standard economic models can be found in Juselius (2006, 2017) and Juselius and Franchi (2007).

To learn about the mechanisms that tend to generate crises, we need to develop methodological principles that can link economic models consistent with self-reinforcing adjustment behavior to the econometric model (here, the CVAR model). My own paper, "Using a Theory-Consistent CVAR Scenario to Test a Real Exchange Rate Model based on Imperfect Knowledge", is an attempt to do so. As such, it also works as a motivating introduction to the main themes of the Special Issue. It addresses the dilemma of unobserved expectations and the crucial role they play in economic models versus a CVAR model based on observable variables. A solution to this dilemma is obtained by introducing a rather weak assumption on the time-series property of the forecast shock, i.e. the deviation between the actual observation at time t and the expected value at time t + 1 made at time t. Given this assumption, the paper derives a theory-consistent CVAR scenario in which basic assumptions of an imperfect knowledge theory model are translated into testable hypotheses of the CVAR's common stochastic trends and cointegration relations. The derived scenario shows that under the assumption of imperfect knowledge expectations, the data are likely to be near I(2). This is because such expectations tend to drive prices away from long-run equilibrium states for extended periods of time and hence generate long persistent swings in the data. An application to the real exchange rate between Germany and the USA shows remarkable support for the derived scenario.

The I(2) model has a rich but also more complex structure than the I(1) model. In particular, the computational complexities behind the estimation of the various structures describing the long run, medium run, and short run are quite daunting. The paper by Jurgen Doornik entitled

"Maximum Likelihood Estimation of the I(2) Model under Linear Restrictions" discusses how to calculate ML estimates of the CVAR model for I(2) data both in its autoregressive and moving average representations. As the ML estimation of I(2) models always requires iteration, the paper discusses different algorithms and offers a new, so-called "triangular form" representation of the I(2) model. While it offers an efficient way of calculating the estimates, the triangular form represents a certain mathematical beauty on its own. The algorithm is implemented in the new software package CATS 3 in OxMetrics (Doornik and Juselius 2017) which allows for a full-fledged I(2) procedure that also calculates ML tests and estimates of the I(2) model under linear restrictions.

While the methods of estimating the different structures of the I(2) model are well-known, either unrestrictedly or subject to just-identifying restrictions, it is more difficult to derive tests of over-identifying restrictions on these structures. In particular, ML tests of over-identifying restrictions on the parameters of common trends are rare or nonexistent, whereas tests of certain non-identifying hypotheses on the common trends can be found. Common for the latter is that they imply the same restriction on the long-run beta structure and, hence, can easily be translated into hypotheses on the cointegration vectors. When the restrictions are over-identifying, it is much more challenging to derive such test procedures. The paper by Peter Boswijk and Paolo Paruolo entitled "Likelihood Ratio Tests of Restrictions on Common Trends Loading Matrices in I(2) VAR Systems" derives a new test for over-identifying restrictions on the common trends loading matrices in an I(2) model. It shows how a fairly complex over-identifying hypothesis on the common trends loadings matrix can be translated into hypotheses on the cointegration parameters, in addition to presenting an algorithm for (constrained) maximum likelihood estimation and providing a sketch of its asymptotic properties. As an illustration, the paper tests an imperfect knowledge hypothesis on the loadings of the common trends discussed in Juselius and Assenmacher (2017) motivated by an analysis of the PPP and UIP between Switzerland and the USA. The hypothesis did not obtain empirical support, implying that the original hypothesis has to be modified to some extent.

The recent theory of imperfect knowledge economics offers an economic framework for addressing certain features in the data, such as long persistent swings away from equilibrium values, which often are associated with financial behavior in asset markets. The paper by Leonardo Salazar entitled "Modeling Real Exchange Rate Persistence in Chile" takes as a starting point the long and persistent swings in the real Chilean dollar exchange rate and uses a monetary model based on imperfect knowledge economics as a theoretical explanation for this persistence. Applying the ideas of Juselius (this issue), he finds that the data cannot be rejected as I(2) and that the results support the hypothesis of error-increasing behavior in prices and interest rates. He finds that persistent movements in the real exchange rate are compensated by similar movements in the interest rate spread, a result that was also found in Juselius (this issue) as well as in Juselius (2006) and Juselius and Assenmacher (2017). However, in the present case the copper price was also needed to explain the deviations of the real exchange rate from its long-run equilibrium value.

Another field where expectations play an important role in price setting is in the housing market. This became painfully obvious when excessive movements in house prices kickstarted the worst recession since the Depression in the 1930s. The paper by Andreas Hetland and Simon Hetland, "Short-Term Expectation Formation Versus Long-Term Equilibrium Conditions: The Danish Housing Market", shows that the long-swings behavior observed in the market price of Danish housing can be understood by studying the interplay between short-term expectations and long-run equilibrium conditions. They introduce an asset market model for housing based on imperfect knowledge in which the demand for housing is affected by uncertainty rather than just risk. Under rather mild assumptions, this leads to other forms of forecasting behavior than usually found when assuming so-called rational expectations. The data were found to be I(2)-consistent with imperfect knowledge models. Using the I(2) cointegrated VAR model, they find that the long-run equilibrium for the housing price corresponds closely to the predictions from the theoretical model. The results of the paper corroborate previous findings that the housing market is well characterized by short-term momentum forecasting behavior.

However, the conclusions have even greater relevance since house prices (through wealth effects) often play an important role in the wider Danish economy, as well as in other developed economies.

Few economic models were able to foresee the great recession, which started a (sometimes heated) debate on the usefulness of standard economic models. Many economists argued that the great recession could not possibly have been predicted: it was a black swan. Many empirical econometricians were less convinced; the long and persistent imbalances had been all but invisible in the period preceding the crisis. Mikael Juselius and Moshe Kim demonstrate in their paper, "Sustainable Financial Obligations and Crisis Cycles", that an econometric model based on cointegration and smooth transition would have been able to foresee three of the most recent economic crises in USA: the savings and loans crisis in 1992, the IT-bobble crisis in 1995, and the great recession in 2008. In all three cases, the paper shows that the amount of credit losses in the household and the business sector exceeded the estimated sustainable debt level approximately 1–2 years before the recession started. This result is obtained by calculating the sustainable level of debt using the financial obligations ratio as a measure of the incipient aggregate liquidity constraint instead of the often used debt-income ratio. An interesting result is that the intensity of the interaction between credit losses and the business cycle was found to depend on whether the credit losses originate in the household or the business sector. For example, the savings and loans crisis originated primarily from losses in the private household sector, the IT crisis from the business sector, and the great recession from both the private and the business sectors. As excessive debt is often the main trigger of a financial crisis, exemplified by the recent crises, failure to foresee and prevent it is likely to cause a breakdown of economic stability. In this sense, the results have important implications for the design of macroprudential policy and countercyclical capital buffers.

Many economists correctly argue that true unit roots are implausible in economic data, as over the very long run this would lead to data properties that are generally not observed: economic data do not tend to move away from equilibrium values forever. This said, data often contain characteristic roots, which are so close to the unit circle that a standard unit root test would not be able to reject the null of unity. Juselius (in this issue) therefore argues that a unit root should not be considered a structural economic parameter (as is frequently done in the literature); rather, one should think of it as a statistical approximation that allows us to structure the data according to their persistency properties. The advantage is that inference can be made about the long run, the medium run, and the short run in the same model. Still, the question of how this affects the probability analysis of the CVAR model has to be addressed. The paper by Massimo Franchi and Søren Johansen entitled "Improved Inference on Cointegrating Vectors in the Presence of a near Unit Root Using Adjusted Quantiles" takes its starting point from the paper by Elliot (1998). The latter shows that correct inference on a cointegrating relation depends in a complex way on whether the model contains a near unit root trend or not, and that the test for a given cointegration vector may have rejection probabilities under the null that deviates from the nominal size by as much as 90%. The present paper extends previous results by Elliot (1998) by using a CVAR model with multiple near unit roots. It derives the asymptotic properties of the Gaussian maximum likelihood estimator and a test of a cointegrating relation in a model with a single near unit root using the two critical value adjustments suggested by McCloskey (2017). A simulation study shows that the latter eliminates the abovementioned serious size distortions and demonstrates that the test has reasonable power for relevant alternatives. By analyzing a number of different bivariate Data Generating Processes, the paper shows that the results are likely to hold more generally.

The focus of empirical work is often on estimating and identifying long-run cointegration relations, rather than common stochastic trends. The latter are intrinsically more difficult as common tends are usually assumed to be functions of unobserved structural shocks, whereas the estimated residuals are not structural as they tend to change every time a new variable is added to the model. In spite of the difficulty, it is of considerable interest to correctly identify the structural trends because they describe the exogenous forces pushing the economy. Failure to do so may lead to a plethora of interpretations often based on the same data. Since it is natural to estimate unobserved common trends based on unobserved components models, this is the starting point for the paper by Søren Johansen and Morten Nyboe Tabor, titled "Cointegration between Trends and Their Estimators in State Space Models and Cointegrated Vector Autoregressive Models". The state space model with an unobserved multivariate random walk and a linear observation equation is studied with the purpose of finding out under which conditions the extracted random walk trend cointegrates with its estimator. The criterion is that the difference between the two should be asymptotically stationary. The paper shows that this holds for the extracted trend given by the linear observation equation, but no longer holds when identifying restrictions are imposed on the trend coefficients in the observation equation. Only when the estimators of the coefficients in the observation equation are consistent at a faster rate than the square root of the sample size will there be cointegration between the identified trend and its estimator. The same results hold when data generated from the state space model are analyzed with a cointegrated vector autoregressive model. The findings are illustrated by a small simulation study.

While panel data models with cointegration are widely used, the role of the deterministic terms in the model is still open to debate. This is addressed in the paper by Uwe Hassler and Mehdi Hosseinkouchack, "Panel Cointegration Testing in the Presence of Linear Time Trends", which considers a class of panel tests of the null hypothesis of no cointegration when the data contain linear time trends. All tests under investigation rely on single equations estimated by least squares, and the tests are either residual-based or not. The focus is on test statistics computed from regressions with intercept only and with at least one of the regressors being dominated by a linear time trend. In such a setting, often encountered in practice, the limiting distributions and critical values provided for the case "with intercept only" are not correct. The paper demonstrates that this leads to size distortions growing with the panel size N. Moreover, it reports the appropriate distributions and shows how correct critical values are obtained.

Today, most econometric packages contain a cointegration routine that calculates estimates and test results using various kinds of algorithms. The more complex the model to be estimated, the more complex the algorithm to be used. Some algorithms may stop at local maxima, while others are more powerful in finding the global maximum. For an applied econometrician, it is a serious problem that the same model applied to the same data may give different results depending on the algorithm used. This is the motivation behind the paper by Jurgen Doornik, Rocco Mosconi, and Paolo Paruolo, titled "Formula I(1) and I(2): Race Tracks for Likelihood Maximization Algorithms of I(1) and I(2) Cointegrated VAR Models". It provides a number of test cases, called circuits, for the evaluation of Gaussian likelihood maximization algorithms of the cointegrated vector autoregressive model. Both I(1) and I(2) models are considered. The performance of algorithms is compared first in terms of effectiveness, defined as the ability to find the overall maximum. The next step is to compare their efficiency and reliability across experiments. The aim of the paper is to commence a collective learning project by the profession on the actual properties of algorithms for CVAR model estimation, in order to improve their quality and, as a consequence, the reliability of empirical research.

Conflicts of Interest: The authors declare no conflict of interest.

References

Elliott, Graham. 1998. On the robustness of cointegration methods when regressors almost have unit roots. *Econometrica* 66: 149–58. [CrossRef]

Doornik, Jurgen, and Katarina Juselius. 2017. *Cointegration Analysis of Time Series Using CATS 3 for OxMetrics*. Richmond: Timberlake Consultants Ltd.

Hoover, Kevin, and Katarina Juselius. 2015. Trygve Haavelmo'S Experimental Methodology and Scenario Analysis in a Cointegrated Vector Autoregression. *Econometric Theory* 31: 249–74. [CrossRef]

Juselius, Katarina. 2006. *The Cointegrated VAR Model*. Oxford: Oxford University Press.

Juselius, Katarina. 2015. Haavelmo's Probability Approach and the Cointegrated VAR model. *Econometric Theory* 31: 213–32. [CrossRef]

Juselius, Katarina. 2017. *A Theory-Consistent CVAR Scenario: Testing a Rational Expectations Based Monetary Model*. Working paper, Department of Economics, University of Copenhagen, Copenhagen, Denmark.
Juselius, Katarina, and Katrin Assenmacher. 2017. Real exchange rate persistence and the excess return puzzle: The case of Switzerland versus the US. *Journal of Applied Econometrics* 32: 1145–55. [CrossRef]
Juselius, Katarina, and Massimo Franchi. 2007. Taking a DSGE Model to the Data Meaningfully. *Economics-The Open-Access, Open-Assessment E-Journal* 1: 1–38. Available online: http://www.economics-ejournal.org/economics/journalarticles/2007-4 (accessed on 12 June 2017). [CrossRef]
McCloskey, Adam. 2017. Bonferroni-based size-correction for nonstandard testing problems. *Journal of Econometrics* 200: 17–35. Available online: http://www.sciencedirect.com/science/article/pii/S0304407617300556 (accessed on 12 June 2017). [CrossRef]

econometrics

MDPI

Article

Using a Theory-Consistent CVAR Scenario to Test an Exchange Rate Model Based on Imperfect Knowledge

Katarina Juselius

Department of Economics, University of Copenhagen, DK-1353 Copenhagen K, Denmark; katarina.juselius@econ.ku.dk; Tel.: +45-35323068

Academic Editor: Marc S. Paolella
Received: 1 March 2017; Accepted: 22 June 2017; Published: 7 July 2017

Abstract: A theory-consistent CVAR scenario describes a set of testable regularieties one should expect to see in the data if the basic assumptions of the theoretical model are empirically valid. Using this method, the paper demonstrates that all basic assumptions about the shock structure and steady-state behavior of an an imperfect knowledge based model for exchange rate determination can be formulated as testable hypotheses on common stochastic trends and cointegration. This model obtaines remarkable support for almost every testable hypothesis and is able to adequately account for the long persistent swings in the real exchange rate.

Keywords: theory-consistent CVAR; imperfect Knowledge; theory-based expectations; international puzzles; long swings; persistence

JEL Classification: F31; F41; G15; G17

1. Introduction

International macroeconomics is known for its many pricing puzzles, including the purchasing power parity (PPP) puzzle, the exchange rate disconnect puzzle, and the forward rate puzzle. The basic problem stems from an inability of standard models based on the rational expectations hypothesis (REH) to account for highly persistent deviations from PPP and uncovered interest parity (UIP). See Engel (2014) and references therein for studies on REH and behavioral models.

Figure 1 illustrates the long swings in the nominal and the real exchange rate that have puzzled economists for decades. The upper panel shows relative prices for the USA and Germany together with the nominal Deutshemark/Dollar rate for the post-Bretton Woods, pre-EMU period. While both series exhibit a similar upward sloping trend defining the long-run fundamental value of the nominal exchange rate, the nominal exchange rate fluctuates around the relative price with long persistent swings. The lower panel shows that the persistent long swings in the real exchange rate (deviation from the PPP) seem to almost coincide with similar long swings in the real interest rate differential.

The theory of imperfect-knowledge-based economics (IKE) developed in Frydman and Goldberg (2007, 2011) shows that the pronounced persistence in the data may stem from forecasting behavior of rational individuals who must cope with imperfect knowledge. Frydman et al. (2008) argues that the persistent swings in the exchange rate around long-run benchmark values are consistent with such forecasting behavior.

Hommes et al. (2005a, 2005b) develops models for a financial market populated by fundamentalists and chartists where fundamentalists use long-term expectations based on economic fundamentals and chartists are trend-followers using short-term expectations. Positive feedback prevails when the latter dominate the market. In these models agents switch endogenously between a mean-reverting fundamentalist and a trend-following chartist strategy. For a detailed overview, see Hommes (2006).

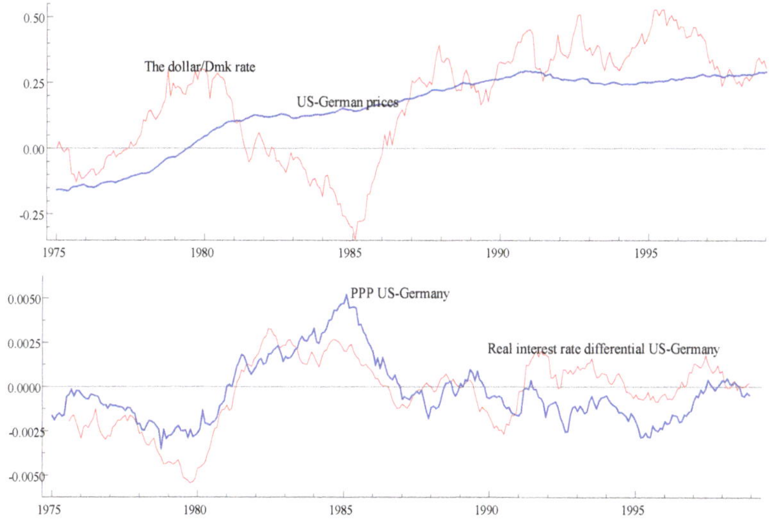

Figure 1. The graphs of the (mean and range adjusted) German-US price differential and the nominal exchange rate (upper panel), and the deviation from purchasing power parity and the real bond rate differential (lower panel).

Consistent with the above theories, Figure 1 shows that there are two very persistent trends in the data, the upward sloping trend in relative prices and the long persistent swings in the nominal exchange rate. It also suggests that the long swings in the real exchange rate and the real interest rate differential are related. Juselius (2009) shows empirically that it is not possible to control for the persistence in the real exchange rate without bringing the interest rates into the analysis.

But, while a graphical analysis can support intuition, it cannot replace hypotheses testing. To be convincing, testing needs to be carried out in the context of a fully specified statistical model. Juselius (2006, 2015) argues that a well-specified Cointegrated Vector AutoRegression (CVAR) model is an approximate description of the data generating process and, therefore, an obvious candidate for such a model. Hoover et al. (2008) argues that the CVAR allows the data to speak freely about the mechanisms that have generated the data. But, since the empirical and the theoretical model represent two different entities, a bridging principle is needed. A so called theory-consistent CVAR scenario (Juselius 2006; Juselius and Franchi 2007; Moller 2008) offers such a principle. It does so by translating basic assumptions underlying the theoretical model into testable hypotheses on the pulling and pushing forces of a CVAR model. One may say that such a scenario describes a specified set of testable empirical regularities one should expect to see in the data if the basic assumptions of the theoretical model were empirically valid. A theoretical model that passes the first check of such basic properties is potentially an empirically relevant model. M. Juselius (2010) demonstrates this for a new Keynesian Phillips curve model. Hoover and Juselius (2015) argues that it may represent a designed experiment for data obtained by passive observations in the sense of Haavelmo (1994).

The purpose of this paper is to derive a CVAR scenario for exchange rate determination assuming expectations are formed in the context of imperfect knowledge. The CVAR model is applied to German-US exchange rate data over the post-Bretton Woods, pre-EMU period which is characterized by pronounced persistence from long-run equilibrium states. The empirical results provide remarkable support for essentially every single testable hypothesis of the imperfect knowledge based scenario.

The paper is organized as follows: Section 2 discusses principles underlying a theory-consistent CVAR scenario, Section 3 introduces an imperfect knowledge based monetary model for exchange rate determination, Section 4 discusses how to anchor expectations to observable variables and derives their time-series properties. Section 5 reports a theory-consistent CVAR scenario, Section 6 introduces the empirical CVAR model, Section 7 tests the order of integration of individual variables/relations and Section 8 reports an identified structure of long-run relations strongly supporting the empirical relevance of imperfect knowledge and self-reinforcing feed-back behavior. Section 9 concludes.

2. Formulating a Theory-Consistent CVAR Scenario[1]

The basic idea of a CVAR scenario analysis is to derive persistency properties of variables and relations that are theoretically consistent and compare these with observed magnitudes measured by the order of integration, such as $I(0)$ for a highly stationary process, $I(1)$ or near $I(1)$ for a first order persistent process, and $I(2)$ or near $I(2)$ for a second order persistent process.[2] One may argue that it is implausible that economic variables move away from their equilibrium values for infinite times and, hence, that most economic relations should be classified as either stationary, *near* $I(1)$ or *near* $I(2)$. But this does not exclude the possibility that over finite samples they exhibit a persistence that is indistinguishable from a unit root or a double unit root process. In this sense the classification of variables into single or double unit roots should be seen as a useful way of classifying the data into more homogeneous groups. For a detailed discussion, see Juselius (2012).

Unobservable expectations are often a crucial part of a theoretical model, whereas the empirical regularities to be uncovered by a CVAR analysis are based on the observed data. Therefore, what we need to do is to derive the persistency property of the *forecast shock*, $f_t = x_t - x^e_{t+1|t}$, as a measure of how the persistency of expectations differ compared to the observed variables. This differs from most work on expectations in economic models where the focus is on *forecast errors* rather than, as here, on *forecast shocks*.

In the discussion below we find it useful to distinguish between the forecast of asset prices for which expectations are crucial and real economy variables, such as consumer goods inflation and real growth rates, for which expectations may matter but only in a subordinate way. The ideas are illustrated with simple examples.

Case 1. Let x_t be an asset price integrated of order one, for example, $x_t = x_{t-1} + \varepsilon_t$ where ε_t is a stationary uncorrelated error. A consistent forecasting rule is formulated as

$$x^e_{t+1|t} = x_t + f_t, \tag{1}$$

where $x^e_{t+1|t}$ denotes the expected value of x_{t+1} formulated at time t and f_t is a forecast shock that may be uncorrelated or correlated over time. The latter is likely to be relevant in an imperfect knowledge economy, where agents may not know whether the random walk model specification is correct or stable over time. For this reason they would be inclined to use all kinds of forecasting rules, such as technical trading rules. Expectations are assumed to influence outcomes, so

$$x_t = x^e_{t|t-1} + \varepsilon_t, \tag{2}$$

where ε_t is an unanticipated forecast error. Inserting (2) in (1) leads to

$$x^e_{t+1|t} = x^e_{t|t-1} + \varepsilon_t + f_t, \tag{3}$$

1 This section is an adaptation of Section 2 in Juselius (2017) where it is used to discuss a rational-expectations-based monetary model.

2 A highly persistent process is one for which a characteristic root is either close to or on the unit circle. See for example (Elliot 1998; Franchi and Johansen 2017) for a theoretical treatment.

showing that the forecast change depends on the most recent forecast error, ε_t, and the forecast shock, f_t. An expression for the data-generating process can be found by inserting $x^e_{t|t-1} = x_{t-1} + f_{t-1}$ in (2)

$$x_t = x_{t-1} + f_{t-1} + \varepsilon_t, \tag{4}$$

i.e., change in the process depends on the previous forecast shock, f_{t-1}, and the forecast error, ε_t.

Now, a "rational expectations" agent, knowing that the random walk is the true model will choose $f_t = 0$. According to (3), the expectations will then follow a random walk and x_t will continue to follow the same model. In a "rational expectations" economy expectations do not change the process x_t.

An "imperfect knowledge" agent, on the other hand, does not necessarily believe there is a true data-generating model. If, instead, he is a chartist then his forecast shocks will tend to be systematically positive/negative depending on whether the market is bullish or bearish. The process x_t will become a random walk with a time-varying drift term, f_{t-1}. If the latter is persistent then x_t may ultimately become *near* $I(2)$. Thus, the variable x_t may be a random walk in a period of regulation when speculative behavior is not a dominant feature and become a *near* $I(2)$ process after deregulation. As another example, let's assume that an imperfect knowledge trader chooses $f_t = \varepsilon_t$, i.e., the forecast shock for the next period's forecast is chosen to be equal to the realized forecast error at time t. In this case, the process will become $x_t = x_{t-1} + \varepsilon_{t-1} + \varepsilon_t$ and the variance of the process Δx_t will be twice as large as the pure random walk. But, given (3) and (4), the forecast error will nonetheless be equal to a random noise, ε_t. Hence, when actual outcomes are influenced by the forecasts, traders in an imperfect knowledge economy may not be making systematic forecast errors in spite of their imperfect knowledge. This is because expectations are likely to change the data-generating process both of x_t and $x^e_{t+1|t}$.

Case 2. Let x_t be an asset price described by (4) where f_t is a very persistent forecast shock. Such a shock can be assumed to be positive when the market is bullish and negative when it is bearish and may be approximated with a first order autoregressive model with a time-varying coefficient $f_t = \rho_t f_{t-1} + \varepsilon_{f,t}$. Juselius (2014) discusses the case where the average of ρ_t, $\bar{\rho}$, is close to 1 and $Var(\varepsilon_{f,t}) \ll Var(\varepsilon_t)$. In this case x_t is integrated of order near $I(2)$, Δx_t contains a near unit root due to the drift term f_t, but this drift term is hardly discernible when the variance of ε_t is much larger than the variance of $\varepsilon_{f,t}$.

A consistent forecasting rule is $x^e_{t+1|t} = x_t + f_t$, so the forecast shock, $f_t = x^e_{t+1|t} - x_t$, is a persistent (*near*) $I(1)$ process. [3]

Case 3. Let x_t be a "real economy" variable integrated of order $I(2)$. The simplest example of an $I(2)$ model is $x_t = x_{t-1} + \Delta x_{t-1} + \varepsilon_t$, in which a consistent forecasting rule is $x^e_{t+1|t} = x_t + \Delta x_t$, so the forecast shock $f_t = x^e_{t+1|t} - x_t = \Delta x_t$ is $I(1)$. Given this assumption, expectations do not change the data-generating process for x_t:

$$x_t = x^e_{t|t-1} + \varepsilon_t = x_{t-1} + \Delta x_{t-1} + \varepsilon_t. \tag{5}$$

The data-generating process for expectations becomes:

$$\begin{aligned} x^e_{t+1|t} &= x^e_{t|t-1} + \Delta x_t + \varepsilon_t, \\ &= x^e_{t|t-1} + \Delta x^e_{t|t-1} + \varepsilon_t + \Delta\varepsilon_t, \end{aligned}$$

showing that expectations also follow an $I(2)$ model, but now with a moving average error.

[3] Juselius (2012) showed for simulated data that the drift term can be quite precisely estimated by a moving average of Δx_t of suitable length.

Even though a variable such as a consumer price index may not in general be subject to speculation, in an imperfect knowledge economy it may nonetheless be indirectly affected by speculative movements in asset prices. This would be the case if there is a two-way interdependency between fundamentals and asset prices owing to self-fulfilling expectations in the financial market.[4] For example, when speculation in foreign currency leads to long persistent swings in the nominal exchange rate, prices are also likely to be affected. See Juselius (2012) for an extended discussion. This means that ε_t in (5) may be affected by forecast shocks in financial markets.

Assumption A exploits these simple ideas:

Assumption A When $x_t \sim I(1)$, $(x^e_{t+1|t} - x_t) = f_t$ is assumed to be $I(0)$, when $x_t \sim$ near $I(2)$ it is assumed to be near $I(1)$ and when $x_t \sim I(2)$ it is assumed to be $I(1)$.

Note that Assumption A disregards $x_t \sim I(3)$, as it is considered empirically implausible, and $x_t \sim I(0)$, as it defines a non-persistent process for which cointegration and stochastic trends have no informational value.

Note also that $x_t \sim I(1)$ implies that $\Delta x_t \sim I(0)$, whereas $x_t \sim I(2)$ implies that $\Delta x_t \sim I(1)$ and $\Delta^2 x_t \sim I(0)$. Given Assumption A, we have that:

Corollary When $x_t \sim I(1)$, x_t, x_{t+1} and $x^e_{t+1|t}$ share the same common stochastic trend of order $I(1)$, i.e., they have the same persistency property. When $x_t \sim I(2)$ or near $I(2)$, Δx_t, Δx_{t+1} and Δx^e_{t+1} share the same common stochastic $I(1)$ trend, i.e., they have the same persistency property.

Consequently, when $x_t \sim I(1)$, $\beta' x_t$, has the same persistency property as $\beta' x^e_{t+1|t}$ or $\beta' x_{t+1}$. When $x_t \sim I(2)$, $\beta' x_t + d' \Delta x_t$ has the same order of integration as $\beta' x_t + d' \Delta x^e_{t+1|t}$ and $\tau' \Delta x_t$ has the same order of integration as $\tau' \Delta x^e_{t+1|t}$ and $\tau' \Delta x_{t+1}$.[5] Thus, Assumption A allows us to make valid inference about a long-run equilibrium relation in a theoretical model even though the postulated behavior is a function of expected rather than observed outcomes.

Based on the above, the steps behind a theory-consistent CVAR scenario can be formulated as follows:

1. Express the expectations variable(s) as a function of observed variables. For example, according to Uncovered Interest Rate Parity (UIP), the expected change in the nominal exchange rate is equal to the interest rate differential. Hence, the persistency property of the latter is also a measure of the persistency property of the unobservable expected change in nominal exchange rate and can, therefore, be empirically tested.
2. For a given order of integration of the unobserved expectations variable and of the forecast shocks, f_t, derive the theory-consistent order of integration for all remaining variables and for the postulated behavioral relations of the system.
3. Translate the stochastically formulated theoretical model into a theory-consistent CVAR scenario by formulating the basic assumptions underlying the theoretical model as a set of testable hypotheses on cointegration relations and common trends.
4. Estimate a well-specified VAR model and check the empirical adequacy of the derived theory-consistent CVAR scenario.

3. Imperfect Knowledge and the Nominal Exchange Rate

While essentially all asset price models assume that today's price depends on expected future prices, models based on rational expectations versus imperfect knowledge differ with respect to how agents are assumed to make forecasts and how they react on forecasting errors. In REH-based

4 Soros (1987) uses the concept of reflexivity for such a situation.

5 Section 6 provides a definition of β, d and τ.

models, agents are adjusting back toward the equilibrium value of the theoretical model after having made a forecast error, implying that expectations are endogenously adjusting to the proposed true model. However, when "perfect knowledge" is replaced by imperfect knowledge, the role of expectations changes.

In IKE-based models, individuals recognize that they do not know the (or may not believe in the existence of a) "true" model. They also revise their forecasting strategies as changes in policy, institutions, and other factors cause the process to undergo structural change at times and in ways that cannot be foreseen. Frydman and Goldberg (2007) show that these revisions (or expectational shocks) may have a permanent effect on market outcomes and thus act as an exogenous force in the model. The Cases 1 and 2 in Section 2 illustrate this important feature of imperfect knowledge.

If PPP prevails in the goods market, one would expect the nominal exchange rate to approximately follow relative prices and the real exchange rate, q_t,

$$q_t = s_t - (p_{d,t} - p_{f,t}) \sim I(0) \tag{6}$$

to be stationary.[6]

If uncovered interest rate parity prevails in the foreign currency market, the interest rate differential, $(i_{d,t} - i_{f,t})$, should reflect the expected change in the exchange rate, $s^e_{t+1|t} - s_t$. But, interest rate differentials tend to move in long persistent swings whereas the change in nominal exchange rates are characterized by a pronounced short-run variability. The excess return puzzle describes the empirical fact that the excess return, exr_t, defined as

$$exr_t = (i_d - i_f)_t - (s^e_{t+1|t} - s_t), \tag{7}$$

often behaves like a nonstationary process. To solve the puzzle it has been customary to add a risk premium, rp_t, to (7), which usually is a measure of the volatility in the foreign currency market. But, although a risk premium can account for exchange rate volatility, it cannot account for the persistent swings in the interest rate differential. To control for the latter, Frydman and Goldberg (2007) propose to add to the UIP an uncertainty premium, up_t, measuring agents' *loss* aversion due to imperfect knowledge and a term measuring the international financial position.[7] Because the time-series property of the latter is difficult to hypothesize about, it will be left out at this stage. Instead, similar to Stillwagon et al. (2017) we incorporate a risk premium, rp_t, to the Uncertainty Adjusted UIP (UA-UIP) now defined as

$$(i_d - i_f)_t = (s^e_{t+1|t} - s_t) + rp_t + up_t, \tag{8}$$

describing an economy in which loss averse financial actors require a minimum return—an uncertainty premium—to speculate in the foreign exchange market. When the exchange rate moves away from its long-run value, the uncertainty premium starts increasing until the direction of the exchange rate reverses towards equilibrium. Frydman and Goldberg (2007) argues that the uncertainty premium is likely to be closely associated with the PPP gap, but that other gaps, for example the current account balance, could play a role as well. Focussing on the PPP gap as a measure of the uncertainty premium, the UA-UIP is formulated as

$$(i_d - i_f)_t = (s^e_{t+1} - s_t) + rp_t + f(p_d - p_f - s)_t. \tag{9}$$

where rp_t is basically associated with market volatility, for example measured by short-term changes in interest rates, inflation rates, nominal exchange rates, etc.

6 The PPP puzzle describes the empirical fact that the real exchange rate often tends to move in long persistent swings and that the volatility of the nominal exchange rate, s_t, is much larger than the one of relative prices.

7 The assumption that agents are loss averse, rather than risk averse, builds on the prospect theory by Kahneman and Tversky (1979).

Thus, the expected change in the nominal exchange rate is not directly associated with the observed interest rate differential but with the interest rate differential corrected for the PPP gap and the risk premium.

4. The Persistence of the PPP Gap

That agents have diverse forecasting strategies is a defining feature of imperfect knowledge based models - bulls hold long positions of foreign exchange and bet on appreciation while bears hold short positions and bet on depreciation.[8] Speculators are likely to change their forecasting strategies depending on how far away the price is from the long-run benchmark value. For example, Hommes (2006) assumes that the proportion of chartists relative to fundamentalists decreases as the PPP gap grows. When the exchange rate is not too far from its fundamental value, the proportion of chartists is high and the rate behaves roughly as a random walk. When it has moved to a far-from-equilibrium region, the proportion of fundamentalists is high and the real exchange rate becomes mean-reverting. This is similar to the assumption made in Taylor and Peel (2000) except that this study attributes the threshold to transactions cost.

Frydman and Goldberg (2007, 2011) explains the persistence of the PPP gap by non-constant parameters due to forecasting under imperfect knowledge. According to this, financial actors are assumed to know that in the long run the nominal exchange rate follows the relative price of the two countries whereas in the short run it reacts on a number of other determinants, z_t, which may include, for example, changes in interest rates, relative incomes and consumption, etc. Therefore, financial actors attach time-varying weights, B_t, to relative prices depending on how far away the nominal exchange rate is from its fundamental PPP value, i.e.,

$$s_t = A + B_t(p_{d,t} - p_{f,t}) + z_t. \tag{10}$$

The change in the nominal exchange rate can then be expressed as:

$$\Delta s_t = B_t \Delta(p_{d,t} - p_{f,t}) + \Delta B_t(p_{d,t} - p_{f,t}) + \Delta z_t.$$

Frydman and Goldberg (2007) make the assumption that $\left|\Delta B_t(p_{d,t} - p_{f,t})\right| \ll \left|B_t \Delta(p_{d,t} - p_{f,t})\right|$. This is backed up by simulations showing that a change in ΔB_t has to be implausibly large for $\Delta B_t(p_{d,t} - p_{f,t})$ to have a noticeable effect on Δs_t. Therefore, we assume that

$$\Delta s_t \simeq B_t \Delta(p_{d,t} - p_{f,t}) + \Delta z_t. \tag{11}$$

To study the properties of this type of time-varying parameter model, Tabor (2017) considers the model:

$$\begin{aligned} \Delta Y_t &= \alpha(Y_{t-1} - \beta_t X_{t-1}) + \varepsilon_{y,t} \\ \Delta X_t &= \varepsilon_{x,t}. \end{aligned} \tag{12}$$

He generates the data with $\alpha = -1$ and $\beta_t = \beta_0 + \rho\beta_{t-1} + \varepsilon_{\beta,t}$ for $\rho = \{0.0, 0.5, 0, 95, 1.0\}$. $\alpha = -1$ implies that the adjustment of Y_t back to $\beta_t' X_t$ is immediate. Instead of estimating a time-varying parameter model, Tabor fits a *constant* parameter CVAR model to the simulated data, so that $(\beta_t - \beta)X_t$ becomes part of the CVAR residual. It corresponds approximately to the forecast shock f_t in the previous section. The simulation results show that the closer ρ is to 1, the more persistent is the estimated gap term, $Y_t - \hat{\beta}' X_t$, and the smaller is the estimated adjustment coefficient α (while still highly significant). As long as $\rho < 1$, the mean of the estimated $\hat{\beta}$ approximately equals its true value β.

[8] Thechnically a speculator could expect a depreciation, but one small enough to be offset by the interest rate differential.

Thus, the pronounced persistence that often characterizes constant-parameter asset price models can potentially be a result of time-varying coefficients due to forecasting under imperfect knowledge.

Assume now that agents are forecasting the change in the nominal exchange rate by using (11), i.e., by relating Δs_t to relative inflation rates with a time-varying coefficient β_t,

$$\Delta s_t = \beta_t \Delta(p_d - p_f)_t + \varepsilon_{s,t}, \tag{13}$$

where $\beta_t = \beta_0 + \rho\beta_{t-1} + \varepsilon_{\beta,t}$ and $E(\beta_t) = (\beta_0/1-\rho) = 1$. If ρ is close, but not equal to one, the Tabor results imply that $\Delta s_t - \Delta(p_d - p_f)_t = \Delta q_t$ is likely to be a persistent near $I(1)$ process and, hence, that q_t is a *near* $I(2)$ process.

The *near* $I(2)$ approximation is useful as it allows for a linear VAR representation and, hence, can make use of a vast econometric literature on estimation and testing. Another option is to use a non-linear adjustment model, for example proposed by Bec and Rahbek (2004).

5. Associating Expectations with Observables in an Imperfect Knowledge Based Model

The first step of a theory-consistent CVAR scenario is to formulate a consistent description of the time series properties of the data given some basic assumptions of agents' expectations formation. In the foreign currency market, expectations are primarily feeding into the model through the UA-UIP condition (9). It states that the expected change in the nominal exchange rate is given by the interest rate differential corrected for an uncertainty and a risk premium. As mentioned above, the risk premium is assumed to be associated with short-term changes in the market such as realized volatilities and changes in the main determinants. The former may be assumed stationary whereas the latter may be empirically *near* $I(1)$. The uncertainty premium is assumed to be associated with a persistent gap effect considered to be *near* $I(2)$ in accordance with the findings in Johansen et al. (2010) and Juselius and Assenmacher (2017). As explained above, the PPP gap effect is likely to be *near* $I(2)$ when the forecast shock of Δs_t is $f_t = \Delta s_t - \beta_t \Delta(p_{d,t} - p_{f,t})$ with $\bar{\beta}_t = 1$. Imperfect knowledge economics would predict that $\beta_t \approx 0$ in the close neighborhood of parity, close to 1 in the far-from-parity region, and between 0 and 1 in the intermediate cases.

If interest rate differentials are affected by a risk and an uncertainty premium, then so are the individual interest rates:

$$i_{j,t} = i_{j,t-1} + \Delta up_{j,t} + \Delta rp_{j,t} + \varepsilon_{j,t} \qquad j = d, f \tag{14}$$

where $\varepsilon_{j,t}$ is a white noise process. The persistency of a *near* $I(2)$ uncertainty premium will always dominate the persistency of a stationary or *near* $I(1)$ risk premium. For notational simplicity, the latter will be part of the error term $\varepsilon_{j,t}$.

The change in the uncertainty premium, Δup_t, is assumed to follow a persistent $AR(1)$ process:

$$\Delta up_{j,t} = \rho_j \Delta up_{j,t-1} + \varepsilon_{up,j,t}, \text{ and } \varepsilon_{up,j,t} \sim Niid(0, \sigma^2_{\varepsilon_{up,,j}}) \qquad j = d, f. \tag{15}$$

The autoregressive coefficient $\rho_{j,t}$ is considered to be approximately 1.0 in periods when the real exchange rate is in the neighborhood of its long-run benchmark value and $\ll 1.0$ when it is far away from this value. Since the periods when $\rho_{j,t} \ll 1.0$ are likely to be short compared to the ones when $\rho_{j,t} \approx 1.0$, the average $\bar{\rho}_j$ is likely to be close to 1.0 so that

$$\Delta up_{j,t} = \sum_{i=1}^{t} \bar{\rho}_j^{t-i} \varepsilon_{up,j,i} + \bar{\rho}_j^t \Delta up_0$$

is a near $I(1)$ process. Integrating (14) over t gives:

$$\begin{aligned} i_{j,t} &= i_{j,0} + \sum_{i=1}^{t} \varepsilon_{j,i} + \sum_{i=1}^{t} \Delta up_{j,i}, \\ &= i_{j,0} + \sum_{i=1}^{t} \varepsilon_{j,i} + up_{j,t}, \qquad j = d, f \end{aligned} \tag{16}$$

where

$$up_{j,t} = \sum_{s=1}^{t} \sum_{i=1}^{s} \bar{\rho}_j^{s-i} \varepsilon_{up,j,i} + \bar{\rho}_j \Delta up_0 \sum_{i=1}^{t} \bar{\rho}_j^i + up_{j,0}.$$

Thus given (15), $up_{j,t}$ is *near* $I(2)$ and so are nominal interest rates. Note, however, that the shocks to the uncertainty premium, while persistent, are likely to be tiny compared to the interest rate shocks, capturing the empirical fact that the variance of the process is usually much larger than the variance of the drift term (for a more detailed discussion, see Juselius (2014)). The process (16) is consistent with persistent swings of shorter and longer durations typical of observed interest rates. The interest rate differential can be expressed as:

$$(i_{d,t} - i_{f,t}) = (i_{d,0} - i_{f,0}) + up_t + \sum_{i=1}^{t} (\varepsilon_{d,i} - \varepsilon_{f,i}). \tag{17}$$

where $up_t = up_{d,t} - up_{f,t}$. The term $\sum_{i=1}^{t}(\varepsilon_{d,i} - \varepsilon_{f,i})$ implies a first order stochastic trend in the interest rate differential, unless $\sum_{i=1}^{t} \varepsilon_{d,i} = \sum_{i=1}^{t} \varepsilon_{f,i}$, which would be highly unlikely in an imperfect knowledge world. As the uncertainty premium, $up_{j,t}$, is assumed to be near $I(2)$, the differential up_t is also near $I(2)$, unless $up_{d,j} - up_{f,j} = 0$. Equality would, however, imply no uncertainty premium in the foreign currency market, which again violates the imperfect knowledge assumption[9].

Approximating up_t with a fraction, ϕ, of the PPP gap gives:

$$(i_{d,t} - i_{f,t}) - \phi(p_{d,t} - p_{f,t} - s_t) = (i_{d,0} - i_{f,0}) + \sum_{i=1}^{t} (\varepsilon_{d,i} - \varepsilon_{f,i}), \tag{18}$$

showing that the interest rate differential corrected for the uncertainty premium is $I(1)$.

The Fisher parity defines the real interest rate as $r_{j,t} = i_{j,t} - \Delta p^e_{j,t+1|t}$. Using $\Delta p^e_{j,t+1|t} = \Delta p_{j,t} + f_{p_j,t}$ we get

$$r_{j,t} = i_{j,t} - \Delta p_{j,t} - f_{p_j,t}, \qquad j = d, f \tag{19}$$

Alternatively, (19) can be expressed for the inflation rate:

$$\Delta p_{j,t} = i_{j,t} - r_{j,t} + f_{p_j,t}, \qquad j = d, f. \tag{20}$$

Inserting (16) in (20) gives:

$$\Delta p_{j,t} = i_{j,0} + \sum_{s=1}^{t} \varepsilon_{j,s} + up_{j,t} - r_{j,t} + f_{p_j,t} \qquad j = d, f. \tag{21}$$

It appears that the inflation rate would be near $I(2)$ (which is implausible) unless $r_{j,t}$ and up_t cointegrate. Goods prices are generally determined by demand and supply in competitive international goods markets and only exceptionally affected by speculation. If nominal interest rates exhibit persistent swings but consumer price inflation does not, then the real interest rate will also exhibit persistent swings. Thus, the uncertainty premium should affect nominal interest rates, but not the price of goods, implying that up_t is part of $r_{j,t}$ rather than the inflation rate. In this case the real interest rate is *near* $I(2)$

9 Brunnermaier et al. (2008) discuss a "rational expectations" model for carry trade where agents demand a premium because of their risk preferences. Under this assumption $up_t \neq 0$ in spite of perfect information.

but, because it cointegrates with the uncertainty premium from *near* $I(2)$ to $I(0)$, i.e., $up_{j,t} - r_{j,t}$ is $I(0)$ in (1), the inflation rate is $I(1)$. This implies a delinking of the inflation rate and the nominal interest rate as a stationary Fisher parity relationship as predicted by Frydman and Goldberg (2007) and shown in Frydman et al. (2008).

Integrating (21) over t gives an expression for prices:

$$p_{j,t} = i_{j,0} \times t + \sum_{s=1}^{t} \sum_{i=1}^{s} \varepsilon_{j,i} + \sum_{i=1}^{t} f_{p_j,i} + p_{j,0}, \qquad j = d, f \tag{22}$$

showing that prices are $I(2)$ around a linear trend.

The inflation spread between the two countries can be expressed as

$$(\Delta p_{d,t} - \Delta p_{f,t}) = (i_{d,0} - i_{f,0}) + \sum_{s=1}^{t} (\varepsilon_{d,s} - \varepsilon_{f,s}) + (f_{p_d,t} - f_{p_f,t}), \tag{23}$$

showing that the inflation spread is $I(1)$. Integrating (23) over t gives an expression for the relative price:

$$p_{d,t} - p_{f,t} = p_{d,0} - p_{f,0} + (i_{d,0} - i_{f,0})t + \sum_{s=1}^{t} \sum_{i=1}^{s} (\varepsilon_{d,i} - \varepsilon_{f,i}) + \sum_{i=1}^{t} (f_{p_d,i} - f_{p_f,i}), \tag{24}$$

showing that the relative price is $I(2)$ with a linear trend.

An expression for the change in nominal exchange rates can be found from the uncertainty adjusted UIP:

$$\Delta s_t = (i_d - i_f)_{t-1} - up_{t-1}. \tag{25}$$

Inserting the expression for $(i_d - i_f)_t$ from (17) gives:

$$\begin{aligned} \Delta s_t &= (i_{d,0} - i_{f,0}) + \sum_{i=1}^{t-1} (\varepsilon_{d,i} - \varepsilon_{f,i}) + up_t - up_{t-1}, \\ &= (i_{d,0} - i_{f,0}) + \sum_{i=1}^{t-1} (\varepsilon_{d,i} - \varepsilon_{f,i}) + \Delta up_t \end{aligned}$$

Summing over t gives an expression for the nominal exchange rate:

$$s_t = s_0 + (i_{d,0} - i_{f,0})t + \sum_{s=1}^{t-1} \sum_{i=1}^{s} (\varepsilon_{d,i} - \varepsilon_{f,i}) + up_t. \tag{26}$$

Thus, the nominal exchange rate contains a local linear trend originating from the initial value of the interest rate differential, an $I(2)$ trend describing the stochastic trend in the relative price and a *near* $I(2)$ trend describing the long swings due to the uncertainty premium.

An expression for the real exchange rate can now be obtained by subtracting (24) from (26):

$$s_t - p_{d,t} + p_{f,t} = (s_0 - p_{d,0} - p_{f,0}) - (\varepsilon_{d,t} - \varepsilon_{f,t}) + up_t - \sum_{i=1}^{t} (f_{p_{d,i}} - f_{p_{f,i}}), \tag{27}$$

showing that the real exchange rate is a *near* $I(2)$ process due to the uncertainty premium. Thus, under imperfect knowledge both the nominal and the real exchange rate will show a tendency to move in similar long swings. Figure 1 illustrates that this has been the case for Germany and the USA in the post-Bretton Woods, pre-EMU period.

Finally, inserting the expression for (23) in (18) gives:

$$\underbrace{\underbrace{\underbrace{(i_{d,t}-i_{f,t})}_{near\ I(2)}-\underbrace{\phi(p_{d,t}-p_{f,t}-s_t)}_{near\ I(2)}}_{\text{near } I(1)}-\underbrace{(\Delta p_{d,t}-\Delta p_{f,t})}_{near\ I(1)}}_{I(0)}=\underbrace{(f_{p_{d,t}}-f_{p_{d,t}})}_{I(0)}, \tag{28}$$

showing that the real interest rate differential cointegrates with the PPP gap to a stationary relation as deduced in Frydman and Goldberg (2007).[10] While the real exchange rate is inherently persistent as discussed in Section 4, the degree of persistence may vary over different sample periods. It may sometimes be very close to $I(2)$, sometimes more like a persistent $I(1)$ process. Whatever the case, the persistency profile of the real exchange rate, the interest rate and the inflation rate differentials should be one degree higher in an imperfect knowledge economy compared to a "rational expectations" economy.

Thus, imperfect knowledge predicts that both exchange rates and interest rates in nominal and real values are integrated of the same order and that the Fisher parity does not hold as a stationary condition.

6. A Theory-Consistent CVAR Scenario for Imperfect Knowledge

The first step in a scenario describes how the underlying stochastic trends are assumed to load into the data provided the theory model is empirically correct. The results of the previous section showed that the data vector $x_t = [p_{d,t}, p_{f,t}, s_t, i_{d,t}, i_{f,t}]$ should be integrated of order two and be affected by two stochastic trends, one originating from twice cumulated interest rate shocks, $\sum_{s=1}^{t}\sum_{i=1}^{s}\varepsilon_{j,i}$, and the other from the uncertainty premium being *near* $I(2)$. Two stochastic $I(2)$ trends that load into five variables implies three relations which are cointegrated $CI(2,1)$[11]. These relations can be decomposed into r relations, $\beta' x_t$, that can become stationary by adding a linear combination of the growth rates, $d'\Delta x_t$, and s_1 linear combinations $\beta'_{\perp 1} x_t$ which can only become stationary by differencing. Thus, stationarity can be achieved by r polynomially cointegrated relations $(\beta' x_t + d'\Delta x_t) \sim I(0)$ and s_1 medium-run relations among the differences $\beta'_{\perp 1}\Delta x_t$. For a more detailed exposition see, for example, (Juselius 2006, chp. 17).

The three $CI(2,1)$ relations are consistent with different choices of r and s_1 as long as $r + s_1 = p - s_2 = 3$ where s_2 is the number of $I(2)$ trends. Theoretically, (18) predicts that $(i_{d,t} - i_{f,t})$ and $(s_t - p_{d,t} + p_{f,t})$ are cointegrated $CI(2,1)$ and (28) that $(i_{d,t} - i_{f,t})$, $(s_t - p_{d,t} + p_{f,t})$ and $(\Delta p_{d,t} + \Delta p_{f,t})$ are cointegrated $CI(2,2)$, so $\{3 \geq r \geq 1\}$. The following two cases satisfy this condition: $\{r = 2, s_1 = 1, s_2 = 2\}$, and $\{r = 3, s_1 = 0, s_2 = 2\}$. Juselius (2017) finds that the trace test supports $\{r = 2, s_1 = 1, s_2 = 2\}$ and the scenario will be formulated for this case. The pushing force of this scenario comprises three autonomous shocks, $u_{1,t}$, $u_{2,t}$ and $u_{3,t}$, two of which cumulate twice to produce the two $I(2)$ trends, while the third shock cumulates only once to produce an $I(1)$ trend. The pulling force consists of two polynomially cointegrated relations and one medium-run relation between growth rates.

Based on the derivations in the previous section, it is possible to impose testable restrictions on some of the coefficients in the scenario. For example, relation (22) assumes that the uncertainty premium does not affect goods prices so that $(c_{21}, c_{22}) = 0$. Relation (27) assumes that the long-run stochastic trend in relative prices and nominal exchange rate, $\sum_{i=1}^{t-1}\sum_{s=1}^{i}(\varepsilon_{d,s} - \varepsilon_{f,s})$, cancels in $(p_d - p_f - s)$, so that $(c_{11} - c_{12}) = c_{13}$. Relation (16) assumes that the relative price trend does not load into the two interest rates, so that $(c_{14} = c_{15} = 0)$. Based on these restrictions, the imperfect knowledge scenario is formulated as:

---

10 Because a risk premium was left out from (14), short-term changes of other important variables are therefore absent in (28).

11 That $\beta' x_t$ is $CI(2,1)$ means that cointegration takes the vector process $x_t \sim I(2)$ down to $I(1)$, i.e., the order of integration 1 step down. If $\beta' x_t$ is $CI(2,2)$, then cointegration takes the $I(2)$ process down to stationarity.

$$\begin{bmatrix} p_d \\ p_f \\ s \\ i_d \\ i_f \end{bmatrix} = \begin{bmatrix} c_{11} & 0 \\ c_{12} & 0 \\ c_{11}-c_{12} & c_{23} \\ 0 & c_{24} \\ 0 & c_{25} \end{bmatrix} \begin{bmatrix} \Sigma\Sigma u_1 \\ \Sigma\Sigma u_2 \end{bmatrix} + \begin{bmatrix} b_{11} & b_{21} & b_{31} \\ b_{12} & b_{22} & b_{32} \\ b_{13} & b_{23} & b_{33} \\ b_{14} & b_{24} & b_{34} \\ b_{15} & b_{25} & b_{35} \end{bmatrix} \begin{bmatrix} \Sigma u_1 \\ \Sigma u_2 \\ \Sigma u_3 \end{bmatrix} + Z_t, \tag{29}$$

where u_1 is a relative price shock and u_2 a shock to the uncertainty premium. Section 2 noted that a risk premium is likely to be near $I(1)$ and thus able to generate an additional trend in the data. Tentatively u_3 is therefore considered a shock to the risk premium and Σu_3 to be a medium-run trend originating from such shocks. Consistent with the derivations in the previous section all variables are assumed to be $I(2)$. Since the two prices and the exchange rate share two stochastic $I(2)$ trends, there exists just one relation, $(p_d - w_1 p_f - w_2 s) \sim I(1)$ with $(w_1, w_2) \neq 1$.

The following three $CI(2,1)$ cointegration relations follow from (29):

1. $\left\{(p_d - p_f - s) - a_1(i_d - i_f) - \gamma_1 t\right\} \sim I(1)$ if $c_{23} + a_1(c_{24} - c_{25}) = 0$
2. $(i_d - a_2 p_d - a_3 s - \gamma_2 t) \sim I(1)$, if $c_{24} - a_3 c_{23} = 0$ and $a_2 c_{11} + a_3(c_{11} - c_{12}) = 0$
3. $(i_f - a_4 p_f - a_5 s - \gamma_3 t) \sim I(1)$, if $c_{25} - a_5 c_{23} = 0$ and $a_4 c_{12} + a_5(c_{11} - c_{21}) = 0$

The first relation corresponds to (18), whereas the two remaining relations, while not explicitly discussed above, are consistent with the theoretical model set-up. The next section will demonstrate that they are also empirically relevant. Note also that the inclusion of a linear trend in the relation means that trend-adjusted price/nominal exchange rate rather than the price itself is the relevant measure. Any linear combination of the three relations are of course also $CI(2,1)$.

The case $(r = 2, s_1 = 1, s_2 = 2)$ implies two multicointegrating relations, $\beta' x_t + d\Delta x_t$, and one medium-run relation between the differences, $\beta_{\perp,1}\Delta x_t$. To obtain stationarity, two of the $CI(2,1)$ relations need to be combined with growth rates in a way that cancels the $I(1)$ trends. As an illustration, the scenario restrictions consistent with stationarity are given below for the first polynomially cointegrated relation given by (28). The scenario restrictions on the remaining two relations can be similarly derived.

1. $\left\{ppp - a_1(i_d - i_f) - a_6(\Delta p_d - \Delta p_f) - \gamma_1 t\right\} \sim I(0)$, if $c_{23} + a_1(c_{24} - c_{25}) = 0$,
   $\{(b_{11} - b_{12} - b_{13}) - a_1(b_{14} - b_{15}) - a_6 c_{11}\} = 0$,
   $\{(b_{21} - b_{22} - b_{23}) - a_1(b_{24} - b_{25}) + a_6 c_{21}\} = 0$, and
   $\{(b_{31} - b_{32} - b_{33}) + a_6(b_{34} - b_{35})\} = 0$
2. $(i_d - a_2 p_d - a_3 s - a_7 \Delta p_d - \gamma_2 t) \sim I(0)$,

   and one medium-run relation, $\beta'_{\perp 1}\Delta x_t$:

   1. $(\Delta p_d + d_1 \Delta p_f + d_2 \Delta s + d_3 \Delta i_f) \sim I(0)$.

Note that linear combinations of the proposed stationary relations are, of course, also stationary.

7. The Empirical Specification of the *CVAR* Model

The empirical analysis is based on German-US data for the post-Bretton Woods, pre-EMU period[12]. The sample starts in 1975:8 and ends in 1998:12 when the Deutshemark was replaced by the Euro. The empirical VAR corresponds to the one in Juselius (2017) and has two lags and contains a few dummy variables, D_t:

---

[12] All estimates are based on a recent Beta version of CATS 3 in OxMetrics Doornik and Juselius (2017).

$$\Delta^2 x_t = \Gamma \Delta x_{t-1} + \Pi x_{t-1} + \mu_0 + \mu_{01} Ds_{91.1,t} + \mu_1 t + \mu_1 t_{91.1} \\ + \phi_1 D_{tax,t} + \phi_2 Dp_{86.2,t} + \phi_3 Dp_{91.2,t} + \varepsilon_t, \tag{30}$$

where $x_t = [p_{d,t}, p_{f,t}, s_t, i_{d,t}, i_{f,t}]$ and p_t stands for CPI prices, s_t for the Dmk/dollar exchange rate, i_t for 10 year bond rates, a subscript d for Germany and a subscript f for the USA, t is a linear trend starting in 1975:3, $t_{91:1,t}$ allows the linear trend to have a different slope from 1991:1 onwards[13], and $Ds_{91:1,t}$ is a step dummy also starting in 1991:1, controlling for the reunification of East and West Germany. $D_{tax,t}$ is an impulse dummy accounting for three different excise taxes introduced to pay for the German reunification, $Dp_{86.2}$ is controlling for a large shock to the US price and bond rate in connection with the Plaza Accord, and $Dp_{91.2}$ accounts for a large shock to the exchange rate after the reunification.

The hypothesis that x_t is $I(1)$ is formulated as a reduced rank hypothesis, $\Pi = \alpha\beta'$, where α is $p \times r$ and β is $p_1 \times r$ with $p_1 = p + 2$ (p variables + 2 deterministic trends) The hypothesis that x_t is $I(2)$ is formulated as an additional reduced rank hypothesis, $\alpha'_{\perp}\Gamma\beta_{\perp} = \xi\eta'$, where ξ, η are $(p - r) \times s_1$ and $\alpha_{\perp}, \beta_{\perp}$ are the orthogonal complements of α, β respectively (Johansen 1992, 1995). The first reduced rank condition is associated with the levels of the variables and the second with the differenced variables. The intuition is that the differenced process also contains unit roots when data are $I(2)$. Juselius (2017) finds that the maximum likelihood trace test (Nielsen and Rahbek 2007) supports the case $\{r = 2, s_1 = 1, s_2 = 2\}$.

Since the $I(2)$ condition is formulated as a reduced rank on the transformed $\mathbf{\Gamma}$ matrix, the latter is no longer unrestricted as in the $I(1)$ model. To circumvent this problem we use the following parameterization (see Johansen 1997, 2006; Doornik and Juselius 2017):

$$\Delta^2 x_t = \alpha \left[\begin{pmatrix} \beta \\ \beta_{01} \\ \beta_0 \end{pmatrix}' \begin{pmatrix} x_{t-1} \\ t_{91:1,t-1} \\ t-1 \end{pmatrix} + \begin{pmatrix} d \\ d_{01} \\ d_0 \end{pmatrix}' \begin{pmatrix} \Delta x_{t-1} \\ D_{s91:1,t-1} \\ 1 \end{pmatrix} \right] \\ + \zeta \begin{pmatrix} \tau \\ \tau_{01} \\ \tau_0 \end{pmatrix}' \begin{pmatrix} \Delta x_{t-1} \\ D_{s91:1,t-1} \\ 1 \end{pmatrix} + \Phi_1 D_{tax,t} + \Phi_2 Dp_{86.2,t} + \phi_3 Dp_{91.2,t} + \varepsilon_t, \tag{31}$$

$$t = 1975.09 - 1998.12$$

where $\tau = [\beta, \beta_{\perp 1}]$ and d is proportional to $\tau_{\perp}$. In (30) an unrestricted constant (and step dummy) will cumulate twice to a quadratic trend, and a linear (broken) trend to a cubic trend. By specifying the broken trend to be restricted to the β part and the differenced broken trend to the d part of model (31) these undesirable effects are avoided. For more details, see Doornik (2017), Kongsted et al. (1999), (Juselius 2006, chp. 17).

8. Testable Hypotheses on Integration and Cointegration

Section 4 found that all the five variables should be individually *(near)* $I(2)$ under imperfect knowledge. The following testable hypotheses represent relevant linear combinations of the variables:

- $(p_{d,t} - p_{f,t}) \sim near\ I(2)$,
- $s_t \sim near\ I(2)$,
- $(i_{d,t} - i_{f,t}) \sim near\ I(2)$,
- $(s_t - p_d - p_f)_t \sim near\ I(2)$,

13 The change in the slope of the trend could possibly be associated with a change in the financial position between the two countries as discussed in Frydman and Goldberg (2007).

- $\left\{(i_{d,t} - i_{f,t}) - b_1(s_t - p_d - p_f)_t\right\} \sim near\ I(1)$

The above hypotheses can be formulated as a known vector b_1 in τ, i.e., $\tau = (b_1, b_{1\perp}\varphi)$ where $b_{1\perp}\varphi$ defines the remaining vectors to be in the orthogonal space of b_1.[14] For example $b_1' = [0,0,0,1,0,0,0]$ tests whether the German bond rate is a unit vector in τ. If not rejected, $b_{d,t}$ can be considered at most $I(1)$, if rejected $I(2)$. Note, however, that Section 4 found that prices and the nominal exchange rate contain both deterministic and stochastic trends and the tests have to take this into account. For example, $H_1' = \begin{bmatrix} 1 & 0 & 0 & 0 & 0 & 0 & 0 \\ 0 & 0 & 0 & 0 & 0 & 0 & 1 \end{bmatrix}$ tests whether trend-adjusted German price is $I(1)$. To allow for a deterministic trend is important as it would otherwise bias the tests towards a rejection of $I(1)$.

Table 1 reports the test results. Except for the German bond rate, the results are supporting the imperfect knowledge hypothesis that all variables are *near* $I(2)$. Even though, the $I(1)$ hypothesis of the nominal and the real exchange rate is borderline acceptable, the low p-value is more in line with *near* $I(2)$ than $I(1)$.[15] That the German bond rate could be rejected as (*near*) $I(2)$ with a p-value of 0.45 may indicate that the German bond rate was less affected by speculative movements than the US rate. Similar results have been found in Juselius and Assenmacher (2017). Hypothesis $\mathcal{H}_9$ corresponds to (18) and support the results in Section 4 that the PPP gap and the interest rate differential should cointegrate from $I(2)$ to $I(1)$.

Table 1. Testing hypotheses of I(1) versus I(2).

		p_d	p_f	s	b_1	b_2	t_{91}	t	$\chi^2(v)$	p-Value
$\mathcal{H}_1$	τ_1'	1	–	–	–	–	*	*	31.9(2)	0.00
$\mathcal{H}_2$	τ_1'	–	1	–	–	–	*	*	32.5(2)	0.00
$\mathcal{H}_3$	τ_1'	1	−1	–	–	–	*	*	24.7(2)	0.00
$\mathcal{H}_4$	τ_1'	–	–	1	–	–	*	*	5.3(2)	0.07
$\mathcal{H}_5$	τ_1'	1	−1	−1	–	–	–	–	8.4(4)	0.07
$\mathcal{H}_6$	τ_1'	–	–	–	1	–	–	–	3.7(4)	0.45
$\mathcal{H}_7$	τ_1'	–	–	–	–	1	–	–	12.6(4)	0.01
$\mathcal{H}_8$	τ_1'	–	–	–	1	−1	–	–	12.4(4)	0.01
$\mathcal{H}_9$	τ_1'	1	−1	−1	a	$-a$	–	–	3.0(5)	0.70

9. The Pulling Forces

The long and persistent swings away from long-run equilibrium values visible in Figure 1 suggest the presence of self-reinforcing feedback mechanisms in the system. Such behavior is likely to show up as a combination of equilibrium error increasing (positive feedback) and error correcting behavior (negative feedback) either in the adjustment of the two polynomially cointegrating relations, $\alpha(\beta' x_t + d'\Delta x_t)$, or in the adjustment to the changes in the τ relations, $\zeta\tau'\Delta x_t$. Juselius and Assenmacher (2017) argue that the adjustment dynamics in the $I(2)$ model, given by α and d, can be interpreted as two levels of equilibrium correction: the d adjustment describing how the growth rates, Δx_t, adjust to the long-run equilibrium errors, $\beta' x_t$ and the α adjustment describing how the acceleration rates, $\Delta^2 x_t$, adjust to the dynamic equilibrium relations, $\beta' x_t + d'\Delta x_t$. The interpretation of d as a medium-run adjustment is, however, conditional on $\alpha \neq 0$.

---

14 Note that in the $I(1)$ model this type of hypothesis is testing whether a variable/relation is $I(0)$, whereas in the $I(2)$ model whether it is $I(1)$.

15 Juselius (2017) shows that a standard rational expectations model is consistent with the real exchange rate behaving like an $I(0)$ or possibly a near-$I(1)$ process.

The adjustment dynamics are illustrated for the variable $x_{i,t}$:

$$\Delta^2 x_{i,t} = \cdots \sum_{j=1}^{r} \alpha_{ij} \sum_{i=1}^{p} (\beta_{ij} x_{i,t-1} + d_{ij} \Delta x_{i,t-1}) + \sum_{j=1}^{r} \zeta_{ij} \sum_{i=1}^{p} (\beta_{ij} \Delta x_{i,t-1}) + \varepsilon_{i,t}, i = 1, ..., p$$

The signs of $\beta, d,$ and α determine whether the variable $x_{i,t}$ is error increasing or error correcting in the medium and the long run. If $\alpha_{ij}\beta_{ij} < 0$ or/and $\alpha_{ij}d_{ij} < 0$, then the acceleration rate, $\Delta^2 x_{i,t}$, is equilibrium correcting to $(\beta_j' x_t + d_j' \Delta x_t)$; if $d_{ij}\beta_{ij} > 0$ (given $\alpha_{ij} \neq 0$), then $\Delta x_{i,t}$, is equilibrium error correcting to $\beta_j' x_t$; if $\zeta_{ij}\tau_{ij} < 0$ then $\Delta^2 x_{i,t}$ is equilibrium correcting to $\tau_j' \Delta x_{t-1}$. In all other cases the system is equilibrium error increasing (except for the cases when the coefficient is zero).

The two stationary polynomially cointegrating relations, $\beta_i' x_t + d_i' \Delta x_t, i = 1, 2$ can be interpreted as dynamic equilibrium relations in the following sense: When data are $I(2)$, $\beta' x_t$ is in general $I(1)$ describing a very persistent static equilibrium error. In a market economy, a movement away from equilibrium would trigger off a compensating movement elsewhere in the system. The $I(2)$ structure tells us that it is the changes of the system, $d'\Delta x_t$, that adjust to the static equilibrium error either in an error-correcting manner bringing $\beta' x_t$ back towards equilibrium, or in an error-increasing manner, pushing $\beta' x_t$ further away from equilibrium.

However, as long as all characteristic roots of the model are inside the unit circle, any equilibrium error increasing behavior is compensated by error correcting behavior somewhere else in the system. For example, speculative behavior may push the real exchange rate away from equilibrium but an increasing uncertainty premium will eventually pull it back toward equilibrium. The largest unrestricted root in our model is 0.48, so the system is stable and all persistent movements in the data are properly accounted for.

Table 2 reports an overidentified structure of $\beta x_t + d'\Delta x_t$ and an unrestricted estimate of $\beta_{\perp 1}$. For a given identified β, the d parameters are uniquely determined as long as d is proportional to $\tau_{\perp}$. See Doornik (2017) in this special issue. The standard errors of β are derived in Johansen (1997) and those of d by the delta method in Doornik (2017).[16] To facilitate interpretation, statistically insignificant adjustment coefficients (with a t-ratio $<|1.4|$) are replaced by an asterisk (*). Error-increasing coefficients are shown in bold face. As discussed above, the α, d and ζ coefficients allow us to investigate how the variables have responded to imbalances in the system.

The β structure contain altogether 6 overidentifying restrictions which are tested with the likelihood ratio test described in Johansen et al. (2010) and accepted with a p-value of 0.72.

The first polynomially cointegrated relation corresponds closely to the Uncertainty Adjusted UIP relation (28):

$$\begin{aligned}(i_{d,t} - i_{f,t}) &= 0.01(p_{d,t} - p_{f,t} - s_t) - 0.16\Delta p_{d,t} - 1.1\Delta p_{f,t} + 0.48\Delta s_t + \\ &\quad 0.0005\Delta i_{d,t} - 0.006\Delta i_{f,t} + 0.013 - 0.006Ds_{91,t} + e_{1,t}\end{aligned}$$

where the PPP gap is a proxy for the uncertainty premium and $d'\Delta x_t \approx (0.16\Delta p_{d,t} + 1.1\Delta p_{f,t} - 0.48\Delta s_t - 0.0005\Delta i_{d,t} + 0.006\Delta i_{f,t})$ can be thought of as a proxy for Δs_{t+1}^e and a risk premium measuring short-term variability in the market. While the coefficient to the PPP is tiny, describing a very slow adjustment to the long-run PPP, the adjustment to the combined (excess return) relation is very fast as measured by the α_1 coefficients. The latter show that in the long run all variables, except for the nominal exchange rate, adjust in an error correcting manner to the disequilibrium $e_{1,t}$. In the medium run, German inflation and the nominal exchange rate are error increasing ($d_{11}\beta_{11}, d_{13}\beta_{13} < 0$) and so are the two interest rates ($d_{14}\beta_{14}, d_{15}\beta_{15} < 0$). Since an increasing PPP gap is likely to cause imbalances

[16] Note that all β coefficients have t ratios that are sufficiently large to be statistically significant also after a near unit root correction. See (Franchi and Johansen 2017; Elliot 1998.)

in the real economy and such imbalances have to be financed, the level of interest rates is likely to respond, which can explain their error-increasing behavior in the medium run.

Altogether the results of the first relation can be interpreted as follows: The PPP gap moves in long persistent swings as a result of error-increasing behavior of the nominal exchange rate and the interest rate differential. As long as the PPP gap and the interest rate differential move in tandem, the long-run equilibrium error, $\beta_1' x_t$, is small and the response of the system is moderate. But when the disequilibrium starts increasing, all variables, except for the nominal exchange rate, will react in an error-correcting manner so as to restore equilibrium.

The second polynomially cointegrated relation contains elements of the relation (19) in Section 4:

$$\begin{aligned} b_{f,t} - 0.89\Delta p_{f,t} &= 0.01(\widehat{p_{f,t} + s_t}) + 0.22\Delta p_{d,t} - 0.0007\Delta i_{d,t} + \\ &\quad 0.0072\Delta i_{f,t} - 0.04 + e_{2,t}. \end{aligned}$$

where $\widehat{x_t}$ stands for "trend-adjusted". An increase/decrease in the US bond rate relative to the US inflation rate (i.e., the real bond rate in (19)) is associated with an increase/decrease in the trend-adjusted US price denominated in Dmk.[17] Each of the d and α coefficients represents error-correcting adjustment, even the nominal exchange rate is error-correcting in α.

The medium-run stationary relation between growth rates, $\beta_{\perp 1}' \Delta x_t$, is given by

$$\begin{aligned} \Delta p_{d,t} &\simeq 0.14\Delta p_{f,t} + 0.30\Delta s_t - 0.33\Delta i_{d,t} + 0.49\Delta i_{f,t} + \\ &\quad 0.0026 - 0.002Ds_{91,t} + e_{3,t} \end{aligned} \tag{32}$$

showing that German inflation rate has been co-moving with US inflation rate, with the change in the nominal exchange rate and with the change in the interest rate differential. The relation resembles relation (28) in differences, except that the coefficients are not consistent with proportional effects. Thus, in the medium run, German price inflation has not fully reacted to changes in the US price and the nominal exchange rate. As a consequence it has contributed to the long swings in the real exchange rate visible in Figure 1. The estimates of ζ_3 in Table 3 show that the German and the US inflation rates are primarily adjusting to this relation, supporting the interpretation of (32) as a medium-run secular trend relationship between inflation rates.

Table 3 also reports the estimated adjustment coefficients ζ of $\beta' \Delta x_t$ where β is given by the estimates of Table 2. It appears that the changes of the two disequilibria have had a very significant effect on both interest rates: $\beta_1' \Delta x_t$ in an error increasing manner and $\beta_2' \Delta x_t$ in an error correcting manner. Interestingly, the nominal exchange rate does not adjust very significantly to any of the three equilibrium errors. Thus, in the medium run speculative movements in the exchange rate seems to have been the main driver in the Dollar-Deutshemark market.[18] Since both bond rates are equilibrium-error increasing in d_1 and ζ_1, the results may tentatively suggest that it is the interest rates that respond to the speculative movements in the nominal exchange. It is also notable that the coefficients on the exchange rate are much larger in absolute value than those on the price levels, suggesting that the changes in the inflation rates were too small to compensate the movements away from long-run equilibrium PPP values caused by financial speculators (trend followers/chartists)[19]. This supports the imperfect knowledge hypothesis that in the medium run the nominal exchange rate tends to move away from its long-run equilibrium values, while in the long run it moves back towards equilibrium.

17 A similar relationship was found in Juselius and Assenmacher (2017) for Swiss-US data and in Juselius and Stillwagon (2017) for UK-US data, both for a more recent period.

18 The latter result is also found in Juselius and Stillwagon (2017).

19 Similar results were found in Juselius and Assenmacher (2017) and in Juselius and Stillwagon (2017).

Table 2. An identified long-run structure in β.

$\tilde{\beta}=(h_1+H_1\varphi_1,\ldots,h_r+H_r\varphi_r)$, $\chi^2(6)=4.60[0.72]$							
	$p_{d,t}$	$p_{f,t}$	s_t	$i_{d,t}$	$i_{f,t}$	$t_{91.1}$	$t^{1)}$
$\tilde{\beta}_1'$	−0.013 [−16.9]	0.031 [16.9]	0.013 [16.9]	1.00	−1.00	−	−
d_1'	**0.16** [3.2]	1.11 [5.3]	**−0.48** [−6.9]	**−0.0005** [−3.4]	**0.0054** [3.2]	0.006 [3.8]	−0.013 [−8.5]
α_1'	0.45 [15.3]	−0.13 [−4.4]	**1.51** [3.1]	−0.01 [−3.8]	0.02 [4.0]		
$\tilde{\beta}_2'$	−	−0.009 [−15.1]	−0.009 [−15.1]	−	1.00	0.002 [2.5]	0.52 [1.5]
d_2'	−0.22 [−1.7]	−0.89 [−5.5]	*	0.0007 [12.8]	−0.0072 [−12.8]	*	0.038 [14.1]
α_2'	0.67 [10.3]	0.40 [6.5]	3.25 [3.0]	−0.03 [−5.0]	*	−	−
$\tilde{\beta}_{\perp,1}'$	1.00	−0.14	−0.30	0.33	−0.49	0.0020	-0.0026

[1)] The trend estimate has been multiplied by 1000. Error-increasing coefficients in bold face. A * means an insignificant coefficient.

Table 3. The adjustment coefficients ζ.

	$\zeta_1(\beta_1'\Delta x_t)$	$\zeta_2(\beta_2'\Delta x)$	$\zeta_3(\beta_{\perp 1}'\Delta x_t)$
$\Delta\Delta p_{d,t}$	*	*	−0.82 [−16.5]
$\Delta\Delta p_{f,t}$	*	*	0.23 [4.7]
$\Delta\Delta s_t$	**13.9** [1.9]	*	*
$\Delta\Delta i_{d,t}$	**0.35** [9.2]	−0.71 [−13.9]	*
$\Delta\Delta i_{f,t}$	**−0.73** [−10.6]	−0.37 [−4.0]	**−0.02** [−2.0]

Coefficients with a $|t-value|<1.3$ is replaced with an *.

10. A Plausible Story

The results generally confirm the hypotheses in Juselius (2012) where prices of tradable goods are assumed to be determined in very competitive customer markets Phelps (1994). Hence, prices are assumed not to be much affected by speculation and, therefore, not to exhibit persistent speculative swings around benchmark values.[20]

A shock to the long-term interest rate (for example, as a result of a domestic increase in sovereign debt) without a corresponding increase in the inflation rate, is likely to increase the amount of speculative capital moving into the economy. The exchange rate appreciates, jeopardizing competitiveness in the tradable sector, the trade balance worsens, and the pressure on the interest rate increases. Under this scenario, the interest rate is likely to keep increasing as long as the structural imbalances are growing, thus generating persistent movements in real interest rates and real exchange rates. The estimates of $\beta' x_t + d'\Delta x_t$ and the error-increasing behavior of the interest rates in d_1 and ζ_1 support this interpretation.

The tendency of the domestic real interest rate to increase and the real exchange rate to appreciate at the same time reduces domestic competitiveness in the tradable sector. In an imperfect knowledge economy in which the nominal exchange rate is determined by speculation, firms cannot in general count on exchange rates to restore competitiveness after a permanent shock to relative costs. Unless firms are prepared to loose market shares, they cannot use constant mark-up pricing as their pricing strategy. See, for example, (Krugman 1986; Phelps 1994; Feenstra 2015). To preserve market shares, they

[20] Energy, precious metals and, recently, grain may be exceptions in this respect.

would have to adjust productivity or profits rather than increasing the product price. Therefore, we would expect customer market pricing (Phelps 1994) to replace constant mark-up pricing, implying that profits are squeezed in periods of persistent appreciation and increased during periods of depreciation. Evidence of a nonstationary profit share co-moving with the real exchange rate has for instance been found in Juselius (2006).

The results showed that German prices have been equilibrium error-increasing ($d_{11}\beta_{11} < 0$) in the medium-run at the same time as the nominal exchange has moved away from its long-run equilibrium value. Thus, Germany's reaction to the long swings in the real exchange rate has been to suppress price changes as a means to preserve competitiveness. US prices, on the other hand, have been error correcting ($d_{12}\beta_{12} > 0$) to the PPP gap, albeit very slowly so, indicating that the USA's reaction has been more prone to letting prices follow the swings in the dollar rate as a result of speculative flows.[21] Judging from the accumulating US trade deficits in this period, US enterprises might have lost market shares accordingly.

To conclude: the IKE behavior of interest rates and the nominal exchange rate seem key for understanding the long swings in the currency market.

11. Conclusions

The paper demonstrates how basic assumptions underlying a theory model can be translated into testable hypotheses on the order of integration and cointegration of key variables and their relationships. The idea is formalized as a theory-consistent CVAR scenario describing the empirical regularities we expect to see in the data if the long-run properties of a theory model are empirically relevant. The procedure is illustrated for a monetary model of real exchange rate determination based on imperfect knowledge expectations.

The empirical results provide overwhelmingly strong support for the informationally less demanding imperfect knowledge type of model. In particular, this model seems able to explain the long and persistent swings in the nominal and the real exchange rate that have puzzled economists for long. This conclusion is strengthened by very similar results based on Danish-German data (Juselius 2006, chp. 21), on Swiss-US data (Juselius and Assenmacher 2017) and on UK-US data (Juselius and Stillwagon 2017). Because of this, it seems that the key for understanding these long swings in exchange rates and interest rates (both real and nominal) is to recognize the importance of imperfect knowledge, reflexivity, and positive and negative feedback mechanisms (Soros 1987; Frydman and Goldberg 2013; Hands 2013; Hommes 2013).

As the real exchange rate and the real interest rate are among the most important determinants for the real economy, the results point to the importance of understanding the underlying cause of the long persistent movements with which they typically evolve over time. The failure of extant models to foresee the recent financial and economic crisis, and to propose adequate policy measures in its aftermath gives a strong argument for this. Without such an understanding financial behavior in the foreign currency and the stock market is likely to continue to generate bubbles and crises with serious implications for the macroeconomy and subsequent political turmoil.

Acknowledgments: I would like to thank Josh Stillwagon for many detailed and highly valuable comments which significantly improved the paper. Valuable comments from Roman Frydman, Michael Goldberg, Kevin Hoover, Søren Johansen, and Mikael Juselius are also gratefully acknowledged.

Conflicts of Interest: The author declares no conflict of interest.

---

[21] Based on the tiny the speed of adjustment coefficient (0.01) it would take on average 6–8 years for the real exchange rate to return to its long-run value if the US inflation rate alone were to adjust. This is slightly higher than the average half-lives reported in the literature. See for example Rogoff (1996).

References

Bec, Frederique, and Anders Rahbek. 2004. Vector Equilibrium Correction Models with Non-Linear Discontinuous Adjustments. *Econometrics Journal* 7: 628–51.

Brunnermaier, Markus K., Stefan Nagel, and Lasse H. Pedersen. 2008. Carry Trades and Currency Crashes. NBER Working Paper 14473, National Bureau of Economic Research, Cambridge, Massachusetts, USA.

Doornik, Jurgen A. 2017. Maximum Likelihood Estimation of the $I(2)$ Model under Linear Restrictions. *Econometrics* 52: 19. doi:10.3390/econometrics5020019.

Doornik, Jurgen and Katarina Juselius. 2017. *Cointegration Analysis of Time Series Using CATS 3 for OxMetrics*. Timberlake Consultants Ltd, Richmond, Surrey, UK.

Elliot, Graham. 1998. The Robustness of Cointegration Methods when Regressors Almost Have Unit Roots. *Econometrica* 66: 149–58.

Engel, Charles. 2014. Exchange Rate and Interest Rate Parity, *Handbook of International Economics*. Amsterdam: Elsevier. vol. 4, chp. 8, pp. 453–522

Feenstra, Robert C. 2015. *Advanced International Trade: Theory and Evidence*, 2nd ed. Princeton: Princeton University Press.

Franchi, Massimo, and Søren Johansen. 2017. Improved inference on cointegrating vectors in the presence of a near unit root using adjusted quantiles. *Econometrics* 52: 19. doi:10.3390/econometrics502002519.

Frydman, Roman, and Michael D. Goldberg. 2007. *Imperfect Knowledge Economics: Exchange rates and Risk*. Princeton: Princeton University Press.

Frydman, Roman, and Michael D. Goldberg. 2011. *Beyond Mechanical Markets: Risk and the Role of Asset Price Swings*. Princeton: Princeton University Press.

Frydman, Roman, and Michael D. Goldberg. 2013. Change and Expectations in Macroeconomic Models: Recognizing the Limits to Knowability. *Journal of Economic Methodology* 20: 118–38.

Frydman, Roman, Michael D. Goldberg, Katarina Juselius, and Søren Johansen. 2008. A Resolution to the Purchasing Power Parity Puzzle: Imperfect Knowledge and Long Swings. Discussion Paper 31, University of Copenhagen, Copenhagen, Denmark.

Haavelmo, Trygve. 1944. The Probability Approach to Econometrics. *Econometrica* 12: 1–118.

Hands, D. Wade. 2013. Introduction to Symposium on Reflexivity and Economics: George Soros's Theory of Reflexivity and the Methodology of Economic Science. *Journal of Economic Methodology* 20: 303–08.

Hommes, Cars H. 2006. Heterogeneous Agent Models in Economics and Finance. In *Handbook of Computational Economics*. Edited by L. Tesfation and K.L. Judd. Amsterdam: Elsevier, vol. 2, chp 23, pp. 1109–86.

Hommes, Cars H. 2013. Reflexivity, Expectations Feedback and Almost Self-Fulfilling Equilibria: Economic Theory, Empirical Evidence and Laboratory Experiments. *Journal of Economic Methodology* 20: 406–19.

Hommes, Cars H., Hai Huang, and Duo Wang. 2005a. A Robust Rational Route to Randomness in a Simple Asset Pricing Model. *Journal of Economic Dynamics and Control* 29: 1043–72. doi:10.1016/j.jedc.2004.08.003.

Hommes, Cars H., Joep Sonnemans, Jan Tuinstra, and Henk van der Velden. 2005b. Coordination of Expectations in Asset Pricing Experiments. *Review of Financial Studies* 18: 955–80. doi:10.1093/rfs/hhi003.

Hoover, Kevin, and Katarina Juselius. 2015. Trygve Haavelmo's Experimental Methodology and Scenario Analysis in a Cointegrated Vector Autoregression. *Econometric Theory* 31: 249–74.

Hoover, Kevin, Søren Johansen, and Katarina Juselius. 2008. Allowing the Data to Speak Freely: The Macroeconometrics of the Cointegrated VAR. *American Economic Review* 98: 251–55.

Johansen, Søren. 1992. A Representation of Vector Autoregressive Processes Integrated of Order 2. *Econometric Theory* 8: 188–202.

Johansen, Søren. 1995. *Likelihood-Based Inference in Cointegrated Vector Autoregressive Models*, 2nd ed. Oxford: Oxford University Press.

Johansen, Soren. 1997. Likelihood Analysis of the $I(2)$ Model. *Scandinavian Journal of Statistics* 24: 433–62.

Johansen, Soren. 2006. Statistical analysis of hypotheses on the cointegrating relations in the $I(2)$ model. *Journal of Econometrics* 132: 81–115.

Johansen, Søren, Katarina Juselius, Roman Frydman, and Michael Goldberg. 2010. Testing Hypotheses in an $I(2)$ Model With Piecewise Linear Trends. An Analysis of the Persistent Long Swings in the Dmk/$ Rate. *Journal of Econometrics* 158: 117–29.

Juselius, Katarina. 2006. *The Cointegrated VAR Model: Methodology and Applications*. Oxford: Oxford University Press.

Juselius, Katarina. 2009. The Long Swings Puzzle. What the data tell when allowed to speak freely. In *The New Palgrave Handbook of Empirical Econometrics*. Edited by T.C. Mills and K. Patterson. London: MacMillan, chp. 8.

Juselius, Katarina. 2012. Imperfect Knowledge, Asset Price Swings and Structural Slumps: A Cointegrated VAR Analysis of Their Interdependence. In *Rethinking Expectations: The Way Forward for Macroeconomics*. Edited by E. Phelps and R. Frydman. Princeton: Princeton University Press.

Juselius, Katarina. 2014. Testing for Near $I(2)$ Trends When the Signal to Noise Ratio Is Small. *Economics-The Open-Access, Open-Assessment E-Journal* 21: 1–30. [CrossRef]

Juselius, Katarina. 2015. Haavelmo's Probability Approach and the Cointegrated VAR model. *Econometric Theory* 31: 213–32.

Juselius, Katarina. 2017. A Theory-Consistent CVAR Scenario: Testing a Rational Expectations Based Monetary Model. Working Paper. University of Copenhagen, Copenhagen, Denmark.

Juselius, Katarina, and Katrin Assenmacher. 2017. Real Exchange Rate Persistence and the Excess Return Puzzle: the Case of Switzerland Versus the US. *Journal of Applied Econometrics*. doi:10.1002/jae.2562.

Juselius, Katarina, and Massimo Franchi. 2007. Taking a DSGE Model to the Data Meaningfully. *Economics-The Open-Access, Open-Assessment E-Journal* 1: 1–38.

Juselius, Katarina, and Josh Stillwagon. 2017. Are outcomes driving expectations or the other way around? An $I(2)$ CVAR analysis of interest rate expectations in the dollar/pound market. *Journal of Applied Econometrics*, under review.

Juselius, Mikael. 2010. Testing Steady-State Restrictions of Linear Rational Expectations Models when Data are Highly Persistent. *Oxford Bulletin of Economics and Statistics* 73: 315–34.

Kahneman, Daniel, and Amos Tversky. 1979. Prospect Theory: An Analysis of Decision Under Risk. *Econometrica* 47: 263–91.

Kongsted, Hans Christian, Anders Rahbek, and Clara Jørgensen. 1999. Trend Stationarity in the ($I2$) Cointegration Model. *Journal of Econometrics* 90: 265–89.

Krugman, Paul. 1986. Pricing to Market When the Exchange Rate Changes. NBER Working Paper 1926, National Bureau of Economic Research, Cambridge, MA, USA.

Nielsen, Heino Bohn, and Anders Rahbek. 2007. The Likelihood Ratio Test for Cointegration Ranks in the $I(2)$ Model. *Econometric Theory* 23: 615–37.

Moller, Niels Framroze. 2008. Bridging Economic Theory Models and the Cointegrated Vector Autoregressive Model. *Economics: The Open-Access, Open-Assessment E-Journal* 2: 36.

Phelps, Edmund S. 1994. *Structural Slumps*. Princeton: Princeton University Press.

Rogoff, Kenneth. 1996. The Purchasing Power Parity Puzzle. *Journal of Economic Literature* 34: 647–68.

Taylor, Mark P., and David A. Peel. 2000. Nonlinear Adjustment, Long-Run Equilibrium and Exchange Rate Fundamentals. *Journal of International Money and Finance* 19: 33–53.

Soros, George. 1987. *The Alchemy of Finance*. Hoboken: John Wiley & Sons.

Stillwagon, Joshua, Michael D. Goldberg, and Nevin Cavusogluc. 2017. New Evidence on the Portfolio Balance Approach to Currency Return. Preprint at the Department of Economics, Trinity College, Hartford, Connecticut, USA.

Tabor, Morten Nyboe. 2017. Time-Varying Cointegration Parameters as a Source of Slow Error-Correction in the Cointegrated VAR Model: A Simulation Study. *Econometrics*, submitted for publication.

econometrics

MDPI

Article

Maximum Likelihood Estimation of the I(2) Model under Linear Restrictions

Jurgen A. Doornik

Department of Economics and Institute for New Economic Thinking at the Oxford Martin School, University of Oxford, Oxford, OX1 3UQ, UK; jurgen.doornik@nuffield.ox.ac.uk

Academic Editor: Katarina Juselius
Received: 27 February 2017; Accepted: 8 May 2017; Published: 15 May 2017

Abstract: Estimation of the I(2) cointegrated vector autoregressive (CVAR) model is considered. Without further restrictions, estimation of the I(1) model is by reduced-rank regression (Anderson (1951)). Maximum likelihood estimation of I(2) models, on the other hand, always requires iteration. This paper presents a new triangular representation of the I(2) model. This is the basis for a new estimation procedure of the unrestricted I(2) model, as well as the I(2) model with linear restrictions imposed.

Keywords: cointegration; I(2); vector autoregression; representation; maximum likelihood estimation; reduced rank regression; generalized least squares

JEL Classification: C32; C51; C61

1. Introduction

The I(1) model or cointegrated vector autoregression (CVAR) is now well established. The model is developed in a series of papers and books (see, e.g., Johansen (1988), Johansen (1991), Johansen (1995a), Juselius (2006)) and generally available in econometric software. The I(1) model is formulated as a rank reduction of the matrix of 'long-run' coefficients. The Gaussian log-likelihood is estimated by reduced-rank regression (RRR; see Anderson (1951), Anderson (2002)).

Determining the cointegrating rank only finds the cointegrating vectors up to a rank-preserving linear transformation. Therefore, the next step of an empirical study usually identifies the cointegrating vectors. This may be followed by imposing over-identifying restrictions. Common restrictions, i.e., the same restrictions on each cointegrating vector, can still be solved by adjusting the RRR estimation; see Johansen and Juselius (1990) and Johansen and Juselius (1992). Estimation with separate linear restrictions on the cointegrating vectors, or more general non-linear restrictions, requires iterative maximization. The usual approach is based on so-called switching algorithms; see Johansen (1995b) and Boswijk and Doornik (2004). The former proposes an algorithm that alternates between cointegrating vectors, estimating one while keeping the others fixed. The latter consider algorithms that alternate between the cointegrating vectors and their loadings: when one is kept fixed, the other is identified. The drawback is that these algorithms can be very slow and occasionally terminate prematurely. Doornik (2017) proposes improvements that can be applied to all switching algorithms.

Johansen (1995c) and Johansen (1997) extend the CVAR to allow for I(2) stochastic trends. These tend to be smoother than I(1) stochastic trends. The I(2) model implies a second reduced rank restriction, but this is now more complicated, and estimation under Gaussian errors can no longer be performed by RRR. The basis of an algorithm for maximum likelihood estimation is presented in Johansen (1997), with an implementation in Dennis and Juselius (2004).

The general approach to handling the I(2) model is to create representations that introduce parameters that vary freely without changing the nature of the model. This facilitates both the statistical analysis and the estimation.

The contributions of the current paper are two-fold. First, we present the triangular representation of the I(2) model. This is a new trilinear formulation with a block-triangular matrix structure at its core. The triangular representation provides a convenient framework for imposing linear restrictions on the model parameters. Next, we introduce several improved estimation algorithms for the I(2) model. A simulation experiment is used to study the behaviour of the algorithms.

Notation

Let α $(p \times r)$ be a matrix with full column rank $r, r \leq p$. The perpendicular matrix $\alpha_{\llcorner}$ $(p \times p{-}r)$ has $\alpha_{\llcorner}' \alpha = 0$. The orthogonal complement $\alpha_{\perp}$ has $\alpha_{\perp}'\alpha = 0$ with the additional property that $\alpha_{\perp}'\alpha_{\perp} = I_{p-r}$. Define $\tilde{\alpha} = \alpha(\alpha'\alpha)^{-1/2}$ and $\bar{\alpha} = \alpha(\alpha'\alpha)^{-1}$. Then, $(\tilde{\alpha} : \alpha_{\perp})$ is a $p \times p$ orthogonal matrix, so $I_p = \tilde{\alpha}\tilde{\alpha}' + \alpha_{\perp}\alpha_{\perp}' = \bar{\alpha}\alpha' + \alpha_{\perp}\alpha_{\perp}' = \alpha\bar{\alpha}' + \alpha_{\perp}\alpha_{\perp}'$.

The (thin) singular value decomposition (SVD) of α is $\alpha = UWV'$, where $U(p \times r), V(r \times r)$ are orthogonal: $U'U = V'V = VV' = I_r$, and W is a diagonal matrix with the ordered positive singular values on the diagonal. If $\text{rank}(\alpha) = s < r$, then the last $r - s$ singular values are zero. We can find $\alpha_{\perp} = U_2$ from the SVD of the square matrix $(\alpha : 0) = (U_1 : U_2)WV' = (U_1 W_1 V_1' : 0)$.

The (thin) QR factorization of α with pivoting is $\alpha P = QR$, with $Q(p \times r)$ orthogonal and R upper triangular. This pivoting is the reordering of columns of α to better handle poor conditioning and singularity, and is captured in P, as discussed Golub and Van Loan (2013, §5.4.2).

The QL decomposition of A can be derived from the QR decomposition of JAJ: $JAJ = QR$, so $A = JJAJJ = JQJJZJ = Q'L$. J is the exchange matrix, which is the identity matrix with columns in reverse order: premultiplication reverses rows; postmultiplication reverses columns; and $JJ = I$.

Let $\bar{\bar{\alpha}} = \Omega^{-1}\alpha\left(\alpha'\Omega^{-1}\alpha\right)^{-1}$, then $\alpha_{\perp}'\Omega\bar{\bar{\alpha}} = 0$.

Finally, $a \leftarrow b$ assigns the value of b to a.

2. The I(2) Model

The vector autoregression (VAR) with p dependent variables and $m \geq 1$ lags:

$$y_t = A_1 y_{t-1} + \ldots + A_m y_{t-m} + \Phi x_t^U + \epsilon_t, \quad \epsilon_t \sim \text{IIN}_p[0_p, \Omega],$$

for $t = 1, \ldots, T$, and with $y_j, j = -m+1, \ldots, 0$ fixed and given, can be written in equilibrium correction form as:

$$\Delta y_t = \Pi_y y_{t-1} + \Gamma_1 \Delta y_{t-1} + \ldots + \Gamma_{m-1}\Delta y_{t-m+1} + \Phi x_t^U + \epsilon_t,$$

without imposing any restrictions. The I(1) cointegrated VAR (CVAR) imposes a reduced rank restriction on $\Pi_y(p \times p)$: $\text{rank}\Pi_y = r$; see, e.g., Johansen and Juselius (1990), Johansen (1995a).

With $m \geq 2$, the model can be written in second-differenced equilibrium correction form as:

$$\Delta^2 y_t = \Pi_y y_{t-1} - \Gamma_y \Delta y_{t-1} + \Psi_1 \Delta^2 y_{t-1} + \ldots + \Psi_{m-2}\Delta^2 y_{t-m+2} + \Phi x_t^U + \epsilon_t. \tag{1}$$

The I(2) CVAR involves an additional reduced rank restriction:

$$\text{rank}(\alpha_{\perp}'\Gamma_y \beta_{y,\perp}) = s,$$

where $\alpha_{\perp}'\alpha = 0$. The two rank restrictions can be expressed more conveniently in terms of products of matrices with reduced dimensions:

$$\Pi_y = \alpha\beta_y', \tag{2}$$

$$\alpha_{\perp}'\Gamma_y\beta_{y,\perp} = \xi\eta_y', \tag{3}$$

where α and β_y are $p \times r$ matrices. The second restriction needs rank s, so ξ and η_y are a $(p-r) \times s$. This requires that the matrices on the right-hand side of (2) and (3) have full column rank. The number of I(2) trends is $s_2 = p - r - s$.

The most relevant model in terms of deterministics allows for linearly trending behaviour: $\Phi x_t^U = \mu_0 + \mu_1 t$. Using the representation theorem of Johansen (1992) and assuming $\mathsf{E}[y_t] = a + bt$ imply:

$$\mu_1 = -\alpha\beta_y' b, \tag{4}$$

$$\mu_0 = -\alpha\beta_y' a + \Gamma_y b, \tag{5}$$

which restricts and links μ_0 and μ_1; we see that $\alpha_\perp' \mu_1 = 0$ and $\alpha_\perp' \mu_0 = \alpha_\perp' \Gamma_y b$.

2.1. The I(2) Model with a Linear Trend

The model (1) subject to the I(1) and I(2) rank restrictions (2) and (3) with $\Phi x_t^U = \mu_0 + \mu_1 t$, subject to (4) and (5) can be written as:

$$\Delta^2 y_t = \alpha\beta' \begin{pmatrix} y_{t-1} \\ t \end{pmatrix} - \Gamma \begin{pmatrix} \Delta y_{t-1} \\ 1 \end{pmatrix} + \Psi_1 \Delta^2 y_{t-1} + \ldots + \Psi_{m-2} \Delta^2 y_{t-m+2} + \epsilon_t, \tag{6}$$

subject to:

$$\alpha_\perp' \Gamma \beta_\perp = \xi \eta', \tag{7}$$

where β is $p_1 \times r$, Γ is $p \times p_1$ and η is $(p_1 - r) \times s$. In this case, $p_1 = p + 1$. Because α is the leading term in (4), we can extend β_y by introducing $\beta_c' = -\beta_y' b$, so $\beta' = (\beta_y' : \beta_c')$. Furthermore, Γ has been extended to $\Gamma = (\Gamma_y : \Gamma_c) = (\Gamma_y : -\mu_0)$.

To see that (6) and (7) remains the same I(2) model, consider $\alpha_\perp' \Gamma_c$ and insert $I_p = \beta_y \overline{\beta}_y' + \beta_{y\perp} \beta_{y\perp}'$:

$$\alpha_\perp' \Gamma_c = -\alpha_\perp' \Gamma_y \overline{\beta}_y \beta_y' b - \alpha_\perp' \Gamma_y \beta_{y\perp} \beta_{y\perp}' b = \alpha_\perp' \Gamma_y \overline{\beta}_y \beta_c' - \xi \eta_y' \beta_{y\perp}' b = \alpha_\perp' \Gamma_y \overline{\beta}_y \beta_c' + \xi \eta_c'.$$

Using the perpendicular matrix:

$$\beta_\llcorner = \begin{pmatrix} \beta_{y\perp} & -\overline{\beta}_y \beta_c' \\ 0 & 1 \end{pmatrix}$$

we see that the rank condition is unaffected:

$$\alpha_\perp' \Gamma \beta_\llcorner = (\alpha_\perp' \Gamma_y \beta_{y\perp} : \xi \eta_c') = \left(\alpha_\perp' \Gamma_y \beta_{y\perp} : \alpha_\perp' [-\Gamma_y \overline{\beta}_y \beta_c' + \Gamma_c]\right) = \xi \left(\eta_y' : \eta_c'\right).$$

A more general formulation allows for restricted deterministic and weakly exogenous variables x_t^R and unrestricted variables x_t^U:

$$\begin{aligned} \Delta^2 y_t &= \Pi \begin{pmatrix} y_{t-1} \\ x_{t-1}^R \end{pmatrix} - \Gamma \begin{pmatrix} \Delta y_{t-1} \\ \Delta x_t^R \end{pmatrix} + \Psi_1 \Delta^2 y_{t-1} + \ldots + \Psi_{m-2} \Delta^2 y_{t-m+2} + \Phi x_t^U + \epsilon_t, \\ &= \Pi w_{2t} - \Gamma w_{1t} + \Psi w_{3t} + \epsilon_t, \end{aligned}$$

where $\Delta^2 x_t^R$, and its lags are contained in x_t^U; this in turn, is subsumed under $w_{3t} = (\Delta^2 y_{t-1}', \ldots, x_t^{U\prime})'$. The number of variables in x_t^R is $p_1 - p$, so Π and Γ always have the same dimensions. Ψ is unrestricted, which allows it to be concentrated out by regressing all other variables on w_{3t}:

$$z_{0t} = \alpha\beta' z_{2t} - \Gamma z_{1t} + \epsilon_t, \quad \epsilon_t \sim \mathsf{IIN}_p[0_p, \Omega]. \tag{8}$$

To implement likelihood-ratio tests, it is necessary to count the number of restrictions:

$$\begin{array}{lrl} \text{restrictions on } \Pi: & (p-r)(p_1-r) & \text{restrictions,} \\ \text{restrictions on } \Gamma: & (p-r-s)(p_1-r-s) = s_2 s_2^* & \text{restrictions,} \end{array}$$

defining $s_2^* = p_1 - r - s$. The restrictions on Π follow from the representation. Several representations of the I(2) model have been introduced in the literature to translate the implicit non-linear restriction (3) on Γ into an explicit part of the model. These representations reveal the number of restrictions imposed on Γ, as is shown below.

First, we introduce the new triangular representation.

2.2. The Triangular Representation

Theorem 1. *Consider the model:*

$$z_{0t} = \Pi z_{2t} - \Gamma z_{1t} + \epsilon_t,$$

with rank restrictions $\Pi = \alpha\beta'$ and $\alpha_\perp'\Gamma\beta_\perp = \xi\eta'$ where α is a $p \times r$ matrix, β is $p_1 \times r$, ξ is $(p-r) \times s$, η is $(p_1 - r) \times s$. This can be written as:

$$z_{0t} = AWB'z_{2t} - AVB'z_{1t} + \epsilon_t, \tag{9}$$

where:

$$W = \begin{pmatrix} 0 & 0 & 0 \\ 0 & 0 & 0 \\ W_{11} & 0 & 0 \end{pmatrix}, \quad V = \begin{pmatrix} V_{31} & 0 & 0 \\ V_{21} & V_{22} & 0 \\ V_{11} & V_{12} & V_{13} \end{pmatrix}. \tag{10}$$

A, B, W_{11}, V_{22} are full rank matrices. A is $p \times p$, and B is $p_1 \times p_1$; moreover, A, B and the nonzero blocks in W and V are freely varying. A and B are partitioned as:

$$A = (A_2 : A_1 : A_0), \quad B = (B_0 : B_1 : B_2),$$

where the blocks in A have s_2, s, r columns respectively; for B, this is: r, s, s_2^*; $p_1 = r + s + s_2^*$. W and V are partitioned accordingly.

Proof. Write $\widetilde{\alpha} = \alpha(\alpha'\alpha)^{-1/2}$, such that $\widetilde{\alpha}'\widetilde{\alpha} = I_r$. Construct A and B as:

$$A = \left(\alpha_\perp\xi_\perp : \alpha_\perp\widetilde{\xi} : \widetilde{\alpha}\right), \quad B = \left(\widetilde{\beta} : \beta_\perp\widetilde{\eta} : \beta_\perp\eta_\perp\right).$$

Now, $A'A = I$ and $B'B = I$. $A(p \times p)$ and $B(p_1 \times p_1)$ are full rank by design. Define $V = A'\Gamma B$:

$$V = \begin{pmatrix} \xi_\perp'\alpha_\perp'\Gamma\widetilde{\beta} & \xi_\perp'\alpha_\perp'\Gamma\beta_\perp\widetilde{\eta} & \xi_\perp'\alpha_\perp'\Gamma\beta_\perp\eta_\perp \\ \widetilde{\xi}'\alpha_\perp'\Gamma\widetilde{\beta} & \widetilde{\xi}'\alpha_\perp'\Gamma\beta_\perp\widetilde{\eta} & \widetilde{\xi}'\alpha_\perp'\Gamma\beta_\perp\eta_\perp \\ \widetilde{\alpha}'\Gamma\widetilde{\beta} & \widetilde{\alpha}'\Gamma\beta_\perp\widetilde{\eta} & \widetilde{\alpha}'\Gamma\beta_\perp\eta_\perp \end{pmatrix} = \begin{pmatrix} V_{31} & 0 & 0 \\ V_{21} & V_{22} & 0 \\ V_{11} & V_{12} & V_{13} \end{pmatrix}.$$

$V_{22} = (\xi'\xi)^{\frac{1}{2}}(\eta'\eta)^{\frac{1}{2}}$ is a full rank $s \times s$ matrix. The zero blocks in V arise because, e.g., $\xi_\perp'\alpha_\perp'\Gamma\beta_\perp = \xi_\perp'\xi\eta' = 0$. Trivially:

$$\Pi = \alpha\beta' = A\begin{pmatrix} 0 & 0 & 0 \\ 0 & 0 & 0 \\ W_{11} & 0 & 0 \end{pmatrix}B' = AWB'.$$

$W_{11} = (\alpha'\alpha)^{\frac{1}{2}}(\beta'\beta)^{\frac{1}{2}}$ is a full rank $r \times r$ matrix. Both W and V are $p \times p_1$ matrices. Because A and B are each orthogonal: $\Gamma = AA'\Gamma BB' = AVB'$.

The QR decomposition shows that a full rank square matrix can be written as the product of an orthogonal matrix and a triangular matrix. Therefore, $AVB' = AL_aL_a^{-1}VL_bL_b^{-1}B' = A_*V_*B_*'$ preserves the structure in V_* when L_a, L_b are lower triangular, as well as that in W_*. This shows that (9) holds for any full rank A and B, and the orthogonality can be relaxed.

Therefore, any model with full rank matrices A and B, together with any W, V that have the zeros as described above, satisfies the I(2) rank restrictions. We obtain the same model by restricting A and B to be orthogonal. □

When Γ is restricted only by the I(2) condition: $\text{rank}\Gamma = r + s + \min(r, s_2)$. Then, V varies freely, except for the zero blocks, and the I(2) restrictions are imposed through the trilinear form of (9). $\Gamma = 0$ implies $V = 0$. Another way to have $s = 0$ is $\Gamma = (\alpha : 0)G$; in that case, $V \neq 0$.

The s_2 restrictions on the intercept (5) can be expressed as $A_2'(\mu_0 - \mu_c) = 0$, using $\mu_c = \Gamma_y \overline{\beta}_y \beta_c'$, or $\mu_0 = (A_1 : A_0)v + \mu_c$, for a vector v of length $r + s$.

2.3. Obtaining the Triangular Representation

The triangular representation shows that the I(2) model can be written in trilinear form:

$$z_{0t} = AWB'z_{2t} - AVB'z_{1t} + \epsilon_t,$$

where A and B are freely varying, provided W and V have the appropriate structure.

Consider that we are given α, β, Γ of an I(2) CVAR with rank indices r, s and wish to obtain the parameters of the triangular representation. First compute $\alpha_\perp' \Gamma \beta_\perp = \xi \eta'$, which can be done with the SVD, assuming rank s. From this, compute A and B:

$$A = (A_2 : A_1 : A_0) = \left(\alpha_\perp \xi_\perp : \alpha_\perp \tilde{\xi} : \alpha\right), \quad B = (B_0 : B_1 : B_2) = (\beta : \beta_\perp \tilde{\eta} : \beta_\perp \eta_\perp).$$

Then, $V = A^{-1}\Gamma B^{-1\prime}$. Because Γ satisfies the I(2) rank restriction, V will have the corresponding block-triangular structure.

It may be of interest to consider which part of the structure can be retrieved in the case where $\text{rank}(\Pi) = r$, but $\text{rank}(\alpha_\perp' \Gamma \beta_\perp) = p - r$, while it should be s. This would happen when using I(1) starting values for I(2) estimation. The off anti-diagonal blocks of zeros:

$$V^* = \begin{pmatrix} V_{31}^* & V_{32}^* & V_{33}^* \\ V_{21} & V_{22} & V_{23}^* \\ V_{11} & V_{12} & V_{13}^* \end{pmatrix} \rightarrow \begin{pmatrix} V_{31} & 0 & V_{33} \\ V_{21} & V_{22} & 0 \\ V_{11} & V_{12} & V_{13} \end{pmatrix} = V \tag{11}$$

can be implemented with two sweep operations:

$$\begin{pmatrix} I_{s_2} & -V_{32}^* V_{22}^{-1} & 0 \\ 0 & I_s & 0 \\ 0 & 0 & I_r \end{pmatrix} V^* \begin{pmatrix} I_r & 0 & 0 \\ 0 & I_s & -V_{22}^{-1} V_{23}^* \\ 0 & 0 & I_{s_2^*} \end{pmatrix}.$$

The offsetting operations affect A_1 and B_1 only, so Π and Γ are unchanged. However, we cannot achieve $V_{33} = 0$ in a similar way, because it would remove the zeros just obtained. The V_{33} block has dimension $s_2 s_2^*$ and represents the number of restrictions imposed on Γ in the I(2) model. Similarly, the anti-diagonal block of zeros in W captures the restrictions on Π.

Note that the $r \times s_2^*$ block V_{13} can be made lower triangular. Write the column partition of V as $(V_{\cdot 1} : V_{\cdot 2} : V_{\cdot 3})$, and use $V_{13} = LQ$ to replace $V_{\cdot 3}$ by $V_{\cdot 3}Q'$ and B_2 by $B_2 Q'$. When $r < s_2^*$, the rightmost $s_2^* - r$ columns of L will be zero, and the corresponding columns of B_2 are not needed to compute Γ. This part can then be omitted from the likelihood evaluation. This is an issue when we propose an estimation procedure in §4.2.1.

2.4. Restoring Orthogonality

Although A and B are freely varying, interpretation may require orthogonality between column blocks. The column blocks of A are in reverse order from B to make V and W block lower triangular. As a consequence, multiplication of V or W from either side by a lower triangular matrix preserves their structure. This allows for the relaxation of the orthogonality of A and B, but also enables us to restore it again.

To restore orthogonality, let $\Gamma = A_* V_* B_*'$, where A_*, B_* are not orthogonal, but with V_* block-triangular. Now, use the QL decomposition to get $A_* = AL$, with A orthogonal and L lower triangular. Use the QR decomposition to get $B_* = BR$, with B orthogonal and R upper triangular. Then, $A_* V_* B_*' = ALV_* R' B' = AVB'$ with the blocks of zeros in V preserved. $A_* W_* B_*'$ must be adjusted accordingly. When β is restricted, B_0 cannot be modified like this. However, we can still adjust $(A_2 : A_1) = A_*$ to get $A_*' A_* = I_{p-r}$ and $A_0' A_* = 0$; with similar adjustments to $(B_1 : B_2)$.

The orthogonal version is convenient mathematically, but for estimation, it is preferable to use the unrestricted version. We do not distinguish through notation, but the context will state when the orthogonal version is used.

2.5. Identification in the Triangular Representation

The matrices A and B are not identified without further restrictions. For example, rescaling α and β as in $\alpha W_{11} \beta' = \alpha' c^{-1} c W_{11} d d^{-1} \beta = \alpha^* c W_{11} d \beta^{*\prime}$ can be absorbed in V:

$$\begin{pmatrix} V_{31} d & 0 & 0 \\ V_{21} d & V_{22} & 0 \\ c V_{11} d & c V_{12} & c V_{13} \end{pmatrix}.$$

When β is identified, W_{11} remains freely varying, and we can, e.g., set $c = W_{11}^{-1}$. However, it is convenient to transform to $W_{11} = I$, so that A_0 and B_0 correspond to α and β. This prevents part of the orthogonality, in the sense that $A_0' A_0 \neq I$ and $B_0' B_0 \neq I$.

The following scheme identifies A and B, under the assumption that B_0 is already identified through prior restrictions.

1. Orthogonalize to obtain $A_0' A_1 = 0, A_0' A_2 = 0, A_1' A_2 = 0$.
2. Choose s full rank rows from B_1, denoted M_{B_1}, and set $B_1 \leftarrow B_1 M_{B_1}^{-1}$. Adjust V accordingly.
3. Do the same for $B_2 \leftarrow B_2 M_{B_2}^{-1}$.
4. Set $A_1 \leftarrow A_1 V_{22}$, $V_{21} \leftarrow V_{22}^{-1} V_{21}$ and $V_{22} \leftarrow I$.
5. $A_2 \leftarrow A_2 M_{A_2}^{-1}$.

The ordering of columns inside A_i, B_i is not unique.

3. Relation to Other Representations

Two other formulations of the I(2) model that are in use are the so-called τ and δ representations. All representations implement the same model and make the rank restrictions explicit. However, they differ in their definitions of freely-varying parameters, so may facilitate different forms of analysis, e.g., asymptotic analysis, estimation or the imposition of restrictions. The different parametrizations may also affect economic interpretations.

3.1. τ Representation

Johansen (1997) transforms (8) into the τ-representation:

$$z_{0t} = \alpha \left(\varrho' \tau' z_{2t} + \psi' z_{1t} \right) + w \kappa' \tau' z_{1t} + \epsilon_t, \tag{12}$$

where $\varrho(p_1 \times r+s)$ is used to recover β: $\beta = \tau\varrho$. The parameters $(\alpha, \varrho, \tau, \psi, \kappa)$ vary freely. If we normalize on $\varrho' = (I_r : 0)$ and adjust κ, τ accordingly, then $\tau = (\beta : \beta_1)$, and:

$$z_{0t} = \alpha\left(\beta' z_{2t} + \psi' z_{1t}\right) + w\kappa'\tau' z_{1t} + \epsilon_t.$$

We shall derive the τ representation. The first step is to define a transformation of $\epsilon_t \sim \mathrm{N}[0, \Omega]$:

$$\begin{pmatrix} \alpha_\perp & \overline{\overline{\alpha}} \end{pmatrix}' \epsilon_t \sim \mathrm{N}\left[0, \begin{pmatrix} \alpha_\perp' \Omega \alpha_\perp & 0 \\ 0 & \left(\alpha' \Omega^{-1} \alpha\right)^{-1} \end{pmatrix}\right]. \tag{13}$$

This splits the p-variate systems into two independent parts. The first has any terms with leading α knocked out, while the second has all leading α's cancelled. The inverse transformation is given by: $(\alpha_\perp : \overline{\overline{\alpha}})^{-1} = (\alpha_\perp - \alpha\overline{\overline{\alpha}}'\alpha_\perp : \alpha)' = (w : \alpha)'$.

The next step is to apply (13) to (8) to create two independent systems and insert $I_p = \overline{\beta}\beta' + \beta_\perp\beta_\perp'$ in the 'marginal' equation:

$$\begin{pmatrix} \alpha_\perp & \overline{\overline{\alpha}} \end{pmatrix}' z_{0t} = \begin{cases} -\alpha_\perp'\Gamma(\overline{\beta}\beta' + \beta_\perp\beta_\perp')z_{1t} + \varepsilon_{1t} & = \kappa'(\beta : \beta_\perp\eta)' z_{1t} + \varepsilon_{1t}, \\ \beta' z_{2t} - \overline{\overline{\alpha}}'\Gamma z_{1t} + \varepsilon_{2t} & = \beta' z_{2t} + \psi' z_{1t} + \varepsilon_{2t}. \end{cases} \tag{14}$$

where $\psi' = -\overline{\overline{\alpha}}'\Gamma$ and $\kappa' = -(\alpha_\perp'\Gamma\overline{\beta} : \xi)$ are freely varying. Removing the transformation:

$$z_{0t} = w'\kappa'(\beta : \beta_\perp\eta)' z_{1t} + \alpha'(\beta' z_{2t} + \psi' z_{1t}) + \epsilon_t$$

and introducing the additional parameters $\tau = (\beta : \beta_\perp\eta)$ and ϱ completes the τ-representation (12). Table 1 provides definitions of the parameters that are used (cf. Johansen (1997, Tables 1 and 2)).

Table 1. Definitions of the symbols used in the τ and δ representations of the I(2) model.

Definition	Dimension
$\tau = (\beta : \beta_\perp\eta)$ when $\varrho' = (I : 0)$	$p_1 \times (r+s)$
$\tau_\perp = \beta_\perp\eta_\perp$	$p_1 \times s_2^*$
$\psi = -(\overline{\overline{\alpha}}'\Gamma)'$	$p_1 \times r$
$\kappa' = -\alpha_\perp'\Gamma\overline{\tau} = -(\alpha_\perp'\Gamma\overline{\beta} : \xi) = (\kappa_1 : \kappa_2)'$	$(p-r) \times (r+s)$
$\delta = -\overline{\alpha}'\Gamma\tau_\perp$	$r \times s_2^*$
$\zeta = -\Gamma\overline{\tau} = (\zeta_1 : \zeta_2)$	$p \times (r+s)$
$w = \alpha_\perp - \alpha\overline{\overline{\alpha}}'\alpha_\perp = \Omega\alpha_\perp\left(\alpha_\perp'\Omega\alpha_\perp\right)^{-1} = \overline{\overline{\alpha_\perp}}$	$p \times (p-r)$
$d = \tau_\perp\delta'$	$p_1 \times r$
$e = \tau\zeta'$	$p_1 \times p$

Corollary 1. *Triangular representation (9) is equivalent to the τ-representation (12) when $A_0'(A_2 : A_1) = 0$.*

Proof. Write $A_* = (A_2 : A_1)$, so $A = (A_* : A_0)$. First, the system (9) is premultiplied by $A^{-1} = \overline{A}'$ and subsequently with a lower triangular matrix L to create two independent subsystems. The matrix L and its inverse are given by:

$$L = \begin{pmatrix} I_{p-r} & 0 \\ -\overline{A}_0' w_* & I_r \end{pmatrix}, \quad L^{-1} = \begin{pmatrix} I_{p-r} & 0 \\ \overline{A}_0' w_* & I_r \end{pmatrix},$$

where $w_* = \Omega\overline{A}_*(\overline{A}_*'\Omega\overline{A}_*)^{-1}$, cf. (14). Because $A_0'A_* = 0$, we have that $A_* + A_0\overline{A}_0'w_* = A_* + (I - A_*\overline{A}_*)'w_* = w_*$, so $AL^{-1} = (w_* : A_0)$. Furthermore: $LW = W$. The identity matrix $L^{-1}L$ can also be inserted directly in (9):

$$\begin{aligned} z_{0t} &= A_0 W_{11} B_0' z_{2t} - (w_* : A_0) L V B' z_{1t} + \epsilon_t \\ &= A_0 W_{11} B_0' z_{2t} - w_* \begin{pmatrix} V_{31} & 0 \\ V_{21} & V_{22} \end{pmatrix} (B_0 : B_1)' z_{1t} + A_0 \overline{A}_0' w_* (V_{11} : V_{12} : V_{13}) B' z_{1t} + \epsilon_t \\ &= \alpha \left[\beta' z_{2t} + \psi' z_{1t}\right] + w\kappa'\tau' z_{1t} + \epsilon_t, \end{aligned}$$

where $\psi' = -\overline{A}_0' w_* (V_{11} : V_{12} : V_{13}) B'$ and $w\kappa' = -w_* \begin{pmatrix} V_{31} & 0 \\ V_{21} & V_{22} \end{pmatrix}$. □

3.2. δ Representation

Paruolo and Rahbek (1999) and Paruolo (2000a) use the δ representation:

$$z_{0t} = \alpha\left(\beta' z_{2t} + \delta\tau_\perp' z_{1t}\right) + \zeta\tau' z_{1t} + \epsilon_t. \tag{15}$$

Here, $(\alpha, \delta, \zeta, \tau = [\beta : \beta_1])$ vary freely. To derive the δ representation, use $\overline{\tau}\tau' + \tau_\perp\tau_\perp' = I_{r+s}$:

$$\begin{aligned} -\Gamma\overline{\tau}\tau' &= -(\Gamma\overline{\beta} : \Gamma\beta_\perp\overline{\eta})\tau' = (\zeta_1 : \zeta_2)\tau' = \zeta\tau', \\ -\Gamma\tau_\perp\tau_\perp' &= -\alpha\overline{\alpha}'\Gamma\tau_\perp\tau_\perp' - \alpha_\perp\alpha_\perp'\Gamma\tau_\perp\tau_\perp' = \alpha\delta\tau_\perp', \end{aligned}$$

and insert in (8). The term with $\alpha_\perp'\Gamma\tau_\perp$ disappears because $\tau_\perp = \beta_\perp\eta_\perp$, so $\alpha_\perp'\Gamma\tau_\perp = \xi\eta'\eta_\perp = 0$.

When β is identified both $\delta\tau_\perp'$ and $\zeta\tau'$ are unique, but not yet ζ or δ. In the τ representation, the variable ψ is also unique with ϱ chosen as $(I : 0)'$ and β identified. Table 2 relates the τ, δ and triangular representations.

Table 2. Links between symbols used in the representations of the I(2) model, assuming $W_{11} = I_r$ and $a_\perp' a_\perp = I$.

$-\Gamma = \alpha\psi' + w\kappa'\tau' = \alpha\delta\tau_\perp' + \zeta\tau' = \alpha d' + e'$			
ζ	=	$\alpha\psi'\overline{\tau} + w\kappa'$	(from $\Gamma\overline{\tau}$)
d'	=	$\psi'\tau_\perp\tau_\perp'$	(from $\Gamma\tau_\perp$)
κ'	=	$\alpha_\perp'\zeta$	(from $\alpha_\perp'\Gamma$)
ψ'	=	$d' + \overline{\overline{\alpha}}'\zeta\tau'$	(from $\overline{\overline{\alpha}}'\Gamma$)
α	=	A_0	
β	=	B_0	
d'	=	$-V_{13}B_2'$	
e'	=	$-A(V_{.1} : V_{.2})(B_0 : B_1)'$	
τ	=	$(B_0 : B_1)$	

Corollary 2. *Triangular representation (9) is equivalent to the δ-representation (15) when $B_2'(B_0 : B_1) = 0$.*

Proof. Write $B_2 = \tau_\perp$ and $(B_0 : B_1) = \tau$. Using the column partitioning if $V = (V_{.1} : V_{.2} : V_{.3})$: $\Gamma\overline{\tau} = AVB'\overline{\tau} = A(V_{.1} : V_{.2})$. From (9):

$$\begin{aligned} z_{0t} &= A_0\left[W_{11}B_0' z_{2t} - V_{13}\tau_\perp' z_{1t}\right] - A(V_{.1} : V_{.2})\tau' z_{1t} + \epsilon_t \\ &= A_0\left[W_{11}B_0' z_{2t} - V_{13}\tau_\perp' z_{1t}\right] - \Gamma\overline{\tau}\tau' z_{1t} + \epsilon_t = \alpha\left[\beta' z_{2t} + \delta\tau_\perp' z_{1t}\right] + \zeta\tau' z_{1t} + \epsilon_t. \end{aligned}$$

□

4. Algorithms for Gaussian Maximum Likelihood Estimation

Algorithms to estimate the Gaussian CVAR are usually alternating over sets of variables. In the cointegration literature, these are called switching algorithms, following Johansen and Juselius (1994).

The advantage of switching is that each step is easy to implement, and no derivatives are required. Furthermore, the partitioning circumvents the lack of identification that can occur in these models and which makes it harder to use Newton-type methods. The drawback is that progress is often slow, taking many iterations to converge. Occasionally, this will lead to premature convergence. Although the steps can generally be shown to be in a non-downward direction, this is not enough to show convergence to a stationary point. The work in Doornik (2017) documents the framework for the switching algorithms and also considers acceleration of these algorithms; both results are used here.

Johansen (1997, §8) proposes an algorithm based on the τ-representation, called τ-switching here. This is presented in detail in Appendix B. Two new algorithms are given next, the first based on the δ-representation, the second on the triangular representation. Some formality is required to describe the algorithms with sufficient detail.

4.1. δ-Switching Algorithm

The free parameters in the δ-representation (15) are $(\alpha, \delta, \zeta, \tau)$ with symmetric positive definite Ω. The algorithm alternates between estimating τ given the rest and fixing τ. The model for τ given the other parameters is linear:

1. To estimate $\tau = [\beta : \beta_1]$, rewrite (15) as:

$$z_{0t} = \alpha\beta' z_{2t} + \zeta_1\beta' z_{1t} + \zeta_2\beta_1' z_{1t} + \alpha d z_{1t} + \epsilon_t,$$

where d replaces $\delta\tau_\perp'$. Then, vectorize, using $\alpha\beta' z_{2t} = \text{vec}(z_{2t}'\beta\alpha') = (\alpha \otimes z_{2t}')\text{vec}\beta$:

$$z_{0t} = (\alpha \otimes z_{2t}' + \zeta_1 \otimes z_{1t}')\text{vec}\beta + (\zeta_2 \otimes z_{1t}')\text{vec}\beta_1 + (\alpha \otimes z_{1t}')\,\text{vec}(d') + \epsilon_t. \quad (16)$$

Given $\alpha, \zeta_1, \zeta_2, \Omega$, we can treat β, β_1 and d as free parameters to be estimated by generalized least squares (GLS). This will give a new estimate of τ.

We can treat d as a free parameter in (16). First, when $r \geq s_2^*$, δ has more parameters than $\tau_\perp$. Second, when $r < s_2^*$, then Γ is reduced rank, and $s_2^* - r$ columns of $\tau_\perp$ are redundant. Orthogonality is recovered in the next step.

2. Given τ and derived $\tau_\perp$, we can estimate α and δ by RRR after concentrating out $\tau' z_{1t}$. Introducing ρ with dimension $(r+s_2^*) \times r$ allows us to write (15) as:

$$z_{0t} = \alpha^*\rho' \begin{pmatrix} \beta' z_{2t} \\ \tau_\perp' z_{1t} \end{pmatrix} + \zeta\tau' z_{1t} + \epsilon_t. \quad (17)$$

RRR provides estimates of α^* and ρ'. Next, $\alpha^*\rho'$ is transformed to $\alpha(I_r : \delta)$, giving new estimates of α and δ. Finally, ζ can be obtained by OLS from (17) given α, δ, τ, and hence, Ω.

The RRR step is the same as used in Dennis and Juselius (2004) and Paruolo (2000b). However, the GLS step for τ is different from both. We have found that the specification of the GLS step can have a substantial impact on the performance of the algorithm.

For numerical reasons (see, e.g. Golub and Van Loan (2013, Ch.5)), we prefer to use the QR decomposition to implement OLS and RRR estimation rather than moment matrices. However, in iterative estimation, there are very many regressions, which would be much faster using precomputed moment matrices. As a compromise, we use precomputed 'data' matrices that are transformed by a QR decomposition. This reduces the effective sample size from T to $2p_1$. The regressions (16) and (17) can then be implemented in terms of the transformed data matrices; see Appendix A.

Usually, starting values of α and β are available from I(1) estimation. The initial τ is then obtained from the marginal equation of the τ-representation, (14a), written as:

$$\alpha_{\perp}' z_{0t} = \kappa'\tau' z_{1t} + \varepsilon_{1t} = \kappa_1'\beta' z_{1t} + \xi\eta'\beta_{\perp}' z_{1t} + \varepsilon_{1t}. \tag{18}$$

RRR of $\alpha_{\perp}' z_{0t}$ on $\beta_{\perp}' z_{1t}$ corrected for $\beta' z_{1t}$ gives estimates of η, and so, τ.

δ-switching algorithm:
To start, set $k = 1$, and choose starting values $\alpha^{(0)}, \beta^{(0)}$, tolerance ε_1 and the maximum number of iterations. Compute $\tau_c^{(0)}$ from (18) and $\alpha^{(0)}, \delta^{(0)}, \zeta^{(0)}, \Omega^{(0)}$ from (17). Furthermore, compute $f^{(0)} = -\log|\Omega^{(0)}|$.

1. Get $\tau_c^{(k)}$ from (16); get the remaining parameters from (17).
2. Compute $f_c^{(k)} = -\log|\Omega_c^{(k)}|$.
3. Enter a line search for τ.
   The change in τ is $\nabla = \tau_c^{(k)} - \tau^{(k-1)}$ and the line search find a step length λ with $\tau^{(k)} = \tau^{(k-1)} + \lambda\nabla$. Because only τ is varied, a GLS step is needed to evaluate the log-likelihood for each trial τ. The line search gives new parameters with corresponding $f^{(k)}$.

T. Compute the relative change from the previous iteration:

$$c^{(k)} = \frac{f^{(k)} - f^{(k-1)}}{1 + |f^{(k-1)}|}.$$

Terminate if:

$$|c^{(k)}| \leq \varepsilon_1 \text{ and } \max_{i,j} \frac{\left|\Pi_{ij}^{(k)} - \Pi_{ij}^{(k-1)}\right|}{1 + \left|\Pi_{ij}^{(k-1)}\right|} \leq \varepsilon_1^{1/2}. \tag{19}$$

Else increment k, and return to Step 1. □

The subscript c indicates that these are candidate values that may be improved upon by the line search. The line search is the concentrated version, so the I(2) equivalent to the LBeta line search documented in Doornik (2017). This means that the function evaluation inside the line search needs to re-evaluate all of the other parameters as τ changes. Therefore, within the line search, we effectively concentrate out all other parameters.

Normalization of τ prevents the scale from growing excessively, and it was found to be beneficial to normalize in the first iteration every hundredth or when the norm of τ gets large. Continuous normalization had a negative impact in our experiments. Care is required when normalizing: if an iteration uses a different normalization from the previous one, then the line search will only be effective if the previous coefficients are adjusted accordingly.

The algorithm is incomplete without starting values, and it is obvious that a better start will lead to faster and more reliable convergence. Experimentation also showed that this and other algorithms struggled more in cases with $s = 0$. To improve this, we generate two initial values, follow three iterations of the τ-switching algorithms, then select the best for continuation. The details are in Appendix C.

4.2. MLE with the Triangular Representation

We set $W_{11} = I$. This tends to lead to slower convergence, but is required when both α and β are restricted. V_{22} is kept unrestricted: fewer restrictions seem to lead to faster convergence. All regressions use the data matrices that are pre-transformed by an orthogonal matrix as described in Appendix A. In the next section, we describe the estimation steps that can be repeated until convergence.

4.2.1. Estimation Steps

Equation (9) provides a convenient structure for an alternating variables algorithm. We can solve three separate steps by ordinary or generalized least squares for the case with orthogonal A:

1. B-step: estimate B, and fix A, V, W, Ω at A_c, V_c, W_c, Ω_c. The resulting model is linear in B:

$$z_{0t} = A_c W_c B' z_{2t} - A_c V_c B' z_{1t} + \varepsilon_t. \tag{20}$$

Estimation by GLS can be conveniently done as follows. Start with the Cholesky decomposition $\Omega_c = PP'$, and premultiply (20) by P^{-1}. Next take the QL decomposition of $P^{-1}A$ as $P^{-1}A = HL$ with L lower diagonal and H orthogonal. Now, premultiply the transformed system by H':

$$H'P^{-1}z_{0t} = LW_c B' z_{2t} - LV_c B' z_{1t} + u_t = \widetilde{W}_c B' z_{2t} - \widetilde{V}_c B' z_{1t} + u_t,$$

which has the unit variance matrix. Because the structures of W and V are preserved, this approach can also be used in the next step.

2. V-step: estimate W, V,, and fix A, B, Ω. This is a linear model in (W, V), which can be solved by GLS as in the B step.
3. A-step: estimate A, Ω and fix W, V, B at W_c, V_c, B_c:

$$z_{0t} = A\left(W_c B_c' z_{2t} - V_c B_c' z_{1t}\right) + \varepsilon_t$$

This is the linear regression of z_{0t} on $W_c B_c' z_{2t} - V_c B_c' z_{1t}$.

The likelihood will not go down when making one update that consists of the three steps given above, provided V is full rank. If that does not hold, as noted at the end of §2.3, some part of B_2 or A_2 is not identified from the above expressions. To handle this, we make the following adjustments to steps 1 and 3:

1a. B-step: Remove the last $s_2^* - \min\{r, s_2^*\}$ columns from B, V and W, as they do not affect the log-likelihood. When iteration is finished, we can add columns of zeros back to W and V and the orthogonal complement of the reduced B to get a rectangular B.

3a. A-step: we wish to keep A invertible and, so, square during iteration. The missing part of A_2 is filled in with the orthogonal complement of the remainder of A after each regression. This requires re-estimation of $V_{.1}$ by OLS.

4.2.2. Triangular-Switching Algorithm

The steps described in the previous section form the basis of an alternating variables algorithm:

Triangular-switching algorithm:
To start, set $k = 1$, and choose $\alpha^{(0)}, \beta^{(0)}$ and the maximum number of iterations. Compute $A^{(0)}$, $B^{(0)}$, $V^{(0)}$, $W^{(0)}$ and $\Omega^{(0)}$.

1.1 B-step: obtain $B^{(k)}$ from $A^{(k-1)}, V^{(k-1)}, W^{(k-1)}, \Omega^{(k-1)}$.
1.2 V step: obtain $W^{(k)}, V^{(k)}$ from $A^{(k-1)}, B^{(k)}, \Omega^{(k-1)}$.
1.3 A step: obtain $A^{(k)}, \Omega^{(k)}$ from $B^{(k)}, V^{(k)}, W^{(k)}$.
1.4 $V_{.1}$ step: if necessary, obtain new $V_{.1}^{(k)}$ from $A^{(k)}, B^{(k)}, V_{.2}^{(k)}, V_{.3}^{(k)}, W^{(k)}$.
2... As steps 2,3,T from the δ-switching algorithm. In this case, the line search is over all of the parameters in A, B, V. □

The starting values are taken as for the δ-switching algorithm; see Appendix C. This means that two iterations of δ-switching are taken first, using only restrictions on β.

4.3. Linear Restrictions

4.3.1. Delta Switching

Estimation under linear restrictions on β or τ of the form:

$$\beta = (H_1\phi_1 : ... : H_r\phi_r) \text{ or } \tau = (H_1\phi_1 : ... : H_{r+s}\phi_{r+s})$$

can be done by adjusting the GLS step in §4.1. However, estimation of α is by RRR, which is not so easily adjusted for linear restrictions. Restricting δ requires replacing the RRR step by regression conditional on δ, which makes the algorithm much slower. Estimation under $\delta = 0$, which implies $d = 0$, is straightforward.

4.3.2. Triangular Switching

Triangular switching avoids RRR, and restrictions on $\beta = B_0$ or $\tau = (B_0 : B_1)$ can be implemented by adjusting the B-step. In general, we can test restrictions of the form:

$$B = \left(H_1\phi_1 : ... : H_{p_1}\phi_{p_1}\right) \text{ and } A = \left(G_1\theta_1 : ... : G_p\theta_p\right).$$

Such linear restrictions on the columns of A and B are a straightforward extension of the GLS steps described above.

Estimation without multi-cointegration is also feasible. Setting $\delta = 0$ corresponds to $V_{13} = 0$ in the triangular representation. This amounts to removing the last s_2^* columns from B, V, W. Boswijk (2010) shows that the test for $\delta = 0$ has an asymptotic $\chi^2(rs_2^*)$ distribution.

Paruolo and Rahbek (1999) derives conditions for weak exogeneity in (15). They decompose this into three sub-hypotheses: $\mathcal{H}_0$: $b'\alpha = 0$, $\mathcal{H}_1$: $b'(\alpha_\perp\xi) = 0$, $\mathcal{H}_2$: $b'\zeta_1 = 0$. These restrictions, taking $b = e_{p,i}$, where $e_{p,i}$ is the i-th column of I_p, correspond to a zero right-hand side in a particular equation in the triangular representation. First is $e'_{p,i}A_0 = 0$ creating a row of zeros in AWB'. Next is $e'_{p,i}A_1 = 0$, which extends the row of zeros. However, A must be full rank, so the final restriction must be imposed on V as $e'_{p,i}AV = (e'_{p,i}A_2 : 0 : 0)V = 0$, expressed as $e'_{p,i}A_2V_{31} = 0$. Paruolo and Rahbek (1999) shows that the combined test for a single variable has an asymptotic $\chi^2(2r + s)$ distribution.

5. Comparing Algorithms

We have three algorithms that can be compared:

1. The δ-switching algorithm, §4.1, which can handle linear restrictions on β or τ.
2. The triangular-switching algorithm proposed in §4.2.2. This can optionally have linear restrictions on the columns of A or B.
3. The improved τ-switching algorithm, Appendix B, implemented to allow for common restrictions on τ.

These algorithms, as well as two pre-existing ones, have been implemented in Ox 7 Doornik (2013).

The comparisons are based on a model for the Danish data (five variables: m_3 = log real money, y = log real GDP, Δp = log GDP deflator, and r_m, r_b, two interest rates); see Juselius (2006, §4.1.1). This has two lags in the VAR, with an unrestricted constant and restricted trend for the deterministic terms, i.e., specification H_l. The sample period is 1973(3) to 2003(1). First computed is the I(2) rank test table.

Table 3 records the number of iterations used by each of the algorithms; this is closely related to the actual computational time required (but less machine specific). All three algorithms converge rapidly to the same likelihood value. Although τ switching takes somewhat fewer iterations, it tends to take a bit more time to run than the other two algorithms. The new triangular I(2) switching procedure is largely competitive with the new δ-switching algorithm.

Table 3. Estimation of all I(2) models by τ, δ and triangular switching; all using the same starting value procedure. Number of iterations to convergence for $\varepsilon_1 = 10^{-14}$.

r\\s_2	τ Switching				δ Switching				Triangular Switching			
	4	3	2	1	4	3	2	1	4	3	2	1
1	19	25	36	34	15	24	37	30	31	31	39	32
2		18	32	25		18	32	34		22	27	50
3			37	23			42	38			50	59
4				29				28				85

To illustrate the advances made with the new algorithms, we report in Table 4 how the original τ-switching, as well as the CATS2 version of δ-switching performed. CATS2, Dennis and Juselius (2004), is a RATS package for the estimation of I(1) and I(2) models, which uses a somewhat different implementation of an I(2) algorithm that is also called δ-switching. The number of iterations of that CATS 2 algorithm is up to 200-times higher than that of the new algorithms, which are therefore much faster, as well as more robust and reliable.

Table 4. Estimation of all I(2) models by old versions of τ, δ switching. Number of iterations to convergence for $\varepsilon_1 = 10^{-14}$.

r\\s_2	Old τ Switching				CATS2 Switching			
	4	3	2	1	4	3	2	1
1	126	198	338	201	5229	8329	8516	5371
2		79	211	229		7234	709	861
3			483	237			550	432
4				4851				5771

6. A More Detailed Comparison

A Monte Carlo experiment is used to show the difference between algorithms in more detail. The first data generation process is the model for the Danish data, estimated with the I(1) and I(2) restrictions r, s imposed. $M = 1000$ random samples are drawn from this, using, for each case, the estimated parameters and estimated residual variance assuming normality. The number of iterations and the progress of the algorithm is recorded for each sample. The maximum number of iterations was set to 10 000, $\epsilon_1 = 10^{-11}$, and all replications are included in the results.

Figure 1 shows the histograms of the number of iterations required to achieve convergence (or 10,000). Each graph has the number of iterations (on a log 10 scale) on the horizontal axis and the count (out of 1000 experiments) represented by the bars and the vertical axis. Ideally, all of the mass is to the left, reflecting very quick convergence. The top row of histograms is for δ switching, the bottom row for triangular switching. In each histogram, the data generation process (DGP) uses the stated r, s values, and estimation is using the correct values of r, s.

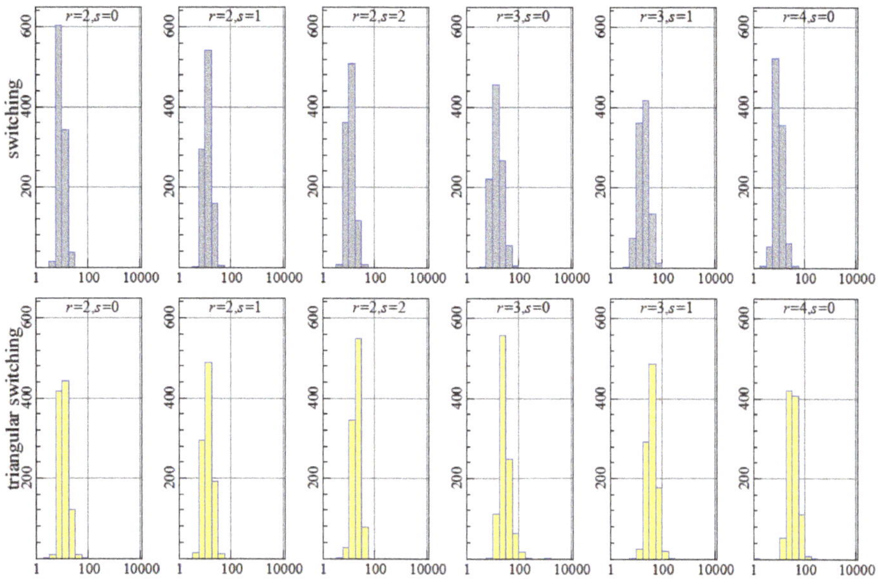

Figure 1. Comparison of algorithms: δ-switching (top row) and triangular-switching (bottom row). Simulating a range of r, s. Number of iterations on the horizontal axis, count (out of 1000) on the vertical.

The histograms show that triangular switching (bottom row) uses more iterations than δ switching (top row), in particular when $s = 0$. Nonetheless, the experiment using triangular switching runs slightly faster as measured by the total time taken (and τ switching is the slowest).

An important question is whether the algorithms converge to the same maximum. The function value that is maximized is:

$$f(\theta) = -\log|\Omega(\theta)|.$$

Out of 10,000 experiments, counted over all r, s combinations that we consider, there is only a single experiment with a noticeable difference in $f(\widehat{\theta})$. This happens for $r = 3, s = 0$, and δ-switching finds a higher function value by almost 0.05. Because $T = 119$, the 0.05 translates to a difference of three in the log-likelihoods.

A second issue of interest is how the algorithms perform when restrictions are imposed. The following restrictions are imposed on the three columns of β with $r = 3$:

	m_3	y	Δp	r_m	r_b	t
β_1'	a	$-a$	0	1	-1	$*$
β_2'	0	$*$	1	$-a$	a	$*$
β_3'	0	0	1	$*$	0	$*$

This specification identifies the cointegrating vectors and imposes two over-identifying restrictions. For $r = 3, s = 0$ this is accepted with a p-value of 0.4, while for $r = 3, s = 1$, the p-value is 0.5 using the model on the actual Danish data. Simulation is from the estimated restricted model.

In terms of the number of iterations, as Figure 2 shows, δ-switching converges more rapidly in most cases. This makes triangular switching slower, but only by about 10%–20%.

Figure 3 shows $f(\widehat{\theta}_\delta) - f(\widehat{\theta}_{\text{triangular}})$, so a positive value means that triangular switching obtained a lower log-likelihood. There are many small differences, mostly to the advantage of δ-switching when

$s = 1$ (right-hand plot), but to the advantage of triangular switching on the left, when $s = 0$. The latter case is also much more noisy.

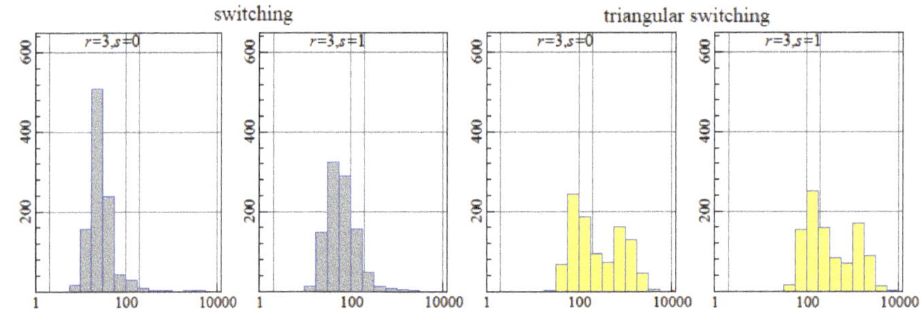

Figure 2. Comparison of algorithms: δ-switching (left two) and triangular-switching (right two). Simulating a range of r, s. Number of iterations on the horizontal axis, count (out of 1000) on the vertical.

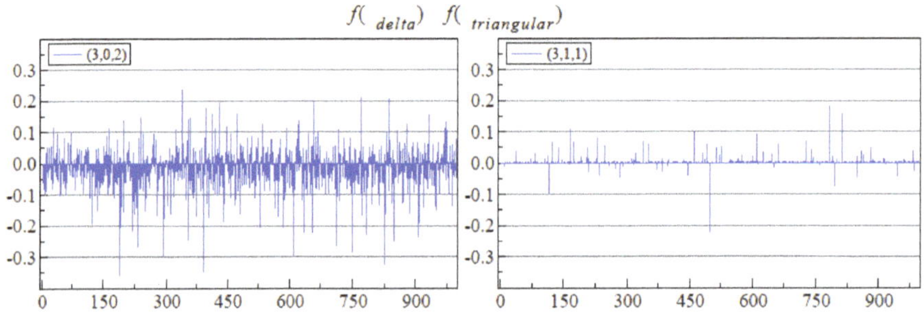

Figure 3. δ-switching function value minus the triangular switching function value (vertical axis) for each replication (horizontal axis). Both starting from their default starting values. The labels are the cointegration indices (r, s, s_2).

6.1. Hybrid Estimation

To increase the robustness of the triangular procedure, we also consider a hybrid procedure, which combines algorithms as follows:

1. standard starting values, as well as twenty randomized starting values, then
2. triangular switching, followed by
3. BFGS optimization (the Broyden-Fletcher, Goldfarb, and Shanno quasi-Newton method) for a maximum of 200 iterations, followed by
4. triangular switching.

This offers some protection against false convergence, because BFGS is based on first derivatives combined with an approximation to the inverse Hessian.

More importantly, we add a randomized search for better starting values as perturbations of the default starting values. Twenty versions of starting values are created this way, and each is followed for ten iterations. Then, we discard half, merge (almost) identical ones and run another ten iterations. This is repeated until a single one is left.

Figure 4 shows that this hybrid approach is an improvement: now, it is almost never beaten by δ switching. Of course, the hybrid approach is a bit slower again. The starting value procedure for δ switching could be improved in the same way.

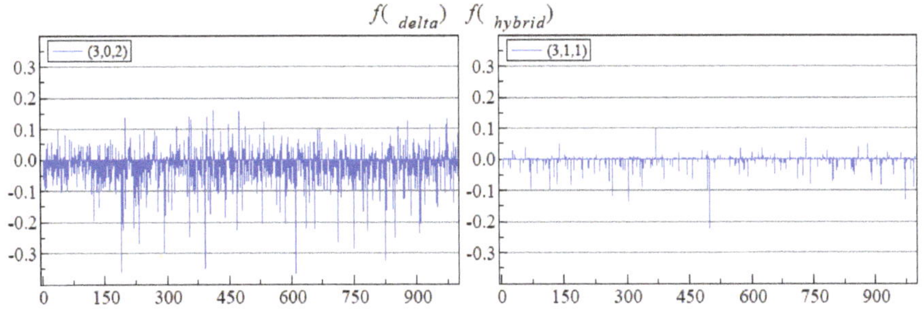

Figure 4. δ-switching function value minus the hybrid triangular-switching function value (vertical axis) for each replication (horizontal axis).

7. Conclusions

We introduced the triangular representation of the I(2) model and showed how it can be used for estimation. The trilinear form of the triangular representation has the advantage that estimation can be implemented as alternating least squares, without using reduced-rank regression. This structure allows us to impose restrictions on (parts of) the A and B matrices, which gives more flexibility than is available in the δ and τ representations.

We also presented an algorithm based on the δ-representation and compared the performance to triangular switching in an application based on Danish data, as well as a parametric bootstrap using that data. Combined with the acceleration of Doornik (2017), both algorithms are fast and give mostly the same result. This will improve empirical applications of the I(2) model and facilitate recursive estimation and Monte Carlo analysis. Expressions for the computation of t-values of coefficients will be reported in a separate paper.

Because they are considerably faster than the previous generation, bootstrapping the I(2) model can now be considered, as Cavaliere et al. (2012) did for the I(1) model.

Acknowledgments: I am grateful to Peter Boswijk, Søren Johansen and Katarina Juselius for providing detailed comments as this paper was developing. Their suggestions have greatly improved the results presented here. Financial support from the Robertson Foundation (Award 9907422) and the Institute for New Economic Thinking (Grant 20029822) is gratefully acknowledged. All computations and graphs use OxMetrics and Ox, Doornik (2013).

Conflicts of Interest: The author declares no conflict of interest.

Appendix A. Estimation Using the QR Decomposition

The data matrices in the I(2) model (8) are $Z_i' = (z_{i1} : \ldots : z_{iT})$ for $i = 0, 1, 2$.

Take the QR decomposition of $(Z_2 : Z_1)$ as $(Z_2 : Z_1)P = QR = Q_z(R_2 : R_1)$ where Q is a $T \times T$ orthogonal matrix and R a $T \times 2p_1$ upper triangular matrix, while Q_z are the $T \times 2p_1$ leading columns of Q and $(R_2 : R_1)$ a $2p_1 \times 2p_1$ upper triangular matrix. P is the orthogonal matrix that captures the column reordering. Then:

$$Q_z'(Z_2 : Z_1) = (R_2 : R_1)P' = (X_2 : X_1),$$

where $(X_2 : X_1)$ is no longer triangular. Introduce:

$$\begin{pmatrix} X_0 \\ X_0^* \end{pmatrix} = Q'Z_0,$$

where $X_0 = Q_z Z_0$ is $2p_1 \times 2p_1$, then:

$$Z_i' Z_j = Z_i' Q Q' Z_j = \begin{cases} X_0' X_0 + X_0^{*\prime} X_0^* & \text{if } i = j = 0, \\ X_i' X_j & \text{otherwise.} \end{cases}$$

Now, e.g., a regression of $A' z_{0t}$ on $B' z_{1t}$ for known A, B:

$$A' z_{0t} = \gamma B' z_{1t} + \epsilon_t, \quad t = 1, ..., T, \tag{A1}$$

has:

$$\widehat{\gamma} = (B' Z_1' Z_1 B)^{-1} B' Z_1' Z_0 A = (B' X_1' X_1 B)^{-1} B' X_1' X_0 A.$$

This is a regression of $X_0 A$ on $X_1 B$. If such regressions need to be done often for the same Z's, it is more efficient to do them in terms of the X_i:

$$A' x_{0i} = \gamma B' x_{1i} + e_i, \quad i = 1, ..., 2p_1,$$

with estimated residual variance:

$$\widehat{\Omega}_e = T^{-1} \left(A' X_0^{*\prime} X_0^* A + \sum_{i=1}^{2p_1} \widehat{e}_i \right).$$

This regression has fewer 'observations', while at the same time avoiding the creation of moment matrices. Precomputed moment matrices would be faster, but not as good numerically. For recursive estimation, it is useful to be able to handle singular regressions because dummy variables can be zero over a subsample; this happens naturally in the QR approach. This approach needs to be adjusted when (A1) also has z_{0t} on the right-hand side, as happens for τ-switching in (A3).

Reduced Rank Regression

Let $\mathrm{RRR}(Z_0, Z_1 | Z_x)$ denote reduced rank regression of z_{0t} on z_{1t} corrected for z_{xt}. Assume that (Z_0, Z_1, Z_x) have been transformed into (X_0, X_1, X_x) using the QR decomposition described above. Concentrating X_x out can be done by regression of (X_0, X_1) on X_x, with residuals (Y, X). Form $S_{00} = Y'Y + X_0^{*\prime} X_0^*$, and decompose using the Cholesky decomposition: $S_{00} = LL'$.

We need to solve the matrix pencil:

$$X' Y S_{00}^{-1} Y' X x = \lambda X' X x.$$

Start by using the QR decomposition $X = QRP'$, $y = P'x$:

$$\begin{aligned} R'Q'YL^{-1\prime}L^{-1}Y'QRy &= \lambda R'Ry, \\ R'W'WRy &= \lambda R'Ry, \\ W'Wz &= \lambda z, \\ U\Sigma^2 U'z &= \lambda z. \end{aligned}$$

The second line introduces $W = L^{-1} Y' Q$; the next line removes R; and the final line takes the SVD of W'. The eigenvalues are the squared singular values that are on the diagonal of Σ^2, and the eigenvectors are $PR^{-1}U$.

When X is singular, as may be the case in recursive estimation, the upper triangular matrix R will have rows and columns that are zero at the bottom and end. These are the same on the left and right of the pencil, so they can be dropped. The resulting reduced dimension R is full rank, and we can set the corresponding rows in the eigenvectors to zero. When the regressors are singular, their corresponding coefficients in β will be set to zero, just as in our regressions.

This approach differs somewhat from Doornik and O'Brien (2002) because of the different structure of S_{00} as a consequence of the prior QR transformation.

Appendix B. Tau-Switching Algorithm

The algorithm of Johansen (1997, §8) is based on the τ-representation and involves three stages:

1. The estimate of τ is obtained by GLS given all other parameters except ψ. Johansen (1997, p. 451) shows the GLS expressions using second moment matrices. Define the orthogonal matrix $\mathrm{A} = (\alpha_\perp : \overline{\alpha})$, then using $\kappa'\tau' z_{1t} = \mathrm{vec}(z_{1t}'\tau\kappa) = (\kappa' \otimes z_{1t})\mathrm{vec}\tau$:

$$\mathrm{A}'z_{0t} = \begin{pmatrix} \kappa' \otimes z_{1t} \\ \varrho' \otimes z_{2t} \end{pmatrix} \mathrm{vec}\tau + \begin{pmatrix} 0 \\ I_r \otimes z_{1t} \end{pmatrix} \mathrm{vec}\psi + \begin{pmatrix} \varepsilon_{1t} \\ \varepsilon_{2t} \end{pmatrix}$$
$$= \left\{ \begin{pmatrix} \kappa' \\ 0 \end{pmatrix} \otimes z_{1t} + \begin{pmatrix} 0 \\ \varrho' \end{pmatrix} \otimes z_{2t} \right\} \mathrm{vec}\tau + \left\{ \begin{pmatrix} 0 \\ I_r \end{pmatrix} \otimes z_{1t} \right\} \mathrm{vec}\psi + u_t. \qquad \text{(A2)}$$

   The error term u_t has variance $\mathrm{A}'\Omega\mathrm{A}$, which is block diagonal. Given $\alpha, \kappa, \rho, \Omega$, (A2) is linear in τ and ψ. The estimates of the latter are discarded.
2. Given just τ, reduced-rank regression of z_{0t} corrected for $\tau' z_{1t}$ on z_{0t} corrected for $z_{1t}, \tau' z_{2t}$ is used to estimate α. Details are in Johansen (1997, p. 450).
3. Given τ and α, the remaining parameters can be obtained by GLS. The equivalence $\overline{\overline{\alpha}}' = \overline{\alpha}' - \overline{\alpha}' w \alpha_\perp'$ is used to write the conditional equation as:

$$\overline{\alpha}' z_{0t} = \gamma' \alpha_\perp' z_{0t} + \varrho' \tau' z_{2t} + \psi' z_{1t} + \varepsilon_{2t}, \qquad \text{(A3)}$$

   from which ϱ and ψ are estimated by regression. Then, κ is estimated from the marginal equation:

$$\alpha_\perp' z_{0t} = \kappa' \tau' z_{1t} + \varepsilon_{1t}. \qquad \text{(A4)}$$

   Together, they give Ω and w. We always transform to set $\varrho' = (I : 0)$, adjusting κ and τ accordingly.

τ-switching algorithm:
To start, set $k = 1$, and choose starting values $\alpha^{(0)}, \beta^{(0)}$, tolerance ε_1 and the maximum number of iterations. Compute $\tau_c^{(0)}$ from (18) and $\kappa^{(0)}, \psi^{(0)}, \Omega^{(0)}$ from (A3) and (A4). Furthermore, compute $f^{(0)} = -\log|\Omega^{(0)}|$.

1. Get $\tau_c^{(k)}$ from (A2). Identify this as follows. Select the non-singular $(r+s) \times (r+s)$ submatrix from τ with the largest volume, say M. We find M by using the first $r+s$ column pivots that are chosen by the QR decomposition of τ (Golub and Van Loan (2013, Algorithm 5.4.1)). Set $\tau_c^{(k)} \leftarrow \tau_c^{(k)} M$. Get $\alpha_c^{(k)}$ by RRR; finally, get the remaining parameters from (A3) and (A4).

2... As steps 2,3,T from the δ-switching algorithm. □

The line search is only for the $p_1 s_2^*$ parameters in τ as part of it is set to a unit matrix every time. The function evaluation inside the line search needs to obtain all of the other parameters as τ changes.

This is the algorithm of Johansen (1997) except for the normalization of τ and the line search. The former protects the parameter values from exploding, while the latter improves convergence speed and makes it more robust. Removing ϱ is largely for convenience: it has little impact on convergence. The τ-switching algorithm is easily adjusted for common restrictions on τ in the form of $\tau = H\widetilde{\tau}$. However, ϱ gets in the way of more general restrictions.

Appendix C. Starting Values

The first starting value procedure is:

1. Set $\alpha^{(-1)}, \beta^{(-1)}$ to their I(1) values (i.e., with full rank Γ).
2. Get $\tau^{(-1)}$ from (A4), then $\Omega^{(-1)}$ from (A3), ignoring restrictions.
3. Take two iterations with the relevant switching algorithm subject to restrictions.

The second starting value procedure is:

1. Get $\alpha^{(-2)}, \beta^{(-2)}$ by RRR from the τ-representation using $\kappa = 0$:

$$z_{0t} = \alpha(\beta' z_{2t} + \psi' z_{1t}) + \epsilon_t.$$

2. Get $\kappa^{(-2)}, w^{(-2)}$ from (A3), (A4).
3. Get $\alpha^{(-1)}, \beta^{(-1)}$ by RRR from the τ-representation:

$$z_{0t} - w\kappa' \beta' z_{1t} = \alpha(\beta' z_{2t} + \psi' z_{1t}) + \epsilon_t.$$

4. Get $\tau^{(-1)}$ from (A4), then $\Omega^{(-1)}$ from (A3), ignoring restrictions.
5. Take two iterations with the relevant switching algorithm subject to restrictions.

Finally, choose the final starting values as those that have the highest function value.

References

Anderson, Theodore W. 1951. Estimating linear restrictions on regression coefficients for multivariate normal distributions. *Annals of Mathematical Statistics* 22: 327–51. (Erratum in Annals of Statistics 8, 1980).

Anderson, Theodore W. 2002. Reduced rank regression in cointegrated models. *Journal of Econometrics* 106: 203–16.

Boswijk, H. Peter. 2010. Mixed Normal Inference on Multicointegration. *Econometric Theory* 26: 1565–76.

Boswijk, H. Peter, and Jurgen A. Doornik. 2004. Identifying, Estimating and Testing Restricted Cointegrated Systems: An Overview. *Statistica Neerlandica* 58: 440–65.

Cavaliere, Giuseppe, Anders Rahbek, and R.A.M. Taylor. 2012. Bootstrap Determination of the Co-Integration Rank in Vector Autoregressive Models. *Econometrica* 80: 1721–40.

Dennis, Jonathan G., and Katarina Juselius. 2004. *CATS in RATS: Cointegration Analysis of Time Series Version 2*. Technical Report. Evanston: Estima.

Doornik, Jurgen A. 2013. *Object-Oriented Matrix Programming using Ox*, 7th ed. London: Timberlake Consultants Press.

Doornik, Jurgen A. 2017. *Accelerated Estimation of Switching Algorithms: The Cointegrated VAR Model and Other Applications*. Oxford: Department of Economics, University of Oxford.

Doornik, Jurgen A., and R. J. O'Brien. 2002. Numerically Stable Cointegration Analysis. *Computational Statistics & Data Analysis* 41: 185–93.

Golub, Gen H., and Charles F. Van Loan. 2013. *Matrix Computations*, 4th ed. Baltimore: The Johns Hopkins University Press.

Johansen, Søren. 1988. Statistical Analysis of Cointegration Vectors. *Journal of Economic Dynamics and Control* 12: 231–54. Reprinted in R. F. Engle, and C. W. J. Granger, eds. 1991. *Long-Run Economic Relationships*. Oxford: Oxford University Press, pp. 131–52.

Johansen, Søren. 1991. Estimation and Hypothesis Testing of Cointegration Vectors in Gaussian Vector Autoregressive Models. *Econometrica* 59: 1551–80.

Johansen, Søren. 1992. A Representation of Vector Autoregressive Processes Integrated of Order 2. *Econometric Theory* 8: 188–202.

Johansen, Søren. 1995a. *Likelihood-based Inference in Cointegrated Vector Autoregressive Models*. Oxford: Oxford University Press.

Johansen, Søren. 1995b. Identifying Restrictions of Linear Equations with Applications to Simultaneous Equations and Cointegration. *Journal of Econometrics* 69: 111–32.

Johansen, Søren. 1995c. A Statistical Analysis of Cointegration for I(2) Variables. *Econometric Theory* 11: 25–59.

Johansen, Søren. 1997. Likelihood Analysis of the I(2) Model. *Scandinavian Journal of Statistics* 24: 433–62.

Johansen, Søren, and Katarina Juselius. 1990. Maximum Likelihood Estimation and Inference on Cointegration—With Application to the Demand for Money. *Oxford Bulletin of Economics and Statistics* 52: 169–210.

Johansen, Søren, and Katarina Juselius. 1992. Testing Structural Hypotheses in a Multivariate Cointegration Analysis of the PPP and the UIP for UK. *Journal of Econometrics* 53: 211–44.

Johansen, Søren, and Katarina Juselius. 1994. Identification of the Long-run and the Short-run Structure. An Application to the ISLM Model. *Journal of Econometrics* 63: 7–36.

Juselius, Katarina. 2006. *The Cointegrated VAR Model: Methodology and Applications*. Oxford: Oxford University Press.

Paruolo, Paolo. 2000a. Asymptotic Efficiency of the Two Stage Estimator in I(2) Systems. *Econometric Theory* 16: 524–50.

Paruolo, Paolo. 2000b. On likelihood-maximizing algorithms for I(2) VAR models. Mimeo. Varese: Universitá dell'Insubria.

Paruolo, Paolo, and Anders Rahbek. 1999. Weak exogeneity in I(2) VAR Systems. *Journal of Econometrics* 93: 281–308.

econometrics

MDPI

Article

Likelihood Ratio Tests of Restrictions on Common Trends Loading Matrices in I(2) VAR Systems

H. Peter Boswijk [1] and Paolo Paruolo [2,*]

1 Amsterdam School of Economics and Tinbergen Institute, University of Amsterdam, 1001 NJ Amsterdam, The Netherlands; h.p.boswijk@uva.nl

2 Joint Research Centre, European Commission, 21027 Ispra (VA), Italy

* Correspondence: paolo.paruolo@ec.europa.eu

Academic Editor: Katarina Juselius
Received: 28 February 2017; Accepted: 21 June 2017; Published: 29 June 2017

Abstract: Likelihood ratio tests of over-identifying restrictions on the common trends loading matrices in I(2) VAR systems are discussed. It is shown how hypotheses on the common trends loading matrices can be translated into hypotheses on the cointegration parameters. Algorithms for (constrained) maximum likelihood estimation are presented, and asymptotic properties sketched. The techniques are illustrated using the analysis of the PPP and UIP between Switzerland and the US.

Keywords: cointegration; common trends; identification; VAR; I(2)

JEL Classification: C32

---

1. Introduction

The duality between the common trends representation and the vector equilibrium-correction model-form (VECM) in cointegrated systems allows researchers to formulate hypotheses of economic interest on any of the two. The VECM is centered on the adjustment with respect to disequilibria in the system; in this way it facilitates the interpretation of cointegrating relations as (deviations from) equilibria.

The common trends representation instead highlights how variables in the system as pushed around by common stochastic trends, which are often interpreted as the main persistent economic factors influencing the long-term. Both representations provide economic insights on the economic system under scrutiny. Examples of both perspectives are given in Juselius (2017a, 2017b)

The common trends and VECM representations are connected through representation results such as the Granger Representation Theorem, in the case of I(1) systems, see Engle and Granger (1987) and Johansen (1991), and the Johansen Representation Theorem, for the case of I(2) systems, see Johansen (1992). In particular, both representation theorems show that the loading matrix of the common stochastic trends of highest order is a basis of the orthogonal complement of the matrix of cointegrating relations. Because of this property, these two matrices are linked, and any one of them can be written as a function of the other one.

This paper focuses on I(2) vector autoregressive (VAR) systems, and it considers the situation where (possibly over-identifying) economic hypotheses are entertained for the factor loading matrix of the I(2) trends. It is shown how they can then be translated into hypotheses on the cointegrating relations, which appear in the VECM representation; the latter forms the basis for maximum likelihood (ML) estimation of I(2) VAR models. In this way, constrained ML estimators are obtained and the associated likelihood ratio (LR) tests of these hypotheses can be defined. These tests are discussed in the present paper; Wald tests on just-identified loading matrices of the I(1) and I(2) common trends have already been proposed by Paruolo (1997, 2002).

The running example of the paper is taken from Juselius and Assenmacher (2015), which is the working paper version of Juselius and Assenmacher (2017). The following notation is used: for a full column-rank matrix a, $\operatorname{col} a$ denotes the space spanned by the columns of a and $a_\perp$ indicates a basis of the orthogonal complement of $\operatorname{col} a$. For a matrix b of the same dimensions of a, and for which $b'a$ is full rank, let $b_a := b(a'b)^{-1}$; a special case is when $a = b$, for which $\bar{a} := a_a = a(a'a)^{-1}$. Let also $P_a := a(a'a)^{-1}a'$ indicate the orthogonal projection matrix onto $\operatorname{col} a$, and let the matrix $P_{a_\perp} = I - P_a$ denote the orthogonal projection matrix on its orthogonal complement. Finally e_j is used to indicate the j-th column of an identity matrix of appropriate dimension.

The rest of this paper is organized as follows: Section 2 contains the motivation and the definition of the problem considered in the paper. The identification of the I(2) common trends loading matrix under linear restrictions is analysed in Section 3. The relationship between the identified parametrization of I(2) common trends loading matrix and an identified version of the cointegration matrix is also discussed. Section 4 considers a parametrization of the VECM, and discusses its identification. ML estimation of this model is discussed in Section 5; the asymptotic distributions of the resulting ML estimator of the I(2) loading matrix and the LR statistic of the over-identifying restrictions are sketched in Section 6. Section 7 reports an illustration of the techniques developed in the paper on a system of US and Swiss prices, interest rates and exchange rate. Section 8 concludes, while two appendices report additional technical material.

2. Common Trends Representation for I(2) Systems

This section introduces quantities of interest and presents the motivation of the paper. Consider a p-variate VAR(k) process X_t:

$$X_t = A_1 X_{t-1} + \ldots + A_k X_{t-k} + \mu_0 + \mu_1 t + \varepsilon_t, \tag{1}$$

where $A_i, i = 1, \ldots, k$ are $p \times p$ matrices, μ_0 and μ_1 are $p \times 1$ vectors, and ε_t is a $p \times 1$ i.i.d. $N(0, \Omega)$ vector, with Ω positive definite. Under the conditions of the Johansen Representation Theorem, see Appendix A, called *the* I(2) *conditions*, X_t admits a common trends I(2) representation of the form

$$X_t = C_2 S_{2t} + C_1 S_{1t} + Y_t + v_0 + v_1 t, \tag{2}$$

where $S_{2t} := \sum_{i=1}^{t} \sum_{s=1}^{i} \varepsilon_s$ are the I(2) stochastic trends (cumulated random walks), $S_{1t} := \Delta S_{2t} = \sum_{i=1}^{t} \varepsilon_i$ is a random walk component, and Y_t is an I(0) linear process.

Cointegration occurs when the matrix C_2 has reduced rank $r_2 < p$, such that $C_2 = ab'$, where a and b are $p \times r_2$ and of full column rank. This observation lends itself to the following interpretation: $b'S_{2t}$ defines the r_2 common I(2) trends, while a acts as the loading matrix of X_t on the I(2) trends. The reduced rank of C_2 implies that there exist $m := p - r_2$ linearly independent cointegrating vectors, collected in a $p \times m$ matrix τ, satisfying $\tau' C_2 = 0$; hence $\tau' X_t$ is I(1). Combining this with $C_2 = ab'$, it is clear that $a = \tau_\perp$, i.e., the columns of the loading matrix span the orthogonal complement of the cointegration space $\operatorname{col} \tau$. Interest in this paper is on hypotheses on $a = \tau_\perp$[1].

Observe that $C_2 = ab'$ is invariant to the choice of basis of either $\operatorname{col} a$ and $\operatorname{col} b$. In fact, (a, b) can be replaced by (aQ, bQ'^{-1}) with Q square and nonsingular without affecting C_2. One way to resolve this identification problem is to impose restrictions on the entries of $a = \tau_\perp$; enough restrictions of this kind would make the choice of $\tau_\perp$ unique. Such an approach to identification is common in confirmatory factor analysis in the statistics literature, see Jöreskog et al. (2016).

If more restrictions are imposed than needed for identification, they are over-identifying. Such over-identifying restrictions on $\tau_\perp$ usually correspond to (similarly over-identifying) restrictions

[1] In the I(2) cointegration literature, $\tau_\perp$ is also referred to as β_2, see the Johansen Representation Theorem in Appendix A.

on τ, see Section 3 below. Although economic hypotheses may directly imply restrictions on the cointegrating vectors in τ, in some cases it is more natural to formulate restrictions on the I(2) loading matrix $\tau_\perp$. This is illustrated by the two following examples.

2.1. Example 1

Kongsted (2005) considers a model for $X_t = (m_t : y_t^n : p_t)'$, where m_t, y_t^n and p_t denote the nominal money stock, nominal income and the price level, respectively (all variables in logs); here ':' indicates horizontal concatenation. He assumes that the system is I(2), with $r_2 = 1$. Given the definition of the variables, Kongsted (2005) considers the natural question of whether real money $m_t - p_t$ and real income $y_t^n - p_t$ are at most I(1). This corresponds to an (over-identified) cointegrating matrix τ and loading vector $\tau_\perp$ of the form

$$\tau = \begin{pmatrix} 1 & 0 \\ 0 & 1 \\ -1 & -1 \end{pmatrix}, \qquad \tau_\perp = \begin{pmatrix} 1 \\ 1 \\ 1 \end{pmatrix}.$$

The form of τ corresponds to the fact that the I(1) linear combinations $\tau' X_t$ are (linear combinations of) $((m_t - p_t) : (y_t^n - p_t))'$, as required. On the other hand, the restriction on $\tau_\perp$ says that each of the three series have exactly the same I(2) trend, with the same scale factor. Both formulations are easily interpretable.

Note that the hypothesis on $\tau_\perp$ involves two over-identifying restrictions (the second and third component are equal to the first component), in addition to a normalization (the first component equals 1). Similarly, the restriction that the matrix consisting of the first two rows of τ equals I_2 is a normalization; the two over-identifying restrictions are that the entries in both columns sum to 0.

As this first example shows, knowing τ is the same as knowing $\tau_\perp$ and vice versa[2].

2.2. Example 2

Juselius and Assenmacher (2015) consider a 7-dimensional VAR with $X_t = (p_{1t} : p_{2t} : e_{12t} : b_{1t} : b_{2t} : s_{1t} : s_{2t})'$ with $r_2 = 2$, where p_{it}, b_{it}, s_{it} are the (log of) the price index, the long and the short interest rate of country i at time t respectively, and e_{12t} is the log of the exchange rate between country 1 (Switzerland) and 2 (the US) at time t. They expect the common trends representation to have a loading matrix $\tau_\perp$ of the form:

$$\tau_\perp = \begin{pmatrix} \phi_{11} & 0 \\ \phi_{21} & \phi_{22} \\ \phi_{31} & \phi_{32} \\ 0 & \phi_{42} \\ 0 & \phi_{52} \\ 0 & \phi_{62} \\ 0 & \phi_{72} \end{pmatrix}. \tag{3}$$

where ϕ_{ij} indicates an entry not restricted to 0.

The second I(2) trend is loaded on the interest rates b_{1t}, b_{2t}, s_{1t}, s_{2t}, as well as on US prices p_{2t} and the exchange rate e_{12t}; this can be interpreted as a financial (or 'speculative') trend affecting world prices. The first I(2) trend, instead, is only loaded on p_{1t}, p_{2t}, e_{12t} and embodies a 'relative price' I(2) trend; it can be interpreted as the Swiss contribution to the trend in prices.

The cointegrating matrix τ in this example is of dimension 7×5. It is not obvious what type of restrictions on τ correspond to the structure in (3). However, it is τ rather than $\tau_\perp$ that enters the likelihood function (as will be analyzed in Section 4). The rest of the paper shows that the restrictions

---

[2] Up to normalizations, see below.

in (3) are over-identifying, how they can be translated into hypotheses on τ, and how they can be tested via LR tests.

3. Hypothesis on the Common Trends Loadings

This section discusses linear hypotheses on $\tau_\perp$ and their relation to τ. First, attention is focused on the case of linear hypotheses on the normalized version $\tau_{\perp c_\perp} := \tau_\perp \left(c_\perp' \tau_\perp\right)^{-1}$ of $\tau_\perp$. Here $c_\perp$ is a full-column-rank matrix of the same dimension of $\tau_\perp$ such that $c_\perp' \tau_\perp$ is square and nonsingular[3]. This normalization was introduced by Johansen (1991) in the context of the I(1) model in order to isolate the (just-) identified parameters in the cointegration matrix.

Later, linear hypotheses formulated directly on $\tau_\perp$ are discussed. The main result of this section is the fact that the parameters of interest appears linearly both in $\tau_{\perp c_\perp}$ *and* in τ_c in the first case; this is not necessarily true in the second case.

The central relation employed in this section (for both cases), is the following identity:

$$\tau_c := \tau \left(c'\tau\right)^{-1} = (I - c_\perp \left(\tau_\perp' c_\perp\right)^{-1} \tau_\perp')\bar{c} = (I - c_\perp \tau_{\perp c_\perp}')\bar{c}, \tag{4}$$

where $\bar{c} := c(c'c)^{-1}$. This identity readily follows from the oblique projections identity

$$I = \tau \left(c'\tau\right)^{-1} c' + c_\perp \left(\tau_\perp' c_\perp\right)^{-1} \tau_\perp',$$

see e.g. Srivastava and Kathri (1979, p. 19), by post-multiplication by $\bar{c}$.

3.1. Linear hypotheses on $\tau_{\perp c_\perp}$

Johansen (1991) noted that the function $a_b := a(b'a)^{-1}$ is invariant with respect to the choice of basis of the space spanned by a. in fact, consider in the present context any alternative basis $\tau_\perp^\star$ of the space spanned by $\tau_\perp$; this has representation $\tau_\perp^\star = \tau_\perp Q$ for Q square and full rank. Inserting $\tau_\perp^\star$ in place of $\tau_\perp$ in the definition of $\tau_{\perp c_\perp} := \tau_\perp \left(c_\perp' \tau_\perp\right)^{-1}$, one finds

$$\tau_{\perp c_\perp}^\star = \tau_\perp^\star \left(c_\perp' \tau_\perp^\star\right)^{-1} = \tau_\perp Q \left(c_\perp' \tau_\perp Q\right)^{-1} = \tau_{\perp c_\perp}.$$

Hence $\tau_{\perp c_\perp}$, similarly to the cointegration matrix in the I(1) model in Johansen (1991), is (just-)identified.

To facilitate stating hypotheses on the unconstrained elements of $\tau_{\perp c_\perp}$, the following representation of $\tau_{\perp c_\perp}$ appears useful:

$$\tau_{\perp c_\perp} = \bar{c}_\perp + c\,\vartheta \tag{5}$$

where ϑ is an $m \times r_2$ matrix of free coefficients in $\tau_\perp$[4]. For example, one may have

$$c_\perp = \begin{pmatrix} 0_{3\times 2} \\ I_2 \end{pmatrix}, \quad c = \begin{pmatrix} I_3 \\ 0_{2\times 3} \end{pmatrix}, \quad \tau_{\perp c_\perp} = \bar{c}_\perp + c \begin{pmatrix} \vartheta_{11} & \vartheta_{12} \\ \vartheta_{21} & \vartheta_{22} \\ \vartheta_{31} & \vartheta_{32} \end{pmatrix} = \begin{pmatrix} \vartheta_{11} & \vartheta_{12} \\ \vartheta_{21} & \vartheta_{22} \\ \vartheta_{31} & \vartheta_{32} \\ 1 & 0 \\ 0 & 1 \end{pmatrix} \tag{6}$$

with $p = 5$, $m = 3$, $r_2 = 2$.

---

3 When $c_\perp' \tau_\perp$ is square and nonsingular, then one can prove that also $c'\tau$ is square and nonsingular, see e.g., Johansen (1996, Exercise 3.7).

4 This equation is obtained by using orthogonal projection of $\tau_{\perp c_\perp}$ on the columns spaces of c and $c_\perp$, and applying the equality $c_\perp' \tau_{\perp c_\perp} = I_{r_2}$ which follows by definition.

Consider over-identifying linear restrictions on the columns of ϑ in (5). Typically, such restrictions will come in the form of zero (exclusion) restrictions or unit restrictions, where the latter would indicate equal loadings of a specific variable and the variable on which the column of $\tau_{\perp c_\perp}$ has been normalized. The general formulation of such restrictions is

$$\vartheta_i = k_i + K_i \phi_i, \quad i = 1, \ldots, r_2, \tag{7}$$

where ϑ_i is the i-th column vector of ϑ, k_i and K_i are conformable vectors and matrices, and ϕ_i contains the remaining unknown parameters in ϑ_i. If only zero restrictions are imposed, then $k_i = 0_m$.

The formulation in (7) includes several notable special cases. For instance, if all $K_i = K$ and $k_i = 0_m$, one obtains the hypothesis that ϑ is contained in a given linear space, $\vartheta = K\phi$. Another example is given by the case where one column ϑ_1 is known, $\vartheta = (k_1 : \phi)$; this corresponds to the choice $\vartheta_1 = k_1$ with K_1 and ϕ_1 void and $k_2 = \ldots = k_{r_2} = 0$, $K_2 = \ldots = K_{r_2} = I$.

The restrictions in (7) may be summarized as

$$\text{vec}\ \vartheta = k + K\phi, \tag{8}$$

where $k = (k_1' : \ldots : k_{r_2}')'$, $K = \text{blkdiag}(K_1, \ldots, K_{r_2})$ and $\phi = (\phi_1' : \ldots : \phi_{r_2}')'$. Here $\text{blkdiag}(B_1, B_2, \ldots, B_n)$ indicates a matrix with the (not necessarily square) blocks $B_1, B_2, \ldots, B_n$ along the main diagonal. Formulation (8) generalises (7).

The main result of this section is stated in the next theorem.

Theorem 1 (Hypotheses on $\tau_{\perp c_\perp}$). *Assume that ϑ satisfies linear restrictions of the type* (8)*; then these restrictions are translated into a linear hypothesis on* vec τ_c *via*

$$\text{vec}\ \tau_c = (\text{vec}\ \bar{c} - (I_m \otimes c_\perp)\mathcal{K}_{m,r_2} k) - (I_m \otimes c_\perp)\mathcal{K}_{m,r_2} K\phi, \tag{9}$$

where $\mathcal{K}_{m,n}$ is the commutation matrix satisfying $\mathcal{K}_{m,n}\,\text{vec}\ A = \text{vec}\ A'$, with A of dimensions $m \times n$, see Magnus and Neudecker (2007).

Proof. Substitute (8) into (4) and vectorize using standard properties of the vec operator, see Magnus and Neudecker (2007). □

The previous theorem shows that, when one can express a linear hypothesis on the coefficients in ϑ that are unrestricted in $\tau_{\perp c_\perp}$, then the same linear hypothesis is translated into a restriction on vec τ_c. Note that the proof simply exploits (4).

Identification of the restricted coefficients ϕ under these hypothesis can be addressed in a straightforward way. In fact, the parameters in ϑ are identified; hence ϕ is identified provided that the matrix K is of full column rank, which in turn will imply that the Jacobian matrix $\partial\, \text{vec}\ \tau_c / \partial \phi' = -(I_m \otimes c_\perp)\mathcal{K}_{m,r_2} K$ in (9) has full column rank.

Because, in practice, econometricians may explore the form of $\tau_\perp$ via unrestricted estimates of $\tau_{\perp c_\perp}$, see Paruolo (2002), before formulating restrictions on $\tau_\perp$, using hypothesis on the unrestricted coefficients in $\tau_{\perp c_\perp}$ appears a natural sequential step.

The next subsection discusses the alternative approach of specifying hypotheses directly on $\tau_\perp$.

3.2. *Linear Hypotheses on $\tau_\perp$*

In case placing restrictions on the unrestricted coefficients in $\tau_{\perp c_\perp}$ is not what the econometrician wants, this subsection considers linear hypothesis on $\tau_\perp$ directly. It is shown that sometimes it is possible to translate linear hypothesis on $\tau_\perp$ into linear hypothesis on $\tau_{\perp c_\perp}$ for some $c_\perp$. It is also shown that this is always possible for $r_2 = 2$, for which a constructive proof is provided.

Analogously to (7), consider linear hypotheses on the columns of $\tau_\perp$, of the following type:

$$\tau_{\perp,i} = h_i + H_i \phi_i, \quad i = 1, \ldots, r_2, \tag{10}$$

summarized as

$$\text{vec}\ \tau_\perp = h + H\phi. \tag{11}$$

In this case, non-zero vectors h_i represent normalizations of the columns of the loading matrix, and as before, ϕ_i collects the unknown parameters in $\tau_{\perp,i}$.

Theorem 2 (Hypotheses on $\tau_\perp$). *Assume that $\tau_\perp = \tau_\perp(\phi)$ satisfies linear restrictions of the type* (11)*, then these restrictions are translated in general into a* non-linear *hypothesis on* vec τ_c *via*

$$\tau_c = (I - c_\perp \left(\tau_\perp(\phi)' c_\perp\right)^{-1} \tau_\perp(\phi)')\bar{c} \tag{12}$$

and the Jacobian of the transformation from ϕ to vec τ_c *is*

$$\mathcal{J}(\cdot) := \frac{\partial\ \text{vec}\ \tau_c(\cdot)}{\partial \phi'} = -(\tau_c(\cdot)' \otimes c_\perp(\tau_\perp(\cdot)' c_\perp)^{-1}) \mathcal{K}_{p,r_2} H. \tag{13}$$

This parametrization is smooth on an open set in the parameter space Φ of ϕ where $c_\perp' \tau_\perp$ is of full rank.

Proof. Equation (12) is a re-statement of (4). Differentiation of (12) delivers (13). □

One can note that the Jacobian matrix in (13) can be used to check local identification using the results in Rothenberg (1971).

The result of Theorem 2 is in contrast with the result of Theorem 1, because the latter delivers a linear hypothesis for τ_c while Theorem 2 gives in general non-linear restrictions on τ_c. One may hence ask the following question: when is it possible to reduce the more general linear hypothesis on $\tau_\perp$ given in (11) to the simpler linear hypothesis on ϑ given in (8)?

In the special case of $r_2 = 2$, the following theorem states that this can be always obtained. This applies for instance to the motivating example (3), where one can choose some $c_\perp$ so that $\tau_\perp' c_\perp$ is equal to the identity, as shown below. Consider the formulation (10) with $r_2 = 2$, and assume that no normalizations have been imposed yet, such that $h_1 = h_2 = 0$. It is assumed that $\tau_\perp$, under the equation-by-equation restrictions, satisfies the usual rank conditions for identification, see Johansen (1995, Theorem 1) :

$$\text{rank}\ R_i' \tau_\perp = 1 \qquad \text{for} \qquad i = 1, 2, \tag{14}$$

where $R_i = H_{i,\perp}$.

Theorem 3 (Case $r_2 = 2$). *Let $\tau_\perp$ obey the restrictions $\tau_\perp = (H_1\phi_1 : H_2\phi_2)$ satisfying the rank conditions* (14)*; then one can choose normalization conditions on ϕ_1 and ϕ_2 so that there exists a matrix $c_\perp$ such that $c_\perp' \tau_\perp = I$. This implies that a hypotheses on $\tau_\perp$ can be stated in terms of ϑ in* (5)*, and, by Theorem 1, a linear hypotheses on* vec ϑ *corresponds to linear hypothesis on* vec τ_c.

Proof. Because $R_1' \tau_\perp = (0 : R_1' H_2 \phi_2)$ has rank 1, one can select (at least) one linear combination of R_1, $R_1 a_1$ say, so that ϕ_2 is normalized to be one in the direction $b_2' := a_1' R_1' H_2$, i.e., $b_2' \phi_2 = 1$. Similarly, $R_2' \tau_\perp = (R_2' H_1 \phi_1 : 0)$ has rank 1, and one can select (at least) one linear combination of R_2, $R_2 a_2$ say, so that ϕ_1 is normalized to be one in the direction $b_1' := a_2' R_2' H_1$, i.e., $b_1' \phi_1 = 1$. Next define $c_\perp = (R_2 a_2 : R_1 a_1)$ which by construction satisfies $c_\perp' \tau_\perp = I_2$. □

The proof of the previous theorem provides a way to construct $c_\perp$ when $r_2 = 2$ and the usual rank condition for identification (14) holds. The rest of the paper focuses attention on the case of linear restrictions on ϑ in (8), which can be translated linearly into restrictions on τ_c as shown in Theorem 1.

3.3. Example 2 Continued

Consider (3); this hypothesis is of type $\tau_\perp = (H_1\phi_1 : H_2\phi_2)$ with

$$H_1 = \begin{pmatrix} I_3 \\ 0_{4\times 3} \end{pmatrix}, \qquad H_2 = \begin{pmatrix} 0_{1\times 6} \\ I_6 \end{pmatrix},$$

and hence $R_1' = (I_4 : 0_{4\times 3})$ and $R_2' = (I_6 : 0_{6\times 1})$. In this case one can define $c = (e_2 : e_3 : e_5 : e_6 : e_7)$ and $c_\perp = (e_1 : e_4)$ where e_j is the j-th column of I_7.

It is simple to verify that, under the additional normalization restrictions $\phi_{11} = 1$ and $\phi_{42} = 1$, $\tau_\perp$ in (3) satisfies $c_\perp' \tau_\perp = I_2$. Therefore, define $\tau_{\perp c_\perp}$ as (3) under these normalization restrictions. Using formula (4) one can see that

$$\tau_c = (I - c_\perp \tau_{\perp c_\perp}')\bar{c} = \begin{pmatrix} -\phi_{21} & -\phi_{31} & 0 & 0 & 0 \\ 1 & 0 & 0 & 0 & 0 \\ 0 & 1 & 0 & 0 & 0 \\ -\phi_{22} & -\phi_{32} & -\phi_{52} & -\phi_{62} & -\phi_{72} \\ 0 & 0 & 1 & 0 & 0 \\ 0 & 0 & 0 & 1 & 0 \\ 0 & 0 & 0 & 0 & 1 \end{pmatrix}, \tag{15}$$

so that vec τ_c is linear in ϕ, as predicted by Theorem 3.

4. The VECM Parametrization

This section describes the I(2) parametrization employed in the statistical analysis of the paper. Consider the following τ-parametrization (τ-par) of the VECM for I(2) VAR systems[5]. See Mosconi and Paruolo (2017):

$$\Delta^2 X_t = \alpha\left(\rho'\tau' X_{t-1} + \psi'\Delta X_{t-1}\right) + \lambda\tau'\Delta X_{t-1} + \Upsilon\Delta^2\mathbb{X}_{t-1} + \varepsilon_t, \tag{16}$$

with $\Upsilon\Delta^2\mathbb{X}_{t-1} = \sum_{j=1}^{k-2}\Upsilon_j\Delta^2 X_{t-j}$. Recall that $m = p - r_2$ is the total number of cointegrating relations, i.e., the number of I(1) linear combinations $\tau' X_t$. The number of linear combinations of $\tau' X_t$ that cointegrate with ΔX_t to I(0), i.e., the number of I(0) linear combinations $\rho'\tau' X_t + \psi'\Delta X_t$, is indicated[6] by $r \le m$. Here α is $p \times r$, τ is $p \times m$ and the other parameter matrices are conformable; the parameters are α, ρ, τ, ψ, λ, Υ, Ω, all freely varying, and Ω is assumed to be positive definite. When λ is restricted as $\lambda = \Omega\alpha_\perp(\alpha_\perp'\Omega\alpha_\perp)^{-1}\kappa'$ with κ' a $(p-r) \times m$ matrix of freely varying parameters, the τ-par reduces to the parametrization of Johansen (1997); this restriction on λ is not imposed here.

4.1. Identification of τ

The parameters in the τ-par (16) are not identified; in particular τ' can be replaced by $B\tau'$ with B square and nonsingular, provided ρ and λ are simultaneously replaced by $B^{-1\prime}\rho$ and λB^{-1}. This is because τ enters the likelihood only via (16) in the products $\rho'\tau' = \rho' B^{-1} B\tau'$ and $\lambda\tau' = (\lambda B^{-1})(B\tau')$. The transformation that generates observationally equivalent parameters, i.e., the post multiplication of τ by a square and invertible matrix B', is the same type of transformation that induces observational

[5] In the general VAR(k) model (1), ε_t in (16) is replaced by $\mu_0 + \mu_1 t + \varepsilon_t$; see Section 4.3 below.
[6] The difference $m - r = p - r - r_2$ is referred to as either s or r_1 in the I(2) cointegration literature, see Appendix A.

equivalence in the classical system of simultaneous equations, see Sargan (1988), or to the set of cointegrating equations in I(1) systems, see Johansen (1995). This leads to the following result.

Theorem 4 (Identification of τ in the τ-par). *Assume that τ_c is specified as the restricted τ_c in (9), which is implied by the general linear hypothesis (8) on $\tau_{\perp c_\perp}$; then the restricted τ_c is identified within the τ-par if and only if*

$$\text{rank}\left(R_\tau'(I_m \otimes \tau)\right) = m^2, \qquad \underset{mp\times m_\tau}{R_\tau} = G_\perp, \qquad G := -(I_m \otimes c_\perp)\mathcal{K}_{m,r_2}K \tag{17}$$

(rank condition), where $m_\tau = mp - \dim\phi$. The corresponding order condition is $m_\tau \geq m^2$, or equivalently $mr_2 \geq \dim\phi$.

Alternatively, consider the general linear hypothesis (11) on $\tau_\perp$; then the constrained τ_c in (12) is identified in a neighborhood of the point $\phi = \phi^\star$ provided the Jacobian $\mathcal{J}(\phi^\star) := \partial \operatorname{vec} \tau_c(\phi^\star)/\partial\phi'$ in (13) is of full rank.

Proof. The rank condition follows from Sargan (1988), given that the class of transformation that induce observational equivalence is the same as the classical one for systems of simultaneous equations. The local identification condition follows from Rothenberg (1971). □

4.2. The Identification of Remaining Parameters

This subsection discusses conditions for remaining parameters of the τ-par to be identified, when τ is identified as in Theorem 4. These additional conditions are used in the discussion of the ML algorithms of the next section.

The VECM can be rewritten as

$$\Delta^2 X_t = \nu\varsigma' \begin{pmatrix} \tau' X_{t-1} \\ \Delta X_{t-1} \end{pmatrix} + \Upsilon\Delta^2 \mathbb{X}_{t-1} + \varepsilon_t, \quad \text{with} \quad \varsigma' := \begin{pmatrix} \rho' & \psi' \\ 0 & \tau' \end{pmatrix}, \qquad \nu := (\alpha : \lambda).$$

One can see that the equilibrium correction terms $\nu\varsigma'\left((\tau' X_{t-1})' : \Delta X_{t-1}'\right)'$ may be replaced by $\nu^\circ\varsigma'^\circ\left((\tau^{\circ\prime} X_{t-1})' : \Delta X_{t-1}'\right)'$ without changing the likelihood, where $\nu^\circ := \nu Q^{-1} = (\alpha A^{-1} : \lambda B^{-1} - \alpha A^{-1} C)$, $\varsigma'^\circ := Q\varsigma' W^{-1}$ and

$$Q := \begin{pmatrix} A & CB \\ 0 & B \end{pmatrix}, \qquad W := \begin{pmatrix} B & 0 \\ 0 & I_p \end{pmatrix}, \qquad \varsigma'^\circ := Q\varsigma' W^{-1} = \begin{pmatrix} A\rho' B^{-1} & A\psi' + CB\tau' \\ 0 & B\tau' \end{pmatrix};$$

here A and B are square nonsingular matrices, and C is a generic matrix. Hence one observes that $(\alpha, \rho, \tau, \psi, \lambda, \Upsilon, \Omega)$ is observationally equivalent to $(\alpha^\circ, \rho^\circ, \tau^\circ, \psi^\circ, \lambda^\circ, \Upsilon, \Omega)$. A, B and C define the class of observationally equivalent transformations in the τ-par for all parameters, including τ. When τ is identified one has $B = I_m$ in the above formulae.

Consider additional restrictions on φ of the type:

$$\underset{m_\varphi \times f_\varphi}{R_\varphi'} \operatorname{vec} \varphi' = q_\varphi, \qquad \varphi' := (\rho' : \psi'). \tag{18}$$

where $f_\varphi = r(p+m)$. The next theorem states rank conditions for these restrictions to identify the remaining parameters.

Theorem 5 (Identification of other parameters in the τ-par). *Assume that τ is identified as in Theorem 4; the restrictions (18) identify φ and all other parameters in the τ-par if and only if (rank condition)*

$$\text{rank}\, R_\varphi' (\varsigma \otimes I_r) = r(r+m) \tag{19}$$

A necessary but not sufficient condition (order condition) for this is that

$$m_\varphi \geq r(r+m). \tag{20}$$

Proof. Because τ is identified, one has $B = I_m$ in Q. For the identification of φ, observe that $\varsigma - \varsigma^\circ = \varsigma(I - Q')$. One finds $\varphi - \varphi^\circ = (\varsigma - \varsigma^\circ)(I_r : 0)' = \varsigma(I_{m+r} - Q')(I_r : 0)'$. Because both φ and φ° satisfy (18), one has $0 = R'_\varphi \operatorname{vec}(\varphi' - \varphi^{\circ\prime}) = R'_\varphi(\varsigma \otimes I_r)\operatorname{vec}((I_r : 0)(I_{r+m} - Q))$. This implies that $(I_r : 0)(I_{m+r} - Q) = 0$, i.e., that both $A = I_r$ and $C = 0_{r \times m}$, and that φ is identified, if and only if $\operatorname{rank} R'_\varphi(\varsigma \otimes I_r) = r(r+m)$. This completes the proof. □

Observe that the identification properties of the τ-par differ from the ones of the parametrization of Johansen (1997), where $\lambda = \Omega\alpha_\perp(\alpha'_\perp\Omega\alpha_\perp)^{-1}\kappa'$ is restricted, and hence the adding-and-subtracting associated with C above is not permitted.

4.3. Deterministic Terms

The τ-par in (16) does not involve deterministic terms. Allowing a constant and a trend to enter the VAR Equation (1) in a way that rules out quadratic trends, one obtains the following equilibrium correction I(2) model—for simplicity still called the τ-par below:

$$\Delta^2 X_t = \alpha\left(\rho'\tau^{\star\prime}X^\star_{t-1} + \psi^{\star\prime}\Delta X^\star_{t-1}\right) + \lambda\tau^{\star\prime}\Delta X^\star_{t-1} + \Upsilon\Delta^2\mathbb{X}_{t-1} + \varepsilon_t. \tag{21}$$

Here $X^\star_{t-1} = (X'_{t-1} : t)'$ so that $\Delta X^\star_{t-1} = (\Delta X'_{t-1} : 1)'$; and $\tau^\star = (\tau' : \tau_1)$ and $\psi^\star = (\psi' : \psi_0)'$.

This parametrization satisfies the conditions of the Johansen Representation Theorem and it generates deterministic trends up to first order, as shown in Appendix A. This is the I(2) model used in the application, with the addition of unrestricted dummy variables.

5. Likelihood Maximization

This section discusses likelihood maximization of the τ-par of the I(2) model (16) under linear, possibly over-identifying, restrictions on $\tau_{\perp c_\perp}$, i.e., on ϑ in (5). The same treatment applies to (21) replacing $(X_{t-1}, \Delta X_{t-1})$ with $(X^\star_{t-1}, \Delta X^\star_{t-1})$, and (τ, ψ), with $(\tau^\star, \psi^\star)$. The formulation (16) is preferred here for simplicity in exposition.

The alternating maximization procedure proposed here is closely related, but not identical, to the algorithms proposed by Doornik (2017b); related algorithms were discussed in Paruolo (2000b). Restricted ML estimation in the I(1) model was discussed in Boswijk and Doornik (2004).

5.1. Normalizations

Consider restrictions (8), which are translated into linear hypotheses on τ_c in (9) as follows

$$\operatorname{vec}\tau_c = (\operatorname{vec}\bar{c} - (I_m \otimes c_\perp)\mathcal{K}_{m,r_2}k) - (I_m \otimes c_\perp)\mathcal{K}_{m,r_2}K\phi =: g + G\phi,$$

where by construction g and G satisfy $(I_m \otimes c')g = \operatorname{vec} I_{rm}$ and $(I_m \otimes c')G = 0$ such that $c'\tau_c = I_m$.

Next, consider just-identifying restrictions on the remaining parameters. For ψ, the linear combinations of first differences entering the multicointegration relations, one can consider

$$c'\psi = 0 \qquad \Longleftrightarrow \qquad \psi = c_\perp\delta', \tag{22}$$

where δ is the $r \times r_2$ matrix of multicointegration parameters. This restriction differs from the restriction $\psi = \tau_\perp\delta'$ which is considered e.g., in Juselius (2017a, 2017b), and it was proposed and analysed by Boswijk (2000).

Furthermore, the $m \times r$ matrix ρ can be normalized as follows

$$d'\rho = I_r \qquad \Longleftrightarrow \qquad \rho = \bar{d} + d_\perp\varrho, \tag{23}$$

where d is some known $m \times r$ matrix, and where ϱ, of dimension $(m-r) \times r$, contains freely varying parameters.

It can be shown that restrictions (22) and (23) identify the remaining parameters using Theorem 5. In fact, (22) and (23) can be written as $\varphi' V = v$ where $V := \text{blkdiag}(d, c)$ and $v := (I_r : 0_{r \times m})$. Vectorizing, one obtains an equation $R'_\varphi \text{vec}\, \varphi' = q_\varphi$ of the form (18) with $R_\varphi = (V \otimes I_r)$ and $q_\varphi = \text{vec}\, v$. The rank condition (19) is satisfied, since $R'_\varphi (\varsigma \otimes I_r) = (V'\varsigma \otimes I_r) = I_{r(m+r)}$ because

$$V'\varsigma = \begin{pmatrix} d'\rho & 0 \\ c'\psi & c'\tau \end{pmatrix} = \begin{pmatrix} I_r & 0 \\ 0 & I_m \end{pmatrix},$$

where the last equality follows from (22) and (23) and $\tau = \tau_c$.

5.2. The Concentrated Likelihood Function

The model (16), after concentrating out the unrestricted parameter matrix Υ, can be represented by the equations

$$Z_{0t} = \alpha(\rho'\tau' Z_{2t} + \psi' Z_{1t}) + \lambda\tau' Z_{1t} + \varepsilon_t(\xi), \tag{24}$$

where ξ indicates the vector of free parameters in $(\alpha, \varrho, \phi, \delta, \lambda)$, Z_{0t}, Z_{1t} and Z_{2t} are residual vectors of regressions of $\Delta^2 X_t$, ΔX_{t-1} and X_{t-1}, respectively, on $\mathbb{X}_{t-1}$;[7] this derivation follows similarly to Chapter 6.1 in Johansen (1996). The associated log-likelihood function, concentrated with respect to Υ, is given by

$$\ell(\xi, \Omega) = -\frac{T}{2} \log |\Omega| - \frac{1}{2} \sum_{t=1}^{T} \varepsilon_t(\xi)' \Omega^{-1} \varepsilon_t(\xi),$$

In the rest of this section, ε_t is used as shorthand for $\varepsilon_t(\xi)$.

Algorithms for the maximization of the concentrated log-likelihood function $\ell(\xi, \Omega)$ are proposed below. The first one, called AL1, considers the alternative maximization of $\ell(\xi, \Omega)$ over $(\alpha, \varrho, \delta, \lambda, \Omega)$ for a fixed value of ϕ (called the α-step), and over (ϕ, δ) for a given value of $(\alpha, \varrho, \lambda, \Omega)$ (called the τ-step).

A variant of this algorithm, called AL2, can be defined fixing δ in the τ-step to the value of δ obtained in the α-step. It can be shown that the increase in $\ell(\xi, \Omega)$ obtained in one combination of α-step and τ-step of AL1 is greater or equal to the one obtained by AL2. The proof of this result is reported in Proposition A1 in Appendix B. Because of this property, and because AL2 may display very slow convergence properties in practice, AL1 is implemented in the illustration below.

The rest of this section presents algorithms AL1 and AL2, defining first the τ-step, then the α-step and finally discussing the starting values, a line search and normalizations.

5.2.1. τ Step

Taking differentials, one has $\text{d}\ell = -\sum_{t=1}^{T} \varepsilon'_t \Omega^{-1} \text{d}\varepsilon_t$. Keeping $(\alpha, \varrho, \lambda)$ fixed, one finds

$$\begin{aligned} -\text{d}\varepsilon_t &= \text{d}\left(\alpha\rho'\tau' Z_{2t} + \alpha\psi' Z_{1t} + \lambda\tau' Z_{1t}\right) \\ &= \left((Z'_{2t} \otimes \alpha\rho') + (Z'_{1t} \otimes \lambda)\right) \text{d}\,\text{vec}\,\tau' + (Z'_{1t} \otimes \alpha)\text{d}\,\text{vec}\,\psi' \\ &= \left((Z'_{2t} \otimes \alpha\rho') + (Z'_{1t} \otimes \lambda)\right) \mathcal{K}_{m,r_1} G\text{d}\phi + (Z'_{1t} c_\perp \otimes \alpha)\text{d}\,\text{vec}\,\delta. \end{aligned}$$

Writing ε_t in terms of ϕ and vec δ, i.e., $\varepsilon_t = Z_{0t} - \left((Z'_{2t} \otimes \alpha\rho') + (Z'_{1t} \otimes \lambda)\right) \mathcal{K}_{m,r_1}(G\phi + g) - (Z'_{1t} c_\perp \otimes \alpha)\,\text{vec}\,\delta$, the first-order conditions $\partial\ell/\partial\phi = 0$ and $\partial\ell/\partial\,\text{vec}\,\delta = 0$ are solved by

---

[7] If a restricted constant and linear trend are included in the model, as in (21), then Z_{1t} and Z_{2t} are defined as the residual vectors of regressions of ΔX^*_{t-1} and X^*_{t-1}, respectively, on $\mathbb{X}_{t-1}$.

$$\begin{pmatrix} \widehat{\phi} \\ \text{vec } \widehat{\delta}' \end{pmatrix} = \begin{pmatrix} G'U_1'\left(\Omega^{-1}\otimes I_T\right)U_1G & G'U_1'\left(\Omega^{-1}\otimes I_T\right)U_2 \\ U_2'\left(\Omega^{-1}\otimes I_T\right)U_1G & U_2'\left(\Omega^{-1}\otimes I_T\right)U_2 \end{pmatrix}^{-1} \cdot$$
$$\cdot \begin{pmatrix} G'U_1'\left(\Omega^{-1}\otimes I_T\right) \\ U_2'\left(\Omega^{-1}\otimes I_T\right) \end{pmatrix} (\text{vec } Z_0 - U_1 g), \tag{25}$$

where $Z_j = (Z_{j1} : \ldots : Z_{jT})', j = 0, 1, 2$, and where $U_1 = (\alpha\rho' \otimes Z_2) + (\lambda \otimes Z_1)$, and $U_2 = (\alpha \otimes Z_1 c_\perp)$. Note that (25) is the GLS estimator in a regression of vec $Z_0 - U_1 g$ on $(U_1 G : U_2)$. This defines the τ-step for AL1.

The τ-step for AL2 is defined similarly, but keeping δ fixed. In this case it is simple to see that

$$\widehat{\phi} = \left(G'U_1'\left(\Omega^{-1}\otimes I_T\right)U_1G\right)^{-1} G'U_1'\left(\Omega^{-1}\otimes I_T\right)(\text{vec } Z_0 - U_1 g - \text{vec } (Z_1\psi\alpha')).$$

5.2.2. α Step

When ϕ is fixed (and hence τ is fixed), one can construct $Z_{3t} = \tau' Z_{1t}$ and

$$Z_{4t} = \begin{pmatrix} \bar{d}'\tau' Z_{2t} \\ d_\perp'\tau' Z_{2t} \\ c_\perp' Z_{1t} \end{pmatrix}, \qquad \gamma = \begin{pmatrix} I_r \\ \varrho \\ \delta' \end{pmatrix}.$$

The concentrated model (24) can then be written as a reduced rank regression:

$$Z_{0t} = \alpha\gamma' Z_{4t} + \lambda Z_{3t} + \varepsilon_t,$$

for which the Guassian ML estimator for α, γ, λ has a closed-form solution, see Johansen (1996). Specifically, let $M_{ij} := T^{-1}\sum_{t=1}^{T} Z_{it}Z_{jt}'$, $i, j = 0, 3, 4$ and $S_{ij} := M_{ij} - M_{i3}M_{33}^{-1}M_{3j}$, $i, j = 0, 4$. If v_i, $i = 1, \ldots, r$, are the eigenvectors corresponding to the largest r eigenvalues of the problem

$$(\mu S_{44} - S_{40}S_{00}^{-1}S_{04})v = 0,$$

and $v = (v_i, \ldots, v_r)$ is the matrix of the corresponding eigenvectors, then the optimal solutions for ϱ, δ, α, λ is given by

$$\widehat{\gamma} = \begin{pmatrix} I_{r_0} \\ \widehat{\varrho} \\ \widehat{\delta}' \end{pmatrix} = v(e'v)^{-1}, \qquad \widehat{\alpha} = S_{04}\widehat{\gamma}(\widehat{\gamma}' S_{44}\widehat{\gamma})^{-1}, \qquad \widehat{\lambda} = (M_{03} - \widehat{\alpha}\widehat{\gamma}' M_{43})M_{33}^{-1},$$

where $e' = (I_r : 0)$. Optimization with respect to $\widehat{\Omega}$ is performed using $\Omega(\xi) = T^{-1}\sum_{t=1}^{T}\varepsilon_t(\xi)\varepsilon_t(\xi)'$ replacing ξ with $\widehat{\xi}$ formed from the previous expressions, namely taking $(\alpha, \varrho, \delta, \lambda)$ equal to $(\widehat{\alpha}, \widehat{\varrho}, \widehat{\delta}, \widehat{\lambda})$ in the above display and $\phi = \widehat{\phi}$ from the τ-step. Using the S_{ij} matrices, one can also compute $\widehat{\Omega}$ directly as $\widehat{\Omega} = S_{00} - S_{04}\widehat{\gamma}(\widehat{\gamma}' S_{44}\widehat{\gamma})^{-1}\widehat{\gamma}' S_{40}$. This completes the definition of the α-step.

5.2.3. Starting Values and Line Search

If the system is just-identified, consistent starting values for all parameters can be obtained by imposing the identifying restrictions on the two-stage estimator for the I(2) model (2SI2), see Johansen (1995) and Paruolo (2000a). In case of over-identification, this method may be used to produce starting values for $(\alpha, \varrho, \lambda)$, which may then be used as input for the first τ-step to obtain starting values for ϕ and δ.

Let η be the vector containing all free parameters in $(\alpha, \varrho, \delta, \lambda)$, and let $\xi := (\phi' : \eta')'$. Denote by $\xi_{j-1} = (\phi_{j-1}' : \eta_{j-1}')'$ the value of ξ in iteration $(j-1)$ of algorithms. Denote as $\widehat{\xi}_j = (\widehat{\phi}_j' : \widehat{\eta}_j')'$ the value of ξ obtained by the application of a τ-step and α-step of algorithms AL1 and AL2 at iteration j starting from ξ_{j-1}. In an I(1) context, Doornik (2017a) found that better convergence properties can be obtained if a line search is added. For this purpose, define the final value of the j-th iteration as

$$\xi_j(\omega) = \xi_{j-1} + \omega(\widehat{\xi}_j - \xi_{j-1})$$

where ω is chosen in $\mathbb{R}_+ = (0, \infty)$ using a line search; note that values of ω greater than 1 are admissible. A simple (albeit admittedly sub-optimal) implementation of the line search is employed in Doornik (2017a); it consists of evaluating the log-likelihood function $\ell(\xi, \Omega(\xi))$ with $\Omega(\xi) = T^{-1} \sum_{t=1}^{T} \varepsilon_t(\xi)\varepsilon_t(\xi)'$ setting ξ equal to $\xi_j(\omega)$ for $\omega \in \{1.2, 2, 4, 8\}$, and in choosing the value of ω with the highest loglikelihood ℓ. This simple choice of line search is used in the empirical illustration.

5.3. Standard Errors

The asymptotic variance matrix of the ML estimators may be obtained from the inverse observed (concentrated) information matrix as usual. Writing (24) as $Z_{0t} = \Pi Z_{2t} + \Gamma Z_{1t} + \varepsilon_t$, and letting $\theta = (\text{vec}\,(\Pi')' : \text{vec}\,(\Gamma')')'$, the observed concentrated information matrix for the reduced-form parameter vector θ is obtained from

$$\mathcal{I}_\theta = -\frac{\partial^2 \ell(\theta)}{\partial\theta\partial\theta'} = \begin{pmatrix} \Omega^{-1} \otimes Z_2'Z_2 & \Omega^{-1} \otimes Z_2'Z_1 \\ \Omega^{-1} \otimes Z_1'Z_2 & \Omega^{-1} \otimes Z_2'Z_2 \end{pmatrix}.$$

This leads to the following information matrix in terms of the parameters (ϕ, η):

$$\mathcal{I}_{\phi,\eta} = \begin{pmatrix} J_\phi' \\ J_\eta' \end{pmatrix} \mathcal{I}_\theta \begin{pmatrix} J_\phi & J_\eta \end{pmatrix},$$

where $J_\phi = \partial\theta/\partial\phi'$ and $J_\eta = \partial\theta/\partial\eta'$. From $\Pi = \alpha\rho'\tau'$ and $\Gamma = \alpha\psi' + \lambda\tau'$, one obtains

$$J_\phi = \begin{pmatrix} \alpha\rho' \otimes I_p \\ \lambda \otimes I_p \end{pmatrix} G.$$

Define $\eta = (\text{vec}\,(\alpha')' : \text{vec}\,(\varrho)' : \text{vec}\,(\delta')' : \text{vec}\,(\lambda')')'$, so that $J_\eta = [J_\alpha : J_\varrho : J_\delta : J_\lambda]$, with

$$J_\alpha = \begin{pmatrix} I_p \otimes \tau\rho \\ I_p \otimes \psi \end{pmatrix}, \quad J_\varrho = \begin{pmatrix} \alpha \otimes \tau d_\perp \\ 0 \end{pmatrix}, \quad J_\delta = \begin{pmatrix} 0 \\ \alpha \otimes c_\perp \end{pmatrix}, \quad J_\lambda = \begin{pmatrix} 0 \\ I_p \otimes \tau \end{pmatrix}.$$

With these ingredients, one finds

$$\widehat{\text{var}}(\widehat{\phi}) = \left(\widehat{J}_\phi'\widehat{\mathcal{I}}_\theta\widehat{J}_\phi - \widehat{J}_\phi'\widehat{\mathcal{I}}_\theta\widehat{J}_\eta(\widehat{J}_\eta'\widehat{\mathcal{I}}_\theta\widehat{J}_\eta)^{-1}\widehat{J}_\eta'\widehat{\mathcal{I}}_\theta\widehat{J}_\phi\right)^{-1},$$

where $\widehat{\mathcal{I}}_\theta$, $\widehat{J}_\phi$ and $\widehat{J}_\eta$ are the expressions given above, evaluated at the ML estimators. Standard errors of individual parameters estimates are obtained as the square root of the diagonal elements of $\widehat{\text{var}}(\widehat{\phi})$. Asymptotic normality of resulting t-statistics (under the null hypothesis), and χ^2 asymptotic null distributions of likelihood ratio test statistics for the over-identifying restrictions, depend on conditions for asymptotic mixed normality being satisfied; this is discussed next.

6. Asymptotics

The asymptotic distribution of the ML estimator in the I(2) model has been discussed in Johansen (1997, 2006). As shown there and discussed in Boswijk (2000), the limit distribution of the ML estimator is not jointly mixed normal as in the I(1) case. As a consequence, the limit distribution of LR test statistics of generic hypotheses need not be χ^2 under the null hypothesis.

In some special cases, the asymptotic distribution of the just-identified ML estimator of the cointegration parameters can be shown to be asymptotically mixed normal. Consider the case $r_1 = 0$ (i.e., $r = m$), and assume as before that no deterministic terms are included in the model. In this case, the limit distribution of the cointegration parameters in Theorem 4 in Johansen (2006), J06 hereafter, can be described in terms of the estimated parameters $\widehat{B}_0 := \bar{\tau}'_\perp(\widehat{\psi} - \psi)$ and $\widehat{B}_2 := \bar{\tau}'_\perp(\widehat{\tau} - \tau)$, where $\widehat{\tau}$ is identified as τ_c with $c = \tau$. Note that the components C and B_1 in the above theorem do not appear here, because $r_1 = 0$. One has

$$\begin{pmatrix} T\widehat{B}_0 \\ T^2\widehat{B}_2 \end{pmatrix} \overset{w}{\to} B^\infty := \left(\int_0^1 H_*(s)H_*(s)'\mathrm{d}s\right)^{-1} \int_0^1 H_*(s)\mathrm{d}W_1(s)$$

with $H_*(u) := (H_0(u)' : H_2(u)')'$,

$$H_{2u} := \int_0^u H_0(s)\mathrm{d}s, \qquad H_0(u) := \tau'_\perp C_2 W(u), \qquad W_1(u) := \left(\alpha'\Omega^{-1}\alpha\right)^{-1} \alpha'\Omega^{-1}W(u),$$

and where $T^{-\frac{1}{2}} \sum_{i=1}^{\lfloor Tu \rfloor} \varepsilon_i \overset{w}{\to} W(u)$, a vector Brownian motion with covariance matrix Ω[8].

As noted in J06, B^∞ has a mixed normal distribution with mean 0, because $H_*(u)$ is a function of $\alpha'_\perp W(u)$, which is independent of $W_1(u)$. Moreover in the case $r_1 = 0$, the C^∞ component of the ML limit distribution does not appear, so that the whole limit distribution of the cointegration parameters is *jointly* mixed normal, unlike in the case $r_1 > 0$.

One can see that hypothesis (8) defines a smooth restriction of the B_2 parameters[9]. More precisely B_2 depends smoothly only on ϕ_2, $B_2 = B_2(\phi_2)$, where ϕ_2 contains the ϕ parameters in (8). Note also that B_0 depends on the parameters in ψ, which are unrestricted by (8); hence B_0 depends only on ϕ_1, $B_0 = B_0(\phi_1)$, where ϕ_1 contains the parameters in δ in (22).

The conditions of Theorem 5 in J06 are next shown to be verified, and hence the LR test of the hypothesis (8) is asymptotically χ^2 with degrees of freedom equal to the number of constraints, in case $r_1 = 0$. In fact, $B_0(\phi_1)$, $B_2(\phi_2)$ are smoothly parametrizated by the continuously identified parameters ϕ_1 and ϕ_2. Because B_2 does not depend on ϕ_1, one easily deduces $\partial B_2/\partial\phi_1 = \partial^2 B_2/\partial\phi_1^2 = 0$ in (37) of J06. Similarly, one has $\phi_1 = \phi_{1B}$ with $\partial B_0/\partial\phi_1$ and $\partial B_2/\partial\phi_2$ of full rank; hence (38) of J06 is satisfied. This shows that the LR statistic is asymptotically χ^2 under the null, for $r_1 = 0$.

In case $r_1 = (m - r) > 0$, the asymptotic distribution of $\widehat{\tau}$ is defined in terms of (B^∞, C^∞) in J06 p. 92, which is not jointly mixed normal. In such cases, Boswijk (2000) showed that inference is mixed normal if the restrictions on $\widehat{\tau}_c$ can be asymptotically linearized in (B^∞, C^∞), and separated into two sets of restrictions, the first group involving B^∞ only, and the second group involving C^∞ only. Because the conditions of Theorem 5 in J06 cannot be easily verified for general linear hypotheses of the form (8) in this case, they will need to be checked case by case. The authors intend to develop more readily verifiable conditions for χ^2 inference on τ in their future research.

7. Illustration

Following Juselius and Assenmacher (2015), consider a 7-dimensional VAR with

$$X_t = (p_{1t} : p_{2t} : e_{12t} : b_{1t} : b_{2t} : s_{1t} : s_{2t})',$$

where p_{it}, b_{it}, s_{it} are the (log of) the price index, the long and the short interest rate of country i at time t respectively, and e_{12t} is the log of the exchange rate between country 1 (Switzerland) and 2 (the US)

---

8 Here $\overset{w}{\to}$ indicates weak convergence and $\lfloor\cdot\rfloor$ denotes the greatest integer part.

9 In the rest of this section the notation ϕ_1, ϕ_2 and $\partial B_i/\partial\phi_j$ are used in accordance to the notation in J06.

at time t. The results are based on quarterly data over the period 1975:1–2013:3. The model has two lags, a restricted linear trend as in (21), which appears in the equilibrium correction only appended to the vector of lagged levels, and a number of dummy variables; see Juselius and Assenmacher (2017), which is an updated version of Juselius and Assenmacher (2015), for further details on the empirical model. The data set used here is taken from Juselius and Assenmacher (2017).

Specification (3) is based on the prediction that $r_2 = 2$. Based on I(2) cointegration tests, Juselius and Assenmacher (2017) choose a model with $r = m = 5$, which indeed implies $r_2 = 2$, but also $r_1 = m - r = 0$; arguably, however, the test results in Table 1 of their paper also support the hypothesis $(r, r_1) = (4, 1)$, which has the same number $r_2 = 2$ of common $I(2)$ trends. The latter model would be selected applying the sequential procedure in Nielsen and Rahbek (2007) using a 5% or 10% significance level in each test in the sequence.

Consider the case $(r, r_1) = (5, 0)$. The over-identifying restrictions on $\tau_\perp$ implied by (3) are incorporated in the parametrization (3), with normalizations $\phi_{11} = \phi_{42} = 1$, which in turn leads to the over-identified structure for τ_c in (15), to be estimated by ML. The restricted ML estimate of $\tau_{\perp c_\perp}$ is (standard errors in parentheses):

$$\widehat{\tau}_{\perp c_\perp} = \begin{pmatrix} 1 & 0 \\ \underset{(0.11)}{1.49} & \underset{(5.23)}{-25.14} \\ \underset{(0.72)}{-1.88} & \underset{(29.81)}{-35.70} \\ 0 & 1 \\ 0 & \underset{(0.53)}{-1.91} \\ 0 & \underset{(0.29)}{1.23} \\ 0 & \underset{(0.95)}{-3.02} \end{pmatrix}.$$

The LR statistics for the 3 over-identifying restrictions equals 16.11. Using the $\chi^2(3)$ asymptotic limit distribution, one finds an asymptotic p-value of 0.001, and hence a rejection of the null hypothesis. This indicates that the hypothesized structure on $\tau_\perp$ is rejected.

For comparison, consider also the case $(r, r_1) = (4, 1)$, for which the LR test for cointegration ranks has a p-value of 0.13. The resulting restricted estimate of $\tau_{\perp c_\perp}$ is:

$$\widehat{\tau}_{\perp c_\perp} = \begin{pmatrix} 1 & 0 \\ \underset{(0.09)}{1.38} & \underset{(5.22)}{-24.67} \\ \underset{(0.56)}{-1.07} & \underset{(22.42)}{-30.10} \\ 0 & 1 \\ 0 & \underset{(0.52)}{-1.75} \\ 0 & \underset{(0.28)}{1.20} \\ 0 & \underset{(1.02)}{-2.97} \end{pmatrix}.$$

The estimates and standard errors are similar to those obtained under the hypothesis $(r, r_1) = (5, 0)$. The LR statistic for the over-identifying restrictions now equals 10.08. If one conjectured that the limit distribution of the LR test is also $\chi^2(3)$ in this case, one would obtain an asymptotic p-value of 0.018, so the evidence against the hypothesized structure of τ appears slightly weaker in this model.

The results for both model $(r, r_1) = (5, 0)$ and for model $(r, r_1) = (4, 1)$ are in line with the preferred specification of Juselius and Assenmacher (2017), who select an over-identified structure for τ, which is not nested in (15), and therefore implies a different impact of the common I(2) trends.

8. Conclusions

Hypotheses on the loading matrix of I(2) common trends are of economic interest. They are shown to be related to the cointegration relations. This link is explicitly discussed in this paper, also for hypotheses that are over-identifying. Likelihood maximization algorithms are proposed and discussed, along with LR tests of the hypotheses.

The application of these LR tests to a system of prices, exchange rates and interest rates for Switzerland and the US shows support for the existence of two I(2) common trends. These may represent a 'speculative' trend and a 'relative prices' trend, but there is little empirical support for the corresponding exclusion restrictions in the loading matrix.

Acknowledgments: Helpful comments and suggestions from two anonymous referees and the Academic Editor, Katarina Juselius, are gratefully acknowledged.

Author Contributions: Both authors contributed equally to the paper.

Conflicts of Interest: The authors declare no conflict of interest.

Appendix A

Theorem A1 (Johansen Representation Theorem). *Let the vector process X_t satisfy $A(L)X_t = \mu_0 + \mu_1 t + \varepsilon_t$, where $A(L) := I_p - \sum_{i=1}^{k} A_i L^i$, a matrix lag polynomial of degree k, and where ε_t is an i.i.d. $(0, \Omega)$ sequence. Assume that $A(z)$ is of full rank for all $|z| < 1 + c$, $c > 0$, with the exception of $z = 1$. Let A, $\dot{A}$ and $\ddot{A}$ denote $A(1)$, the first and second derivative of $A(z)$ with respect to z, evaluated at $z = 1$; finally define $\Gamma = \dot{A} - A$. Then X_t is I(2) if and only if the following conditions hold:*

(i) $A = -\alpha\beta'$ *where* α, β *are* $p \times r$ *matrices of full column rank* $r < p$,
(ii) $P_{\alpha_\perp}\Gamma P_{\beta_\perp} = \alpha_1\beta_1'$ *where* α_1, β_1 *are* $p \times r_1$ *matrices of full column rank* $r_1 < p - r$,
(iii) $\alpha_2'\Theta\beta_2$ *is of full rank* $r_2 := p - r - r_1$, *where* $\Theta := \frac{1}{2}\ddot{A} + \dot{A}\bar{\beta}\bar{\alpha}'\dot{A}$, $\alpha_2 := (\alpha, \alpha_1)_\perp$ *and* $\beta_2 := (\beta, \beta_1)_\perp$,
(iv) $\mu_1 = \alpha\beta_D$ *for some* β_D,
(v) $\alpha_2'\mu_0 = \alpha_2'\Gamma\bar{\beta}\beta_D$.

Under these conditions, X_t admits a common trends I(2) representation of the form

$$X_t = C_2 \sum_{i=1}^{t}\sum_{s=1}^{i} \varepsilon_s + C_1 \sum_{i=1}^{t} \varepsilon_i + C^\star(L)\varepsilon_t + v_0 + v_1 t, \tag{A1}$$

where

$$C_2 = \beta_2(\alpha_2'\Theta\beta_2)^{-1}\alpha_2', \tag{A2}$$

$C^\star(L)\varepsilon_t$ is an I(0) linear process, and v_0 and v_1 depend on the VAR coefficients and on the initial values of the process.

Proof. See Johansen (1992), Johansen (2009) and Rahbek et al. (1999), which also contain expressions for C_1, $C^*(L)$ and (v_0, v_1). □

It is next shown that conditions (*iv*) and (*v*) are satisfied by the τ-par (21). In fact, condition (*iv*) holds for $\beta_D = \rho'\tau_1$. Note that $\Gamma = \alpha\psi' + \lambda\tau'$, $\beta = \tau\rho$ and $P_{\alpha_\perp}\Gamma P_{\beta_\perp} = P_{\alpha_\perp}\lambda\tau' P_{\beta_\perp} = \alpha_1\beta_1'$. The l.h.s. of (*v*) is

$$\alpha_2'\mu_0 = \alpha_2'\lambda\tau_1. \tag{A3}$$

Next write the r.h.s. of (*v*) using $\tau'\tau\rho(\rho'\tau'\tau\rho)^{-1}\rho' = I - \rho_\perp(\rho_\perp'(\tau'\tau)^{-1}\rho_\perp)^{-1}\rho_\perp'(\tau'\tau)^{-1}$ by oblique projections; one finds

$$\begin{aligned}\alpha_2'\Gamma\bar{\beta}\beta_D &= \alpha_2'\lambda\tau'\tau\rho(\rho'\tau'\tau\rho)^{-1}\rho'\tau_1 \\ &= \alpha_2'\lambda\tau_1 - \alpha_2'\lambda\rho_\perp(\rho_\perp'(\tau'\tau)^{-1}\rho_\perp)^{-1}\rho_\perp'(\tau'\tau)^{-1}\tau_1 = \alpha_2'\lambda\tau_1\end{aligned} \tag{A4}$$

where the last equality holds because $\alpha_2'\lambda\rho_\perp = 0$, as shown below. Note in fact that $\beta_1 = \bar{\tau}\rho_\perp$ lies in $\text{col}\,\beta_\perp$ and α_2 lies in $\text{col}\,\alpha_\perp$; hence one can write

$$\alpha_2'\lambda\rho_\perp = \alpha_2'\lambda\tau'\bar{\tau}\rho_\perp = \alpha_2'P_{\alpha_\perp}\lambda\tau'P_{\beta_\perp}\beta_1 = \alpha_2'P_{\alpha_\perp}\Gamma P_{\beta_\perp}\beta_1 = \alpha_2'\alpha_1\beta_1'\beta_1 = 0.$$

Hence, because (A3) equals (A4), condition (v) is satisfied.

Appendix B

This Appendix contains a proof that the increase in ℓ in one combination of α-step and τ-step of AL1 is greater or equal to the one obtained by AL2. In order to state the argument in somewhat greater generality, define a parameter vector θ partitioned in 3 components, denoted $(\theta_1, \theta_2, \theta_3)$, where each θ_j represents a subvector of parameters, respectively of dimensions n_1, n_2, n_3. Let $\ell(\theta)$ be the log-likelihood function. Define also the following switching algorithms, both starting at the same initial value $(\theta_1^{(j-1)}, \theta_2^{(j-1)}, \theta_3^{(j-1)})$:

Definition A1. ALGO1 *(3 way switching)*

Step 1: *for fixed* θ_1, *maximize* ℓ *with respect to* (θ_2, θ_3);
Step 2: *for fixed* θ_2, *maximize* ℓ *with respect to* (θ_1, θ_3).

Let $\ell(\theta^{(1,j)})$ *be the value of* ℓ *corresponding to the application of step 1 and 2 of* ALGO1.

Definition A2. ALGO2 *(Pure switching)*

Step 1: *for fixed* θ_1, *maximize* ℓ *with respect to* (θ_2, θ_3);
Step 2: *for fixed* (θ_2, θ_3), *maximize* ℓ *with respect to* θ_1.

Let $\ell(\theta^{(2,j)})$ *be the value of* ℓ *corresponding to the application of step 1 and 2 of* ALGO2.

Proposition A1 (Pure versus 3-way switching). *One has* $\ell(\theta^{(1,j)}) \geq \ell(\theta^{(2,j)})$.

Proof. In order to see this, let

$$(\theta_2^\star, \theta_3^\star) = \arg\max_{\theta_2,\theta_3} \ell(\theta_1^{(j-1)}, \theta_2, \theta_3).$$

Step 1 is the same for ALGO1 and ALGO2. In the second step of ALGO1 one considers

$$\ell(\theta^{(1,j)}) = \max_{\theta_1,\theta_3} \ell(\theta_1, \theta_2^\star, \theta_3), \tag{A5}$$

while for ALGO2 one considers

$$\ell(\theta^{(2,j)}) = \max_{\theta_1} \ell(\theta_1, \theta_2^\star, \theta_3^\star). \tag{A6}$$

The conclusion that $\ell(\theta^{(1,j)}) \geq \ell(\theta^{(2,j)})$ follows from the fact that the maximization problem (A6) is a constrained version of (A5) under $\theta_3 = \theta_3^\star$. □

It is simple to observe that the argument of the proof implies that the larger the dimension of n_3, the better.

References

Boswijk, H. Peter. 2000. Mixed normality and ancillarity in I(2) systems. *Econometric Theory* 16: 878–904.

Boswijk, H. Peter, and Jurgen A. Doornik. 2004. Identifying, estimating and testing restricted cointegrated systems: An overview. *Statistica Neerlandica* 58: 440–65.

Doornik, Jurgen A. 2017a. Accelerated estimation of switching algorithms: The cointegrated VAR model and other applications. Working paper, University of Oxford, Oxford, UK.

Doornik, Jurgen A. 2017b. Maximum likelihood estimation of the I(2) model under linear restrictions. *Econometrics* 5: 19.

Engle, Robert F., and Clive W. J. Granger. 1987. Co-integration and error correction: Representation, estimation, and testing. *Econometrica* 55: 251–76.

Johansen, Søren. 1991. Estimation and hypothesis testing of cointegration vectors in Gaussian vector autoregressive models. *Econometrica* 59: 1551–80.

Johansen, Søren. 1992. A representation of vector autoregressive processes integrated of order 2. *Econometric Theory* 8: 188–202.

Johansen, Søren. 1995. Identifying restrictions of linear equations with applications to simultaneous equations and cointegration. *Journal of Econometrics* 69: 111–32.

Johansen, Søren. 1996. *Likelihood-Based Inference in Cointegrated Vector Autoregressive Models*, 2nd printing. Oxford: Oxford University Press.

Johansen, Søren. 1997. A likelihood analysis of the I(2) model. *Scandinavian Journal of Statistics* 24: 433–62.

Johansen, Søren. 2006. Statistical analysis of hypotheses on the cointegrating relations in the I(2) model. *Journal of Econometrics* 132: 81–115.

Johansen, Søren. 2009. Representation of cointegrated autoregressive processes with application to fractional processes. *Econometric Reviews* 28: 121–45.

Jöreskog, Karl G., Ulf H. Olsson, and Fan Y. Wallentin. 2016. *Multivariate Analysis with LISREL*. Basel: Springer International Publishing.

Juselius, Katarina. 2017a. A theory consistent CVAR scenario for a standard monetary model using data-generated expectations. Working paper, University of Copenhagen, Copenhagen, Denmark.

Juselius, Katarina. 2017b. Using a theory-consistent CVAR scenario to test an exchange rate model based on imperfect knowledge. Working paper, University of Copenhagen, Copenhagen, Denmark.

Juselius, Katarina, and Katrin Assenmacher. 2015. Real exchange rate persistence: The case of the Swiss franc-US dollar rate. SNB Working paper 2015-03, Swiss National Bank, Zürich, Switzerland.

Juselius, Katarina, and Katrin Assenmacher. 2017. Real Exchange Rate Persistence and the Excess Return Puzzle: The Case of Switzerland Versus the US. *Journal of Applied Econometrics*, forthcoming. doi:10.1002/jae.2562.

Kongsted, Hans Christian. 2005. Testing the nominal-to-real transformation. *Journal of Econometrics* 124: 205–25.

Magnus, Jan R., and Heinz Neudecker. 2007. *Matrix Differential Calculus with Applications in Statistics and Econometrics*, 3rd ed. New York: Wiley.

Mosconi, Rocco, and Paolo Paruolo. 2017. Cointegration and error correction in I(2) vector autoregressive models: Identification, estimation and testing. Mimeo, Polictenico di Milano, Milano, Italy.

Nielsen, Heino Bohn, and Anders Rahbek. 2007. The likelihood ratio test for cointegration ranks in the I(2) model. *Econometric Theory* 23: 615–37.

Paruolo, Paolo. 1997. Asymptotic inference on the moving average impact matrix in cointegrated I(1) VAR systems. *Econometric Theory* 13: 79–118.

Paruolo, Paolo. 2000a. Asymptotic efficiency of the two stage estimator in I(2) systems. *Econometric Theory* 16: 524–50.

Paruolo, Paolo. 2000b. On likelihood-maximizing algorithms for I(2) VAR models. Mimeo, University of Insubria, Varese, Italy.

Paruolo, Paolo. 2002. Asymptotic inference on the moving average impact matrix in cointegrated I(2) VAR systems. *Econometric Theory* 18: 673–90.

Rahbek, Anders, Hans Christian Kongsted, and Clara Jørgensen. 1999. Trend-stationarity in the I(2) cointegration model. *Journal of Econometrics* 90: 265–89.

Rothenberg, Thomas J. 1971. Identification in parametric models. *Econometrica* 39: 577–91.

Sargan, J. Denis. 1988. *Lectures on Advanced Econometric Theory* (edited by Meghnad Desai). Oxford: Basil Blackwell.

Srivastava, Muni S., and C. G. Kathri. 1979. *An Introduction to Multivariate Statistics*. New York: North Holland.

econometrics

Article

Modeling Real Exchange Rate Persistence in Chile

Leonardo Salazar

Department of Economics and Finance, Universtiy of Bío-Bío, Avenida Collao 1202, Concepción, Chile; lsalazar@ubiobio.cl; Tel.: +56-41-3111481

Academic Editor: Katarina Juselius
Received: 28 February 2017; Accepted: 30 June 2017; Published: 7 July 2017

Abstract: The long and persistent swings in the real exchange rate have for a long time puzzled economists. Recent models built on imperfect knowledge economics seem to provide a theoretical explanation for this persistence. Empirical results, based on a cointegrated vector autoregressive (CVAR) model, provide evidence of error-increasing behavior in prices and interest rates, which is consistent with the persistence observed in the data. The movements in the real exchange rate are compensated by movements in the interest rate spread, which restores the equilibrium in the product market when the real exchange rate moves away from its long-run benchmark value. Fluctuations in the copper price also explain the deviations of the real exchange rate from its long-run equilibrium value.

Keywords: exchange rate; long swings; I(2) analysis

JEL Classification: C32; F31; F41; G15

1. Introduction

The purchasing power parity (PPP) theory establishes that identical goods will have the same price in different economies when prices are expressed in the same currency (Krugman et al. 2011). In other words, the aggregate relative prices between two countries should be equal to the nominal exchange rate between them (Taylor and Taylor 2004).[1]

The PPP has been broadly used in economics, in both theoretical models and empirical applications. For instance, a number of general equilibrium models use the PPP as an equilibrium condition; that is, the PPP is assumed to hold over time, and the main results in these models rely on the PPP assumption (Duncan and Calderón 2003). In addition, estimates of PPP exchange rates are used to compare national income levels, determining the degree of misalignment of the nominal exchange rate around relative prices and the appropriate policy response (Sarno and Taylor 2002).

However, empirical evidence shows that over time, the nominal exchange rate exhibits long and persistent swings around relative prices. Specifically, while the ratio of domestic to foreign good prices changes slowly over time, the nominal exchange rate exhibits long and persistent swings away from its benchmark value. Consequently, these persistent swings are observed in the real exchange rate. See Figure 1 for the Chilean case.

Long and persistent fluctuations in the real exchange rate (RER) may generate allocative effects on the economy. Indeed, the competitiveness of a country might be negatively affected by a prolonged real appreciation (Mark 2001). Furthermore, these fluctuations might affect domestic real interest rates, wages, unemployment, and output, generating structural slumps in economies (Phelps 1994).

[1] This concept is known as absolute PPP.

Frydman and Goldberg (2007) developed a monetary model based on imperfect knowledge economics (IKE), know as IKE-based model, that was proposed as a solution to the puzzle of the long swings in exchange rates. Its empirical validity has been tested by Johansen et al. (2010), Juselius (2017a), and Juselius and Assenmacher (2017). For instance, using a cointegrated vector autoregressive (CVAR) scenario,[2] Juselius (2017a) argues, based on German-US data, that the IKE-based scenario is empirically supported by every testable hypothesis that describes the underlying assumptions of this model.

Departures from PPP have also been related to theories were the markup over costs of firms operating on imperfectly competitive markets is negatively affected by the inflation rate. For instance, Bacchiocchi and Fanelli (2005) found that persistent deviations from PPP in France, the United Kingdom and Germany, versus the United States, might be attributed to the presence of $I(2)$ stochastic trends in prices which can be associated with inflation rates that reduces the markup of profit-maximizing firms acting on imperfectly competitive markets.

The evidence on PPP is generally mixed and the results depend on the covered period, the variables included in the analysis, and the econometric methodology used to test the PPP hypothesis.[3]

In the case of Chile, the evidence is also mixed, and the results depend primarily on the methodology used to test the PPP hypothesis. On the one hand, when augmented Dickey-Fuller (ADF) test is used in a single equation that includes the nominal exchange rate, domestic price, and foreign price, the PPP hypothesis seems to hold. That is, RER is found to be a stationary process (Délano and Valdés 1998; Duncan and Calderón 2003). On the other hand, if multivariate cointegration techniques are used, the results show that RER behaves as a nonstationary $I(1)$ process. However, it cointegrates with other $I(1)$ variables to a stationary process. Indeed, there is evidence of cointegration between RER, productivity, net foreign assets, government expenditures, and terms of trade (Céspedes and De Gregorio 1999) and between RER and black exchange rates (parallel market) (Diamandis 2003). It also seems that the stationarity of RER depends on the analyzed period; for instance, Délano and Valdés (1998) shows that RER behaves as an $I(0)$ process when the period 1830–1995 is considered but as an $I(1)$ process in the period 1918–1995.

The Chilean economy, similar to other economies in South America, depends strongly on its commodities prices. Copper is the main export commodity in Chile; it accounted for 54% of Chile's exports, 14% of fiscal revenue, and 13% of nominal GDP in 2012 (Wu 2013). Chile has become increasingly important in the world copper market because its share of global production has increased to somewhat more than a third since the late 1960s (De Gregorio and Labbé 2011).

A number of studies have analyzed how copper prices affect the Chilean economy through its effects on nominal exchange rates, terms of trade, and business cycles. The results suggest that a positive shock to the copper price leads to appreciation in nominal and real exchange rates, output expansion, and an increased inflation rate (Cowan et al. 2007; Medina and Soto 2007).

In the long run, copper prices appear to explain most of the fluctuations in the Chilean peso, but in the short run, other factors, including interest rate spread, global financial risk, and local pension funds foreign exchange derivative position, may explain these fluctuations (Wu 2013). The fact that RER has acted as a shock absorber due to the flexible exchange rate regime, a rule-based fiscal policy, and a flexible inflation targeting system might explain why the Chilean economy has become increasingly resilient to copper price shocks in the last 25 years (De Gregorio and Labbé 2011).

This paper finds, based on the estimation of a CVAR model, that the long and persistent swings in the real exchange rate are compensated by movements in the interest rate spread, which restores the equilibrium in the product market when the real exchange rate moves away from its long-run benchmark value. Fluctuations in the copper price also explain the deviations of the real exchange

[2] A CVAR scenario tests the empirical consistency of the basic underlying assumptions of a model rather than imposing them on the data from the outset (Juselius 2017a).

[3] Duncan and Calderón (2003), and Froot and Rogoff (1995) present a thorough review of the literature on PPP testing.

rate from its long-run equilibrium value. The latter is consistent with the finding that in commodity exporters economies, variations in exchange rates are not random, but tightly linked to movements in commodity prices (Kohlscheen et al. 2017). Additionally, the results indicate error-increasing behavior in prices and interest rates, which is consistent with the persistence in the data.

The paper is organized as follows. Section 2 presents a theoretical framework based on IKE for exchange rate determination. Section 3 introduces the cointegrated vector of autoregressive model for variables that are integrated of order 2, $I(2)$. Section 4 presents stylized facts about Chilean data. Section 5 shows an empirical analysis of the data and presents a long-run structure. Section 6 concludes.

2. Theoretical Framework

2.1. Parity Conditions

This subsection introduces one of the most important parity conditions of open-economy macroeconomic models: the purchasing power parity (PPP) condition. This parity condition states that once converted to a common currency, via nominal exchange rate, national price levels should equalize (Bacchiocchi and Fanelli 2005). The absolute form (or strong form) of the PPP condition is expressed as:

$$P_{d,t} = S_t P_{f,t} \tag{1}$$

where $P_{d,t}$ is the domestic price level, $P_{f,t}$ is the foreign price level, S_t is the nominal exchange rate defined as the domestic-currency price in a unit of foreign currency, and t stands for time.

If p_d, p_f and s are, respectively, the natural logarithm of P_d, P_f, and S, Equation (1) can be rewritten as:

$$p_{d,t} = p_{f,t} + s_t \tag{2}$$

and the long-run PPP condition is expressed as:

$$p_{d,t} - p_{f,t} - s_t = \mu + ppp_t \tag{3}$$

where μ is a constant that reflects differences both in units of measure and in base-year normalization of price indices (Mark 2001), and ppp_t is a stationary error term that represents the deviations from PPP.[4] If the PPP condition holds in the goods market, then by definition, the log of the real exchange rate,[5] q_t, behaves as a stationary process, that is:

$$q_t = s_t + p_{f,t} - p_{d,t} \sim I(0). \tag{4}$$

Moreover, deviations from the uncovered interest parity (UIP) condition, that is, the excess returns on foreign exchange, er_t, would be stationary,[6] so that:

$$er_t = \left(i_d - i_f\right) - \left(s^e_{t+1} - s_t\right) \sim I(0) \tag{5}$$

where i_d and i_f are, respectively, the domestic and foreign interest rated and the superscript e denotes an expected value.

Empirical evidence finds, however, that the real exchange rates and excess returns behave as nonstationary processes, suggesting that the assumptions behind Equations (4) and (5) are

---

4 In empirical testing, the PPP condition is normally replaced by $s_t = \mu + \gamma_1 p_{d,t} + \gamma_2 p_{f,t} + ppp_t$, where $\gamma_1 = -\gamma_2 = 1$ is expected.

5 The real exchange rate is defined as $Q_t = S_t \frac{P_{f,t}}{P_{d,t}}$. It corresponds to the ratio of the foreign price level and the domestic price level, once the foreign price has been converted to the domestic currency through the nominal exchange rate.

6 If deviations from PPP are assumed to be near $I(1)$, the deviations from UIP also behave as nonstationary, near-$I(1)$ processes.

untenable when using real data (see Juselius 2010, 2017a, 2017b; Juselius and Assenmacher 2017; Johansen et al. 2010; and Frydman and Goldberg 2007).

2.2. Persistence in the Data

This subsection[7] presents a theoretical framework, developed in Juselius (2017a) and based on IKE, that is consistent with the long and persistent swings in the real exchange rate. The model assumes that the nominal exchange rate is mainly driven by relative prices, that is:

$$s_t = B_0 + B_{1,t}\left(p_d - p_f\right)_t + \nu_t \tag{6}$$

where ν_t is a standard i.d.d. Gaussian error term that captures changes in interest rates and income. B_0 is a constant term, and $B_{1,t}$ is a time-varying coefficient that represents the weight to relative prices in financial actors' forecasts. Generally, the weight depends on how far the nominal exchange is from its long-run benchmark value. Based on (6), changes in the nominal exchange can be expressed as:

$$\triangle s_t = B_{1,t}\triangle\left(p_d - p_f\right)_t + \triangle B_{1,t}\left(p_d - p_f\right)_t + \triangle\nu_t. \tag{7}$$

One can assume, as in Frydman and Goldberg (2007), that $\left|B_{1,t}\triangle\left(p_d - p_f\right)_t\right| \gg \left|\triangle B_{1,t}\left(p_d - p_f\right)_t\right|$,[8] so that:

$$\triangle s_t \simeq B_{1,t}\triangle\left(p_d - p_f\right)_t + \triangle\nu_t. \tag{8}$$

Before estimating the above model using the CVAR, the issue of time-varying parameters must be addressed. Tabor (2014) simulates data for the process $y_t = \beta_t' x_t + \varepsilon_t$ where x_t is nonstationary $I(1)$, ε_t is an i.i.d. Gaussian error term and $\beta_t = \beta + Z_t$ where $Z_t = \varrho Z_{t-1} + \varepsilon_{Z,t}$ and $\varrho < 1$. Tabor (2014) showed that when a CVAR model is applied to the simulated data, the estimated cointegrated coefficient corresponds to $E\left(\beta_t\right)$. Hence, based on this result, one can argue that the CVAR model may be used to estimate average long-run relationships when the underlying data-generating process involves bounded-parameter instability.

Then, the change in the real exchange rate should behave as a near $I(1)$ process provided that $B_{1,t} = B + \rho B_{1,t-1} + \varepsilon_{B_1,t}$ with $\rho < 1$, but close to one. Juselius (2014) argues that the latter behavior can be used to approximate the the change in the real exchange rate through the following process:

$$\triangle q_t = a_t + \nu_{q,t} \tag{9}$$

where $\nu_{q,t}$ is an i.i.d. Gaussian error term and the time-varying drift term, a_t, measures the appreciation or depreciation of the real exchange rate due to changes in individual forecasting strategies.[9] This drift is assumed to follow a mean zero stationary autoregressive process, so that:

$$a_t = \rho_t a_{t-1} + \nu_{a,t} \tag{10}$$

---

7 This subsection is based mainly on Juselius (2017a), Juselius and Assenmacher (2017), and Frydman and Goldberg (2007, 2011).

8 This assumption is based on simulations that show that $\triangle B_{1,t}$ has to be extremely large for $\triangle B_{1,t}\left(p_d - p_f\right)_t$ to have a marked effect on $\triangle s_t$. Frydman and Goldberg (2007) use this assumption ("conservative revision") in their IKE-based monetary model to illustrate the fact that forecasting behavior is led by new realizations of the causal variables, $\triangle\left(p_d - p_f\right)_t$, rather than revision of forecasting strategies, $\triangle B_{1,t}$.

9 This is consistent with the FG IKE-based model developed by Frydman and Goldberg (2007), which assumes that individuals recognize their imperfect knowledge about the underlying processes that drive outcomes. Thus, they use a multitude of forecasting strategies that are revised over time in a way that cannot be fully prespecified. Indeed, given the diversity of forecasting strategies, this model assumes two kinds of individuals in the foreign currency market: bulls, who speculate on the belief that the asset price will rise, and bears, who speculate on its fall.

where $\nu_{a,t}$ is an i.i.d. Gaussian error term and ρ_t is a time-varying coefficient that is close to one when the real exchange rate is in the vicinity of its long-run benchmark value, and otherwise $\rho_t \ll 1$.[10] The average of this coefficient, $\bar{\rho}$, is generally close to one whenever the sample period is sufficiently long (Juselius 2017a). Then, a_t describes a persistent near $I(1)$ process, and modeling the real exchange rate as a near $I(2)$ process is consistent with swings of shorter and longer duration, implying that the length of these swings is not predictable (Frydman and Goldberg 2007).

Since excess return on the foreign exchange rate is often found to behave like a nonstationary process—the excess return puzzle—it has been argued that volatility in the foreign currency market should be taken into account. Specifically, a risk premium, rp, might be added to (5) to obtain a stationary relationship. However, it is unlikely that a risk premium, assumed to be stationary, accounts for the persistent swings in the real interest rate spread. Frydman and Goldberg (2007), in their FG IKE-based model, proposed to replace the uncovered interest rate parity, UIP, condition—the market clearing mechanism between the expected change in the nominal exchange rate and the nominal interest rate spread—by an uncertainty adjusted uncovered interest rate parity (UA-UIP) condition, that is defined as:

$$\left(i_d - i_f\right)_t = \left(s_{t+1}^e - s_t\right) + rp_t + up_t \tag{11}$$

where up_t stands for an uncertainty nonstationary premium, a measure of agents' loss averseness.[11] The interest rate spread corrected for the uncertainty premium is a minimum return that agents require to speculate in the foreign exchange market. This premium starts increasing when the nominal exchange rate moves away from its long-run benchmark value and decreases when the nominal exchange rate moves toward equilibrium. In the foreign exchange market, the uncertainty premium is related to the PPP gap (Frydman and Goldberg 2007). Then, the UA-UIP is formulated as:

$$\left(i_d - i_f\right)_t = \left(s_{t+1}^e - s_t\right) + rp_t + f\left(p_d - p_f - s_t\right). \tag{12}$$

This equation suggests that in a world of imperfect knowledge, the expected change in the nominal exchange rate may not be directly related to the interest rate spread, but to the spread corrected by the PPP gap and the risk premium. The latter might be associated with short-term changes in interest rates, inflation rates and nominal exchange rates (Juselius 2017a).

2.3. Theory-Consistent CVAR Scenario Results

A consequence of the UA-UIP condition is that both domestic and foreign interest rates are affected by the uncertainty premium. Juselius (2017a) suggests the following data-generating process to describe changes in the interest rate:

$$\Delta i_{j,t} = \omega_{j,t} + \Delta rp_{j,t} + \nu_{j,t} \tag{13}$$

where $\nu_{j,t}$ is a white nose error term and $j = d, f$. The term $\omega_{j,t}$ stands for changes in the domestic uncertainty premium, $\omega_{j,t} = \Delta up_{j,t}$, and is assumed to follow a mean zero stationary autoregressive process:

$$\omega_{j,t} = \rho_{j,t}^{\omega}\omega_{j,t-1} + \nu_{j,t}^{\omega} \tag{14}$$

where $\nu_{j,t}^{\omega}$ is a stationary error term. The time-varying autoregressive coefficient, $\rho_{j,t}^{\omega}$, is assumed to be almost on the unit circle when the nominal exchange rate is in the vicinity of its long-run

10 When periods where a_t is far from its benchmark value are shorter compared with the near vicinity periods, it describes a persistent but mean-reverting process.

11 Frydman and Goldberg (2007) extend the concept of loss aversion given by Kahneman and Tversky (1979) to the concept of endogenous loss aversion, which says that the greater the potential loss, the higher the degree of loss aversion. This definition establishes that the UA-UIP equilibrium exists.

benchmark value—the relative price—otherwise the coefficient is strictly less than one. Nevertheless, $\rho_j^{\tilde{w}} \approx 1$ provided that periods where the coefficient is close to one are much longer than otherwise. When $\rho_j^{\tilde{w}} \approx 1$, (14) describes a near $I(1)$ domestic uncertainty premium. Consequently, under IKE, the interest rate change behaves as a persistent near $I(1)$ process, implying that nominal interest rates are near $I(2)$.

Using a CVAR scenario, Juselius (2017a) demonstrates that the following hypotheses are consistent with IKE:

$$s_t \sim \text{near } I(2) \tag{15}$$

$$\left(p_{d,t} - p_{f,t}\right) \sim \text{near } I(2) \tag{16}$$

$$\left(i_{d,t} - i_{f,t}\right) \sim \text{near } I(2) \tag{17}$$

$$\left(s_t + p_{f,t} - p_{d,t}\right) \sim \text{near } I(2) \tag{18}$$

$$\left\{\left(i_{d,t} - i_{f,t}\right) - c\left(s_t + p_{f,t} - p_{d,t}\right)\right\} \sim \text{near } I(1) \tag{19}$$

where c is a constant coefficient. These relationships show that when allowing for IKE, real exchange rate, interest rate spread, and relative price are likely to behave as near $I(2)$.

3. The CVAR Model and the $I(2)$ Representation

A VAR model in second order differences is expressed as:[12]

$$\triangle^2 x_t = \mathbf{\Pi} x_{t-1} - \mathbf{\Gamma} \triangle x_{t-1} + \sum_{i=1}^{k-2} \mathbf{\Psi}_i \triangle^2 x_{t-1} + \mathbf{\Phi} \boldsymbol{D}_t + \boldsymbol{\mu}_0 + \boldsymbol{\mu}_1 t + \boldsymbol{\varepsilon}_t \tag{20}$$

where $x_t' = \left[x_{1,t}, x_{2,t}, \ldots, x_{p,t}\right]$ is a p-dimensional vector of stochastic variables, $\boldsymbol{D}_t$ is a matrix of deterministic terms (shift dummies, seasonal dummies, etc) with coefficient matrix $\mathbf{\Phi}$. $\mathbf{\Pi}, \mathbf{\Gamma}$ are $p \times p$ coefficient matrices, $\boldsymbol{\mu}_0$ is an unrestricted constant, t is an unrestricted trend with coefficient matrix $\boldsymbol{\mu}_1$, and $\boldsymbol{\varepsilon}_t$ is a multivariate white noise process, that is $\boldsymbol{\varepsilon}_t \sim$ i.i.d.$\mathcal{N}_p\left(\mathbf{0}, \mathbf{\Omega}\right)$.

If $\mathbf{\Pi}$ has reduced rank, $0 < r < p$, it can be decomposed into $\mathbf{\Pi} = \boldsymbol{\alpha}\boldsymbol{\beta}'$, where $\boldsymbol{\alpha}$ and $\boldsymbol{\beta}$ are $p \times r$ matrices of full column rank. The orthogonal complement of matrix z is denoted as $z_\perp$, and $\bar{z} = z\left(z'z\right)^{-1}$. Structuring the $I(2)$ representation of the CVAR model is a bit more complicated, and additional definitions must be given. The $I(2)$ model is defined by the two following reduced rank restrictions:

$$\begin{aligned} \mathbf{\Pi} &= \boldsymbol{\alpha}\boldsymbol{\beta}' \\ \boldsymbol{\alpha}_\perp' \mathbf{\Gamma} \boldsymbol{\beta}_\perp &= \boldsymbol{\xi}\boldsymbol{\eta}' \end{aligned} \tag{21}$$

where $\boldsymbol{\xi}$ and $\boldsymbol{\eta}$ are $(p-r) \times s_1$ matrices, s_1 is the number of $I(1)$ trends, or unit root processes, and it is such that $p - r = s_1 + s_2$, where s_2 is the number of $I(2)$ trends, or double unit root processes, in vector $\boldsymbol{x}_t$. Whereas the first rank condition in (21) is associated with the variables in levels, the second rank condition is related to the differentiated variables.

$\boldsymbol{\beta}_\perp$ and $\boldsymbol{\alpha}_\perp$ can, respectively, be decomposed into $\boldsymbol{\beta}_\perp = \left[\boldsymbol{\beta}_{\perp 1}, \boldsymbol{\beta}_{\perp 2}\right]$ and $\boldsymbol{\alpha}_\perp = \left[\boldsymbol{\alpha}_{\perp 1}, \boldsymbol{\alpha}_{\perp 2}\right]$. Matrices $\boldsymbol{\alpha}_{\perp 1} = \overline{\boldsymbol{\alpha}_\perp}\boldsymbol{\eta}$ and $\boldsymbol{\beta}_{\perp 1} = \overline{\boldsymbol{\beta}_\perp}\boldsymbol{\eta}$ are of dimension $p \times s_1$. Matrices $\boldsymbol{\alpha}_{\perp 2} = \boldsymbol{\alpha}_\perp \boldsymbol{\xi}_\perp$ and $\boldsymbol{\beta}_{\perp 2} = \boldsymbol{\beta}_\perp \boldsymbol{\eta}_\perp$ have dimension $p \times s_2$.

[12] This section is based mainly on Doornik and Juselius (2017) and Juselius (2006).

Using the Johansen (1997) parametrization, model (20) can be written as follows:

$$\begin{aligned}\triangle^2 x_t =& \alpha\left(\rho'\tau' x_{t-1} + d'\triangle x_{t-1}\right) + \zeta'\tau'\triangle x_{t-1} + \sum_{i=1}^{k-2}\Lambda_i \triangle^2 x_{t-i} + \\ & \Phi D_t + \mu_0 + \mu_1 t + \varepsilon_t\end{aligned} \tag{22}$$

where $\rho = [\mathbf{I}, 0]'$, $\tau = [\beta, \beta_{\perp 1}]$, $d' = -\left(\left(\alpha'\Omega^{-1}\alpha\right)^{-1}\alpha\Omega^{-1}\Gamma\right)\tau_{\perp}\left(\tau_{\perp}'\tau_{\perp}\right)^{-1}\tau_{\perp}'$, $\zeta = [\zeta_1, \zeta_2]'$ is a matrix of medium-run adjustment.

In this model, the term in $(\cdot)$ represents the long-run equilibrium or polynomially cointegrating relationships. The term $\zeta'\tau'\triangle x_{t-1}$ can be interpreted as a medium-run equilibrium relationship, defining the $r + s_1$ relationship that needs to be differentiated to become stationary.

The moving average (MA) representation of the $I(2)$ model is expressed as:

$$\begin{aligned}x_t =& C_2 \sum_{i=1}^{t}\sum_{s=1}^{i}\underbrace{\left(\varepsilon_s + \Phi D_s + \mu_0 + \mu_1 s\right)}_{\varepsilon_s} + C_1 \sum_{i=1}^{t}\underbrace{\left(\varepsilon_i + \Phi D_i + \mu_0 + \mu_1 i\right)}_{\varepsilon_i} + \\ & C^*(L)\left(\varepsilon_t + \Phi D_t + \mu_0 + \mu_1 t\right) + A + Bt\end{aligned} \tag{23}$$

where $C_2 = \beta_{\perp 2}\left(\alpha_{\perp 2}'\Theta\beta_{\perp 2}\right)^{-1}\alpha_{\perp 2}'$, $\beta' C_1 = \bar{\alpha}'\Gamma C_2$, $\beta_{\perp 1}' C_1 = \overline{\alpha_{\perp 1}}'\left(\mathbf{I}_p - \Theta C_2\right)$, and $\Theta = \Gamma\bar{\beta}\bar{\alpha}'\Gamma + \left(\mathbf{I}_p - \sum_{i=1}^{k-2}\Lambda_i\right)$. A and B are functions of both the initial values and the model parameters (Johansen 1992).[13]

Matrix C_2 can be expressed as $C_2 = \breve{\beta}_{\perp 2}\alpha_{\perp 2}'$, where $\breve{\beta}_{\perp 2} = \beta_{\perp 2}\left(\alpha_{\perp 2}'\Theta\beta_{\perp 2}\right)^{-1}$, so that $\alpha_{\perp 2}'\sum_{i=1}^{t}\sum_{s=1}^{i}\varepsilon_s$ can be interpreted as the measure of the s_2 trends which load into the variables in x_t with the weights $\breve{\beta}_{\perp 2}$ (Juselius 2006).

The likelihood ratio test for the joint hypothesis of r cointegrating relationships and s_1 and s_2 trends, labeled $\mathcal{H}(r, s_1, s_2)$, versus $\mathcal{H}(p)$ is given by:

$$-2\log Q\left(\mathcal{H}(r, s_1, s_2) \mid \mathcal{H}(p)\right) = -T\log\left|\tilde{\Omega}^{-1}\hat{\Omega}\right| \tag{24}$$

where $\tilde{\Omega}$ and $\hat{\Omega}$ are, respectively, the covariance matrices estimated under $\mathcal{H}(r, s_1, s_2)$ and $\mathcal{H}(p)$.[14]

4. Stylized Facts

Figure 1a shows the evolution of the natural logarithm (log) of the nominal exchange rate, measured as Chilean pesos (CLP) per US dollar (USD) and the log of the relative prices, measured as the ratio between the Chilean consumer price index (CPI) and the US CPI. Relative prices exhibit a positive but decreasing slope, reflecting the fact that from 1986 until 1999, Chilean prices were growing faster than US prices, but after 1999 the growth in relative prices decreased. This might be associated with the partial implementation of inflation targeting in Chile in 1990, which reduced annual inflation from 26% in 1990 to 3% in 1997. In the same panel, the nominal exchange rate undergoes long and persistent swings around relative prices, suggesting that PPP may hold only as a very long-run condition.

---

13 From the MA representation (23), it follows that the unrestricted constant, μ_0, cumulates once to a linear trend and twice to a quadratic trend. In addition, the unrestricted trend, μ_1, cumulates once to a quadratic trend and twice to a cubic trend. To avoid the latter, quadratic and cubic trends have been restricted to zero in the subsequent analysis. For further information, see Chapter 17 in Juselius (2006).

14 The distribution of the this is found in Johansen (1995) provided that model (22) does not restrict deterministic components; otherwise see Rahbek et al. (1999).

Figure 1b shows the PPP gap, defined as the difference between the log of relative prices and the log of the nominal exchange rate. The deviations exhibit long persistent swings, but it seems that the upward trend in relative prices is canceled by the upward trend in nominal exchange rate.

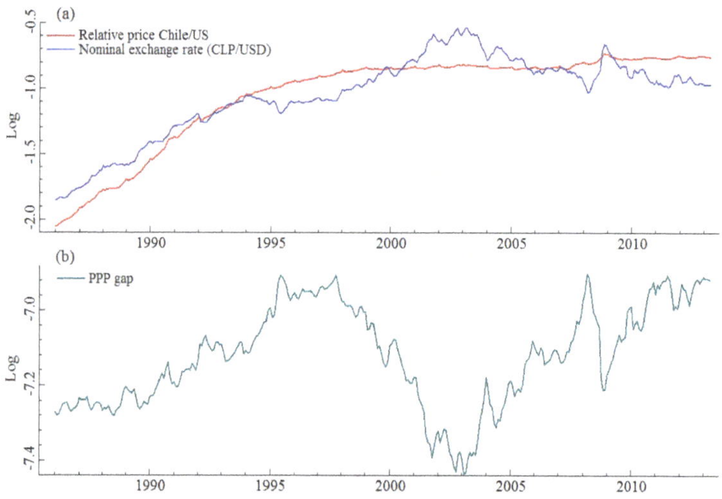

Figure 1. (**a**) Nominal exchange rate (CLP/USD) and relative prices (Chilean CPI/US CPI); (**b**) Deviations from PPP. Monthly data 1986:1–2013:04. CLP: Chilean peso, USD: U.S. dollar.

Figure 2a shows that relative inflation rates exhibit a high persistence, which is corroborated by the 12-month moving average. This persistence seems, however, to decrease steadily beginning in 1990, which may be associated with the implementation of inflation targeting in Chile in 1990. In Figure 2b shows the changes in the nominal exchange rate, which seems stationary. Nevertheless, the 12-month moving average exhibits some persistence around the mean. It also appears that appreciations and depreciations are more volatile since 2000, which might be related to the free-floating exchange rate regime that was implemented by the Central Bank of Chile in September 1999. Figure 2c, shows that changes in the PPP gap behave as a persistent but mean-reverting process. The 12-month moving average exhibits persistence around the mean that seems higher since 2000.

Figure 3a,b show, respectively, the Chilean interest rate and its first difference. The latter exhibits a large decrease in volatility since 2000. This might be associated with two major reforms that were introduced in the Chilean financial market between 2000 and 2001. While the first reform, promulgated in 2000, gave greater protection to both domestic and foreign investors, the second reform, enacted in 2001, liberalized the financial system, implying, among other things, capital account deregulation.

When the Chilean interest rate and its first difference are compared with their US counterparts, which are shown in Figure 3c,d, an important difference in levels and volatility is noticeable. The Chilean interest rate has been historically higher than the US interest rate, and this seems to have changed since 2000. The latter is clearly reflected in the interest rate spread shown in Figure 3e. The changes in the interest rate spread shown in Figure 3f seem to mimic the changes in the Chilean interest rate volatility.

Figure 4a plots the copper price and the PPP gap. Two facts are noticeable. First, it seems that both variables are positively co-moving over time, suggesting that there is a negative relationship between copper prices and real exchange rates. Second, since 2005, the copper price has been higher than in the previous years, which might be associated with an increase in world copper demand. The decrease of in the copper price observed in 2008 was mainly caused by lower copper demand due to the international financial crisis. Figure 4b shows that the copper price was more volatile at the beginning and end of the sample, and its 12-month moving average suggests some persistence around its mean.

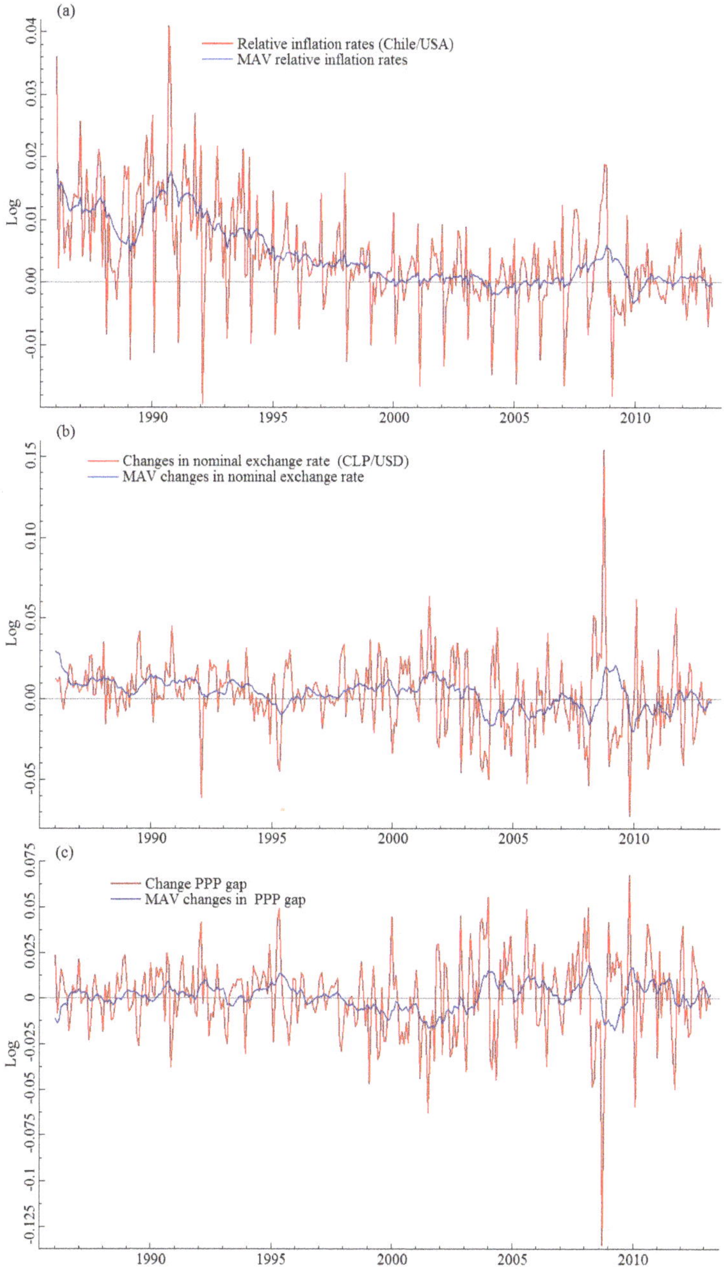

Figure 2. (**a**) Relative inflation rates (Chile/US); (**b**) Changes in nominal exchange rate (CLP/USD); (**c**) Change in the PPP gap. Monthly data 1986:1–2013:4. MAV is the 12-month moving average process.

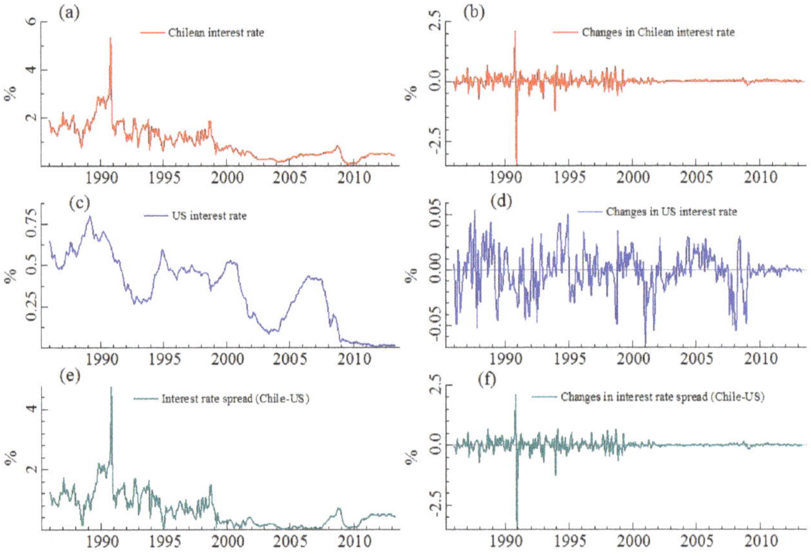

Figure 3. (**a**) Chilean interest rate; (**b**) Changes in Chilean interest rate; (**c**) US interest rate; (**d**) Changes in US interest rate; (**e**) Interest rate spread (Chile-US); (**f**) Changes in interest rate spread. Monthly data: 1986:1–2013:4.

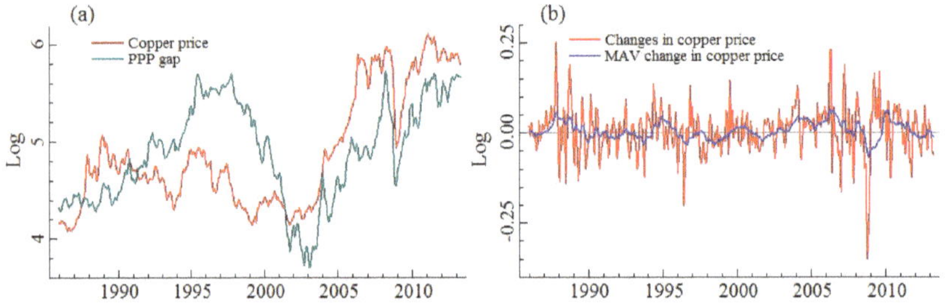

Figure 4. (**a**) Copper price and PPP gap; (**b**) Changes in the copper price. Monthly data 1986:1–2013:4. MAV is the 12-month moving average of the changes in copper price. PPP gap is calculated as the difference between the log of relative prices and the log of the nominal exchange rate.

This section discussed the pronounced persistence exhibited in the data. For instance, the graphical analysis seems to suggest that nominal exchange rate, real exchange rate, and relative prices behave as a nonstationary near $I(2)$ process. However, this persistence has to be formally tested, which is done in Section 5.

5. Empirical Model Analysis

The monthly data cover the period 1986:1–2013:4 and the baseline model, which contains three lags,[15] is expressed as:

---

[15] Appendix B presents the selection of the number of lags.

$$\Delta^2 x_t = \alpha \left[\tilde{\rho}' \underbrace{\begin{pmatrix} \tau \\ \tau_0 \end{pmatrix}'}_{\tilde{\tau}'} \underbrace{\begin{pmatrix} x_{t-1} \\ t-1 \end{pmatrix}}_{\tilde{x}_{t-1}} + \underbrace{\begin{pmatrix} d \\ d_0 \end{pmatrix}'}_{\tilde{d}'} \underbrace{\begin{pmatrix} \Delta x_{t-1} \\ \mathbf{1} \end{pmatrix}}_{\Delta \tilde{x}_{t-1}} \right] + \zeta' \tilde{\tau}' \Delta \tilde{x}_{t-1} + \Lambda_1 \Delta^2 x_{t-1} + \Phi_p D_{p,t} + \Phi_s D_{s,t} + \varepsilon_t \tag{25}$$

where $x_t' = [p_{d,t}, p_{f,t}, s_t, cp_t, i_{d,t}, i_{f,t}]$, $p_{d,t}$ is the Chilean CPI, $p_{f,t}$ is the US CPI, s_t is the nominal exchange rate, defined as CLP per USD, cp_t is the copper price, $i_{d,t}$ is the Chilean interest rate, and $i_{f,t}$ is the US interest rate.[16] All variables except interest rates are in natural logarithms. $\tilde{\rho} = [\rho, 0]$ and picks out the r cointegrating vectors, including the restricted trend, **1** is a vector of constant terms and t is a linear trend. $D_{p,t}$ is a (9×1) vector of intervention dummies,[17] and $D_{s,t}$ is a (11×1) vector of centered seasonal dummies.[18] The software CATS 3 for OxMetrics (Doornik and Juselius 2017) was used in the econometric analysis.

Table 1 reports the residual misspecification tests of model (25).[19] The upper part indicates that the hypotheses of normality and non-ARCH of orders 1 and 2 can be rejected but not the hypothesis of non-autocorrelation. The univariate tests, reported in the lower part, show that all equations exhibit residual non-normality and that only the residuals of the copper price do not show ARCH effects. It appears that the normality problem is due to excess kurtosis rather than excess skewness. Financial variables usually exhibit non-normality and ARCH problems, but adding more dummy variables is not necessarily a solution (Juselius 2010). Moreover, VAR estimates are robust for moderately excess kurtosis (Gonzalo 1994; Juselius 2006).

Table 1. Misspecification tests for CVAR model (25).

Multivariate Specification Tests				
Autocorrelation		**Normality**	**ARCH**	
Order 1: χ^2 (36)	Order 2: χ^2 (36)	χ^2 (12)	Order 1: χ^2 (441)	Order 2: χ^2 (882)
45.25 [0.14]	41.66 [0.24]	128.94 [0.00]	514.01 [0.01]	1007.42 [0.00]

Univariate Specification Tests						
Equation	$\Delta^2 p_{d,t}$	$\Delta^2 p_{f,t}$	$\Delta^2 s_t$	$\Delta^2 cp_t$	$\Delta^2 i_{d,t}$	$\Delta^2 i_{f,t}$
ARCH Order 2: χ^2 (2)	27.92 [0.00]	11.15 [0.00]	6.57 [0.04]	0.88 [0.64]	21.93 [0.00]	23.27 [0.00]
Normality χ^2 (2)	12.83 [0.00]	15.99 [0.00]	12.86 [0.00]	34.31 [0.00]	36.05 [0.00]	6.26 [0.04]
Skewness	0.23	0.07	−0.12	0.03	0.02	−0.17
Kurtosis	3.99	4.12	3.98	4.81	4.87	3.60
S.E.$\times 10^3$	4.38	1.96	16.68	52.17	1.51	0.15

[·] is the p-value of the test; S.E. is the residual standard error.

16 Appendix A presents the source, description, and transformation of the data. Dataset and code to replicate the results are available from the author.
17 Appendix C specifies the intervention dummies and their estimated coefficients.
18 Initially, the cointegration space considered a broken linear trend that started in September 1999, corresponding to the beginning of the floating exchange rate regime in Chile. However, this broken linear trend was revealed to be non-significant. The potential effect of the new regime on the nominal exchange rate was, possibly, offset by changes in the Chilean inflation rate and/or interest rate.
19 For a thorough description of the tests see Doornik and Juselius (2017).

5.1. Rank Determination

Table 2 reports the $I(2)$ trace test and shows the maximum likelihood test of the joint hypothesis of (r, s_1), which corresponds to the two rank restrictions in (21), together with simulated p-values of the trace test. The standard test procedure starts with the most restricted model, $(r = 0,\ s_1 = 0,\ s_2 = 6)$, which is reported in the first row with a likelihood ratio test of 1120.90; it then continues from this point to the right, and row by row, until the first joint hypothesis is not rejected. The first rejection corresponds to the case $(r = 2,\ s_1 = 2,\ s_2 = 2)$ with a p-value of 0.12. The case $(r = 1,\ s_1 = 4,\ s_2 = 1)$ is also not rejected, though with a lower p-value of 0.07.

Table 2. Simulated asymptotic distribution of the cointegration rank indices model (25).

$p-r$	r	$s_2=6$	$s_2=5$	$s_2=4$	$s_2=3$	$s_2=2$	$s_2=1$	$s_2=0$
6	0	1120.90 [0.00]	797.61 [0.00]	582.76 [0.00]	425.17 [0.00]	314.38 [0.00]	232.61 [0.00]	195.29 [0.00]
5	1		579.62 [0.00]	413.11 [0.00]	289.11 [0.00]	179.09 [0.00]	96.24 [0.07]	92.28 [0.01]
4	2			286.97 [0.00]	169.23 [0.00]	84.13 [0.12]	59.00 [0.39]	53.96 [0.18]
3	3				76.83 [0.17]	47.78 [0.61]	31.90 [0.77]	28.59 [0.48]
2	4					26.20 [0.86]	18.59 [0.74]	16.60 [0.37]
1	5						9.31 [0.65]	7.13 [0.28]

p is the number of variables in vector x; r is the number of cointegrating relationships; s_1 and s_2 are, respectively, the number of $I(1)$ and $I(2)$ trends.

As a robustness check, Table 3 reports the seven largest characteristic roots for $r = 2$, and $r = 6$. The unrestricted model, $(r = 6,\ s_1 = 0,\ s_2 = 0)$, has six large roots: five almost on the unit circle and one large but less close to 1 (0.82). Under the assumption that $x_t \sim I(1)$, that is $(r = 2,\ s_1 = 4,\ s_2 = 0)$, there would be two large roots (0.98 and 0.82) in the model. Under such persistence, treating the process x_t as $I(1)$ is likely to yield unreliable inference (Johansen et al. 2010).

Therefore, the reduced rank model should account for 6 unit roots. The case $(r = 2,\ s_1 = 2,\ s_2 = 2)$ implies six characteristic roots to be on the unit circle and leaves 0.56 as the largest unrestricted root. Thus, based on the above discussion, the analysis considers the case $(r = 2,\ s_1 = 2,\ s_2 = 2)$, which implies $x_t \sim$ near $I(2)$.

Table 3. Model adequacy.

Seven Largest Characteristic Roots							
Model	Moduli						
$(r = 6,\ s_1 = 0,\ s_2 = 0)$	0.98	0.98	0.98	0.95	0.95	0.82	0.56
$(r = 2,\ s_1 = 4,\ s_2 = 0)$	1.00	1.00	1.00	1.00	0.98	0.82	0.56
$(r = 2,\ s_1 = 2,\ s_2 = 2)$	1.00	1.00	1.00	1.00	1.00	1.00	0.56

r is the number of cointegrating relationships; s_1 and s_2 are, respectively, the number of $I(1)$ and $I(2)$ trends.

5.2. Partial System

The copper price was found to be a strong exogenous variable based on $\chi^2\,(15) = 13.83$ with p-value of 0.05. Thus, copper price is pushing the system but not adjusting to it. Because the copper price is internationally determined, this finding is economically plausible. Therefore, a partial system can be modeled with vector $x'_t = \left\{x'_{1,t}, x'_{2,t}\right\}$, where $x'_{1,t} = \left[p_{d,t}, p_{f,t}, s_t, i_{d,t}, i_{f,t}\right]$ and $x'_{2,t} = [cp_t]$. Then, Equation (25) is reformulated as:

$$\begin{aligned}\triangle^2 x_{1,t} =& \alpha\left(\tilde{\rho}'\tilde{\tau}'\tilde{x}_{t-1}+\tilde{d}'\triangle\tilde{x}_{t-1}\right)+\zeta'\tilde{\tau}'\triangle\tilde{x}_{t-1}+ \\ &+\Lambda_1\triangle^2 x_{1,t-1}+\sum_{j=0}^{1}\pi_j\triangle^2 x_{2,t-i}+\Phi_p D_{p,t}+\Phi_s D_{s,t}+\varepsilon_t\end{aligned} \tag{26}$$

where the left-hand side excludes the acceleration rate of the copper price and the right-hand side adds two second-order lagged differences of the copper price.

In the full model (25) the number of $I(2)$ trends was $s_2 = 2$. In the partial model (26) the number of $I\,(2)$trends decreases by one because the copper price was found to be an exogenous variable. This suggests that one of the previous two $I\,(2)$ trends is now accounted for the exogenous copper price. Therefore, the following analysis considers the case $(r = 2, s_1 = 2, s_2 = 1)$.

5.2.1. Testing Non-Identifying Hypotheses in the $I(2)$ Model

- **Same restrictions on all $\tilde{\tau}$**

The hypothesis of same restrictions on all $\tilde{\tau}$ is formulated as $\mathbf{R}'\tilde{\tau} = \mathbf{0}$, where $\mathbf{R}$ is of dimension $p_1 \times (p_1 - m)$, p_1 is the dimension of $\tilde{x}$ and m is the number of free parameters. The test is asymptotically $\chi^2\left((r+s_1)\left(p_1-m\right)\right)$ distributed (Johansen 2006).

The upper part of Table 4 reports three hypothesis restrictions on all $\tilde{\tau}$. The null hypothesis $\mathcal{H}_1$ entails that the nominal to real transformation may be used (Kongsted 2005). That is, x_t that is near $I(2)$ can be transformed into the $I(1)$ vector $\check{x}_t' = \left[ppp_t, \triangle p_{d,t}, \triangle p_{f,t}, i_{d,t}, i_{f,t}, cp_t\right]$ without loss of information (Johansen et al. 2010). The result of $\mathcal{H}_1$ indicates that the PPP restriction can be rejected; that is, the transformation $\left(p_{d,t} - p_{f,t} - s_t\right)$ is not statistically supported.

The null hypothesis $\mathcal{H}_2$ entails price homogeneity. That is, vector x_t can be transformed into $\check{x}_t' = \left[p_{d,t} - p_{f,t}, s_t, \triangle p_{d,t}, i_{d,t}, i_{f,t}, cp_t\right]$ without loss of information. The result of $\mathcal{H}_2$ indicates that price homogeneity can be rejected; that is, the transformation $\left(p_d - p_f\right)_t$ is not statistically supported. Finally, the result of hypothesis $\mathcal{H}_3$ indicates that the restricted linear trend is no long-run excludable.

- **A known vector in $\tilde{\tau}$**

In this case, a variable or relationship can be tested to be $I(1)$ in the $I(2)$ model. The restriction is expressed as $\tilde{\tau} = (\mathbf{b}, \mathbf{b}_\perp\boldsymbol{\varphi})$ where $\mathbf{b}$ is a $p_1 \times n$ known vector, n is the number of known vectors in $\tilde{\tau}$, and $\boldsymbol{\varphi}$ is a matrix of unknown parameters. The test is asymptotically $\chi^2\left((p_1 - r - s_1)\,n\right)$ distributed unless $\mathbf{b}$ is also a vector in $\tilde{\boldsymbol{\beta}}$ (Johansen 1996). Thus, $\mathbf{b} \in \mathrm{sp}\left(\tilde{\boldsymbol{\beta}}\right)$ must be checked to ensure the correct distribution of the test. If the hypothesis $\tilde{\tau} = (\mathbf{b}, \mathbf{b}_\perp\boldsymbol{\varphi})$ is not rejected and $\mathbf{b} \notin \mathrm{sp}\left(\tilde{\boldsymbol{\beta}}\right)$, then the analyzed variable, or relationship, can be considered $I(1)$.

The lower part of Table 4 reports the test results[20] of which hypotheses $\mathcal{H}_4$ to $\mathcal{H}_7$ and $\mathcal{H}_9$ are consistent with the CVAR scenario based on IKE under which nominal exchange rate, prices, relative prices, and nominal interest rate are likely to behave as a near $I(2)$ process. According to IKE, the real exchange rate is likely to behave as a near $I(2)$ process, but the result of $\mathcal{H}_8$ indicates that the hypothesis of the real exchange rate being $I(1)$ cannot be rejected based on a p-value of 0.11. This is, nevertheless, consistent with the high persistence observed in the real exchange rate. In addition, the result of $\mathcal{H}_{10}$ indicates that the copper price is likely to behave as near $I(2)$.

---

20 The hypothesis $\mathbf{b}_i \in \mathrm{sp}\left(\tilde{\boldsymbol{\beta}}\right)$ was rejected in all cases, except for the Chilean interest rate based on $\chi^2\,(5) = 10.42$ with a p-value of 0.06 and for the interest rate spread based on $\chi^2\,(5) = 6.80$ with a p-value of 0.23. Thus, the hypotheses $i_{d,t} \sim I(1)$ and $\left(i_{d,t} - i_{f,t}\right) \sim I(1)$ are not presented because the distribution of the test is not necessarily χ^2.

Table 4. Restrictions on $\tilde{\tau}$.

Hypothesis	Matrix Restriction Design	Distribution	p-Value
PPP restriction $\mathcal{H}_1 : \mathbf{R}_1'\tilde{\tau} = 0$	$\mathbf{R}_1' = \begin{bmatrix} 1 & 1 & 0 & 0 & 0 & 0 & 0 \\ 1 & 0 & 1 & 0 & 0 & 0 & 0 \end{bmatrix}$	$\chi^2(8) = 40.70$	0.00
Price homogeneity $\mathcal{H}_2 : \mathbf{R}_2'\tilde{\tau} = 0$	$\mathbf{R}_2' = [1,1,0,0,0,0,0]$	$\chi^2(4) = 38.66$	0.00
Excludable trend $\mathcal{H}_3 : \mathbf{R}_3'\tilde{\tau} = 0$	$\mathbf{R}_3' = [0,0,0,0,0,0,1]$	$\chi^2(4) = 39.14$	0.00
Chilean price $\mathcal{H}_4 : \tilde{\tau} = (\mathbf{b}_1, \mathbf{b}_{1\perp}\varphi)$	$\mathbf{b}_1 = [1,0,0,0,0,0,0]$	$\chi^2(3) = 25.15$	0.00
US price $\mathcal{H}_5 : \tilde{\tau} = (\mathbf{b}_2, \mathbf{b}_{2\perp}\varphi)$	$\mathbf{b}_2 = [0,1,0,0,0,0,0]$	$\chi^2(3) = 27.19$	0.00
Relative price $\mathcal{H}_6 : \tilde{\tau} = (\mathbf{b}_3, \mathbf{b}_{3\perp}\varphi)$	$\mathbf{b}_3 = [1,-1,0,0,0,0,0]$	$\chi^2(3) = 24.74$	0.00
Nominal exchange rate $\mathcal{H}_7 : \tilde{\tau} = (\mathbf{b}_4, \mathbf{b}_{4\perp}\varphi)$	$\mathbf{b}_4 = [0,0,1,0,0,0,0]$	$\chi^2(3) = 14.15$	0.00
PPP gap $\mathcal{H}_8 : \tilde{\tau} = (\mathbf{b}_5, \mathbf{b}_{5\perp}\varphi)$	$\mathbf{b}_5 = [1,-1,-1,0,0,0,0]$	$\chi^2(3) = 6.01$	0.11
US interest rate $\mathcal{H}_9 : \tilde{\tau} = (\mathbf{b}_6, \mathbf{b}_{6\perp}\varphi)$	$\mathbf{b}_6 = [0,0,0,0,1,0,0]$	$\chi^2(3) = 10.07$	0.01
Copper price $\mathcal{H}_{10} : \tilde{\tau} = (\mathbf{b}_7, \mathbf{b}_{7\perp}\varphi)$	$\mathbf{b}_7 = [0,0,0,0,0,1,0]$	$\chi^2(3) = 28.25$	0.00

5.2.2. Testing Identifying Restrictions on the Long-Run Structure

To identify plausible economic relationships among the variables, a set of restrictions, $\mathcal{H}_{\tilde{\beta}} : \tilde{\beta} = (\mathbf{H}_1\vartheta_1, \ldots, \mathbf{H}_r\vartheta_r)$, must be imposed on $\tilde{\beta} = \tilde{\tau}\tilde{\rho}$, where $\mathbf{H}_i$ is a $p_1 \times m_i$ restriction matrix, ϑ_i is a $m_i \times 1$ vector of unknown parameters, and m_i is the number of free parameters in $\tilde{\beta}_i$. The test is asymptotically χ^2 distributed with degrees of freedom equal to $\sum_{i=1}^{r}((p_1 - m_i) - (r-1))$ (Johansen et al. 2010).

Furthermore, to understand the persistence observed in the variables in the system, it is useful to study the signs and significance of the coefficients in β, d, and α. Juselius and Assenmacher (2017) suggest that the different types of adjustment for the variable $x_{i,t}$, $i = 1, 2, \ldots, p$, may be illustrated using the expression $\Delta^2 x_{it} = \sum_{j=1}^{r} \alpha_{ij} \sum_{m=1}^{p} (\beta_{mj} x_{m,t-1} + d_{mj}\Delta x_{m,t-1}) + \cdots + \varepsilon_{it}$, which corresponds to the i-th equation in the baseline empirical model (25). The error correcting- and error-increasing behavior of the variables can be analyzed using the following rules:

- If $d_{ij}\beta_{ij} > 0$ (given $\alpha_{ij} \neq 0$), then $\Delta x_{i,t}$ is equilibrium error correcting to $\beta_j' x_{t-1}$ (medium run).
- If $\alpha_{ij}\beta_{ij} < 0$, then the acceleration rate $\Delta^2 x_{i,t}$ is equilibrium error correcting to the polynomially cointegrated relation $\left(\beta_j' x_{t-1} + d_j' \Delta x_{t-1}\right)$ (long run).

In all other cases, there is equilibrium error increasing behavior.

The selected case, $(r = 2,\ s_1 = 2,\ s_2 = 1)$, entails two stationary polynomially cointegrating relationships, $\tilde{\beta}_i'\tilde{x}_t + \tilde{d}_i'\Delta\tilde{x}_t$, where $\tilde{\beta}_i' = \tilde{\rho}_i'\tilde{\tau}_i'$ and $i = 1, 2$. Table 5 reports an identified long-run structure on $\tilde{\beta}$, together with unrestricted estimates of $\tilde{d}$ and restricted estimates of α, which could not be rejected based on $\chi^2(9) = 6.75$ with a p-value of 0.66.[21] To facilitate interpretation, a coefficient in boldface (italics) stands for equilibrium error-correcting (increasing) behavior. Table 3 showed that all eigenvalues are inside the unit circle, so that the system is stable and any error-increasing behavior is compensated by error-correcting behavior.

[21] The estimated long-run $\tilde{\beta}$ structure is identified. That is, $r-1$ restrictions were imposed, at least, on each of the vectors. See Doornik and Juselius (2017) for further information.

Table 5. The estimated long-run $\tilde{\beta}$ structure $(\chi^2(9) = 6.75\ [0.66])$. *t*-values are given in $(\cdot)$, "-" is a zero restriction. A coefficient in boldface (italics) stands for equilibrium error-correcting (increasing) behavior.

	$p_{d,t}$	$p_{f,t}$	s_t	$i_{d,t}$	$i_{f,t}$	cp_t	$t \times 10^3$	c
$\tilde{\beta}_1'$	−0.01 (−3.9)	0.01 (3.9)	0.01 (3.9)	1.00	−1.00	0.002 (2.8)	-	
$\tilde{d}_1'$	**−0.52** (−8.5)	−0.07 (−8.5)	−0.44 (−8.6)	**0.0006** (8.5)	0.0006 (8.6)	−0.03 (−1.8)		−0.06 (−4.2)
α_1'	*−0.36* (−3.0)	-	-	**−0.26** (−5.9)	-			
$\tilde{\beta}_2'$	−0.03 (−14.2)	0.28 (17.4)	-	1.00	−1.00	-	−0.47 (−16.3)	
$\tilde{d}_2'$	**−1.21** (−8.4)	*−0.17* (−8.5)	−1.01 (−8.4)	**0.001** (8.3)	0.001 (8.7)	−0.05 (−1.6)		−1.13 (−16.8)
α_2'	**0.58** (9.7)	*0.05* (3.0)	0.37 (2.5)	*0.06* (3.0)	-			

The first polynomially cointegrating relationship, $\tilde{\beta}_1'\tilde{x}_t + \tilde{d}_1'\triangle\tilde{x}_t$, is interpreted as the UA-UIP condition:[22]

$$\left(i_d - i_f\right)_t = 0.01ppp_t - 0.002cp_t + 0.52\triangle p_{d,t} - 0.0006\triangle i_{d,t} + 0.06 + \hat{v}_{1,t} \tag{27}$$

where $\hat{v}_{1,t} \sim I(0)$ is the equilibrium error. The equation shows that the interest rate spread has been positively co-moving with the PPP gap—a measure of the risk premium—and the copper price. This relationship resembles the UA-UIP condition, Equation (12), where the term $(0.51\triangle p_d - 0.0007\triangle i_d)_t$ is likely to be related to the expected change in the nominal exchange rate and to a risk premium. Moreover, Equation (27) indicates that the uncovered interest parity is stationary after being adjusted by the PPP gap—the uncertainty premium—and copper price.

Equation (27) shows that, exactly as the IKE theory predicts, movements in the interest rate spread co-move with swings in the real exchange rate. That is, the interest rate spread moves in a compensatory manner to restore the equilibrium in the product market when the nominal exchange rate has been away from its benchmark value.

The copper price also enters the relationship that describes the excess returns under IKE, though with a small coefficient. A higher copper price increases the dollar supply in Chile, generating an appreciation of the exchange rate and, consequently, a larger PPP gap. This indicates that the Chilean economy might be affected by the so called commodity super-cycle (Erten and Ocampo 2013) through the effects that fluctuations in the copper price have on the real exchange rate and, consequently, on competitiveness.

The adjustment coefficients show that the Chilean interest rate is equilibrium error correcting in the long and medium run. The domestic price is equilibrium error increasing in the long run but equilibrium error correcting in the medium run. Thus, if the domestic price is above its long-run benchmark value, in the medium run both the domestic inflation rate and changes in the domestic interest rate will tend to increase, generating an increase in the equilibrium error term $\hat{v}_{1,t}$. In the long run, however, the domestic price will tend to increase, which generates a decrease in $\hat{v}_{1,t}$. To restore the long-run equilibrium, the domestic interest rate starts increasing.

The second polynomially cointegrating relationship, $\tilde{\beta}_2'\tilde{x}_t + \tilde{d}_2'\triangle\tilde{x}_t$, can be interpreted as a long-run relationship between the interest rate spread, trend-adjusted prices, and changes in the nominal exchange rate and is expressed as:

22 When $\alpha_{ij} = 0$, the corresponding d_{ij} is not shown in Equations (27) and (28). Furthermore, only d_{ij} coefficients with a $|\text{t-value}| \geq 2.5$ are shown.

$$\left(i_{d,t} - i_{f,t}\right) = 0.03\tilde{p}_{d,t} - 0.28\tilde{p}_{f,t} + 1.21\triangle p_{d.t} + 0.17\triangle p_{f,t} + 1.01\triangle s_t - 0.001\triangle i_{d,t} + 1.13 + \hat{v}_{2,t} \quad (28)$$

where $\tilde{p}_{f,t}$ and $\tilde{p}_{d,t}$ are, respectively, the trend-adjusted prices in US and Chile and $\hat{v}_{2,t} \sim I(0)$ is the equilibrium error. The equation shows that the interest rate spread is positively co-moving with the relative trend-adjusted level of prices, domestic and foreign inflation rates, and changes in both nominal exchange rate and domestic interest rate. This relationship might describe a central bank's reaction rule.

The Chilean trend-adjusted price, $\tilde{p}_{d,t}$, might tentatively be interpreted as a proxy for a long-run indicator of the inflation target. That is, given the US interest rate and US trend-adjusted price, if the domestic price is above (below) its long-run trend, the central bank may use contractionary (expansionary) monetary policy that increases (decreases) the domestic interest rate. The above argument may be used to explain the relationship between the interest rate spread and the changes in the nominal exchange rate. For example, the central bank may use contractionary monetary policy to counteract inflationary pressures due to exchange rate depreciation.

The adjustment coefficients show that when the interest rate spread has been under its long-run value, the domestic inflation rate and the domestic interest rate will tend to decrease in the medium run. Furthermore, the domestic price is equilibrium error correcting to the central bank's reaction rule in the long run, whereas the domestic interest rate is equilibrium error increasing in the long run. Then, if the interest rate spread is under its long-run equilibrium value, the domestic interest rate will tend to decrease. This generates further decreases in the equilibrium error $\hat{v}_{2,t}$. However, at the same time, the domestic price will tend to decrease, so it starts to restore the equilibrium.

Figure 5 shows the graph of the polynomial cointegration relationships and despite some signs of volatility change, they seem mean-reverting.

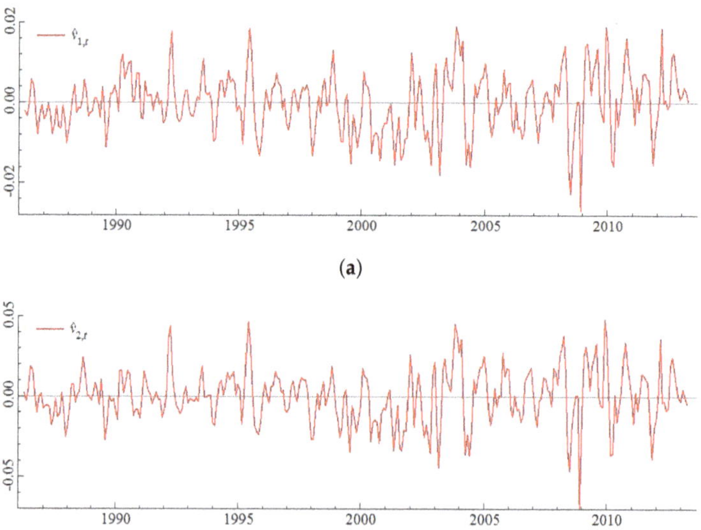

(b)

Figure 5. Polynomial cointegrating relationships. The graphs are corrected by short-run effects (for further details, see Juselius (2006)). **(a)** $\tilde{\beta}_1'\tilde{x}_t + \tilde{d}_1'\triangle\tilde{x}_t$: UA-UIP condition; **(b)** $\tilde{\beta}_2'\tilde{x}_t + \tilde{d}_2'\triangle\tilde{x}_t$: Central bank reaction's rule.

5.2.3. The Common Stochastic Trends

Table 6 reports the estimated $I(2)$ trend, $\boldsymbol{\alpha}_{\perp 2}$, and its respective estimated loading, $\breve{\boldsymbol{\beta}}_{\perp 2}$. The former may be interpreted as a relative price shock because it loads into prices and exchange rate rather than into exchange rate and interest rates. The estimate of $\boldsymbol{\alpha}_{\perp 2}$ suggests, however, that only shocks to the US price have generated the $I(2)$ trend. The coefficients in $\breve{\boldsymbol{\beta}}_{\perp 2}$ indicate that the $I(2)$ trend loads into nominal exchange rate and relative prices with coefficients of the same sign but different magnitude, which is consistent with the results of hypotheses $\mathcal{H}_4$, $\mathcal{H}_5$, and $\mathcal{H}_7$ in Table 4 that prices and exchange rate behave as a near $I(2)$ process. Equations (29) and (30) show, respectively, the $I(2)$ properties of the relative price and PPP gap.

The relative price is expressed as:

$$\left(p_{d,t} - p_{f,t}\right) = (0.25 - 0.03)\, \boldsymbol{\alpha}'_{\perp 2} \sum_{i=1}^{t} \sum_{s=1}^{i} \hat{\boldsymbol{\varepsilon}}_s. \tag{29}$$

The loading coefficients to the Chilean CPI and US CPI have the same sign but not the same size. Its difference, 0.22, has to be significant because the result of hypothesis $\mathcal{H}_6$ in Table 4 showed that the relative price is likely to behave as a near $I(2)$ process. The positive loading is consistent with the upward sloping trend in Figure 1a.

The PPP gap is expressed as:

$$\left(p_{d,t} - p_{f,t} - s_t\right) = (0.25 - 0.03 - 0.22)\, \boldsymbol{\alpha}'_{\perp 2} \sum_{i=1}^{t} \sum_{s=1}^{i} \hat{\boldsymbol{\varepsilon}}_s. \tag{30}$$

The long-run stochastic trend in relative prices and nominal exchange rate cancels out. This is consistent with both the result of hypothesis $\mathcal{H}_8$ in Table 4, which showed that deviations from PPP are likely to behave as an $I(1)$ process, and the long swings in Figure 1b.

The MA representation suggests that the Chilean economy is primarily affected by external shocks, which is natural when a small and open economy is participating in global markets. Chile has one of the most open economies in the world and also a developed financial market that is almost fully integrated into international markets.

Table 6. MA representation. $(\cdot)$ is the t-value. c_{ij} are constant terms.

$$\begin{bmatrix} p_d \\ p_f \\ s \\ i_d \\ i_f \end{bmatrix}_t = \underbrace{\begin{bmatrix} 0.25 \\ 0.03 \\ 0.22 \\ -0.00 \\ -0.00 \end{bmatrix}}_{\breve{\boldsymbol{\beta}}_{\perp 2}} \left[\boldsymbol{\alpha}'_{\perp 2} \sum_{i=1}^{t} \sum_{s=1}^{i} \hat{\boldsymbol{\varepsilon}}_s\right] + \begin{bmatrix} c_{11} & c_{12} & c_{13} \\ c_{21} & c_{22} & c_{23} \\ c_{31} & c_{32} & c_{33} \\ c_{41} & c_{42} & c_{43} \\ c_{51} & c_{53} & c_{53} \end{bmatrix} \begin{bmatrix} \boldsymbol{\alpha}'_{\perp 2} \sum_{i=1}^{t} \hat{\boldsymbol{\varepsilon}}_i \\ \boldsymbol{\alpha}'_{\perp 1,1} \sum_{i=1}^{t} \hat{\boldsymbol{\varepsilon}}_i \\ \boldsymbol{\alpha}'_{\perp 1,2} \sum_{i=1}^{t} \hat{\boldsymbol{\varepsilon}}_i \end{bmatrix} + \begin{bmatrix} b_{11} \\ b_{21} \\ b_{31} \\ b_{41} \\ b_{51} \end{bmatrix} t$$

$$\boldsymbol{\alpha}'_{\perp 2} = \begin{bmatrix} \underset{(-0.7)}{-0.07} & \mathbf{1.00} & \underset{(-0.3)}{-0.03} & \underset{(1.1)}{0.16} & \underset{(0.3)}{0.33} \end{bmatrix}$$

6. Conclusions

The long and persistent swings of the real exchange rate have for a long time puzzled economists. Recent models that build on IKE seem to provide theoretical explanations for this persistence.

This paper has analyzed the empirical regularities behind the PPP gap and the uncovered interest rate parity in Chile. The results, based on an $I(2)$ cointegrated vector autoregressive model, gave support for the theoretical exchange rate model based on imperfect knowledge, which assumes that individuals use a multitude of forecasting strategies that are revised over time in ways that cannot be fully prespecified. This is further supported by the results that showed a complex and fairly informative mix of error-increasing and error-correcting behavior.

The results showed that, exactly as the IKE theory predicts, movements in the interest rate spread co-move with swings in the real exchange rate. That is, the interest rate spread moves in a compensatory manner to restore the equilibrium in the product market when the real exchange rate has been away from its long-run value. The copper price also explain the deviations of the real exchange rate from its long-run equilibrium value. Copper is the main export commodity in Chile and accounts for a large share in total exports; its price fluctuations seems to affect the real exchange rate through its effect on the exchange market.

Altogether, the results indicate that when the interest rate spread is corrected by the uncertainty premium (the PPP gap) and by the fluctuations in the copper price one gets a stationary market-clearing mechanism.

Conflicts of Interest: The author declares no conflict of interest.

Appendix A. Data

Table A1 describes the variables used in this study, their sources, notations, and transformations.

Table A1. Data Description.

Variable	Description	Source	Transformation
$p_{d,t}$	Chilean Consumer Price Index	Central Bank of Chile	Natural logarithm
$p_{f,t}$	US Consumer Price Index	Bureau of Labor Statistics, United States	Natural logarithm
s_t	Nominal exchange rate (Chilean pesos per US dollar)	Central Bank of Chile	Natural logarithm
$i_{d,t}$	1-year Chilean average weighted rates of all transactions in the month by financial commercial banks in Chilean pesos (nominal). Nominal interest rates are annualized (base 360 days) using the conversion of simple interest.	Own elaboration based on data from the Central Bank of Chile	The original variable was divided by 1200 to make it comparable with monthly data
$i_{f,t}$	United States interest rate, Constant Maturity Yields, 1 Year, Average, USD	Own elaboration based on data from the International Monetary Fund	The original variable was divided by 1200 to make it comparable with monthly data
cp_t	Real copper price (USD cents./lb.)	Comisión Chilena del Cobre	Natural logarithm

Appendix B. Lag-Length Selection

Table A2 reports the lag-length selection and lag reduction test. The upper part suggests that $k = 2$ should be selected based on SC and H-Q criteria. However, there is evidence of autocorrelation of order 1 and 2 when $k = 2$. If $k = 3$ is selected, the hypotheses of autocorrelation of orders 1 and 3 can be rejected. The lower part of Table A2 shows that only the reduction from 4 to 3 lags cannot be rejected.

Table A2. Lag-length selection model and lag reduction test.

Lag-Length Selection				
Lag: k	SC	H-Q	LM(1)	LM(k)
4	−63.42	−65.35	0.34	0.52
3	−63.97	−65.62	0.13	0.38
2	**−64.28**	**−65.71**	0.05	0.04
1	−64.02	−65.20	0.00	0.00

Table A2. *Cont.*

Lag Reduction		
Reduction from - to	**Test**	***p*-Value**
VAR(4) - VAR(3)	$\chi^2\,(36) = 41.55$	0.24
VAR (3) - VAR(2)	$\chi^2\,(36) = 95.74$	0.00
VAR(2)-VAR(1)	$\chi^2\,(36) = 291.88$	0.00

SC: Schwarz Criterion, H-Q: Hannan-Quinn Criterion; LM(i) stands for a LM-test for autocorrelation of order i; a number in boldface stands for the lowest criteria value.

Appendix C. Dummy Variables

In model (25), nine dummies were incorporated. Table A3 describes the economic facts that justify the dummies, and Table A4 reports its estimated coefficients.

Table A3. Dummy justification.

Dummy	Variable	Justification
P 1990:9	$+p_d$	The Central Bank of Chile started the partial implementation of an inflation targeting system
T 1990:11	$+i_d$	INA
P 1993:12	$-i_d$	INA
P 1998:9	$+i_d$	Central Bank of Chile increased the real monetary policy interest rate from 8.5% to 14%
P 2005:9	$+p_f$	Energy costs increased sharply. Overall, the index for energy commodities (petroleum-based energy)
P 2006:04	$+cp$	The copper price increased in 30% in April triggered by the lower inventories and higher demand
P 2008:10	$-p_f, +s$	The energy index fell 8.6% and the transportation index fell in 5.4% in October . The nominal exchange rate depreciated 12% due to the dollar strengthening in international markets
P 2008:11	$-p_f$	The overall CPI index decreased mainly due to a decrease in energy prices, particularly gasoline .
P 2010:2	$+s, +p_d$	The nominal exchange rate depreciated due to changes in the forward position of the pension funds

P and *T* stand for a permanent dummy, $(0,\ldots,0,1,0,\ldots,0)$, and a transitory dummy, $(0,\ldots,0,1,-1,0,\ldots,0)$, respectively. The signs "$-$" and "$+$" stand for decreases and increases, respectively; INA official information regarding the variable increase or decrease is not available.

Table A4. Estimated outlier coefficients.

Dummy	$\Delta^2 p_d$	$\Delta^2 p_f$	$\Delta^2 s$	$\Delta^2 cp$	$\Delta^2 i_d$	$\Delta^2 i_f$
P 1990:9	0.01 (5.08)	*	*	*	*	*
T 1990:11	*	*	*	*	0.02 (18.44)	*
P 1993:12	*	*	*	*	−0.009 (−5.68)	*
P 1998:9	*	*	*	*	0.005 (3.32)	*
P 2005:9	*	0.01 (4.62)	*	*	*	*
P 2006:4	*	*	*	0.21 (3.98)	*	*
P 2008:10	*	−0.01 (−5.361)	0.14 (8.48)	−0.25 (−4.54)	*	*
P 2008:11	*	−0.01 (−6.73)	*	*	*	*
P 2010:2	0.01 (2.88)	*	0.07 (4.18)	*	*	*

$(\cdot)$ is the t-value. * stands for a $|\text{t-value}| \leq 2.0$; *P* and *T* stand, respectively, for a permanent and a transitory dummy.

References

Bacchiocchi, Emanuele, and Luca Fanelli. 2005. Testing the PPP through I (2) cointegration techniques. *Journal of Applied Econometrics* 20: 749–70.

Céspedes, Luis.F., and José De Gregorio. 1999. Tipo de cambio real, desalineamiento y devaluaciones: teoría y evidencia para Chile. Unpublished paper, University of Chile, Santiago, Chile, March.

Cowan, Kevin, David Rappoport, and Jorge Selaive. 2007. *High Frequency Dynamics of the Exchange Rate in Chile.* Santiago: Central Bank of Chile.

De Gregorio, José, and Felipe Labbé. 2011. *Copper, the Real Exchange Rate and Macroeconomic Fluctuations In Chile.* Santiago: Central Bank of Chile.

Délano, Valentín, and Rodrigo Valdés. 1998. Productividad y Tipo Cambio Real en Chile. *Central Bank of Chile Working Paper* 38: 1–19.

Diamandis, Panayiotis F. 2003. Market efficiency, purchasing power parity, and the official and parallel markets for foreign currency in Latin America. *International Review of Economics & Finance* 12: 89–110.

Doornik, Jurgen A., and Katarina Juselius. 2017. *Cointegration Analysis of Time Series Using CATS 3 for OxMetrics.* London: Timerlake Consultants Ltd.

Duncan, Roberto, and César Calderón. 2003. Purchasing Power Parity in an Emerging Market Economy: A Long-Span Study for Chile. *Estudios de Economía* 30: 103–132.

Erten, Bilge, and José Antonio Ocampo. 2013. Super cycles of commodity prices since the mid-nineteenth century. *World Development* 44: 14–30.

Froot, Kenneth A., and Kenneth Rogoff. 1995. Perspectives on PPP and long-run real exchange rates. In *Handbook of International Economics*. Amsterdam: Elsevier, Volume 3, pp. 1647–88.

Frydman, Roman, and Michael D. Goldberg. 2011. *Beyond Mechanical Markets: Asset Price Swings, Risk, and The Role of the State.* Princeton: Princeton University Press.

Frydman, Roman, and Michael D. Goldberg. 2007. *Imperfect Knowledge Economics: Exchange Rates and Risk.* Princeton: Princeton University Press.

Gonzalo, Jesus. 1994. Five alternative methods of estimating long-run equilibrium relationships. *Journal of Econometrics* 60: 203–33.

Johansen, Søren. 1992. A representation of vector autoregressive processes integrated of order 2. *Econometric Theory* 8: 188–202.

Johansen, Søren. 1995. A statistical analysis of cointegration for I(2) variables. *Econometric Theory* 11: 25–59.

Johansen, Søren. 1996. *Likelihood-Based Inference in Cointegrated Vector Autoregressive Models.* Oxford: Oxford University Press.

Johansen, Søren. 1997. Likelihood analysis of the I(2) model. *Scandinavian Journal of Statistics* 24: 433–62.

Johansen, Søren. 2006. Statistical analysis of hypotheses on the cointegrating relations in the I(2) model. *Journal of Econometrics* 132: 81–115.

Johansen, Søren, Katarina Juselius, Roman Frydman, and Michael Goldberg. 2010. Testing hypotheses in an I(2) model with piecewise linear trends. An analysis of the persistent long swings in the Dmk/$ rate. *Journal of Econometrics* 158: 117–29.

Juselius, Katarina. 2006. *The Cointegrated VAR Model: Methodology and Applications.* Oxford: Oxford University Press.

Juselius, Katarina. 2010. *Imperfect Knowledge, Asset Price Swings and Structural Slumps: A Cointegrated VAR Analysis of Their Interdependence.* Technical Report. Copenhagen: Department of Economics, University of Copenhagen.

Juselius, Katarina. 2014. Testing for Near I(2) Trends When the Signal-to-Noise Ratio Is Small. *Economics: The Open-Access, Open-Assessment E-Journal* 8: 2014-21. doi:10.5018/economicsejournal.ja.2014-21.

Juselius, Katarina. 2017a. Using a Theory-Consistent CVAR Scenario to Test an Exchange Rate Model Based on Imperfect Knowledge. Unpublished manuscript, Department of Economics, University of Copenhagen, Copenhagen, Demark.

Juselius, Katarina. 2017b. A Theory Consistent CVAR Scenario for a Standard Monetary Model Using Data-Generated Expectaions. Unpublished manuscript, Department of Economics, University of Copenhagen, Copenhagen, Denmark.

Juselius, Katarina, and Katrin Assenmacher. 2017. Real exchange rate persistence and the excess return puzzle: The case of Switzerland versus the US. *Journal of Applied Econometrics*, doi:10.1002/jae.2562.
Kahneman, Daniel, and Amos Tversky. 1979. Prospect theory: An analysis of decision under risk. *Econometrica* 47: 263–91.
Kohlscheen, Emanuel, Fernando Avalos, and Andreas Schrimpf. 2017. When the Walk Is Not Random: Commodity Prices and Exchange Rates. *International Journal of Central Banking*, June.
Kongsted, Hans Christian. 2005. Testing the nominal-to-real transformation. *Journal of Econometrics* 124: 205–25.
Krugman, Paul R., Maurice Obstfeld, and Marc Melitz. 2011. *International Economics: Theory and Policy*, 9th ed. Boston: Addison-Wesley.
Mark, Nelson C. 2001. *International Macroeconomics and Finance: Theory and Econometric Methods*, 1st ed. Malden: Wiley-Blackwell.
Medina, Juan Pablo, and Claudio Soto. 2007. *Copper Price, Fiscal Policy and Business Cycle in Chile.* Documentos de Trabajo. Santiago: Banco Central de Chile, p. 1.
Phelps, Edmund S. 1994. *Structural Slumps: The Modern Equilibrium Theory of Unemployment, Interest, and Assets.* Harvard: Harvard University Press.
Rahbek, Anders, Hans Christian Kongsted, and Clara Jørgensen. 1999. Trend stationarity in the I(2) cointegration model. *Journal of Econometrics* 90: 265–89.
Sarno, Lucio, and Mark P. Taylor. 2002. *The Economics of Exchange Rates.* Cambridge: Cambridge University Press.
Tabor, Morten Nyboe. 2014. Essays on Imperfect Knowledge Economics, Structural Change, And Persistence in the Cointegrated VAR Model. Ph.D. thesis, University of Copenhagen, Copenhagen, Denmark.
Taylor, Alan M., and Mark P. Taylor. 2004. The Purchasing Power Parity Debate. *Journal of Economic Perspectives* 18: 135–58.
Wu, Yi. 2013. *What Explains Movements in the Peso/Dollar Exchange Rate?* IMF Working papers No. 13/171, International Monetary Fund, Washington, DC, USA.

econometrics

MDPI

Article

Short-Term Expectation Formation Versus Long-Term Equilibrium Conditions: The Danish Housing Market

Andreas Hetland * and Simon Hetland

Department of Economics, University of Copenhagen, 1353 Copenhagen K, Denmark; bhp240@ku.dk
* Correspondence: lxs601@ku.dk; Tel.: +45-20422606

Academic Editor: Katarina Juselius
Received: 28 February 2017; Accepted: 25 August 2017; Published: 4 September 2017

Abstract: The primary contribution of this paper is to establish that the long-swings behavior observed in the market price of Danish housing since the 1970s can be understood by studying the interplay between short-term expectation formation and long-run equilibrium conditions. We introduce an asset market model for housing based on uncertainty rather than risk, which under mild assumptions allows for other forms of forecasting behavior than rational expectations. We test the theory via an $I(2)$ cointegrated VAR model and find that the long-run equilibrium for the housing price corresponds closely to the predictions from the theoretical framework. Additionally, we corroborate previous findings that housing markets are well characterized by short-term momentum forecasting behavior. Our conclusions have wider relevance, since housing prices play a role in the wider Danish economy, and other developed economies, through wealth effects.

Keywords: asset pricing; cointegration; $I(2)$ analysis; housing market; imperfect knowledge; Knightian uncertainty; long swings

JEL Classification: C32; C51; D81; E22; G12

1. Introduction

Changes in housing prices, and in turn changes in housing wealth, exert substantial effects on the economy: increased housing wealth is strongly associated with increased aggregate consumption, cf. Case et al. (2005), and vice versa, cf. Case et al. (2013). Housing wealth has (together with pension wealth) also been found to be a primary driver of the share of total wealth accruing to the middle class,[1] cf. Saez and Zucman (2016). For example, higher housing prices have historically been associated with the middle class owning a greater share of total wealth, and thereby with a lower level of inequality. Consequently, understanding the drivers and dynamics of housing prices is of material importance to economists and policy makers alike.

The market price of housing has a tendency to undergo prolonged periods of increases that outpace both incomes and other prices, see e.g., Case et al. (2003) for a study of the US housing market. We have observed similar long-swings patterns in the Danish housing market, see Figure 1.[2] The Danish national price index for housing increased by 65% between 2003:Q1 and 2007:Q4, while the general price level increased by only 8% over the same period, meaning that housing outpaced inflation by 57 percentage points. In 2008, the housing boom turned to bust as the global economy fell in to recession. Danish house prices fell by 17% between 2008:Q1 and 2012:Q4, while the general price level increased by 10%, closing most of the gap created during the boom years. Moreover, prolonged

[1] Defined by the authors as the share of total wealth owned by the bottom 90% of the population.
[2] The data we use has been provided by the Danish Central Bank. We refer to Section 3.1 for further details.

deviations are not just a phenomenon of the relatively recent past. Housing price changes have either persistently outpaced or fallen behind consumer price inflation since the late 1970s. For example, housing prices slumped during the late 1980s and early 1990s, with inflation outpacing house price increases by 43 percentage points between 1986:Q1 and 1993:Q2. The house price increases then accelerated and had completely closed the gap by 1998:Q2.

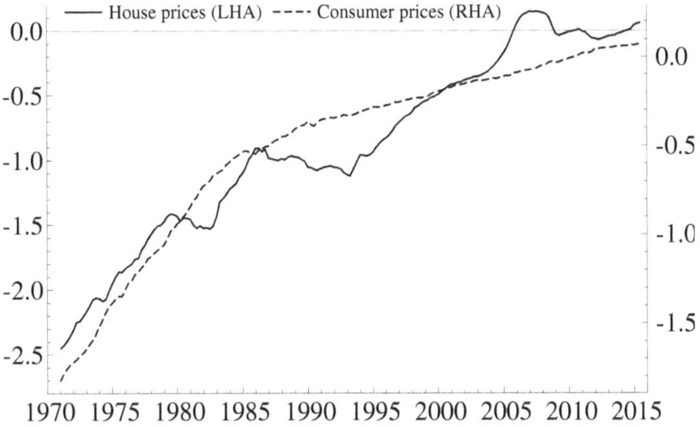

Figure 1. Danish house and consumer price indices between 1971:Q1 and 2015:Q3, log-levels.

Given that housing prices play an important role in the wider economy, the determinants of the market price of housing have been the focus of numerous studies. In this paper, we focus on the approach which treats housing as a carry-generating physical asset that can be reproduced at the cost of construction, cf. Poterba (1984). This approach falls under the general asset pricing theory, which typically represents the uncertainty associated with the future value of an asset in the form of a probability distribution, cf. e.g., Björk (2009). Investors' expectation of the future value of the asset is then assumed to follow the mathematical expectation with respect to this probability distribution. This is known as rational expectations in the wider context of economic modelling, cf. e.g., Muth (1961) and Sargent and Wallace (1975). However, in the case of housing, several studies from the US have found evidence in support of individual investors forming their expectations based on extrapolation of recent price changes, see Case and Shiller (1989), Poterba (1991), Case et al. (2003), Shiller (2008), and Piazzesi and Schneider (2009). As remarked in these studies, the observed momentum-based expectation formation appears incompatible with the assumption of rational expectations.

Some have argued that rational expectations-based approaches conflate the fundamentally different notions of risk and uncertainty, where the former may be expressed as a probability distribution while the latter cannot, see e.g., Savage (1951), Rutherford (1984), Lawson (1988) and Binmore (2009). This distinction has important implications for the appropriateness of rational expectations, and has gained traction with central bank economists in recent years, see e.g., King (2004), Carney (2016) and ECB (2016). More generally this type of thinking has led to alternative paradigms for expectation formation. For example, Akerlof and Shiller (2009) argue that investor psychology is driven by "animal spirits" such as confidence, money illusion and narratives. Frydman et al. (2007) advances the imperfect knowledge economics theory, in which individuals change their forecasting strategies in ways that need not be given by expectations with respect to a model-implied probability distribution. Elsewhere in the field of psychology, large-scale forecasting experiments have led to the finding that while "forecasting is often viewed as a statistical problem, [...] forecasts can be improved with behavioural interventions [... such as] training, teaming, and tracking.", cf. Mellers et al. (2014), which suggests that, in practice, expectation formation for macroeconomic outcomes goes beyond the problem of identifying an appropriate statistical model.

In this paper we seek to explain the long-swings dynamic in Danish housing prices (Figure 1). We do this by developing an asset market model based on uncertainty rather than risk, which allows other forms of forecasting behavior than rational expectations, such as momentum-based forecasting (cf. e.g., Case et al. (2003)). However, since we do not have survey data of individual expectations in the Danish housing market, we introduce the assumption that the expectation errors are stationary (Assumption A in Juselius (2017b)). Additionally, we introduce the notion of a gap effect as a measure of the required uncertainty premium, cf. Frydman et al. (2007), specified in terms of Tobin's q, cf. Tobin (1969). This uncertainty-based asset market approach produces a set of testable hypotheses on the long-run relationships governing the Danish housing prices, which we confront with the data via a cointegrated vector autoregressive (CVAR) model, see e.g., Juselius (2007) and Johansen (1996). The CVAR model provides a general-to-specific framework, which allows us to start the empirical analysis with a sufficiently well-specified, unrestricted VAR model of the Danish housing market, and then impose restrictions corresponding to hypotheses arising from the theoretical model, cf. e.g., Hoover et al. (2008). Importantly, this approach also allows us to infer the process by which the market adjusts when out of equilibrium; specifically, the interplay between long-run and medium-run dynamics may be able to explain long swings around the equilibrium, cf. Juselius and Assenmacher (2016, Section 5) .

The paper proceeds as follows: in Section 2, we introduce the theoretical framework for the uncertainty-based no-arbitrage condition, and derive a set of empirically testable hypotheses. Section 3 specifies an $I(2)$ CVAR model and tests the hypotheses presented in Section 2. Finally, we conclude in Section 4.

2. The Theoretical Framework

We here develop an uncertainty-based theoretical framework for housing markets with the purpose of guiding us to a set of testable hypotheses on the long-run equilibrium for housing prices. Our framework is based on uncertainty rather than risk for the reasons outlined in Section 1, and the aim is to develop a model which is simple, yet realistic enough to be empirically relevant. In the following we: introduce the classic deterministic asset-market approach to the housing market in Section 2.1; incorporate risk into the asset market model in Section 2.2; further amend the model to allow for uncertainty in Section 2.3; and finally we derive testable hypotheses from the uncertainty-based model in Section 2.4. We will confront these with historical data for the Danish housing market in Section 3.

2.1. An Asset-Market Approach to Housing

We follow the asset-market approach to modeling the price of residential housing, which was originally introduced in Poterba (1984), and rests on the premise that the price of an asset should be characterized by the absence of arbitrage opportunities. This approach centers on the equilibrium condition that individuals invest in housing until the marginal value of housing equals its cost. In line with Poterba (1984), we make several simplifying assumptions to make this condition explicit: at each point in time t, the housing stock depreciates at a rate of δ_t; housing is taxed at a rate of μ_t; all investors face a marginal income tax rate θ_t, from which they may deduct property taxes; investors may borrow or lend any amount at a nominal interest rate i_t. We assume for ease of presentation that each of these quantities are constant between periods.

The cost of a single unit of housing with nominal price, denoted $P_{h,t}$ (not in logarithmic terms), is $\omega_t P_{h,t}$, where ω_t is the sum of after-tax depreciation, property taxes, mortgage interest payments, and the opportunity cost of owning housing stock, minus the nominal capital gain

$$\omega_t = \delta_t + (1 - \theta_t)(i_t + \mu_t) - \pi_{h,t}, \tag{1}$$

where $\pi_{h,t} := dP_{h,t}/P_{h,t}dt$. The benefit of owning a unit of housing is the nominal rental income, R_t, produced (or saved in the case of owner-occupied housing). In the housing market equilibrium, investors (including home owners) will price housing such that the marginal cost equals the marginal benefit of housing; formally $R_t = \omega_t P_{h,t}$, which we can rewrite as the first-order differential equation for changes in the nominal housing price

$$dP_{h,t} = c_t P_{h,t} dt\,, \tag{2}$$

where we have defined the user cost rate $c_t := \delta_t + (1-\theta_t)(i_t + \mu_t) - R_t/P_{h,t}$. We assume that the ratio $R_t/P_{h,t}$ is constant to simplify the exposition. For a given initial house price $P_{h,0}$, Equation (2) determines the nominal capital gain needed to induce investors to hold the existing housing stock.

2.2. A Risk-Based Asset-Market Approach

We next extend the no-arbitrage condition given by Equation (2) to a simple setting involving market risk. Specifically, we consider the simple case where the price of housing is given by the geometric Brownian motion

$$dP_{h,t} = (c_t + rp_t)\, P_{h,t} dt + \omega_t P_{h,t} dW_t\,, \tag{3}$$

where rp_t denotes a risk premium, dW_t is a Wiener process under the physical measure, denoted $\mathbb{P}$, and ω_t denotes the volatility of the house price changes. Investors require the risk premium rp_t to undertake the risk ω_t; the larger the risk, the larger the required premium.

Omitting here the full details, the fundamental theorem of asset pricing, see e.g., Björk (2009, Section 5.5), implies that if, and only if, there is no arbitrage in the housing market, then the current price of housing, $P_{h,t}$, must satisfy

$$P_{h,t} = E^{\mathbb{Q}}\left[P_{h,t+1} \mid \mathcal{F}_t\right] e^{-c_t}\,, \tag{4}$$

where $\mathbb{Q}$ denotes the risk-neutral measure. That is, Equation (4) states the current price of housing is equal to the discounted expected future price under the risk-neutral measure, conditional on the available information, $\mathcal{F}_t$.

Under standard regularity conditions, Girsanov's theorem tells us we can re-weigh the expectation in Equation (4) from the risk-neutral measure, $\mathbb{Q}$, to the physical measure, $\mathbb{P}$. If the investor preferences are not risk neutral then $\mathbb{P}$ will be different from $\mathbb{Q}$, such that an additional term compensating for taking on market risk enters the discount factor

$$P_{h,t} = E^{\mathbb{P}}\left[P_{h,t+1} \mid \mathcal{F}_t\right] e^{-c_t - rp_t}\,. \tag{5}$$

Next, we apply the log-transformation to Equation (5).[3] Noting that we have assumed the user cost rate and risk premium to be constant between periods, we have that

$$p^{e,\mathbb{P}}_{h,t+1|t} - p_{h,t} = c_t + rp_t\,, \tag{6}$$

where we have denoted the logarithm of the expected price by $p^{e,\mathbb{P}}_{h,t+1|t} := \log E^{\mathbb{P}}\left[P_{h,t+1} \mid \mathcal{F}_t\right]$.

Equation (6) constitutes what we will refer to as the *risk-adjusted no-arbitrage condition* from standard asset pricing theory. This equation states that for there to be no arbitrage opportunities in the housing market, the price of housing must be given by the present value of the expected price one period in the future, where the expectation is with respect to the physical measure $\mathbb{P}$, which follows

[3] We generally let lower case letters denote logarithmic values, e.g., $p_{h,t} := \log(P_{h,t})$. The exception being rates, e.g., c_t.

from our simple model given by Equation (3). The discount factor reflects the opportunity cost under the physical measure, i.e., the user cost rate plus a premium demanded for undertaking risk.

While this risk-based asset price model is a stepping stone on our way to introduce uncertainty, we note that richer and more realistic dynamics are also possible in risk-based settings. For example, the $\mathbb{P}$-dynamics in Equation (3) may depend on the other variables such as net investments. We will not pursue these here.

2.3. An Uncertainty-Based Asset-Market Approach

If the housing market is better characterized by uncertainty than risk, then it becomes necessary to revisit the no-arbitrage condition in Equation (6). Recall that recognizing that a setting involves uncertainty implies that it is not feasible to attribute the known outcomes with unambiguous probabilities; in turn, the mathematical expectation operator in Equation (6) is not defined. We assume that investors form subjective expectations under uncertainty, but these do not necessarily follow from a model such as Equation (3). We return to the expectations formation under uncertainty in Section 2.3.1. For now, we simply denote the subjective expectations of the future house prices given the information available at time t as $p^e_{h,t+1|t}$. Based on this, we re-formulate Equation (6) as

$$p^e_{h,t+1|t} - p_{h,t} = c_t + up_t\,, \tag{7}$$

where up_t denotes an uncertainty premium. We will refer to Equation (7) as the *uncertainty-adjusted no-arbitrage* (UANA) condition. This equation states that for there to be no arbitrage in the housing market, the subjective expectation of the one-period return must equal the user cost rate plus a premium compensating for undertaking uncertainty, which is conceptually similar to the risk-adjusted no-arbitrage condition in Equation (6), except in Equation (7) the expectations are not generated by solving a stochastic model.

2.3.1. Expectation Formation under Uncertainty

Investors form subjective expectations of future house price changes, but these expectations are inherently unobservable. To relate the expectations in Equation (7) to the realized prices, we introduce Assumption A from Juselius (2017a).

Assumption A: The expectation errors of the future price levels, defined as

$$e_{t+1} := p^e_{h,t+1|t} - p_{h,t+1}\,, \tag{8}$$

are stationary; more precisely, $e_{t+1} \sim I(0)$.

This assumption implies that investors are able to assess the order of integration of house prices, $p_{h,t}$, such that the expectation errors are stationary, but not necessarily uncorrelated over time. This specification of investors' expectation formation is far less restrictive than rational expectations, and so does not preclude e.g., momentum-based forecasting.

2.3.2. The Uncertainty Premium and the Gap Effect

In a similar type of uncertainty-based asset pricing framework, Frydman et al. (2007) have introduced the notion of a gap effect to characterize the uncertainty premium. In general terms, the gap effect is defined as the difference between the current asset price and its perceived long-run fair value. In the context of housing, the Tobin's q measure, which is the ratio of the price to reproduction cost, cf. Tobin (1969), is an appropriate long-term benchmark. In the following, we will refer to Tobin's q in logarithmic terms, i.e., the difference $p_{h,t} - p_{b,t}$. Intuitively, if the price of a unit of housing is above the cost of building such a unit, then there is an incentive to construct and sell new houses until either the increased demand for construction supplies and labor pushes the cost up, the increased supply of homes pushes the price of housing down, or a combination of both. All else equal, this dynamic will tend to pull the Tobin's q ratio towards unity in the long run.

We specify the uncertainty premium as being proportional to Tobin's q (in logarithmic terms), measured using the nominal housing index, $p_{h,t}$, and the nominal price index for construction costs, $p_{b,t}$. Specifically,

$$up_t = \sigma(p_{h,t} - p_{b,t}) \, , \tag{9}$$

where σ is a positive scalar; that is, the further in excess of a Tobin's q value of one, the higher the required premium. When Tobin's q is less than unity, the premium will be negative, i.e., the required expected return will be less than the user cost rate, c_t. Substituting Equation (9) into the UANA condition in Equation (7) yields,

$$p^e_{h,t+1|t} - p_{h,t} = c_t + \sigma(p_{h,t} - p_{b,t}) \, . \tag{10}$$

In conclusion, introducing uncertainty in terms of subjective expectations and potential loss, as measured by the gap effect, results in an equilibrium condition remarkably similar to that arising from the deterministic framework originally introduced in Poterba (1984), but with an additional term accounting for the uncertainty premium as measured by Tobin's q. We now turn our attention to the testable hypotheses arising from the above framework.

2.4. Testable Hypotheses

We use Assumption A combined with with the gap effect to restate the UANA condition in terms of realized, contemporary price changes. We first rewrite the left-hand side of Equation (10) as

$$p^e_{h,t+1|t} - p_{h,t} = \Delta p_{h,t} + \Delta^2 p_{h,t+1} + e_{t+1} \, , \tag{11}$$

noting that $\Delta^2 p_{h,t+1} = \Delta p_{h,t+1} - \Delta p_{h,t}$. If the price of housing $p_{h,t}$ is non-stationary in the sense that it is integrated of order one or two, then the term $\Delta^2 p_{h,t+1}$ will be stationary. As such, under Assumption A, Equations (10) and (11) suggest the cointegration relation

$$\Delta p_{h,t} = c_t + \sigma(p_{h,t} - p_{b,t}) + w_t \, , \tag{12}$$

where $w_t := -\left(\Delta^2 p_{h,t+1} + e_{t+1}\right) \sim I(0)$ denotes stationary deviations from the long-run equilibrium.

Considering the potential for each of the variables $p_{h,t}$, $p_{b,t}$ and c_t to be either $I(1)$ or $I(2)$, there are eight different potentially relevant scenarios. We here limit our attention to scenarios where cointegration to stationarity remains a possibility, and where the price indices have the same order of integration. This leaves three different relevant scenarios.

In the first scenario, we have that $p_{h,t} \sim I(1)$, $p_{b,t} \sim I(1)$ and $c_t \sim I(1)$, such that

$$\underset{I(0)}{\Delta p_{h,t}} = \underset{I(1)}{c_t} + \sigma\underset{I(1)}{(p_{h,t} - p_{b,t})} + \underset{I(0)}{w_t} \, , \tag{13}$$

where the user cost rate, c_t, cointegrates with Tobin's q from $I(1)$ to stationarity.

In the second scenario, if $p_{h,t} \sim I(2)$, $p_{b,t} \sim I(2)$ and $c_t \sim I(1)$ then

$$\underset{I(1)}{\Delta p_{h,t}} = \underset{I(1)}{c_t} + \sigma\underset{I(1)}{(p_{h,t} - p_{b,t})} + \underset{I(0)}{w_t} \, , \tag{14}$$

where the house and construction prices, $p_{h,t}$ and $p_{b,t}$, cointegrate from $I(2)$ to $I(1)$, such that Tobin's q is $I(1)$ and cointegrates with the user cost rate, c_t, and the house price changes $\Delta p_{h,t}$ to stationarity.

Third, and last, if $p_{h,t} \sim I(2)$, $p_{b,t} \sim I(2)$ and $c_t \sim I(2)$ then

$$\underset{I(1)}{\Delta p_{h,t}} = \underset{I(2)}{c_t} + \sigma\underset{I(2)}{(p_{h,t} - p_{b,t})} + \underset{I(0)}{w_t}, \tag{15}$$

where the user cost rate, c_t, cointegrates with Tobin's q from $I(2)$ to $I(1)$, which in turn cointegrates with the changes in house prices, $\Delta p_{h,t}$ to stationarity. Only one, if any, of the three scenarios will find empirical support. We will introduce the cointegrated VAR model to investigate which one in the following section.

3. Specifying an $I(2)$ CVAR Model for the Danish Housing Market

We now turn our attention to confronting the hypotheses derived from the theoretical framework presented in Section 2 with historical data for the Danish housing market. Specifically, to investigate the empirical relevance of the cointegrating relations in Section 2.4, we here introduce the $I(2)$ cointegrated vector autoregressive (CVAR) model. The method applied to arrive at a well-specified, properly identified system is outlined in Juselius (2007), while a mathematical exposition of the model, estimation and inference can be found in Johansen (1996). An appealing feature of the CVAR framework is that through testing and subsequently imposing restrictions on an unrestricted VAR, such as rank restrictions, zero parameter restrictions, and other restrictions, we arrive at a more parsimonious model with economically interpretable coefficients. As such, specifying a CVAR with an over-identified long-run structure adheres to the general-to-specific procedure outlined in e.g., Campos et al. (2005).

In the following we: introduce the information set in Section 3.1; define the $I(2)$ cointegrated VAR model in Section 3.2; develop a sufficiently well-specified unrestricted VAR model in Sections 3.3–3.5; determine the cointegration rank in Section 3.6; test the theory-derived hypotheses and interpret the over-identified long-run structure of the cointegrated VAR model in Sections 3.7–3.9; finally, we summarize the empirical findings in Section 3.10.

3.1. The Information Set

Our empirical analysis is based on variables that are part of the "MONA" database maintained by the Danish Central Bank, cf. Danmarks Nationalbank (2003). This database contains quarterly observations of variables for the Danish economy from 1971:Q1 to 2015:Q3.[4] We define the information set for our empirical analysis as: the nominal price index for goods, measured as the GDP deflator, denoted $p_{c,t}$; the nominal price index for construction costs, $p_{b,t}$; and the nominal price index for single family houses in Denmark, $p_{h,t}$. We also include the user cost rate of housing investments, c_t, which is the post-tax nominal interest rate on a highly rated bond. Since this rate represents the opportunity costs of investing in housing (i.e., the carry), depreciation and convenience yield are included and have been assumed to stay constant at 1% and 4%, respectively; an assumption similar to those made in Danmarks Nationalbank (2003, chp. 3). Finally, we also include the net investments in housing in fixed prices, Δh_t, i.e., the first-differenced real housing stock in log terms, h_t. All variables, apart from the user cost rate, c_t, are transformed with the natural logarithm. We combine these five variables in our data column vector, x_t, which we define as

$$x_t = [\ p_{c,t} \quad p_{b,t} \quad p_{h,t} \quad c_t \quad \Delta h_t\ ]'. \tag{16}$$

The levels, first-, and second differences of the data is shown in Figure A1 in Appendix A.

[4] The dataset and variable definitions are available from the authors on request. The empirical analysis is carried out in OxMetrics v.7.1 using the Cointegration Analysis of Time Series (CATS) package v.3C.

3.2. The I(2) Cointegrated VAR Model

We formulate the $I(2)$ CVAR model in terms of acceleration rates, changes and levels (see Juselius (2007)), and use the maximum likelihood parametrization introduced by Johansen (1997). The model is shown here with $k = 2$ lags to simplify the presentation

$$\begin{aligned}\Delta^2 x_t &= \alpha\left(\beta' x_{t-1} + d'\Delta x_{t-1}\right) + \zeta\tau'\Delta x_{t-1} \\ &\quad + \mu_0 + \mu_1 t + \Phi_s D_{s,t} + \Phi_p D_{p,t} + \Phi_{tr} D_{tr,t} + \epsilon_t \\ \epsilon_t &\sim N_p(0,\Omega), \qquad t = 1,\ldots,T.\end{aligned} \tag{17}$$

Here α is a $p \times r$ matrix of adjustment coefficients, β is a $p \times r$ matrix describing long-run relationships among the variables, p is the dimension of the data vector, r is the number of multicointegration relations, s_1 is the number of cointegration relations that only become stationary by differencing, s_2 is the number of stochastic $I(2)$ trends, and $p = r + s_1 + s_2$. Moreover, $d = -((\alpha'\Omega^{-1}\alpha)^{-1}\alpha'\Omega^{-1}\Gamma)\tau_\perp(\tau_\perp'\tau_\perp)^{-1}\tau_\perp'$ is a $p \times r$ matrix of coefficients, where $\Gamma = -(\alpha d' + \zeta\tau')$. The d matrix is determined such that $(\beta' x_{t-1} + d'\Delta x_{t-1}) \sim I(0)$. Additionally, $\tau = [\beta, \beta_{\perp 1}]$ is a $(p+1) \times (r + s_1)$ matrix which describe stationary relationships among the differenced variables, where $\beta_{\perp 1}$ is the orthogonal complement of $[\beta, \beta_{\perp 2}]$. Finally, ζ is a $p \times (p - s_2)$ matrix of restricted medium-run adjustment coefficients. We follow Rahbek et al. (1999) and restrict the constant term to be in $d'\Delta x_{t-1}$ and the deterministic trend to be in $\beta' x_{t-1}$.

3.3. Lag Length Selection

Given the data vector defined in Equation (16) for the period 1971:Q1–2015:Q3 we determine the appropriate number of lags and deterministic components required to obtain a sufficiently well-specified model. First, we choose the lag length by starting with a model with $k = 4$ lags and then reduce the number of lags by removing one at a time until a LM-test is rejected and the Schwarz, Hannan-Quinn and Akaike information criteria are minimized (these are given in Table A1 in Appendix A). Based on this procedure, we choose the lag length $k = 2$. Secondly, fitting the CVAR model commonly requires a number of deterministic components to obtain a sufficiently well-specified model, e.g., shift, permanent, and/or transitory dummies. These components become necessary when the structure captured by the unrestricted VAR model falls short of explaining large movements in the data. Such a large movement could for instance be the enactment of a political reform, which changes the institutional features of the economy, or it could be a natural event affecting the economy.

3.4. Dummy Specification

We follow the method of Juselius (2007, chp. 6.6) to determine which dummies to include. This approach is based on the sequential identification of large outliers (defined as a standardized residual greater than 3.5) until a sufficiently well-specified model has been obtained. In an iterative manner, we include one dummy at a time to investigate if the specified dummy results in a well-specified model. Following this method, our final specification includes six permanent intervention dummies,[5] two transitory dummies, and three centered quarterly dummies to control for seasonality at the quarterly frequency. We specify the dummies as follows (omitting seasonal dummies)

$$D_s' = \mathbf{0}\,,\; D_p' = \left[D_{p75:1,t}\; D_{p82:1,t}\; D_{p83:1,t}\; D_{p87:1,t}\; D_{p93:1,t}\; D_{p93:3,t}\right] \text{ and } D_{tr}' = \left[D_{tr00:1,t}\; D_{tr08:1,t}\right]. \tag{18}$$

[5] In this specification there are still two large outliers remaining; 1972 Q2 and 1994 Q1, respectively. We have chosen not to include dummies for these outliers as this re-introduces residual autocorrelation. We find that including additional dummies does not produce a better model specification than the one presented here.

Reassuringly, most of the dummies coincide with economic events that we would not expect to be captured by the structure of the unrestricted VAR model. The dummies $D_{p75:1,t}$ and $D_{p83:1,t}$ are included to reduce skewness in c_t; the latter is included due to a big drop in the interest rate following the transition to a fixed exchange rate regime in 1983, whereas the former accounts for a correction from a spike in interest rates in 1975 following turbulence in the money market. The dummy $D_{p87:1,t}$ accounts for the tax reform enacted that year, which is significant in both c_t and $p_{h,t}$. The dummy $D_{p93:3,t}$ is included to correct for a large outlier in $p_{b,t}$ in the third quarter of 1993, which coincides with the abolishment of mixed loans. The dummy, $D_{tr00:1,t}$, accounts for the December storm of 1999, which caused a rise and a drop in Δh_t. The final dummy, $D_{tr08:1,t}$ accounts for the initial shocks of the financial crisis which caused a large transitory shock to Δh_t. As a robustness measure, we have also estimated the model without any dummies (included in Appendix B), where we are able to retrace the main conclusions from the analysis.

3.5. Misspecification Tests

Once the lag length and deterministic components have been chosen, we examine if the assumption on IID multivariate normality of the model innovations holds. To this end, we present a selection of common misspecification tests for the unrestricted VAR(2) in Table 1.

Table 1. Misspecification tests for the unrestricted VAR(2) model.

Multivariate Tests					
No-autocorrelation	LM(1)	$\chi^2(25) = 34.46$	$p = 0.10$		
	LM(2)	$\chi^2(25) = 24.82$	$p = 0.47$		
Normality	Doornik-Hansen	$\chi^2(10) = \mathbf{90.16}$	$p = 0.00$		
No-ARCH	LM(1)	$\chi^2(225) = \mathbf{481.45}$	$p = 0.00$		
	LM(2)	$\chi^2(450) = \mathbf{721.72}$	$p = 0.00$		
Univariate Tests					
	$\Delta^2 p_{c,t}$	$\Delta^2 p_{b,t}$	$\Delta^2 p_{h,t}$	$\Delta^2 c_t$	$\Delta^3 h_t$
No-ARCH	**17.34** [0.00]	3.06 [0.22]	3.52 [0.17]	**30.13** [0.00]	**24.77** [0.00]
Skewness	−0.25	0.22	0.01	−0.29	0.37
Kurtosis	4.85	5.55	4.19	4.33	4.68
Normality	**20.67** [0.00]	**33.95** [0.00]	**11.54** [0.00]	**27.14** [0.00]	**21.18** [0.00]
R^2	63%	54%	57%	58%	48%

Notes: Bold font indicates that the hypothesis is rejected at the 5% significance level. Graphical representations of the residual analysis can be found in Figure A2 in Appendix A. We use the multivariate tests for ARCH-effects and autocorrelation presented in Godfrey (1988) and the univariate and multivariate normality test from Doornik and Hansen (2008). The p-values for the univariate tests are shown in square brackets.

The hypotheses of no residual autocorrelation of order 1 and 2 are not rejected, which is necessary for a model to be dynamically complete. The residuals for the construction costs, $p_{b,t}$, and housing price, $p_{h,t}$, show no signs of ARCH effects. However, the residuals for the consumer price index, $p_{c,t}$, the user cost rate, c_t, and the net investments, Δh_t, do not pass the no-ARCH test. The ARCH effects in the consumer prices, $p_{c,t}$, may in part be attributed to the regime change in 1983, before which there were higher, more volatile price changes than after. The inference is robust to moderate ARCH effects, cf. Rahbek et al. (2002) and Cavaliere et al. (2010), and as such the presence ARCH effects should not invalidate inference based on our unrestricted VAR model. We note that the presence of ARCH effects is likely to contribute to excess kurtosis, and as such it is not surprising that the univariate tests of non-normality are rejected primarily due to excess kurtosis. Non-normality due to skewness is, on the other hand, a concern for inference, cf. Juselius (2007, chp. 4.3). That said, not much skewness remains in the residuals, indicating that the rejection of normality is not sufficient to invalidate inference. In sum, considering that the unrestricted VAR model is only misspecified in terms of ARCH effects and kurtosis-induced non-normality, to which the inference is robust, and given that inclusion of further dummies does not resolve these issues, we conclude that this specification constitutes an appropriate basis for further analysis.

3.6. Rank Determination

Given our sufficiently well-specified unrestricted VAR model, we proceed to determine the appropriate reduced ranks of the Π and Γ matrices. Similar to the $I(1)$ analysis, exploring whether $x_t \sim I(1)$ is facilitated by the reduced rank hypothesis $\Pi = \alpha\beta'$, implicitly assuming that Γ is full rank. Examining whether $x_t \sim I(2)$ is facilitated by the additional reduced rank hypothesis $\alpha'_{\perp}\Gamma\beta_{\perp} = \xi\eta'$, where $\alpha_{\perp}$ and $\beta_{\perp}$ are the orthogonal complements of α and β, respectively. The determination of the reduced rank indices is based on the maximum likelihood trace test procedure proposed by Bohn Nielsen and Rahbek (2007).[6] As an alternative to the analytical distribution of the rank test, one can also use critical values from a bootstrap procedure, which is outlined for the $I(1)$ model in Cavaliere et al. (2012). We refrain from using the bootstrap procedure here, as the asymptotic properties have not been shown for the $I(2)$ model yet.

Table 2 presents the $I(2)$ trace tests for rank r equal to 2 and 3, as well as the modulus of the six largest characteristic roots of the model. The trace test starts with the most restricted model $\{r = 0,\ s_1 = 0,\ s_2 = 5\}$, recalling that s_2 is the number of $I(2)$ trends, and proceeds until a reduced rank specification not rejected, and is nested in models that are also not rejected. The most restricted model we show in Table 2 is $\{r = 2,\ s_1 = 0,\ s_2 = 3\}$. The models become less and less restricted as the table is read row-wise.

Table 2. Determination of the two rank indices.

Rank Test Statistics						
$p - r$	r	$s_2 = 4$	$s_2 = 3$	$s_2 = 2$	$s_2 = 1$	$s_2 = 0$
3	2		134.9 [0.00]	69.8 [0.05]	55.2 [0.04]	53.4 [0.00]
2	3			44.3 [0.13]	28.6 [0.23]	23.2 [0.10]
Six Largest Roots						
Unrestricted VAR	0.98	0.94	0.92	0.92	0.65	0.42
Case 1: $r = 2$						
$r = 2, s_1 = 1, s_2 = 2$	1.00	1.00	1.00	1.00	1.00	0.47
$r = 2, s_1 = 2, s_2 = 1$	1.00	1.00	1.00	1.00	0.79	0.51
$r = 2, s_1 = 3, s_2 = 0$	1.00	1.00	1.00	0.99	0.79	0.51
Case 2: $r = 3$						
$r = 3, s_1 = 0, s_2 = 2$	1.00	1.00	1.00	1.00	0.66	0.53
$r = 3, s_1 = 1, s_2 = 1$	1.00	1.00	1.00	0.87	0.72	0.51
$r = 3, s_1 = 2, s_2 = 0$	1.00	1.00	0.98	0.88	0.65	0.52

Note: The p-values for the $I(2)$ rank test are given in square brackets below the test result.

The trace test suggests either $\{r = 2,\ s_1 = 1,\ s_2 = 2\}$ or $\{r = 3,\ s_1 = 0,\ s_2 = 2\}$. The first specification is borderline rejected (p-value of 4.6%), and it is nested in two models that are rejected (p-values of 4.0% and 0.0% respectively). The second specification is not rejected (p-value of 12.6%) and is nested in models that are also not rejected. Both specifications leave no large characteristic roots; the largest remaining root has modulus 0.47 and 0.66, respectively, indicating no residual unit roots. The first specification points to five unit roots, whereas the second specification points to four

[6] Earlier work on $I(2)$ rank tests include Rahbek et al. (1999) and Johansen (1995). Work on the distribution for the $I(2)$ rank test include Doornik (1998) and Johansen (1996).

unit roots. The modulus of the unrestricted VAR points to four unit roots, corresponding to the second specification.

Taking this into account, we proceed with the second specification, as the rank test is not rejected nor nested in models which are rejected. Moreover, there is significant error correction and stationarity in all cointegrating relations (we return to this point in Section 3.8). The chosen specification implies two stochastic $I(2)$ trends ($s_2 = 2$) and three polynomially cointegrating relations ($r = 3$), $\beta' x_t + d'\Delta x_t$, which achieve stationarity.

3.7. Hypothesis Testing

Before identifying a long-run structure, we examine if certain variables, or linear combinations of variables, relating to the UANA condition outlined in Equations (13)–(15), are found to be $I(1)$. This is done by estimating the CVAR under the reduced rank conditions, $\{r = 3,\ s_1 = 0,\ s_2 = 2\}$, also using the numerical maximum likelihood procedure outlined by Johansen (1997). Following the estimation, we impose restrictions on the $\tau = [\beta, \beta_{\perp 1}]$ vectors (see Johansen (2006, Proposition II)). This lets us examine the persistency properties of the different variables in the information set and allows us to examine how the UANA condition outlined in Section 2.4 may hold.

First, we examine if any of the variables are $I(1)$, by imposing restrictions on one τ vector. The test results are displayed in the upper half of Table 3 and we note all variables seem to be driven by one or more $I(2)$ trends, as all the hypotheses are rejected. This indicates that c_t, $p_{h,t}$, and $p_{b,t}$ are driven by $I(2)$ trends, and that they may cointegrate from $I(2)$ to $I(1)$ to form the right hand side of the UANA condition in Equation (15).

Table 3. Hypotheses.

Hypothesis	Test Statistic	*p*-Value
$p_{c,t} \sim I(1)$	$\chi^2(3) = \mathbf{21.83}$	$p = 0.00$
$p_{b,t} \sim I(1)$	$\chi^2(3) = \mathbf{21.17}$	$p = 0.00$
$p_{h,t} \sim I(1)$	$\chi^2(3) = \mathbf{14.86}$	$p = 0.00$
$c_t \sim I(1)$	$\chi^2(3) = \mathbf{15.31}$	$p = 0.00$
$\Delta h_t \sim I(1)$	$\chi^2(3) = \mathbf{14.47}$	$p = 0.00$
Long-run price homogeneity	$\chi^2(4) = \mathbf{25.57}$	$p = 0.00$
$p_{b,t} - p_{c,t} \sim I(1)$	$\chi^2(2) = \mathbf{9.28}$	$p = 0.01$
$p_{h,t} - p_{c,t} \sim I(1)$	$\chi^2(2) = \mathbf{11.49}$	$p = 0.00$
$p_{h,t} - p_{b,t} \sim I(1)$	$\chi^2(2) = \mathbf{10.14}$	$p = 0.01$
$c_t + \sigma(p_{h,t} - p_{b,t}) \sim I(1)$	$\chi^2(1) = 0.30$	$p = 0.58$

Note: We allow for a restricted trend in the lower half of the table. Bold font indicates that the hypothesis is rejected at the 5% significance level.

Next, by imposing restrictions on multiple τ vectors, we examine if any linear combinations of the variables in x_t are $I(1)$. The test results are shown in the bottom half of Table 3. The first test is a joint test for long-run price homogeneity; that is, we test whether $p_{b,t} - p_{c,t} \sim I(1)$ and $p_{h,t} - p_{c,t} \sim I(1)$ hold jointly. The nominal price indices would then share the same nominal $I(2)$ trend, while the real house and construction prices would be $I(1)$, which corresponds to classical dichotomy holding in the long-run, cf. Kongsted (2005). However, the joint test for long-run price homogeneity is rejected with a test statistic of $\chi^2(4) = 25.57$ and a p-value of practically zero. Testing the hypothesis for $p_{b,t} - p_{c,t} \sim I(1)$ returns a test statistic of $\chi^2(2) = 9.28$ with a p-value of $p = 0.01$, which we reject at a 5% critical level. The hypothesis for $p_{h,t} - p_{c,t} \sim I(1)$ is rejected with a test statistic of $\chi^2(2) = 11.49$ and a p-value of practically zero. The hypothesis for $p_{h,t} - p_{b,t} \sim I(1)$ corresponds to the second scenario for the UANA condition, given in Equation (14). In this scenario $p_{h,t} - p_{b,t}$ would cointegrate from $I(2)$ to $I(1)$, which could cointegrate with c_t and $\Delta p_{h,t}$ to stationarity. This scenario is based on the premise that $c_t \sim I(1)$, which we have already rejeced, and we likewise reject the test for $p_{h,t} - p_{b,t} \sim I(1)$ with a test statistic of $\chi^2(2) = 10.14$ and the p-value of $p = 0.01$. Therefore, the hypothesis for the UANA condition in Equation (14) is rejected.

The final hypothesis test corresponds to the third scenario for the UANA condition in Section 2.4, seen in Equation (15). Given the premises that $c_t \sim I(2)$, $p_{h,t} - p_{b,t} \sim I(2)$, and $\Delta p_{h,t} \sim I(1)$, we may still find that there is cointegration between the user cost rate and the relation for Tobin's q expressed in the price indices. The test for whether $c_t + \sigma(p_{h,t} - p_{b,t}) \sim I(1)$ is not rejected with a p-value of $p = 0.58$. Based on this test, it appears that there is support for the UANA condition proposed in Equation (15). However, we still have to establish that $c_t + \sigma(p_{h,t} - p_{b,t})$ cointegrates with $\Delta p_{h,t}$ from $I(1)$ to $I(0)$ for the UANA condition in Equation (15) not to be rejected by the data.

We are now ready to specify an over-identified long-run structure. This will allow us to investigate if the UANA condition in Equation (15) holds empirically, and we may examine if the equilibrium-correcting behavior of the UANA condition can explain the long-swings dynamic in the housing prices introduced in Section 1.

3.8. An Over-Identified Long-Run Structure

For the chosen rank specification, $\{r = 3,\ s_1 = 0,\ s_2 = 2\}$, there will be three polynomially cointegrating relations, $\beta_i' x_t + d_i' \Delta x_t$ for $i = 1, 2, 3$, but no stationary medium-run relations in the growth rates, $\beta'_{\perp 1} \Delta x_t$, due to no cointegration in the differences, $s_1 = 0$. We impose over-identifying restrictions on β' by testing reduced rank hypotheses on $\Pi = \alpha\beta'$ in a fashion parallel to that of an $I(1)$ analysis. We obtain an identified long-run structure by first imposing the UANA condition from Section 2.4. The UANA condition in itself is is not rejected, and we identify the second and third cointegrating relations by applying an inductive approach, in which we restrict a single variable at a time until we cannot restrict the system further.

The data lends support to a relation between the user cost rate, c_t, the price of construction, $p_{b,t}$, and the price of housing, $p_{h,t}$, in line with Equation (15); a relation between the net housing investments, Δh_t, the price of construction, $p_{b,t}$, and the price of housing, $p_{h,t}$; and a relation between the net housing investments, Δh_t, the consumer price level, $p_{c,t}$, and the user cost rate, c_t. We determine the over-identified long-run structure to be

$$\begin{bmatrix} \beta_1' \\ \beta_2' \\ \beta_3' \end{bmatrix} = \begin{bmatrix} 0 & \beta_{12} & -\beta_{12} & \beta_{14} & 0 & \beta_{16} \\ 0 & \beta_{22} & \beta_{23} & 0 & \beta_{25} & \beta_{26} \\ \beta_{31} & 0 & 0 & \beta_{34} & \beta_{35} & \beta_{36} \end{bmatrix}, \tag{19}$$

with the test statistic $\chi^2(1) = 0.30$, corresponding to $p = 0.58$. The cointegrating relations are shown graphically in Figures 2 and 3. We return to the intuition of this specification in the interpretations of the cointegrating relations in Section 3.9.

Imposing the identification scheme on the $I(2)$ model in Equation (17) results in the estimated long-run structure presented in Table 4. The asymptotic distribution of the standard errors for β are derived in Johansen (1997) and the standard errors for d are calculated using the delta method in Doornik (2016). Unfortunately, we are unable to test joint restrictions on the elements in d, which prevents us from assessing whether we can reduce the presence of first differences further.[7]

[7] An anonymous referee kindly made us aware of a recently published alternative identification scheme, which allows for more restrictions in the over-identified long-run structure, cf. Mosconi and Paruolo (2017). Unfortunately, this procedure has not yet been implemented in the software at our disposal, but it is of interest for future research.

Table 4. An identified long-run structure in β.

	$p_{c,t}$	$p_{b,t}$	$p_{h,t}$	c_t	Δh_t	Det $^{a)}$
β_1'	0.000 [–]	0.025 [10.2]	−0.025 [−10.2]	1.000 [–]	0.000 [–]	6.28×10^{-4} [12.4]
d_1'	−0.077 [−0.5]	0.073 [0.7]	0.683 [6.8]	0.016 [3.8]	0.009 [2.3]	−0.187 [−24.3]
α_1	−0.473 [−0.6]	10.500 [4.9]	10.600 [5.0]	−0.776 [−2.6]	−0.196 [−3.6]	
β_2'	0.000 [–]	0.030 [21.0]	−0.017 [−21.0]	0.000 [–]	1.000 [–]	3.97×10^{-5} [2.1]
d_2'	0.357 [8.6]	0.260 [9.3]	0.050 [1.9]	−0.005 [−5.2]	−0.007 [−7.0]	−0.013 [−4.5]
α_2	−0.487 [−0.4]	−15.500 [−5.2]	−15.700 [−5.3]	1.160 [2.8]	0.255 [3.4]	
β_3'	0.012 [13.2]	0.000 [–]	0.000 [–]	−0.535 [−89.6]	1.000 [–]	-3.04×10^{-3} [−13.6]
d_3'	0.321 [4.6]	0.160 [3.4]	−0.353 [−8.2]	−0.013 [−7.5]	−0.011 [−6.3]	0.090 [26.2]
α_3	−1.240 [−0.9]	18.700 [4.9]	19.300 [5.1]	−1.230 [−2.3]	−0.346 [−3.6]	

Notes: t-statistics are given in brackets below the estimate. $a)$ A restricted trend is included in β' and a restricted constant in d'.

3.9. Interpreting the Long-Run Structure

We interpret a polynomially cointegrating relation as a dynamic equilibrium the same way as Juselius (2007): if $x_t \sim I(2)$, then $\beta' x_t \sim I(1)$ and we can interpret it as an equilibrium error with a high degree of persistence. This means that we can interpret α and d as two levels of equilibrium correction: α describes how the acceleration rates, $\Delta^2 x_t$, adjust to the dynamic equilibrium relations, $\beta' x_t + d' \Delta x_t$, and d describes how the growth rates, Δx_t, adjust to the long-run equilibrium error, $\beta' x_t$ (i.e., describing a medium-run adjustment, conditional on $\alpha \neq 0$). We say that a variable $x_{j,t}$, for $j = 1, 2, \ldots, 5$, is equilibrium error correcting in the long run if $\alpha_{ij}\beta_{ij} < 0$ and/or $\alpha_{ij} d_{ij} < 0$, and it is error correcting in the medium run if $d_{ij}\beta_{ij} > 0$. If we reverse the inequalities, the system is equilibrium error increasing. It is of particular interest that a variable can be error correcting in the long run ($\alpha_{ij}\beta_{ij} < 0$), while being error increasing in the medium run ($d_{ij}\beta_{ij} < 0$), or vice versa. This type of interplay between long-run and medium-run dynamics can lead to persistent swings around the long-run equilibrium, which we refer to as "long-swings dynamics" in line with Juselius and Assenmacher (2016, Section 5).

We translate the parameter estimates in Table 4 into three univariate equations, which govern the long-run error-correction mechanisms of the system, i.e., the cointegrating relations. These can be rearranged to facilitate interpretation. We do this in the following subsections.

3.9.1. The Uncertainty-Adjusted No-Arbitrage Condition

We interpret the first of the three cointegrating relations in terms of the uncertainty-adjusted no-arbitrage condition presented in Section 2.4, specifically Equation (15). The first cointegrating relation is given by

$$0.025 p_{b,t} - 0.025 p_{h,t} + c_t + 6.28 \times 10^{-4} t + 0.683 \Delta p_{h,t} + 0.016 \Delta c_t + 0.009 \Delta^2 h_t + 0.187 \sim I(0), \quad (20)$$

where we include the levels from β_1' and first differences from d_1' that are significant at the 95% critical level. We rearrange the terms in Equation (20) to relate it to the UANA condition in Equation (15):

$$\begin{aligned} \Delta p_{h,t} = & -1.464 c_t + 0.037 (p_{h,t} - p_{b,t}) \\ & - 0.013 \Delta^2 h_t - 0.023 \Delta c_t + 0.274 - 6.28 \times 10^{-4} t + u_{1,t}, \end{aligned} \quad (21)$$

where $u_{1,t} \sim I(0)$ denotes the stationary error component. As suggested by the uncertainty-based asset price approach presented in Section 2.3, the price level of housing, $p_{h,t}$, and the cost of construction, $p_{b,t}$, enter with the same coefficient and opposite sign to form Tobin's q. The user cost rate, c_t, is also present but enters with a negative coefficient. Based on asset pricing theory the user cost rate, c_t, should have entered with a positive coefficient as it represents the carry, or opportunity cost, of buying the asset. We may attempt to understand the negative coefficient on c_t by the dynamic that, in practice, a higher user cost rate would make housing less affordable, which in turn would preclude some investors from entering the housing market as they will be able to borrow less, all else equal. In addition to the levels predicted by the theory, we also find that the changes in net housing investments, $\Delta^2 h_t$, and the user cost rate Δc_t are significant.

As such, we reject the exact specification of the UANA condition as it is presented in Equation (15), noting that the primary implication from the original framework resulting in Equation (2) appears to be inconsistent with the data. However, we do find that realized changes in the price of housing, $\Delta p_{h,t}$, are positively related to Tobin's q. This is in support of the contribution made to the theory by specifying the uncertainty premium in terms of a gap effect. That said, while there are more terms present in Equation (21) than predicted, the cointegrating relation does indicate that the UANA condition in Equation (15) provides an empirically relevant characterization of the price formation in the Danish housing market over the period under consideration.

Turning our attention to the medium- and long-term dynamics, the α_1 and d_1' coefficients reveal that the price of housing, $p_{h,t}$, is strongly error correcting in the long run with respect to this cointegrating relation, but the d' coefficient suggests that the change in the price of housing, $\Delta p_{h,t}$, is error increasing in the medium run. This dynamic implies that the price of housing is prone to overshooting its long-term equilibrium level given by Equation (21). This type of overshooting is consistent with momentum-based forecasting behavior. That is, if investors base their expectations on recent price changes, then the persistence in the realized price changes will increase, cf. e.g., Shiller (2008), leading to overshooting behavior in the medium run. We return to this point in Section 3.10. We also note that the construction price index, $p_{b,t}$, is error increasing in the long run, and the change in the housing stock, Δh_t is (borderline) error correcting in the long run. Finally, the user cost rate, c_t, is (borderline) error correcting in both the medium- and long run. Moreover, graphical inspection of the cointegrating relation in the sample reveals that the relation is stationary and it exhibits relatively little persistence, see Figure 2.

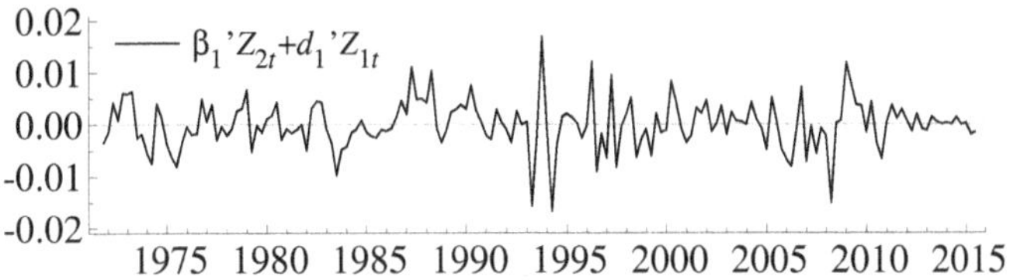

Figure 2. The first cointegration relation, see Equation (21).

3.9.2. Net Housing Investments

We interpret the second and third cointegrating relations as characterizing the long-run equilibrium of net housing investments. These relations are not implied by our theoretical framework in Section 2, instead we have identified them inductively by imposing zero restrictions on the long-run structure. In the Equations (22) and (23), we include the levels from β' and differences from d' that are significant at the 95% critical level.

The second of the three cointegrating relations is given by,

$$\begin{aligned}\Delta h_t = &+0.017(p_{h,t} - p_{b,t}) - 0.013p_{b,t} \\ &- 0.357\Delta p_{c,t} - 0.260\Delta p_{b,t} + 0.005\Delta c_t + 0.007\Delta^2 h_t \\ &+ 0.010 - 3.97 \times 10^{-5} t + u_{2,t},\end{aligned} \tag{22}$$

where $u_{2,t} \sim I(0)$ denotes the stationary error component. We interpret Equation (22) as characterizing the net housing investment in equilibrium as approximately proportional to Tobin's q. The levels of the variables $\{p_{h,t}, p_{b,t}, \Delta h_t\}$ cointegrate from $I(2)$ to $I(1)$, and in turn with the significant first-differences, $\{\Delta p_{c,t}, \Delta p_{b,t}, \Delta c_t, \Delta^2 h_t\}$, from $I(1)$ to $I(0)$ to achieve stationarity. While $p_{h,t}$ and $p_{b,t}$ do not enter with the same coefficient, they are of roughly the same magnitude and enter with opposite signs. The α_2 and d_2' coefficients reveal that the net housing investments, Δh_t, exhibits error-increasing behavior with respect to this cointegrating relation in both the long and medium run. If there is a positive deviation from the cointegrating relation as a result of Tobin's q being above unity, then we would expect this to cause the net investments to increase. We note that the price level of housing, $p_{h,t}$, is error increasing with respect to the this cointegrating relation in the long run. On the other hand, the price index of building costs, $p_{b,t}$, is error correcting in both the long and medium run. Finally, the user cost, c_t is (borderline) error correcting in the long run. Figure 3a shows this cointegrating relation.

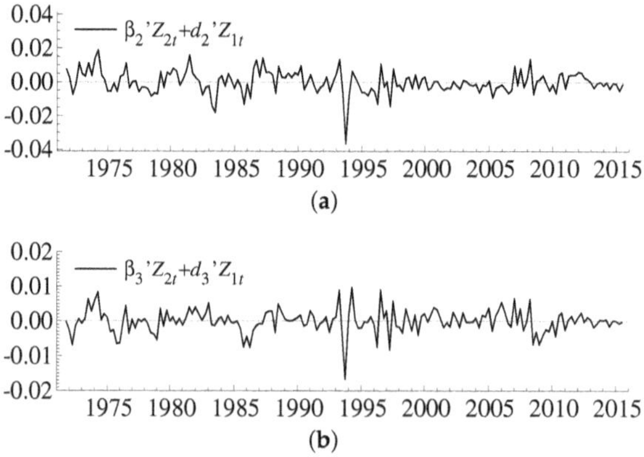

Figure 3. The second and third cointegration relations. (**a**) The second cointegration relation, see Equation (22). (**b**) The third cointegration relation, see Equation (23).

The third and final cointegration relation is a linear combination of the housing prices, $p_{c,t}$, the building costs, $p_{b,t}$, and the net investment in housing, Δh_t, which cointegrate to cancel out the $I(2)$ trends, and in turn cointegrate with the first differences to $I(0)$. The cointegrating relation is given by,

$$\begin{aligned}\Delta h_t = &- 0.012p_{c,t} + 0.535c_t \\ &- 0.321\Delta p_{c,t} - 0.160\Delta p_{b,t} + 0.353\Delta p_{h,t} + 0.013\Delta c_t + 0.011\Delta^2 h_t \\ &- 0.090 + 3.04 \times 10^{-3} t + u_{3,t},\end{aligned} \tag{23}$$

where $u_{3,t} \sim I(0)$ denotes the stationary error component. Equation (23) is somewhat difficult to interpret in isolation. Considering the error-correcting properties, α_3 and d_3' reveal that the housing investments, Δh_t, error correct in the long run, and error increases in the medium run with respect to this cointegrating relation. Furthermore, the user cost rate, c_t is error increasing in the long run, and error correcting in the medium run. Intuitively, if the user cost rate rises above its long-run value relative to the housing investments, we expect a negative effect on the housing investments, as a higher user cost rate will discourage investments. Finally, the construction price index, $p_{b,t}$, is error increasing in the long run, while the house price index, $p_{h,t}$, error corrects in the long run. Figure 3b shows this cointegrating relation.

3.10. Summary of Empirical Findings

In summary, we find strong evidence in support of the housing price, as well as remaining variables in our information set, defined in Equation (16), being integrated of order two, i.e., highly persistent. Moreover, we strongly reject that the $I(2)$ dynamics can be appropriately accounted for by simply transforming to real variables, i.e., we reject long-run price homogeneity. Rather, we find that the uncertainty-adjusted no-arbitrage (UANA) condition, given in Equation (15), provides an empirically relevant characterization of the long-run house price equilibrium. Furthermore, the error-correction dynamics estimated via the cointegrated VAR model can help explain the long-swings behavior in the housing price, observed in Figure 1.

On the last point, it is instructive to construct an informal example of how long-swings behavior associated with the cointegrating relation in Equation (21) relates to our theoretical framework in Section 2 in combination with momentum-based forecasting. Suppose that, at some point in time, the expected future price change is greater than the sum of the current user cost rate and the uncertainty premium; that is, there is arbitrage according to the UANA condition in Equation (12). Investors will then respond by buying housing, pushing the housing price up in the process, which increases Tobin's q (all else equal), and in turn the required uncertainty premium in the next quarter.

This pattern may continue quarter after quarter until Tobin's q has been increased to the point where the expected price change for the next quarter is less than or equal to the sum of the user cost rate and the uncertainty premium. Given the momentum in the price of housing and individual forecasts, the result can be a persistent swing upwards in the price until the required uncertainty premium has become too large relative to investors' expectations of the price change in the next quarter. At this point, further price increases will result in overshooting relative to the long-run equilibrium as well as further increases in the uncertainty premium. In this situation there is also arbitrage, but in the other direction, which will lead to investors selling housing. In turn, the momentum in housing prices will decrease, or even turn (all else equal), and the process will go into reverse. The result is in this case a persistent swing downwards in the price of housing until the required uncertainty premium has become small enough for investors to find housing attractive again relative to their expectations of future price changes.

In practice, all else is not equal, and changes in the user cost rate, building costs, and housing investments will also affect the price of housing. For example, if Tobin's q is greater than unity then the housing stock is smaller than what is demanded by investors, and so net investments will increase to generate profit from the discrepancy between the price at which housing is sold relative to its cost of construction. That is, we would expect a positive association between Tobin's q and net investments, which aligns well with our interpretation of the second cointegration relation in Equation (22).

4. Conclusions

The primary contribution of this paper was to establish that the long-swings behavior observed in the market price of Danish housing since the 1970s can be understood by studying the interplay between short-term expectation formation and long-run equilibrium conditions. We have introduced an asset market model for housing based on uncertainty rather than risk, which under mild assumptions allows for other forms of forecasting behavior than rational expectations. We have tested the theory via an $I(2)$ cointegrated VAR model and found that the long-run equilibrium for the housing price corresponds closely to the predictions from the theoretical framework. Additionally, we have corroborated previous findings that housing markets are well characterized by short-term momentum forecasting behavior. Our conclusions have wider relevance, since housing prices play a role in the wider Danish economy, and other developed economies, through wealth effects. In sum, the CVAR model and the uncertainty-based asset market approach provide a useful framework to analyzing and understanding price formation and net investments in the Danish housing market.

Supplementary Materials: The following are available online at http://www.mdpi.com/2225-1146/5/3/40/s1: the original data from the MONA database, cf. Danmarks Nationalbank (2003), and Ox code to transform the variables into the data vector in Equation (16).

Acknowledgments: We gratefully acknowledge comments by two anonymous referees that have led to substantial improvements of the paper. We also thank the editor, Prof. Katarina Juselius, for constructive feedback, and the assistant editors, Lu Liao and Nancy Zhang, for assisting in the publication process. All errors and omissions are the sole responsibility of the authors.

Author Contributions: The authors contributed jointly to the paper.

Conflicts of Interest: The authors declare no conflict of interest.

Appendix A. Supplementary Material

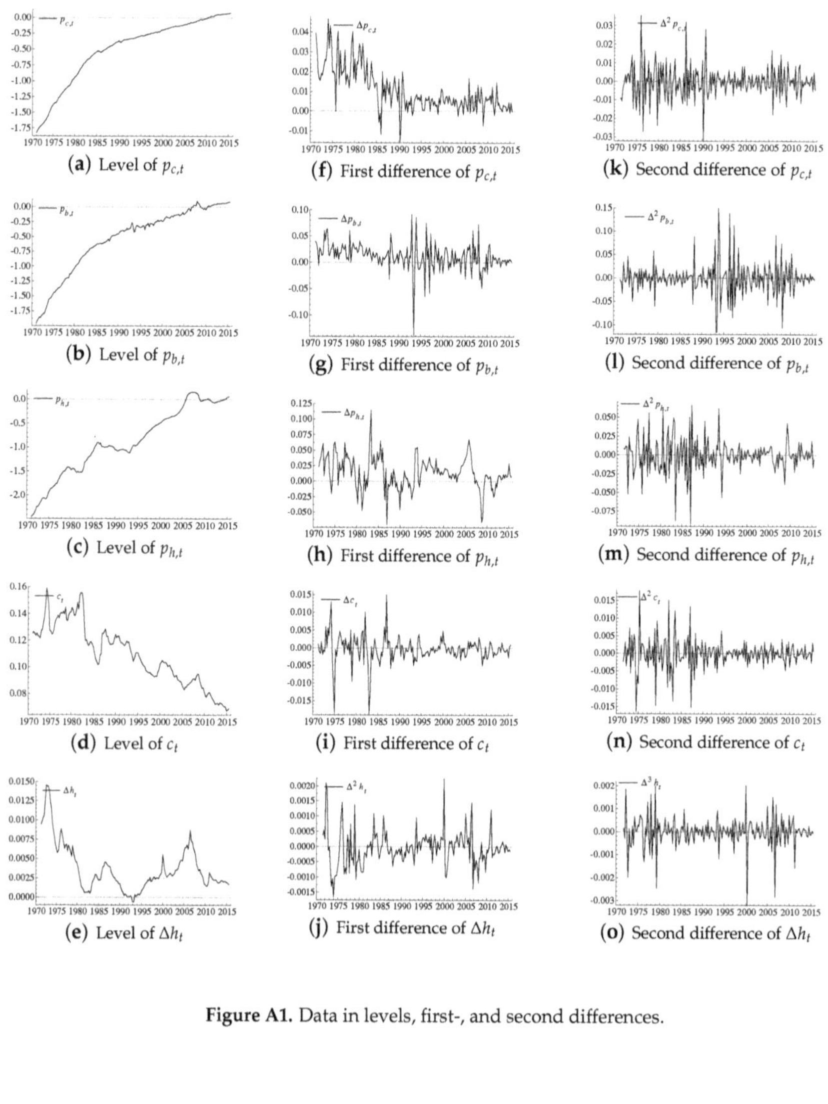

(**a**) Level of $p_{c,t}$; (**b**) Level of $p_{b,t}$; (**c**) Level of $p_{h,t}$; (**d**) Level of c_t; (**e**) Level of Δh_t; (**f**) First difference of $p_{c,t}$; (**g**) First difference of $p_{b,t}$; (**h**) First difference of $p_{h,t}$; (**i**) First difference of c_t; (**j**) First difference of Δh_t; (**k**) Second difference of $p_{c,t}$; (**l**) Second difference of $p_{b,t}$; (**m**) Second difference of $p_{h,t}$; (**n**) Second difference of c_t; (**o**) Second difference of Δh_t

Figure A1. Data in levels, first-, and second differences.

Table A1. Lag-length determination.

Lags	Log-likelihood	SC	HQ	AIC	LM-test
$k = 4$	3406.56	−35.45	−36.80	−37.72	−
$k = 3$	3395.29	−36.06	−37.14	−37.88	$F(25, 540) = 0.77$ [0.79]
$k = 2$	3375.61	−36.58	−37.39	−37.94	$F(50, 664) = 1.08$ [0.34]

Note: The LM-test is nested in $k = 4$. The preferred model minimizes the information criteria.

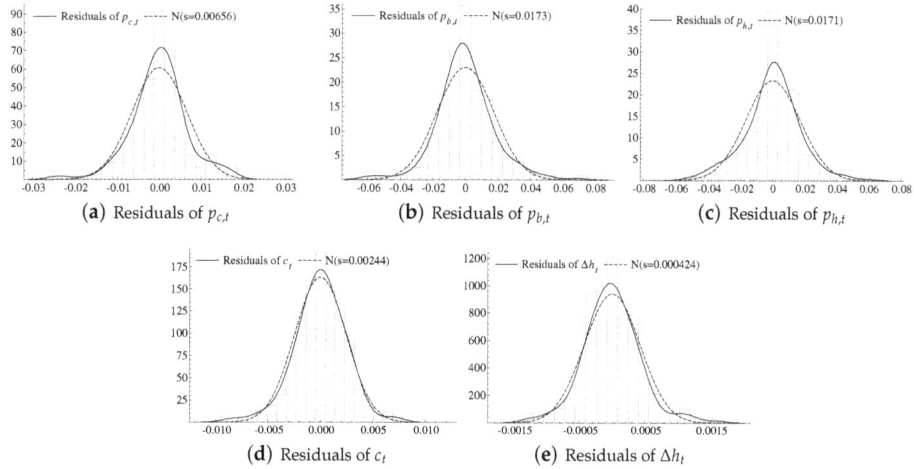

(**a**) Residuals of $p_{c,t}$ (**b**) Residuals of $p_{b,t}$ (**c**) Residuals of $p_{h,t}$

(**d**) Residuals of c_t (**e**) Residuals of Δh_t

Figure A2. Residuals from the unrestricted CVAR model with lag order 2.

Appendix B. Specification without Dummies

The VAR(2) model with no dummies has more traces of ARCH effects, kurtosis and skewness than the specification with dummies, as shown in Table A2. From Table A3 the rank test indicates a rank of $\{r = 4, s_1 = 0, s_2 = 1\}$. We find the same main conclusion, namely that the UANA condition exists in the over-identified long-run structure (which is not rejected, $\chi^2(2) = 0.21$, p-value of 0.90), despite the rank test pointing to a different rank. We also find that there are long swings in the house prices, i.e., the house price is error increasing in the medium run and error correcting in the long run as seen in Table A4.

Table A2. Misspecification tests for the specification with no dummies.

Multivariate tests					
No-autocorrelation	LM(1)	$\chi^2(25) = 26.4$	$p = 0.39$		
	LM(2)	$\chi^2(25) = 28.4$	$p = 0.29$		
Normality	Doornik-Hansen	$\chi^2(10) = \mathbf{238.6}$	$p = 0.00$		
No-ARCH	LM(1)	$\chi^2(225) = \mathbf{341.0}$	$p = 0.00$		
	LM(2)	$\chi^2(450) = \mathbf{630.0}$	$p = 0.00$		
Univariate tests					
	$\Delta^2 p_{c,t}$	$\Delta^2 p_{b,t}$	$\Delta^2 p_{h,t}$	$\Delta^2 c_t$	$\Delta^3 h_t$
No-ARCH	**17.57** [0.00]	**29.19** [0.00]	**9.61** [0.00]	5.75 [0.06]	**16.35** [0.00]
Skewness	−0.21	0.44	−0.26	−0.058	0.87
Kurtosis	4.59	9.15	4.75	7.72	6.05
Normality	**16.88** [0.00]	**107.61** [0.00]	**19.07** [0.00]	**84.71** [0.00]	**25.33** [0.00]
R^2	61%	32%	46%	27%	35%

Notes: Bold font indicates that the hypothesis is rejected at the 5% significance level. We use the multivariate tests for ARCH-effects and autocorrelation presented in Godfrey (1988) and the univariate and multivariate normality test from Doornik and Hansen (2008). The p-values for the univariate tests are shown in square brackets.

Table A3. $I(2)$ rank test for the specification with no dummies.

$p-r$	r	$s_2 = 4$	$s_2 = 3$	$s_2 = 2$	$s_2 = 1$	$s_2 = 0$
2	3			56.1 [0.01]	37.1 [0.03]	30.3 [0.01]
1	4				16.9 [0.13]	7.7 [0.28]

Note: The p-values for the $I(2)$ rank test are given in square brackets.

Table A4. Over-identified long-run structure for the specification with no dummies.

	$p_{c,t}$	$p_{b,t}$	$p_{h,t}$	c_t	Δh_t	$Det^{a)}$
β_1'	0.000	0.028 [7.2]	−0.028 [−7.2]	1.000	0.000	0.001 [15.1]
d_1'	0.393 [6.9]	0.393 [6.9]	0.697 [6.9]	0.009 [7.0]	−0.001 [−7.0]	−0.205 [−25.6]
α_1	−0.533 [−5.0]	0.238 [0.7]	0.532 [1.7]	−0.027 [−0.5]	−0.039 [−5.1]	
β_2'	0.000	0.002 [8.3]	0.000	0.000	1.000	−0.000 [−12.1]
d_2'	−0.117 [−10.5]	−0.117 [−10.5]	−0.208 [−10.5]	−0.003 [−10.5]	0.000 [10.5]	0.009 [8.4]
α_2	−7.610 [−5.7]	0.715 [0.2]	3.310 [0.8]	1.530 [2.4]	−0.377 [−4.0]	
β_3'	0.000	0.000	0.000	0.112 [17.2]	1.000	0.000
d_3'	−0.127 [−11.6]	−0.127 [−11.6]	−0.225 [−11.6]	−0.003 [−11.5]	0.000 [11.5]	−0.001 [−9.3]
α_3	6.540 [6.5]	2.220 [0.7]	0.611 [0.2]	−1.590 [−3.3]	0.220 [3.1]	
β_4'	1.000	-1.000	0.000	0.000	0.000	0.001 [8.8]
d_4'	0.340 [2.3]	0.340 [2.3]	0.603 [2.3]	0.008 [2.3]	−0.001 [−2.3]	−0.153 [−8.1]
α_4	−0.042 [−2.1]	0.385 [6.2]	0.107 [1.8]	−0.010 [−1.1]	−0.004 [−2.9]	

Notes: t-statistics are given in brackets below the estimate. $a)$ A restricted trend is included in β' and a restricted constant in d'.

References

Akerlof, George A., and Robert J. Shiller. 2009. *Animal Spirits: How Human Psychology Drives the Economy, and Why It Matters for Global Capitalism*. Princeton and Oxford: Princeton University Press, pp. 1–248.

Binmore, Ken. 2009. *Rational Decisions (The Gorman Lectures in Economics)*. Princeton and Oxford: Princeton University Press.

Björk, Tomas. 2009. *Arbitrage Theory in Continuous Time*, 3rd ed. Oxford: Oxford University Press, pp. 1–560.

Bohn Nielsen, Heino, and Anders Rahbek. 2007. The Likelihood Ratio Test for Cointegration Ranks in the I(2) Model. *Econometric Theory* 23: 615–37.

Campos, Julia, Neil R. Ericsson, and David F. Hendry. 2005. General-to-Specific Modeling: An Overview and Selected Bibliography. International Finance Discussion Papers No. 838, Board of Governors of the Federal Reserve System, Washington, USA.

Carney, Mark. 2016. Uncertainty, the Economy and Policy. Speech, Bank of England. Available online: http://www.bankofengland.co.uk/publications/Documents/speeches/2016/speech915.pdf (accessed on 31 August 2017).

Case, Karl E., John M. Quigley, and Robert J. Shiller. 2003. Home-buyers, Housing and the Macroeconomy. In *Assets Prices and Monetary Policy*. Edited by Anthony Richards and Tim Robinson. Sydney: Reserve Bank of Australia, pp. 149–88.

Case, Karl E., John M. Quigley, and Robert J. Shiller. 2005. Comparing Wealth Effects: The Stock Market versus the Housing Market. *Advances in Macroeconomics* 5: 1–32.

Case, Karl E., John M. Quigley, and Robert J. Shiller. 2013. Wealth effects revisited: 1978–2009. *Critical Finance Review* 2: 101–28.

Case, Karl E., and Robert J. Shiller. 1989. The Efficiency of the Market for Single-Family Homes. *The American Economic Review* 79: 125–37.

Cavaliere, Giuseppe Cavaliere, Anders Rahbek, and A. M. Robert Taylor. 2010. Cointegration Rank Testing Under Conditional Heteroskedasticity. *Econometric Theory* 26: 1719–60.

Cavaliere, Giuseppe Cavaliere, Anders Rahbek, and A. M. Robert Taylor. 2012. Bootstrap Determination of the Co-Integration Rank in Vector Autoregressive Models. *Econometrica* 80: 1721–40.

Danmarks Nationalbank. 2003. *MONA—En Kvartalsmodel af Dansk Økonomi*. Copenhagen: Danmarks Nationalbank.

Doornik, Jurgen A. 1998. Approximations to the asymptotic distribution of cointegration tests. *Journal of Economic Surveys* 12: 573–93.

Doornik, Jurgen A. 2016. Estimation of the I(2) Model. Institute for Economic Modelling, Oxford Martin School, and Economics Department, University of Oxford, Oxford, UK.

Doornik, Jurgen A., and Henrik Hansen. 2008. An omnibus test for univariate and multivariate normality. *Oxford Bulletin of Economics and Statistics* 70: 927–39.

ECB. 2016. The Impact of Uncertainty on Activity in the Euro Area. ECB Economic Bulletin, European Central Bank, Frankfurt am Main, Germany.

Frydman, Roman, Michael D. Goldberg, and Edmund S. Phelps. 2007. *Imperfect Knowledge Economics: Exchange Rates and Risk*. Princeton and Oxford: Princeton University Press.

Godfrey, L. G. 1988. *Misspecification Tests in Econometrics*. Cambridge: Cambridge University Press.

Hoover, Kevin D., Søren Johansen, and Katarina Juselius. 2008. Allowing the Data to Speak Freely: The Macroeconometrics of the Cointegrated Vector Autoregression. *The American Economic Review* 98: 251–55.

Johansen, Søren. 1995. A statistical analysis of cointegration for I(2) variables. *Econometric Theory* 11: 25–59.

Johansen, Søren. 1996. *Likelihood-Based Inference in Cointegrated Vector Autoregressive Models (Advanced Texts in Econometrics)*. Oxford: Oxford University Press.

Johansen, Søren. 1997. Likelihood analysis of the I(2) model. *Scandinavian Journal of Statistics* 24: 433–62.

Johansen, Søren. 2006. Statistical analysis of hypotheses on the cointegrating relations in the I(2) model. *Journal of Econometrics* 132: 81–115.

Juselius, Katarina. 2007. *The Cointegrated VAR Model: Methodology and Applications (Advanced Texts in Econometrics)*. Oxford: Oxford University Press.

Juselius, Katarina. 2017a. A Theory-Consistent CVAR Scenario for a Standard Monetary Model using Data-Generated Expectations. Discussion Papers, Department of Economics, University of Copenhagen, Copenhagen, Denmark.

Juselius, Katarina. 2017b. Using a Theory-Consistent CVAR Scenario to Test an Exchange Rate Model Based on Imperfect Knowledge. Discussion Papers, Department of Economics, University of Copenhagen, Copenhagen, Denmark.

Juselius, Katarina, and Katrin Assenmacher. 2016. Real Exchange Rate Persistence and the Excess Return Puzzle: The Case of Switzerland Versus the US. Discussion Papers, Department of Economics, University of Copenhagen, Copenhagen, Denmark.

King, Mervyn. 2004. What Fates Impose: Facing up to Uncertainty. Available online: http://www.bankofengland.co.uk/archive/Documents/historicpubs/speeches/2004/speech234.pdf (accessed on 31 August 2017).

Kongsted, Hans Christian. 2005. Testing the nominal-to-real transformation. *Journal of Econometrics* 124: 202–25.

Lawson, Tony. 1988. Probability and Uncertainty in Economic Analysis. *Journal of Post Keynesian Economics* 11: 38–65.

Mellers, Barbara, Lyle Ungar, Jonathan Baron, Jaime Ramos, Burcu Gurcay, Katrina Fincher, Sydney E. Scott, Don Moore, Pavel Atanasov, Samuel A. Swift, and et al. 2014. Psychological strategies for winning a geopolitical forecasting tournament. *Psychological Science* 25: 1106–15.

Mosconi, Rocco, and Paolo Paruolo. 2017. Identification conditions in simultaneous systems of cointegrating equations with integrated variables of higher order. *Journal of Econometrics* 198: 271–76.

Muth, John F. 1961. Rational expectations and the theory of price movements. *Econometrica* 29: 315–35.

Piazzesi, Monika, and Martin Schneider. 2009. Momentum Traders in the Housing Market: Survey Evidence and a Search Model. *American Economic Review* 99: 406–11.

Poterba, James M. 1984. Tax Subsidies to Owner-Occupied Housing: An Asset-Market Approach. *The Quarterly Journal of Economics* 99: 729–52.

Poterba, James M. 1991. House price dynamics: The role of tax policy and demography. *Brookings Papers on Economic Activity* 1991: 143–203.

Rahbek, Anders, Ernst Hansen, and Jonathan G. Dennis. 2002. ARCH Innovations and Their Impact on Cointegration Rank Testing. Working Paper, Centre for Analytical Finance, University of Copenhagen, Copenhagen, Denmark.

Rahbek, Ander, Hans Christian Kongsted, and Clara Jørgensen. 1999. Trend Stationarity in the I(2) Cointegration Model. *Journal of Econometrics* 90: 265–89.

Rutherford, Malcolm. 1984. Rational Expectations and Kenyesian Uncertainty: A critique. *Journal of Post Keynesian Economics* VI: 377–87.

Saez, Emmanuel, and Gabriel Zucman. 2016. Wealth Inequality in the US Since 1913: Evidence from Capitalized Income Data. *The Quarterly Journal of Economics* 131: 519–78.

Sargent, Thomas J., and Neil Wallace. 1975. Rational expectations, the optimal monetary instrument, and the optimal money supply rule. *Journal of Political Economy* 83: 241–54.

Savage, Leonard J. 1951. *The Foundations of Statistics*. New York: Wiley.

Shiller, Robert J. 2008. Understanding Recent Trends in Housing Prices and Home Ownership. In Proceedings of "Housing, Housing Finance and Monetary Policy" Jackson Hole Conference Series, Federal Reserve Bank of Kansas City, Kansas City, USA, pp. 85–123.

Tobin, James. 1969. A General Equilibrium Approach to Monetary Theory. *Journal of Money, Credit and Banking* 1: 15–29.

econometrics

MDPI

Article

Sustainable Financial Obligations and Crisis Cycles

Mikael Juselius [1,*,†] and Moshe Kim [2]

1 Monetary Policy and Research Department, Bank of Finland, P.O. Box 160, FI-00101 Helsinki, Finland
2 Department of Economics, University of Haifa, Mount Carmel, Haifa 31905, Israel; kim@econ.haifa.ac.il
* Correspondence: mikael.juselius@bof.fi; Tel.: +358-50-521-7287
† Disclaimer: the views presented here are the authors' and do not necessarily represent those of the Bank of Finland.

Academic Editors: Katarina Juselius and Marc S. Paolella
Received: 28 February 2017; Accepted: 13 June 2017; Published: 22 June 2017

Abstract: The ability to distinguish between sustainable and excessive debt developments is crucial for securing economic stability. By studying US private sector credit loss dynamics, we show that this distinction can be made based on a measure of the incipient aggregate liquidity constraint, the financial obligations ratio. Specifically, as this variable rises, the interaction between credit losses and the business cycle increases, albeit with different intensity depending on whether the problems originate in the household or the business sector. This occurs 1–2 years before each recession in the sample. Our results have implications for macroprudential policy and countercyclical capital-buffers.

Keywords: debt sustainability; credit losses; financial crises; financial obligations; smooth transition regression; non-linear cointegration

JEL Classification: E32; E44; G01

---

1. Introduction

The concern that private sector debt accumulations can become excessive, threatening both real and financial stability, has gained considerable momentum during the past decade. To assess the importance of such considerations empirically, one must be able to separate sustainable debt developments from excessive buildups. By studying US aggregate credit loss dynamics over the period 1985–2010, we show that the upper limit for sustainable debt developments is determined by the strength of the incipient aggregate liquidity constraint, as measured by the financial obligations ratio. In particular, we find that both household and business sector financial obligations ratios act as regime switching variables. Once they move beyond critical levels, the interaction between business cycle fluctuations and credit losses starts to intensify. This occurs in either the household or the business sector 1–2 years prior to each economic downturn in our sample. The more severe recessions ensue when both sectors are affected simultaneously. In contrast to existing cross-sectional studies on individual episodes of financial distress, we do not find that leverage, as measured by the debt to income ratio, to be informative in this respect. These patterns suggest that increasing liquidity problems associated with excessive aggregate debt accumulations can undermine both real and financial stability.

The idea that credit cycles can be a source of real fluctuations is by now well established in a large body of theoretical work on financial frictions. For instance, Bernanke et al. (1999) show that feedback between firms' net worth and their borrowing opportunities can generate credit booms which result in increased investments. Similarly, by focusing on households, Kiyotaki and Moore (1997) demonstrate that increases in house prices raise the value of collateral available to households, increasing their borrowing opportunities and thereby their consumption spending. In both cases, there is a financial accelerator effect which tends to reinforce the business cycle. More recent contributions along these lines include Kiyotaki and Gertler (2010), and references therein.

While the aforementioned literature is mainly concerned with the amplifying effect of credit on ordinary macroeconomic shocks, there is also a risk that aggregate debt can reach excessive and inefficient levels. For example, Lorenzoni (2008) and Miller and Stiglitz (2010) discuss how self-reinforcing processes between net worth and borrowing can lead to asset price bubbles and excessive leverage under the assumptions that agents have limited commitment in financial contracts or dispersed beliefs. Because banks can have incentives to reduce their lending standards during upturns, the problem may be further exacerbated (Ruckes 2004; Dell'Ariccia and Marquez 2006). When aggregate debt reaches unsustainable levels, debt holders become highly vulnerable to any common negative shock which reduces their net worth, as it constrains their refinancing ability. In such situations, they may attempt to sell off assets and reduce spending to meet their debt obligations. Campello et al. (2010), for instance, document such alterations in behavior among financially constrained firms during the recent financial crisis. However, such actions can be contagious as they tend to reinforce the negative effects of the initial shock, triggering off a self-reinforcing downward spiral which can lead to a severe recession or even a systemic financial crisis (e.g., Gai et al. (2008)).

Theoretical predictions of this type have been lent considerable credibility by empirical studies that find a close association between high aggregate debt to income ratios (leverage) and subsequent credit and output losses[1]. For example, King (1994) documents this type of relationship across countries in connection with the early 1990s recession. More recently, Mian and Sufi (2010) obtain similar results by exploiting US cross-county variation from the recent financial crisis. However, because these studies focus on cross-section variation from individual episodes of financial distress, they tend to overlook the persistent upward trend that has been present in US debt to income ratios for the past 30 years. Because such long-run developments probably impinge on the cross-section in a uniform way, most of the cross-sectional variation will be due to possibly excessive short-run accumulations. If so, this would explain why the past studies find a seemingly close relationship between leverage and losses. The question remains, however: If high aggregate leverage was one of the major factors behind the early 1990s recession, as suggested by King (1994), then how could even higher and increasing debt ratios be sustained during the two following decades?

To make progress, it seems crucial to be able to distinguish between *sustainable* and *excessive* debt developments already from the outset. This is recognized by Borio and Lowe (2002) and Borio and Drehmann (2009) who construct early warning indicators of systemic banking crises based on leverage and asset price gaps. While the indicators perform well both in and out of sample, the gaps are, however, constructed using the Hodrick-Prescott filter rather than motivated by economic rationale. Thus, there is a risk of mistaking sustainable debt developments for excessive buildups. For example, if a credit boom lasts for a long time the filtered trend will eventually catch up, producing a gap which is close to zero or even negative. Similar problems can occur if the true underlying trend in debt-to-income suddenly changes. This suggests that the debt to income ratio should be detrended using economic rather than statistical criteria.

The most likely explanation for the upward trend in leverage during the recent decades is the concurrent decline in real interest rates, documented for example in Caballero et al. (2008), among others. Indeed, the optimal (sustainable) allocation of aggregate debt in a dynamic stochastic environment should vary with changes in the terms of credit (see e.g., Stein (2006)). If this is the case, a more appropriate alternative measure for the burden imposed by private sector indebtedness is given by the financial obligations ratio constructed by the Federal Reserve (see Dynan et al. (2003)). By consisting of interest payments and repayments on debt divided by income, the financial obligations ratio captures the incipient aggregate liquidity constraints of borrowers (Hall 2011). Rising financial obligations, for instance, indicate that borrowers have less leeway to smooth their consumption or make new

[1] Several empirical studies also attempt to quantify the relative importance of the financial accelerator for output fluctuations. See for instance, Gertler and Lown (1999), Meier and Müller (2006), Gilchrist et al. (2009), and references therein.

investments, and are also more vulnerable to income and interest rate shocks. This may not be a problem as long as the business cycle is benign and banks' lending standards are soft. However, when the business cycle turns, the liquidity constraints start to bind for more and more borrowers, forcing them in arrears and ultimately to default, thereby driving up banks' losses.

To investigate this possibility, we compare the ability of the financial obligations ratio for explaining US banking sector credit losses with that of the debt-to-income ratio. Focusing on credit losses instead of output losses also allows us to assess the differential roles that business and household loans play in generating real and financial weakness (see e.g., Iacoviello (2005))[2]. We allow the two debt measures to enter credit loss determination both linearly, in line with the literature on financial accelerators, as well as non-linearly, to capture altered behavior and contagion effects during episodes in which aggregate credit constraints become binding. In the latter case, each debt measure is allowed to enter the empirical model as a regime switching variable which smoothly increases the interaction between credit losses and the business cycle once it exceeds an estimated critical threshold.

Applying this approach to quarterly US data from 1985Q1 to 2010Q2, we find evidence of significant nonlinearities in the credit loss data, associated with the episodes of severe financial distress in our sample. This seems consistent with theories that allow for excessive aggregate buildups of credit. However, we do not find any significant temporal relationship, linear or otherwise, between aggregate leverage and credit losses. Replacing leverage by the financial obligations ratio, we find that the latter significantly enters credit loss determination as a regime switching variable of the type described above. Hence, based on this variable we can adequately account for the nonlinear dynamics inherent in aggregate credit losses. In addition, we are able to accurately estimate the parameters of the transition function which determines the weights given to the high and low credit loss regimes as a smooth function of the financial obligations ratio. We refer to the half way point between regimes as the maximum sustainable debt burden (MSDB).

By further distinguishing between total debt and real estate related debt in both the household and business sector, we gain important insights into how these different debt categories contribute to aggregate credit loss dynamics. For the household sector we find that the financial obligations ratio, specifically associated with real estate debt, exceeds an estimated MSDB threshold of 10.1% at two intervals over the sample period. The first interval is 1989Q2–1992Q1, i.e., MSDB is exceeded roughly one year prior to the recession in the early 1990's and returns to the sustainable region at the bottom of the recession. The second starts in 2005Q1, more than two years before the recent crisis, and continues to the end of the sample in 2010Q2, by which time the financial obligations ratio has not yet returned to the sustainable region. Both of these episodes are associated with massive credit losses and an unusually large number of bank failures, but differ with respect to the severity and length of the ensuing recession. This difference appears to be related to size with which the financial obligations ratio exceeded the MSDB estimate on each occasion.

For the business sector, we similarly find that major credit losses ensue when the associated financial obligations ratio crosses its MSDB estimate of 10.4% into the unsustainable region. This happens 1–2 years prior to each of the three US recessions in the sample but, as exemplified by the recession in the early 2000s, does not necessarily lead to large-scale bank failures. While the credit losses associated with excessive business loans seem less detrimental to financial stability than those associated with households' real estate loans, they may, nevertheless, exert a significant effect on the business cycle.

The observation that the financial obligations ratio in excess of its MSDB level precede economic downturns could be useful in designing capital standards for banks (Drehmann et al. 2010; Repullo et al. 2010) and for implementing more general macro prudential policies (e.g., Borio (2009)).

[2] The temporal association between credit losses and output losses is very strong as can be seen by comparing panels (a) and (e) of Figure 1.

For instance, our analysis suggests that credit risk assessment based on financial obligations ratios could lead to more countercyclical capital standards. Similarly, the financial obligations ratios, in particular those related to real estate debt, may be useful for macro prudential policy as early warning indicators of such long-term debt accumulations which may eventually threaten financial stability[3]. Our results also suggest a channel through which monetary policy may affect financial stability under certain conditions. For instance, an interest rate increase, intended to curb inflationary pressure, can impinge on financial stability in periods when aggregate debt is close to or above the sustainable level. This is because an interest rate increase directly raises the financial obligations of borrowers, which in turn can make credit losses both more likely and more severe.

The rest of the paper is organized as follows: Section 2 introduces the data, whereas Section 3 discusses methodology and statistical models. The results are presented in Sections 4 and 5 concludes.

2. Data

This section introduces quarterly US time-series data of the key variables, spanning the sample 1985Q1–2010Q2. We first introduce credit loss rates and indicators of the business cycle, and discuss their temporal association graphically. Then, in Section 2.2, we present two different measures of aggregate debt and relate their dynamics to that of the credit loss rates. Detailed descriptions of the variables and their sources are provided in Appendix A.

2.1. Credit Losses and Business Cycle Indicators

As a measure of credit losses we use the net charge-off rate on loans held by all insured commercial US banks. The banks are required to charge off an estimate of the current amount of loans and leases that are not likely to be collected, or are more than 120 days delinquent, from their loan loss allowance[4]. The net change-off rate is the current period change-offs minus recoveries. Hence, it constitutes the most accurate and timely estimate of credit losses that are available for US banks.

We distinguish between losses on total loans (TL), real estate loans (RL), and business loans (BL), denoted $loss_t^{TL}$, $loss_t^{RL}$, and $loss_t^{BL}$, respectively. The loss rate on total loans, depicted in panel (a) of Figure 1, shows peaks at the low point of each of the three US recessions in the sample (as indicated by a standard output gap measure, $ygap_t = y_t - y_t^*$, depicted in panel e of the figure), with the most recent one being almost twice as severe as the previous ones. This pattern, however, is not preserved over different loan categories. For example, the loss rate on real estate loans (panel b) peaks only twice over the sample, first during the recession in the early 1990s and next during the recent financial crisis. As can be seen from panel (d) of the figure, both of these occasions are associated with large-scale bank failures. In contrast, the loss rate on business loans (panel c) displays peaks of roughly equal magnitude at each of the three recessions. In this sense, it more closely resembles the term-spread, $term_t = fundr_t - govr_t$, depicted in panel (g), where $fundr_t$ is the federal funds rate and $govr_t$ is the yield of 10-year treasury securities. We also note that losses on business loans seem less strongly connected to bank failures, as exemplified by the early 2000s recession.

3 This conjecture has recently been corroborated in a subsequent paper by Drehmann and Juselius (2012), who construct debt service ratios, a more narrow counterpart to the financial obligations ratio, for 27 countries. They find that the debt service ratio produce more accurate early warning signals than other extant measures 1–2 years ahead of systemic banking crises, whereas the credit-to-GDP gap have superior performance at longer horizons.

4 See the Federal Financial Institutions Examination Council's "Instructions for Preparation of Consolidated Reports of Condition and Income (FFIEC 031 and 041)" and the Generally Accepted Accounting Principles (GAAP).

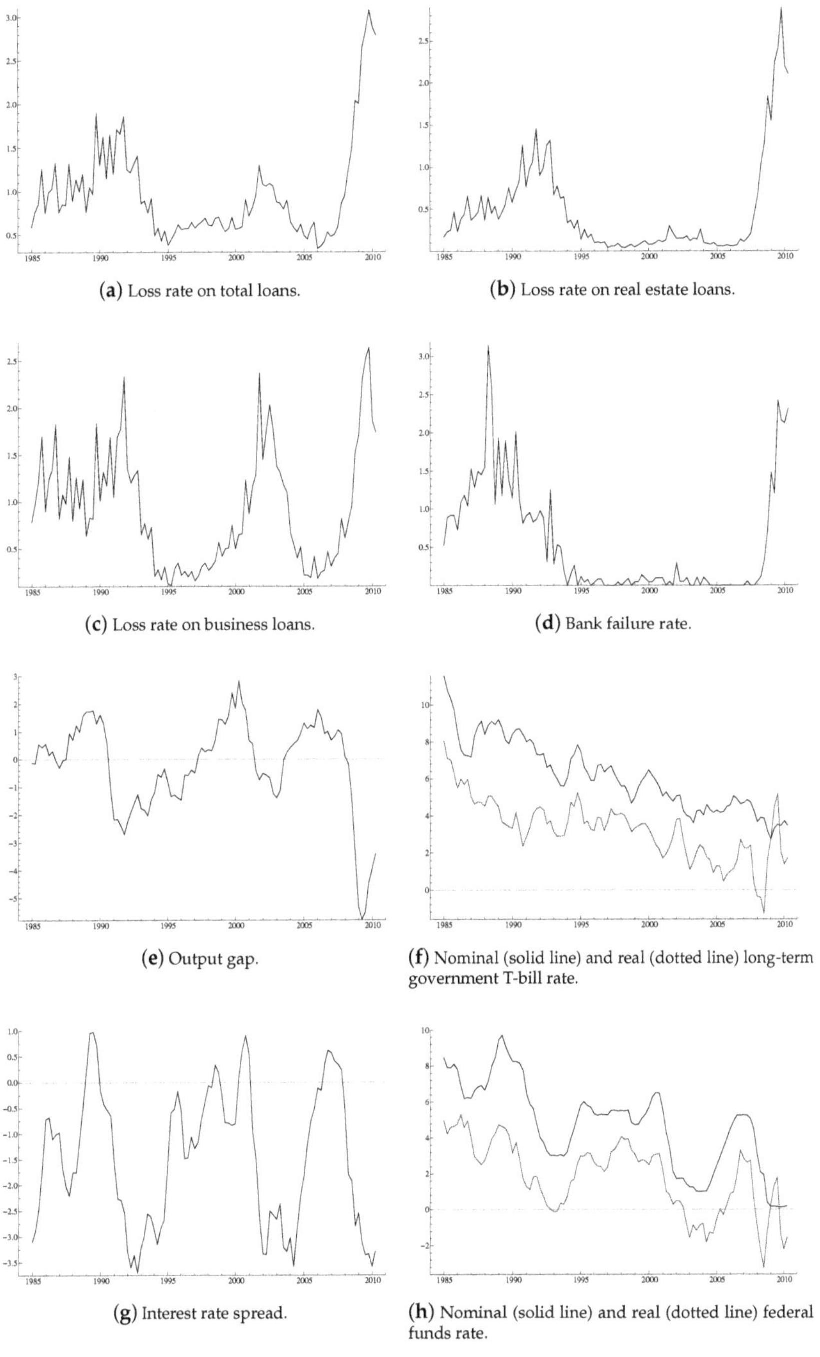

(a) Loss rate on total loans.

(b) Loss rate on real estate loans.

(c) Loss rate on business loans.

(d) Bank failure rate.

(e) Output gap.

(f) Nominal (solid line) and real (dotted line) long-term government T-bill rate.

(g) Interest rate spread.

(h) Nominal (solid line) and real (dotted line) federal funds rate.

Figure 1. Credit loss rates and various indicators of financial, monetary, and real conditions in the United Sates. The real (ex-post) interest rates are constructed using the 4-quarter moving average inflation rate to facilitate the exposition.

This ocular evidence suggests that there may be significant interactions between credit losses across different loan categories and the business cycle, potentially reinforcing each other. For instance, deep recessions and financial instability appear to be more closely associated with losses on real estate loans than losses on business loans, whereas the latter seems more related to ordinary business cycle fluctuations. The question is whether a suitable measure of the aggregate debt burden, either the conventional leverage or the financial obligations ratio that we propose in this paper, can predict when such interactions become pivotal[5].

2.2. Leverage vs. Financial Obligations

Panels (a)–(d) in Figure 2 depict the household (H) and business (B) sector debt-to-income ratios, distinguishing between total and real estate loans (RL), respectively. We use these ratios as a measure of leverage and denote them by $lev_t^{i,j}$, where $i = H, B$ and $j = TL, RL$. By comparing panels (a) and (b), as well as panels (c) and (d), it can be seen that real estate loans comprise more than two thirds of total loans in the household sector, but less than 10% of total loans in the business sector. Moreover, business sector leverage appears to be more volatile than household sector leverage. This points to potentially important disparities between the processes which generate excessive debt in the two sectors.

One potential problem with using the leverage variables for determining debt sustainability is their clear upward trends over the sample. This either implies that debt in the two sectors did not reach excessive levels until possibly just before the recent crisis or, alternatively, that the associated critical threshold must have been time-varying. The evidence in King (1994), for example, would argue against the former case, whereas estimation is problematic in the latter.

The likely reasons for the growth displayed by the debt-to-income ratios are changes in the terms of credit, as discussed in the introduction. For instance, both the federal funds rate and the long-term interest rate have been declining over the entire sample, as is evident from panels (f) and (h) in Figure 1.

A measure that explicitly accounts for changes in the terms of credit is the financial obligations ratio, reported by the Federal Reserve. It is broadly defined as the ratio of financial obligations, consiting mostly of interest payments and amortizations, to income[6]. As the Federal Reserve only reports this measure for the household sector, we construct a corresponding measure for the business sector by using the federal funds rates as the relevant interest rate, a fixed maturity of 3 years[7], and a linear amortization schedule. Panels (e)–(h) in Figure 2 depict the financial obligations ratios, denoted by for_t^{ij}, where i corresponds to the two sectors and j to the two loan categories. These ratios show less persistent growth and a stronger tendency to revert back to some benchmark value, compared to the leverage variables. Moreover, given that a large fraction of debt outstanding has longer maturity than one quarter, the per-period financial obligations ratios are considerably lower than the corresponding debt to income ratio as can clearly be seen from the figure.

The differences in the dynamic behavior between the leverage variables and the financial obligations ratios indicate that much of the upward trend in the former is due to changes in the terms of credit. Hence, the financial obligations ratio is more likely to be informative about the limits to private sector indebtedness than leverage.

5 In the empirical analysis, we also control for a number of other variables including real house prices, deviations from a standard Taylor's rule, the real exchange rate, the unemployment rate, and the inflation rate.

6 The numerator also includes rent payments on tenant-occupied property, auto lease payments, homeowners' insurance, and property tax payments.

7 This value lies between the average maturities on firms' bank loans reported in Stohs and Mauer (1996) and Berger et al. (2005). We checked robustness of the results below by assuming 2 and 4 years maturities. The results did not change significantly and are available upon request.

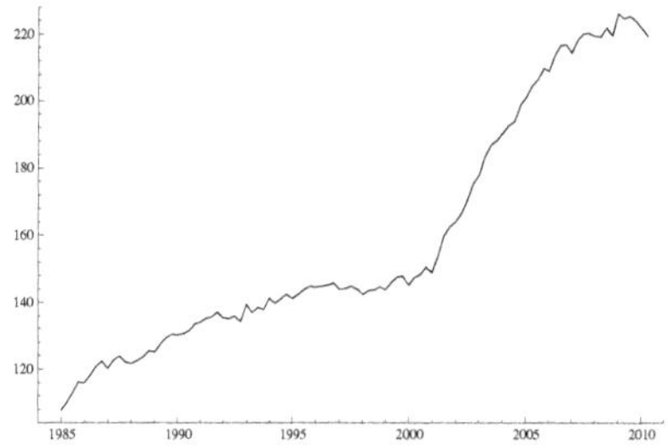

(a) Total leverage in the household sector.

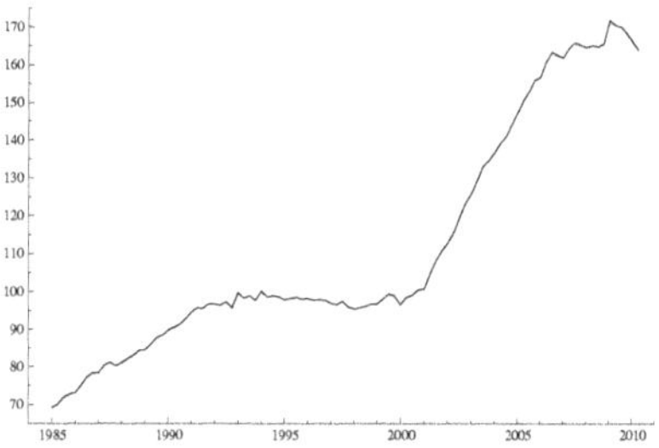

(b) Real estate leverage in the household sector.

(c) Total leverage in the business sector.

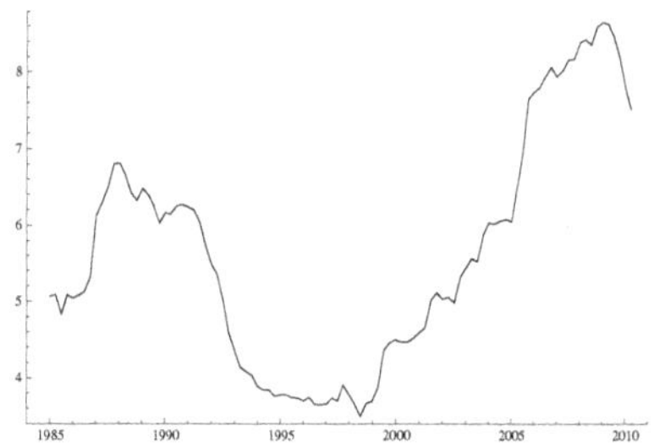

(d) Real estate leverage in the business sector.

(e) Total financial obligations in the household sector.

(f) Total financial obligations in the household sector

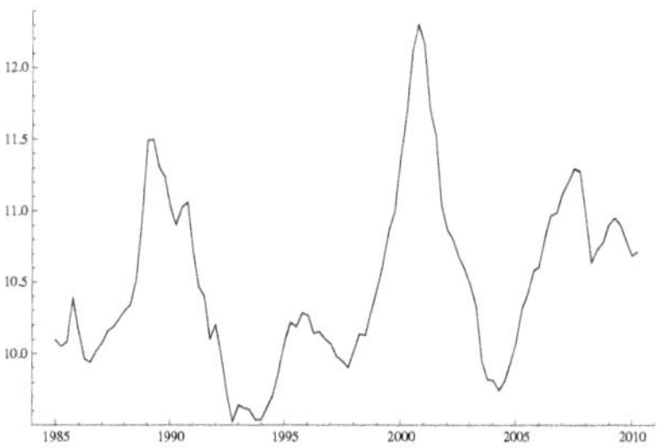

(g) Total financial obligations in the business sector.

(h) Real estate financial obligations in the business sector.

Figure 2. Indicators of leverage and financial obligations in the household and business sectors.

3. Methodology

In this section, we present our empirical strategy for determining the role of aggregate debt variables in credit loss determination and discuss statistical models which can be used for its implementation. We first document that our credit loss variables display considerable variability at frequencies close to zero. This suggest that standard cyclical variables, such as output gaps or credit spreads, may not be able to fully account for the variation in them. We then consider two alternative sources for the persistence, both related to the aggregate debt variables.

The first possibility is that the persistence of the credit loss rates is directly (linearly) inherited from the debt variables. This would be in line with existing empirical work on financial accelerators (e.g., Gertler and Lown 1999; Gilchrist et al. 2009). Because the economic models which underlie such accelerator effects typically exclude credit rationing (see e.g., Bernanke et al. (1999)), they seem more relevant as descriptions of credit market and business cycle interactions during normal (stable) times. To allow for this possibility we approximate the persistence in the credit loss rates and the debt variables by unit-roots and test for cointegration between them.

If the persistence cannot be accounted for linearly, a second possibility is that it stems from threshold dynamics related to excessive debt. For example, Leybourne et al. (1998) and Nelson et al. 2001 find that such non-linear dynamics can give rise to the appearance of stochastic trending. To study this possibility, we use the debt measures as transition variables in *nonlinear* regime-switching models for the credit loss rates. The idea is to capture increases in the interaction between credit losses and the business cycle which may arise if aggregate debt is allowed to reach excessive levels (see e.g., Miller and Stiglitz (2010)). The reason is that borrowers who are at the limits of their credit constraints may not be able to smooth their consumption or make optimal investments as they have to honor their debt obligations in the wake of a negative shock. Campello et al. (2010), for example, document significant changes in the investment and employment decisions of credit constrained firms during the recent financial crisis. If the proportion of constrained borrowers is large, this type of behavior can easily reinforce the negative effects of the initial shock, thereby creating increased feedback between loan defaults and the business cycle. An additional benefit of this modeling strategy is that it allows us to estimate a critical threshold for each debt variable above which it becomes excessive, provided that nonlinear transition-dynamics are present[8].

3.1. Statistical Models

A convenient way of testing for linear long-run co-movement between the credit loss rates and the debt variables is to model them jointly in a cointegrated VAR model

$$\Delta \boldsymbol{y}_t = \sum_{i=1}^{k-1} \Gamma_i \Delta \boldsymbol{y}_{t-i} + \Pi \boldsymbol{y}_{t-1} + \Phi \boldsymbol{d}_t + \varepsilon_t \tag{1}$$

where $\boldsymbol{y}_t = (loss_t^h, ygap_t, term_t, fundr_t, debt_t)'$ for $h = TL, RL, BL$, $debt_t$ is successively one of the debt measures presented in Section 2.2, i.e., $lev_t^{j,i}$ or $for_t^{j,i}$ for $j = H, B$ and $i = TL, RL$, $\boldsymbol{d}_t$ is a vector consisting of a constant and seasonal dummies (and possibly other dummies defined in the text), $\varepsilon_t \sim N_p(0, \Sigma)$, and k is the lag-length. This setting implies that we only consider each debt variable separately rather than jointly. Note that we also include the federal funds rate as a separate variable in the system. This is to allow for possibility that the decline in interest rates over

8 The precision with which the critical thresholds can be estimated depends more on the relative number of observations in each regime than the number of transitions between regimes. For instance, while our sample contains only two episodes of severe household sector financial distress, the number of observations associated with these events is 34, i.e., approximately one third of the entire sample.

the past decades have reduced credit risks associated with the existing stock of loans in banks' loan portfolios (see e.g. Altunbas et al. (2010)).

Cointegration in (1) can be tested by the likelihood ratio (LR) test for the rank of Π (Johansen (1996)). If the rank, r, is equal to the number of variables in the system, p, then $\boldsymbol{y}_t$ is stationary, i.e., $\boldsymbol{y}_t \sim I(0)$. If $0 < r < p$, then $\Pi = \alpha\beta'$, where α and β are two $(p \times r)$ matrices of full column rank and $\beta'\boldsymbol{y}_{t-1}$ describes the cointegration relationships. In this case $\boldsymbol{y}_t \sim I(1)$ and cointegrated with r cointegration vectors, β, and $p - r$ common stochastic trends, assuming that the "no $I(2)$ trends" condition $\left|\alpha'_\perp(I - \sum_{i=1}^{k-1}\Gamma_i)\beta_\perp\right| \neq 0$ is met, where $\perp$ denotes orthogonal complements. For example, any variable in $\boldsymbol{y}_t$ that is stationary *a priori*, such as the term spread and the output gap, is expected to increase r by one and add a unit-vector to β. If $r = 0$, then $\boldsymbol{y}_t \sim I(1)$ and the process is not cointegrated. A testing sequence that ensures correct power and size starts from the null hypothesis of rank zero and then successively increases the rank by one until the first non-rejection. When $0 < r < p$, it is possible to test the hypothesis that a variable, $y_{i,t}$ say, is weakly exogenous with respect to the long-run parameters of the model. The test of this hypothesis is asymptotically χ^2, and amounts to imposing zero-restrictions on a row of α corresponding to $y_{i,t}$.

If the persistence in the credit loss rates cannot be explained linearly, there is still a possibility that it stems from important nonlinearities. To allow for this possibility, we specify a smooth transition regression (STR) model for the credit loss rates. As we do not expect to find strong nonlinearities in the other variables[9], we focus on a single-equation model to keep the analysis tractable, rather than attempt to estimate a full-fledged multivariate STR model (see van Dijk et al. (2002)). In particular, the model takes the form

$$loss_t^h = (1 - \varphi(debt_t))(\mu_1 + \gamma_1'\boldsymbol{x}_t) + \varphi(debt_t)(\mu_2 + \gamma_2'\boldsymbol{x}_t) + \boldsymbol{\psi}'\boldsymbol{d}_t + v_t \quad (2)$$

where, $\boldsymbol{x}_t = (ygap_t, term_t, debt_t)'$ is a vector of potentially difference stationary explanatory variables, $\boldsymbol{d}_t$ is a vector of deterministic terms define above, and v_t is assumed to be a mean zero stationary disturbance term[10]. We note that the stationarity assumption on the disturbance term implies that $loss_t^h$ and $\boldsymbol{x}_t$ are either linearly or non-linearly cointegrated. Thus, verifying this assumption ensures model consistency, as well as safeguards against spurious results, for example due to growth correlations over time.

Our primary interest lies in the transition function

$$\varphi(debt_t) = \frac{1}{1 + e^{-\kappa_1(debt_t - \kappa_2)}}$$

which determines the relative weights between regimes 1 and 2, and has the properties $0 \leq \varphi(debt_t) \leq 1$ and $\varphi(\kappa_2) = 1/2$. We use $debt_t$ as the primary transition variable, i.e., we successively try one of the leverage or financial obligations ratios as arguments in $\varphi(\cdot)$[11]. Hence, for positive κ_1 and κ_2, say, (2) captures gradual changes in the effect (given by $\varphi(\cdot)(\gamma_1 - \gamma_2)$) of the cyclical variables in $\boldsymbol{x}_t$ on credit losses, as the debt variable increases. The halfway point between regimes, which we will loosely refer to as the maximum sustainable debt burden (MSDB), is determined by the κ_2 and the speed of the transition is determined by κ_1.

We apply a linearity test by Choi and Saikkonen (2004) to identify the statistically significant transition variables. The test is based on a Taylor series approximation of (2), which under the null hypothesis of linearity will not contain any significant second (or higher) order polynomial terms.

9 Both the output gap and the term structure should be stationary. Moreover, credit losses reduce the credit aggregates so that even if they affect output debt to GDP ratios would not move too much.

10 See Saikkonen and Choi (2004) for a discussion of this model.

11 We also tried the other variables in x_t, as well as real house prices. None, of these variables produced superior results in the sense discussed in Section 4.2.

However, under the STR alternative, all significant higher order terms will involve the transition variable. Hence, statistically valid transition variables can be detected by applying the test successively to each variable from the set of potential transition variables. Such information may be helpful in distinguishing between competing explanations for the recent crisis, such as lax monetary policy or excessive debt.

4. Results

This section reports the main empirical findings. Section 4.1 first investigates whether the observed persistence in the credit loss rates is due to exogenous factors or related to (transitory) regime shifts, or both. Next, Section 4.2 compares the ability of leverage and the financial obligations ratio for explaining shifts in credit loss dynamics. Section 4.3 reports the estimates associated with regime shift dynamics, and shows that they are informative about debt sustainability.

4.1. Linearity vs. Regime Shifts

We find that all credit loss rates show significant variation at frequencies close to zero, indicating the presence of cycles of longer duration than the available sample. This can be clearly seen from the spectral densities reported in Figure 3. Moreover, the unit-root hypothesis cannot be rejected for any of the loss rates using standard Augmented Dickey-Fuller (ADF) tests. We also find that our leverage variables, financial obligations ratios, and the federal funds rate (see Figures 1 and 2) all display similar stochastic trending[12]. Hence, each of the latter variables may conceivably be a source of persistence in the credit loss rates.

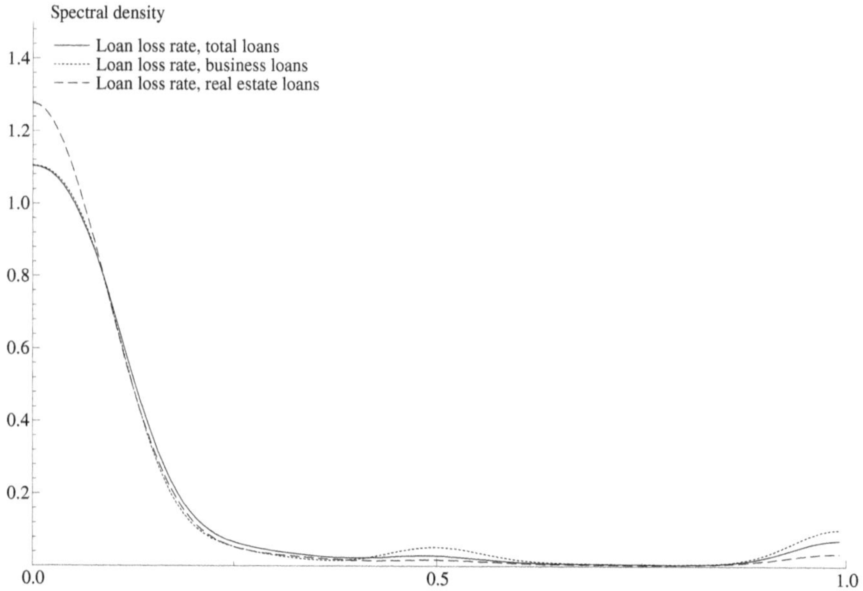

Figure 3. Spectral densities of the credit loss rates.

12 The only exception is the financial obligations ratio on total business loans which is found to be stationary. These results are available upon request.

While unit-roots are a convenient way of capturing the persistence in the credit loss rates, giving such roots a structural interpretation in this context does not seem reasonable. Instead, the persistence is more likely to reflect breaks or other types of nonlinearities, possibly associated with the recent crisis and its aftermath. For this reason, we adopt a cautious approach, initially restricting our attention to the pre-crisis sample 1985Q1–2006Q4, where regime shift dynamics are less likely to have played a dominant role in credit loss determination. We model credit loss rates jointly with the other variables to see if we can identify the source of the persistence in them, i.e., we estimate (1) with $y_t = (loss_t^h, ygap_t, term_t, fundr_t, debt_t)'$ for $h = TL, RL, BL$ and $debt_t$ successively indicating one of the debt variables in Section 2.2. We are especially interested to see if the persistent debt variables are relevant in this regard.

Applying the LR test for cointegration rank, as well as tests for unit-vectors in β, we find that: (i) unit-roots in the credit loss rates cannot be rejected in the pre-crisis sample; (ii) none of the other persistent debt variables are linearly cointegrated with the loss rates; and (iii) that the output gap and the term spread are stationary (i.e., they have corresponding unit vectors in β)[13]. The only variable that is linearly cointegrated with the loss rates is the nominal federal funds rate, suggesting that the declining interest rates during the past decades have reduced credit risk, consistent with Altunbas et al. (2010).

We next ask if the pre-crisis sample cointegration results continue to hold once the recent crisis period is included. For simplicity, we do this within a smaller model with $y_t = (loss_t^h, fundr_t)'$, $k = 2$, a restricted constant, three centered seasonal dummies, and transitory impulse dummies (reported in Appendix A), but the results remain the same if we also include the stationary variables and the debt variables. Table 1 reports the results of the LR test for the rank of Π and tests of weak exogeneity (conditional on $r = 1$). The upper part of the table confirms the cointegration results for the pre-crisis sample. As can be seen, $r = 0$ is always rejected, whereas $r \leq 1$ cannot be rejected in this sample. Moreover, we cannot reject the hypothesis that the federal funds rate is weakly exogenous. The lower part of the table shows that the cointegration results break-down in the full sample from 1985Q1 to 2010Q2. This is likely caused by a transitory but influential change in the process that govern short-run credit losses associated with the crisis.

Table 1. Linear cointegration results. Notes: The rows labeled "$r = 0$" and "$r \leq 1$" report the p-values of the LR tests for the rank of Π. The following two rows report the p-values from testing weak exogeneity for both of the variables in y_t. Boldface values indicate significance at the 5% level.

Linear Cointegration Results				
1985Q1–2006Q4				
y_t'	$r = 0$	$r \leq 1$	$\alpha_{loss} = 0$	$\alpha_{fundr} = 0$
$(loss_t^{TL}, fundr_t)'$	**0.00**	0.38	**0.00**	0.42
$(loss_t^{RL}, fundr_t)'$	**0.01**	0.79	**0.00**	0.13
$(loss_t^{BL}, fundr_t)'$	**0.00**	0.19	**0.00**	0.54
1985Q1–2010Q2				
y_t'	$r = 0$	$r \leq 1$	$\alpha_{loss} = 0$	$\alpha_{fundr} = 0$
$(loss_t^{TL}, fundr_t)'$	0.96	0.98	–	–
$(loss_t^{RL}, fundr_t)'$	0.95	0.94	–	–
$(loss_t^{BL}, fundr_t)'$	0.27	0.29	–	–

13 These results are omitted for brevity, but are available upon request. We also tried per capita GDP, the inflation rate, the unemployment rate, and the real exchange rate. None of these were found to be both cointegrated and weakly exogenous with respect to the credit loss rates.

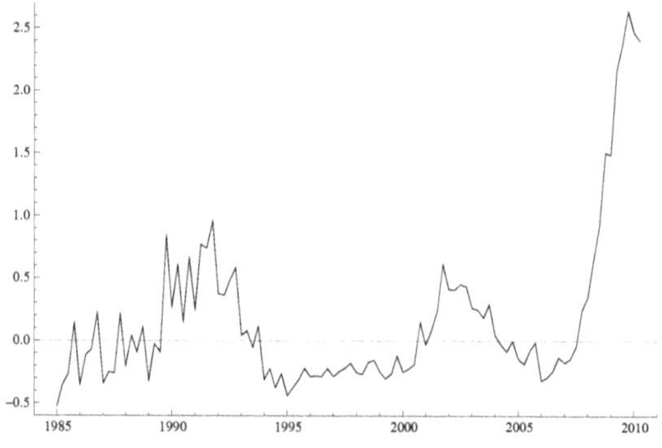

(**a**) Filtered Loss rate on total loans.

(**b**) Filtered loss rate on business loans.

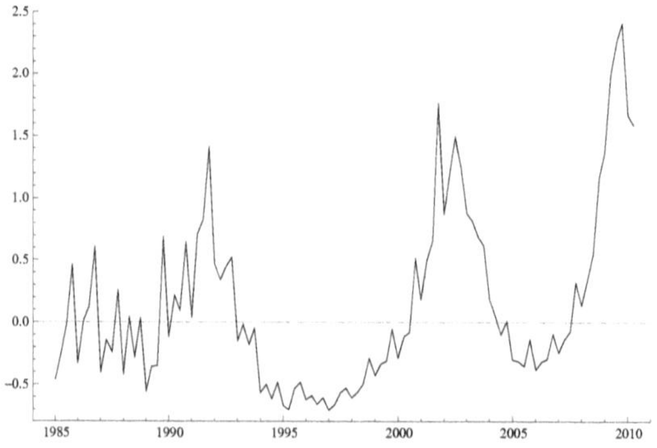

(**c**) Filtered loss rate on real estate loans.

Figure 4. Credit loss rates with stochastic trend component removed.

The presence of a small downward trend associated with the long-term decline in the federal funds rate is a nuisance, as there is a risk that it can be mixed-up with the type of nonlinearity that are the main focus of the study. For this reason, we estimate it by Hodrick-Prescott filtering the federal funds rate and remove it from the credit loss rates based on the pre-crisis cointegration estimates[14]. The adjusted loss rates are depicted in Figure 4. Comparing these loss rates with the unadjusted ones in Figure 1, reveals that the effect of the detrending is relatively small. The main change is a relative reduction in the loss rates at the beginning of the sample compared to the rates at the end.

Having controlled for linear stochastic trends in the loss rates, we proceed to test the null hypothesis of linearity against the STR model alternative in (2) using a test by Choi and Saikkonen (2004). Initial modeling suggested that none of the debt variables (which successively enter through $debt_t$) yielded significant coefficients in γ_1 or γ_2, i.e., the two regimes. Hence, we excluded them from x_t altogether. Similarly, the output gap, $ygap_t$, was never significant in the model for the loss rate on business loans, $loss_t^{BL}$, and was therefore excluded from this model. This has very little effect on the estimated regime switching dynamics, but improves the precision of the γ_1 and γ_2 estimates. We consistently apply these restrictions in the subsequent analysis, using $x_t = (term_t, ygap_t)'$ in the models for losses on total loans and real estate loans and $x_t = term_t$ in the model for losses on business loans.

Given the indicated choices of x_t, Table 2 reports the results of the linearity tests corresponding to each of the individual debt variables. For the pre-crisis period, the results in the upper part of the table show that the null hypothesis of linearity cannot be rejected in any of the models[15]. However, turning to the lower part of Table 2, we see that the null hypothesis of linearity is rejected for several potential transition variables in the full sample. For instance, in the model for the loss rate on real estate loans, $loss_t^{RL}$, there seems to be significant nonlinearities associated with household and business sector real estate debt-to-income, as well as the household sector's real estate financial obligations ratio. In the model for the loss rate on business loans, $loss_t^{BL}$ on the other hand, all debt-to-income ratios and the financial obligations ratio in the business sector, are significant. The results of the model for the loss rate on total loans, $loss_t^{TL}$ are, by and large, a combination of the results from the models of $loss_t^{RL}$ and $loss_t^{BL}$. Hence, while regime shifts do not play a very dominant role in the pre-crisis period, they seem crucial for describing credit loss dynamics in the full sample, and in particular during the recent financial crisis.

Table 2. Tests of linearity against a STR alternative. Boldface values indicate rejection of the null hypothesis at the 5% significance level.

Tests of Linearity vs. Regime Shifts								
				1985Q1–2006Q2				
	$lev_t^{H,TL}$	$lev_t^{H,RL}$	$lev_t^{B,TL}$	$lev_t^{B,RL}$	$for_t^{H,TL}$	$for_t^{H,RL}$	$for_t^{B,TL}$	$for_t^{B,RL}$
$loss_t^{TL}$	0.828	0.719	0.535	0.419	0.963	0.406	0.780	0.570
$loss_t^{RL}$	0.363	0.597	0.489	0.688	0.108	0.085	0.221	0.583
$loss_t^{BL}$	0.370	0.408	0.072	0.256	0.132	0.929	0.141	0.420
				1985Q1–2010Q2				
	$lev_t^{H,TL}$	$lev_t^{H,RL}$	$lev_t^{B,TL}$	$lev_t^{B,RL}$	$for_t^{H,TL}$	$for_t^{H,RL}$	$for_t^{B,TL}$	$for_t^{B,RL}$
$loss_t^{TL}$	**0.016**	**0.013**	**0.011**	**0.012**	0.181	**0.041**	0.411	**0.037**
$loss_t^{RL}$	0.059	**0.042**	0.052	**0.021**	0.738	**0.018**	0.940	0.054
$loss_t^{BL}$	**0.048**	**0.049**	**0.006**	**0.029**	0.058	0.151	**0.021**	0.064

14 This is statistically justified if the federal funds rate is strongly exogenous and the Hodrick-Prescott filtered trend provides an accurate estimate of the underlying trend in the federal funds rate. We found some evidence in favor of strong exogeneity for the federal funds rate by testing additional restrictions on the short-term dynamics. While there is no guarantee that the Hodrick-Prescott trend is an accurate estimate of the underlying trend, we checked robustness by estimating (2) with $loss_t^h$ on the left hand side and $\gamma_0 i_t^M$ added to the right hand side. This does not change the results below to any significant degree.

15 This does not, however, imply that such shifts are not present in the pre-crisis sample, but rather that the resulting dynamics are of a lesser magnitude and, hence, not likely to be confused with long-run movements in the credit loss rates.

4.2. Leverage vs. Financial Obligations

Next we estimate (2) for each the three credit loss rates, $loss_t^h$, with x_t as in the previous section, and $debt_t$ in $\varphi(\cdot)$ successively equal to one of the transition variable candidates that has a significant entry in Table 2. Before we turn to the estimates, it is worthwhile to ask if the resulting regressions can account for the persistence in the credit loss rates associated with the crisis period. To this end, we apply both ADF tests and and (KPSS) stationarity tests to the residual. While these tests are strictly not valid for the residuals from (2), which are mixture processes, this technicality may not be so important in practice[16]. Nevertheless, these results should be viewed with some caution.

When the leverage variables, $lev_t^{i,j}$, are used we find that the stationarity of the residual cannot be secured in most cases. This can be seen from Table 3 which reports (ADF) unit-root and (KPSS) stationarity tests for the residual. In only two cases, $lev_t^{B,RL}$ in the equation for $loss_t^{TL}$ and $lev_t^{H,RL}$ in the equation for $loss_t^{BL}$, do the tests conclusively yield stationary residuals. In both of these cases, however, the estimated parameters of $\varphi(\cdot)$ are such that regime 2 never occurs within the sample. In one case ($lev^{B,RL}$ in the equation for $loss_t^{BL}$), the tests yield inconclusive results. These results suggest that non-linear cointegration is generally rejected when the leverage variables are used, implying they cannot adequately account for the large and persistent fluctuations in the credit loss rates associated with the regime-shift dynamics.

Table 3. Tests for non-linear cointegration. The null hypothesis of the Augmented Dickey-Fuller (ADF) test is that the residual from (2), with explained and transition variable as indicated in the columns, is a unit-root process. A constant and seasonal dummies were included, and lag-length was chosen based in the AIC information criterion. The 10%, 5%, and 1% critical values for this test are −2.58, −2.89, and −3.50, respectively. The null hypothesis of the Kwiatkowski–Phillips–Schmidt–Shin (KPSS) test is that the aforementioned residual is stationary. The bandwidth was set to 2 in each case. The 10%, 5%, and 1% critical values for this test are 0.35, 0.46, and 0.74, respectively. Rejections of the null hypothesis at the 10%, 5% and 1% significance levels are indicated by ⋆, ⋆⋆, and ⋆⋆⋆, respectively. † Estimated values for κ_1 and κ_2 imply that regime 2 occurs outside the rage of $debt_t$.

Unit-Root and Stationarity Tests								
				Explained Variable: $Loss_t^{TL}$				
$debt_t$:	$lev_t^{H,TL}$	$lev_t^{H,RL}$	$lev_t^{B,TL}$	$lev_t^{B,RL}$	$for_t^{H,TL}$	$for_t^{H,RL}$	$for_t^{B,TL}$	$for_t^{B,RL}$
ADF:	−1.99	−0.51	−2.08	−3.55 ***†	–	−4.84 ***	–	−3.49 **
$KPSS$:	0.38 *	1.11 ***	0.37 *	0.09 †	–	0.24	–	0.24
				Explained Variable: $Loss_t^{RL}$				
$debt_t$:	$lev_t^{H,TL}$	$lev_t^{H,RL}$	$lev_t^{B,TL}$	$lev_t^{B,RL}$	$for_t^{H,TL}$	$for_t^{H,RL}$	$for_t^{B,TL}$	$for_t^{B,RL}$
ADF:	–	−1.90	–	−2.41	–	−4.31 ***	–	–
$KPSS$:	–	0.63 **	–	0.52 **	–	0.12	–	–
				Explained Variable: $Loss_t^{BL}$				
$debt_t$:	$lev_t^{H,TL}$	$lev_t^{H,RL}$	$lev_t^{B,TL}$	$lev_t^{B,RL}$	$for_t^{H,TL}$	$for_t^{H,RL}$	$for_t^{B,TL}$	$for_t^{B,RL}$
ADF:	−2.36	−3.16 **†	−2.58 *	−2.57	–	–	−5.08 ***	–
$KPSS$:	0.37 *	0.30 †	0.84 ***	0.31	–	–	0.20	–

In contrast, when the financial obligations ratios are used, both the ADF and the KPSS tests conclusively support the stationarity of the residuals as can be seen from Table 3. Moreover, in all of these cases the estimated parameters of $\varphi(\cdot)$ yield regime transitions inside the range of the relevant financial obligations ratio. In the model for losses on total loans, $loss_t^{TL}$ both the financial obligations

[16] Applying a more appropriate test, such as the one in Saikkonen and Choi (2010) which is based on the KPSS test, is left for future work.

ratios associated with real estate debt in the household and business sectors, $for_t^{H,RL}$ and $for_t^{B,RL}$, have significant entries in Table 2. We choose the former financial obligations ratio as it produces a somewhat better fit and higher likelihood than the latter. Based on these results, the leverage variables do not seem to signal an impending crisis with sufficient precision, whereas the Financial obligations ratios seem more relevant in this respect.

4.3. Explaining Credit Losses

Table 4 reports the key parameter estimates of the STR models. As can be seen from the table, both the estimated coefficients measuring the speed of transition between regimes, κ_1, and the estimated thresholds, κ_2, are positive, indicating that regime 2 dominates for values *above* κ_2. Furthermore, the estimates of κ_1 indicate that speeds of transitions between regimes are rather fast in all cases. The two regimes are characterized by the parameters γ_{term} and γ_{ygap}, describing the effect of of the term spread, $term_t$ and the output gap, $ygap_t$, on credit losses, $loss_t^h$, in each regime (except in the equation for $loss_t^{BL}$ where only $term_t$ enter the regimes). The parameters in the first regime are generally negative but not significant, whereas in the second regime both parameters become negative and significant. It is notable that the effect on credit losses from a change in the output gap or the interest rate spread is much larger in the second regime. Therefore, the financial system becomes much more exposed to real economic fluctuations when the financial obligations ratios are above the estimated threshold values. Thus, the second regime describes unstable periods where even small negative shocks can lead to massive credit losses. In this sense, the threshold values, κ_2, can be viewed as estimates of the *maximum sustainable debt burden* (MSDB) with respect to a given credit category. Our estimates suggest that both total debt and real estate debt become unsustainable (i.e., susceptible to high loss rates) when the financial obligation ratio associated with households real estate loans exceed 10.19% and 10.08%, respectively. Similarly, business debt becomes unsustainable when the financial obligations ratio associated with total business loans exceeds 10.44%.

The results in Table 4 are robust to more general specifications of (2). For example, adding auto-regressive lags to the equation yields a well-specified model with approximately constant parameters that displays both quantitatively and qualitatively similar results. Moreover, the model also compares favorably to a simple Markov-Switching specification of (2). This suggests that conditioning the transition dynamics on the financial obligations ratio is indeed beneficial for describing credit loss dynamics. The details of these robustness checks are reported in Appendix B.

Table 4. Estimated transition parameters and regime coefficients from STR models of the adjusted credit loss rates. Boldface values indicate significance at the 5% level (standard errors in parenthesis).

STR Estimates							
		Transition Parameters		Regime 1		Regime 2	
Equ.	$debt_t$	κ_1	κ_2	γ_{term}	γ_{ygap}	γ_{term}	γ_{ygap}
$loss_t^{TL}$	$for_t^{H,RL}$	**12.678** (5.630)	**10.192** (0.056)	−0.063 (0.034)	0.002 (0.045)	**−0.276** (0.094)	**−0.224** (0.051)
$loss_t^{RL}$	$for_t^{H,RL}$	**3.609** (1.128)	**10.079** (0.106)	−0.023 (0.041)	−0.051 (0.038)	**−0.267** (0.099)	**−0.243** (0.049)
$loss_t^{BL}$	$for_t^{B,TL}$	**2.318** (0.968)	**10.44** (0.199)	**−0.249** (0.085)	-	**−0.619** (0.119)	-

The relationship between the financial obligations ratio and the credit losses can also be presented graphically. The upper panel of Figure 5 depicts the loss rate on real estate loans, and the lower panel depicts the financial obligations ratio related to household real estate debt along with a line demarking the corresponding MSDB estimate. The periods during which the second regime dominates are demarked by grey bars in the figure. As can be seen, there are only two unstable periods in the sample. The first begins in 1989Q2, roughly one year in advance of the recession in the early 1990s, and ends at its bottom. The second begins in 2005Q1, over two years in advance of the recent crisis, and has not yet ended by the last observation in our sample (2010Q2). Hence, in retrospect this MSDB estimate would have signaled a significant increase in credit risk a full two years before the onset of the crisis. In addition, the magnitude and duration by which the financial obligations ratio exceed the MSDB line may explain both the severity and length of the ensuing downturns. We leave this interesting aspect for future work.

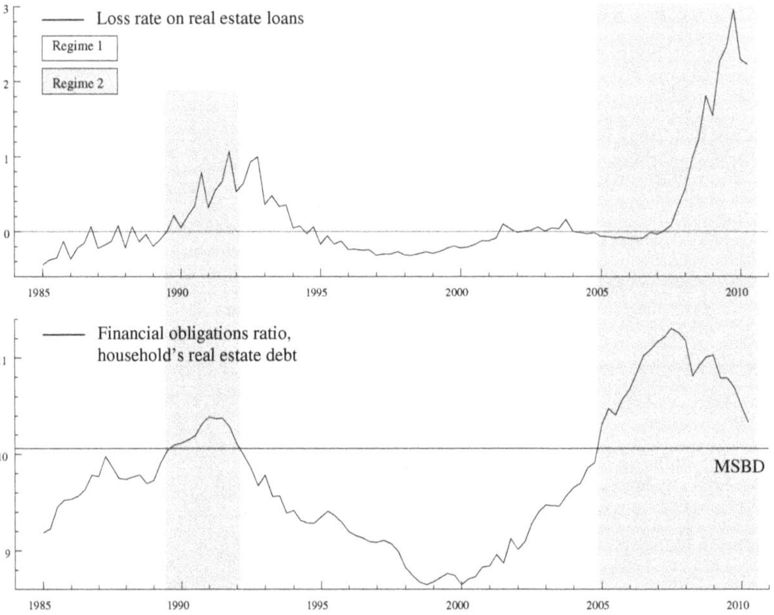

Figure 5. Transitions in the loss rate on real estate loans. The upper panel depicts the loss rate on real estate loans, whereas the lower panel depicts the financial obligations ratio associated with household's real estate debt and the corresponding MSDB estimate. Episodes when regime 2 dominate are demarked by grey bars.

Similarly, Figure 6 depicts the loss rate on business loans and the corresponding financial obligations ratio. As can be seen form the figure, there are three unstable periods in our sample, each beginning between 1–2 years prior to one of the three known US recessions in the sample, and ending roughly at their low points. Prior to the 1990s recession, the MSDB of business loans is exceeded in 1988Q2, a full year earlier than the MSDB of households real estate loans. However, prior to the recent crisis the relative timing is reversed, i.e., the household sector MSDB was exceeded first. Finally, we note that it is possible to construct the business sector financial obligations ratio for earlier dates than those in our estimation sample. Hence, as a tentative test of the out-of-sample performance of the business sector MSDB, we checked whether it predicts the deep recession in the early 1980's[17]. We find that the financial obligations ratio crosses the MSDB line from below in 1980Q4, three quarters before the onset of the early 80's recession, and returns to the sustainable region at bottom of the recession. Since this pattern is in accordance with the within-sample results, it gives some additional support to our estimates.

[17] It is more difficult to conduct a similar test for the household sector, as the Federal Reserve does not record financial obligations ratios before 1985.

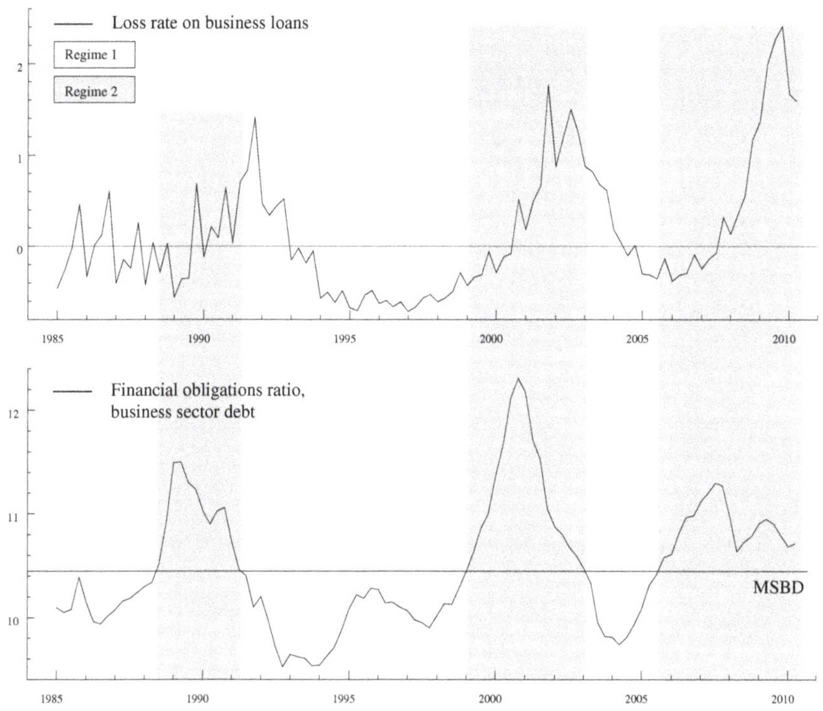

Figure 6. Transitions in the loss rate on business loans. The upper panel depicts the loss rate on business loans, whereas the lower panel depicts the financial obligations ratio associated with total business sector debt and the corresponding MSDB estimate. Episodes when regime 2 dominate are demarked by grey bars.

5. Conclusions

When do aggregate debt accumulations become excessive, compromising both macroeconomic and financial stability? By studying US credit loss dynamics over the period 1985–2010, we show that it is the strength of the aggregate liquidity constraint, as measured by the financial obligations ratio, which determines the upper limit for sustainable debt developments. In contrast to previous studies which use cross-sectional data, we do not find the debt-to-income ratio, or leverage, to be particularly relevant in this respect. The reason for this finding seems to be that a large part of the growth trend in leverage during the past decades was in fact sustainable and due to a concurrent decline in the real interest rate. Because this trend is likely to have a uniform effect on the cross-sections, most of the cross-sectional variation in leverage will be due to excessive buildups which, thereby, generate seemingly strong association with subsequent credit losses.

We find that the private sector financial obligations ratio displays a cyclical pattern, reaching unsustainable levels 1–2 years prior to each of the three US recessions in our sample. This pattern is, however, not identical among households and businesses. For instance, the household sector cycle seems to be approximately twice as long as the corresponding business sector cycle. Thus, the household sector financial obligations ratio only reached unsustainable levels prior to the deep recessions in the early 1990s and late 2000s, whereas the Business sector financial obligations ratio reached unsustainable levels prior to each of the three recessions. These results suggest that the distinction between excessive financial obligations in the household and business sectors may be important for understanding why some recessions become deep and prolonged while others do not. However, They also indicate that the financial obligations ratio may be useful as an early warnings indicator.

While our empirical approach seems promising in the sense of successfully spotting buildups of excessive aggregate debt, several interesting avenues for future research remain to be explored. For instance, because different types of households are likely to differ with respect the tightness of their financial constraints (Hall (2011)), it might be worthwhile to decompose the financial obligations ratio according to such characteristics as age and income. This may significantly improve our ability to detect excessive debt accumulations, especially when population cohorts change along these dimensions. It is also conceivable that our framework can be extended to an analysis of public sector debt, which could potentially be very valuable in light of the ongoing US and European sovereign debt crisis. As a final remark, we note that the recurrent nature of excessive debt accumulations suggests that the underlying credit market behavior is systematic, which seems inconsistent with the basic assumptions of most theoretical models. Asset price models that incorporate imperfect knowledge and heterogeneous expectations (e.g., Frydman and Goldberg (2009) and Burnside et al. (2016)) are able to generate pervasive boom and busts as a consequence of the market's allocation of capital and, hence, seem more promising in this respect.

Appendix A

Detailed definitions of the variables used in the analysis are provided in Table A1.

Table A1. Variable definitions and sources.

Data and Definitions	
Variable:	Definition:
$loss_t^h$	Net charge-off rate on loans, all insured US commercial banks. h = TL (total loans), RL (real estate loans), and BL (business loans). Source: FRS (Bank Assets & Liabilities)
$lev_t^{i,j}$	Debt-to-income ratio (in %). $i = H$ (households'), B (Nonfarm nonfinancial corporate business). $j = TL$ (total loans), RL (real estate loans). Household income: total wages and salaries. Business income: Value added in non farm business. Sources: FRS (Flow of Funds Accounts) and BEA (National Economic Accounts).
$for_t^{i,j}$	Financial obligations ratio. i and j are as above. For $i = H$ the series are taken from the FRS (Household Finance). For $i = B$ the definition is $l_t^{Bj} i_t^M/400 + l_t^{Bj}/12$.
$fundr_t$	Effective federal fund rate (3-month average). Source: FRS (Interest Rates)
$govr_t$	Yield on 10-year Treasury securities. Source: FRS (Interest Rates)
$term_t$	$fundr_t - govr_t$
$ygap_t$	$100(y_t - y_t^*)$, where y_t is log real output and y_t^* is the OECD production function
	based level of potential output. Source: OECD.

Sources: Federal Reserve System (FRS), Bureau of Economic Analysis (BEA), Bureau of Labor Statistics (BLS), OECD databases (OECD), Federal Housing Finance Agency (FHFA).

The underlying data are publicly available at the listed sources. To check robustness, we considered several alternative measures. For instance, we used the household debt service ratio (FRS) instead of for^{HT}, deviations between real and Hodric-Prescott filtered GDP and the unemployment gap (congressional budget office definition) instead of $ygap_t$, and the difference between corporate BAA and AAA bonds instead of $term_t$. This did not produce significant changes to the results.

A few transitory impulse dummies were used in connection with the VAR estimates in Section 4.1. These dummies (labeled $DYYQ$) take the value 1 at date YYQ and –1 at the consecutive date, where YY and Q refer to the year and quarter digits, respectively. The model for $\boldsymbol{y}_t = (loss_t^{TL}, fundr_t)'$ includes $D894$, the model for $\boldsymbol{y}_t = (loss_t^{RL}, fundr_t)'$ includes $D904$, $D914$ and $D923$, and the model for $\boldsymbol{y}_t = (loss_t^{BL}, fundr_t)'$ includes $D894$ and $D014$.

Appendix B

In this section we test robustness of the results reported in the main text with respect to alternative specifications. We begin by comparing the results in Table 4 with those obtained from a dynamic specification of (2). We also report the results from break-point Chow tests for these models. Finally, to assess the value added of the financial obligations ratios for explaining regime-switching in credit loss rates, we compare the weights to Regime 2 from models in Table 4 with the ones obtained from a simple Markov-Switching (MS) dynamic regression specification of (2).

The results in Section 4.2 indicate that the STR models for the credit loss rates in conjunction with the financial obligations ratios can produce stationary residuals. These residuals are, however, severely auto-correlated and show other signs of misspecification as well. As this can affect both the precision and consistency of the estimates reported in Table 4, we re-estimate the STR models using a dynamic specification of the form

$$\widetilde{loss}_t^h = \sum_{i=1}^{4} \rho_i \widetilde{loss}_{t-i}^h + (1 - \varphi(debt_t))(\mu_1 + \gamma_1' x_t) + \varphi(debt_t)(\mu_2 + \gamma_2' x_t) + \boldsymbol{\psi}' \boldsymbol{d}_t + v_t \quad \text{(A1)}$$

where $\widetilde{loss}_t^h = loss_t^h - strend_t^h$ for $h = TL, RL, BL$, and $\boldsymbol{x}_t$ and $\boldsymbol{d}_t$ are as in Section 4.3. Table A2 reports the estimates. As can be seen from the table, the estimated parameters of the transition function, κ_1 and κ_2, are fairly close to the ones reported in Table 4. The biggest difference with respect to these parameters occurs in the model for losses on real estate loans, where κ_2 increases from 10.08 to 10.92. While this increase is substantial, the speed of adjustment is now reduced from 3.61 to 2.50. This has the effect of widening the transition region, producing very similar regimes as before. At the same time, however, it becomes less appropriate to interpret κ_2 as a maximum sustainable debt burden.

The effect of the explanatory variables, as given by γ_1 and γ_2, cannot easily be compared to the estimates in Table 4. The reason is the contemporaneous effects in Table A2 will be reinforced by the auto regressive terms. The long run (steady state) effects are given by $\gamma_j / 1 - \sum \rho_i$. In the models for $\widetilde{loss}_t^{TL}$, $\widetilde{loss}_t^{RL}$, and $\widetilde{loss}_t^{BL}$, the sums of auto-regressive coefficients are 0.88, 0.81, and 0.83, respectively, as can be seen from Table A2, giving long-run multipliers of 8.3, 5.3, and 5.9. This implies that the effects of the explanatory variables are larger than what is immediately apparent from the table. Overall, the same general patter that was found in Table 4 seems to hold for the dynamic versions of the model: the effects in Regime 1 are smaller in magnitude and insignificant, whereas the effects in Regime 2 are large and often significant. Hence, we conclude that the patterns and results reported in the main text are broadly robust to dynamic extensions of the models.

Table A2 also report the results of several misspecification tests. It can be seen from the table that the residuals of the three models are reasonably well behaved. While there are still some signs of auto-correlation, in particular in the model for real estate losses, the effect on the results are nevertheless likely to be minor. Also, the normality assumption is rejected at the 5% significance level in all three models due to a few outliers. To investigate the parameter stability of the models, Figure A1 shows the results from recursive break-point Chow tests. Values above the black dotted line indicate rejection of parameter stability at the 1% significance level. As can be seen from the figure, all three models seem to display reasonable parameter stability.

Table A2. Estimated transition parameters and regime coefficients from dynamic versions of the STR models for the credit loss rates. Boldface values indicate significance at the 5% level (standard errors in parenthesis). The null hypothesis of no auto-correlation (AR) in up to five lags of the residual is tested by a Lagrange multiplier test. A similar test is conducted on the squared residuals to test for the null of no auto-regressive conditional heteroscedasticity (ARCH). The last row reports the adjusted coefficient of determination.

Dynamic STR Estimates			
	Model		
Explained:	$\widetilde{loss}_t^{TL}$	$\widetilde{loss}_t^{RL}$	$\widetilde{loss}_t^{BL}$
$debt_t$:	$for_t^{H,RL}$	$for_t^{H,RL}$	$for_t^{B,TL}$
	Parameters		
ρ_1	**0.67** (0.10)	**0.50** (0.10)	**0.59** (0.11)
ρ_2	**0.47** (0.12)	0.21 (0.11)	**0.31** (0.13)
ρ_3	**−0.52** (0.12)	−0.19 (0.12)	−0.20 (0.12)
ρ_4	**0.26** (011)	**0.29** (0.11)	0.13 (0.12)
κ_1	29.80 (28.02)	**2.50** (1.28)	3.37 (1.96)
κ_2	**10.34** (0.03)	**10.92** (0.62)	**10.72** (0.24)
$\gamma_{1,term}$	0.02 (0.02)	0.01 (0.02)	0.01 (0.05)
$\gamma_{1,ygap}$	0.00 (0.02)	0.01 (0.02)	–
$\gamma_{2,term}$	−0.02 (0.05)	−0.25 (0.22)	**−0.21** (0.10)
$\gamma_{2,ygap}$	**−0.08** (0.03)	−0.24 (0.23)	–
	Misspecification		
AR	0.18	**0.01**	0.05
ARCH	0.97	0.16	0.15
Normality	**0.00**	**0.01**	**0.02**
R^2	0.96	0.97	0.90

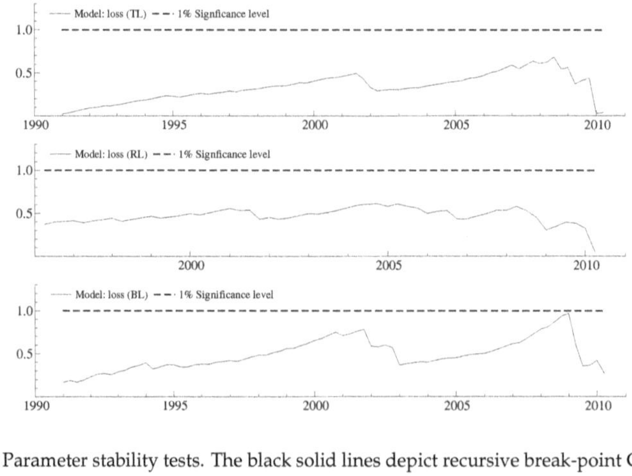

Figure A1. Parameter stability tests. The black solid lines depict recursive break-point Chow tests for the models in Table A2. Twenty quarters were used to initialize the recursions. Values above the dotted black line indicate rejection of parameter stability at the 1% significance level.

As a final assessment of the model, we compare the results in Table 4, which are based on the STR specification in (2), with an analogous MS model. In particular, the latter model has exactly the same explanatory variables and two regimes, but replaces the transition function, $\varphi(\cdot)$, with a unobserved random variable which follows a Markov chain. Hence, comparing the two models allows us to assess the benefits of having the financial obligations ratio as a specific transition variable: if the two model yield identical regimes, the value added of conditioning on this variable is limited. The estimates, of the MS-model (available upon request) are qualitatively in line with the ones for the STR model in Table 4, i.e., the effects of the cyclical variables are generally insignificant in Regime 1 and significantly negative in Regime 2. As a first statistical assessment of the MS model, we check if it produces stationary residuals for each of the three loss rates. The ADF-test statistics on the residuals of $loss_t^{TL}$, $loss_t^{RL}$, and $loss_t^{BL}$ are -2.66, -3.25, and -4.73, respectively. This implies that we cannot reject the unit-root hypothesis for the residuals of the equation for the loss rate on total loans. For the loss rate on real estate loans we reject this hypothesis at the 5%, but not on the 1% significance level, whereas the residual of the equation for losses on business loans is clearly stationary. In all three cases, however, the residual persistence of the STR model is less than that of the MS model.

Figure A2 depicts the weights to (or probabilities of) Regime 2 which are implied by the STR and MS models. While the two types of models yield transitions between regimes which are broadly reminiscent of each other, there are nevertheless several sharp differences as is clear from the figure. The most wide dispersion between the regimes is obtained with respect to the models for losses on total loans (upper panel). The regime classification of the MS model for this loss rate, does not seem to be entirely reasonable. In particular, the episodes in the "bad" regime which are associated with the crisis periods in the early 1990s and late 2000s are very long, for instance starting the the late 1999's for the latter crisis. Moreover, the strength of Regime 2 declines just prior to the crisis. These results indicate that the MS model for losses on total loans may not be able to characterize the data adequately, which is also evidenced by the failure to reject the unit-root hypothesis for the residuals of this equation. Turning to the models for the two remaining loss rates, we see that the transition patterns are more closely aligned. However, there is a clear tendency for the STR regimes to increase and decline approximately one year before the MS regimes. The only exception to this pattern is during the early 90's recession in the model for losses on real estate loans, where the MS transition moves more sharply around the crisis date than the one obtained from the STR model.

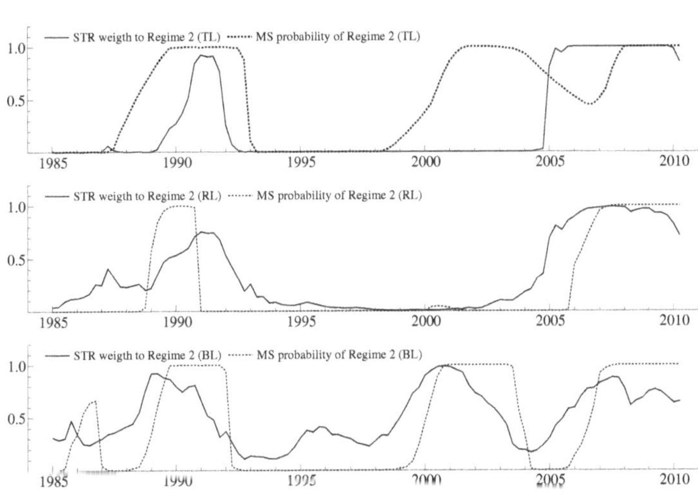

Figure A2. Estimated weights/probabilities to Regime 2 implied by the STR and the MS models.

Taken together, these results point to substantial differences between the predictions of the two types of models. While the STR model is more demanding, as it requires successful specification of the transition variable, it nevertheless delivers significant pay-offs in terms of statistical fit, early warnings, and economic interpretation.

Acknowledgments: We thank Michael Goldberg and Katarina Juselius for giving us extensive feedback on an earlier version of this paper. We have also benefited from numerous valuable comments and suggestions provided by Sigbjørn Attle Berg, Claudio Borio, Diana Bonfim, Stephen Cecchetti, Andrew Filardo, Staffan Ringbom, Jerome Stein, Paul Wachtel, and participants at presentations given at the Bank for International Settlements, 17th Dubrovnik Economic Conference, Bank of Finland, Norges Bank, Van Leer Jerusalem Institute, the 14th DNB Annual Research Conference, and 21st EC-squared conference. Remaining errors and omissions are our own.

Author Contributions: Mikael Juselius and Moshe Kim developed the analysis and drafted the article. Mikael Juselius collected the data, implemented the analysis in CATS in RATS, PcGive and GAUSS, and interpreted the results. Both authors contributed to the critical revision of the article.

Conflicts of Interest: The authors declare no conflict of interest.

References

Altunbas, Yener, Leonardo Gambacorta, and David Marques-Ibanez. 2010. Does Monetary Policy Affect Bank Risk-Taking? *BIS Working Papers*, No. 298. Available online: http://www.bis.org/publ/work298.htm (accessed on 6 November 2012).

Berger, Allen N., Marco A. Espinosa-Vega, Nathan H. Miller, and W. Scott Frame. 2005. Debt maturity, risk, and asymmetric information. *The Journal of Finance* 60: 2895–923.

Bernanke, Ben S., Mark Gertler, and Simon Gilchrist. 1999. The financial accelerator in a quantitative business cycle framework. In *Handbook of Macroeconomics*. Edited by John B. Taylor and Michael Woodford. Amsterdam: North-Holland, vol. 1.

Borio, Claudio. 2009. Implementing the macroprudential approach to financial regulation and supervision. *Banque de France Financial Stability Review* 13: 31–41.

Borio, Claudio, and Mathias Drehmann. 2009. Assessing the risk of banking crises-revisited. *BIS Quarterly Review*, March. Available online: http://www.bis.org/publ/qtrpdf/r_qt0903e.htm (accessed on 6 November 2012).

Borio, Claudio, and Philip Lowe. 2002. Asset prices, financial and monetary stability: Exploring the nexus. *BIS Working Papers*, No. 114. Available online: http://www.bis.org/publ/work114.htm (accessed on 6 November 2012).

Burnside, Craig, Martin Eichenbaum, and Sergio Rebelo. 2016. Understanding booms and busts in housing markets. *Journal of Political Economy* 124(4): 1088–147.

Caballero, Ricardo J., Emmanuel Farhi, and Pierre-Olivier Gourinchas. 2008. An equilibrium model of "global imbalances" and low interest rates. *American Economic Review* 98: 358–93.

Campello, Murillo, John R. Graham, and Campbell R. Harvey. 2010. The real effects of financial constraints: Evidence from a financial crisis. *Journal of Financial Economics* 97: 470–87.

Choi, In, and Pentti Saikkonen. 2004. Testing linearity in cointegrating smooth transition regressions. *Econometrics Journal* 7: 341–65.

Dell'Ariccia, Giovanni, and Robert Marquez. 2006. Lending booms and lending standards. *The Journal of Finance* 61: 2511–46.

Drehmann, Mathias, Claudio Borio, Leonardo Gambacorta, Gabriel Jiménez, and Carlos Trucharte. 2010. Countercyclical capital buffers: Exploring options. *BIS Working Papers*, No. 317. Available online: http://www.bis.org/publ/work317.htm (accessed on 6 November 2012).

Drehmann, Mathias, and Mikael Juselius. 2012. Do debt service costs affect macroeconomic and financial stability? *BIS Quarterly Review*, September. Available online: http://www.bis.org/publ/qtrpdf/r_qt1209e.htm (accessed on 6 November 2012).

Dynan, Karen, Kathleen Johnson, and Karen Pence. 2003. Recent changes to a measure of US household debt service. *Federal Reserve Bulletin* 89: 417–26.

Frydman, Roman, and Michael D. Goldberg. 2009. Financial markets and the state: Price swings, risk, and the scope of regulation. *Capitalism and Society* 4: 1–43.

Gai, Prasanna, Sujit Kapadia, Stephen Millard, and Ander Perez. 2008. Financial innovation, macroeconomic stability and systemic crises. *The Economic Journal* 118: 401–26.

Gertler, Mark, and Cara S. Lown. 1999. The information in the high-yield bond spread for the business cycle: Evidence and some implications. *Oxford Review of Economic Policy* 15: 132–50.

Gilchrist, Simon, Vladimir Yankov, and Egon Zakrajšek. 2009. Credit market shocks and economic fluctuations: Evidence from corporate bond and stock markets. *Journal of Monetary Economics* 56: 471–93.

Hall, Robert. 2011. The long slump. *American Economic Review* 101(2): 431–69.

Iacoviello, Matteo. 2005. House prices, borrowing constraints, and monetary policy in the business cycle. *American Economic Review* 95: 739–64.

Johansen, Søren. 1996. *Likelihood-Based Inference in Cointegrated Vector Auto-Regressive Models*. Oxford: Oxford University Press.

King, Mervyn. 1994. Debt deflation: Theory and evidence. *European Economic Review* 38: 419–55.

Kiyotaki, Nobuhiro, and Mark Gertler. 2010. Financial intermediation and credit policy in business cycle analysis. In *Handbook of Monetary Economics*. Edited by Benjamin M. Friedman and Michael Woodford. Amsterdam: Elsevier.

Kiyotaki, Nobuhiro, and John Moore. 1997. Credit cycles. *Journal of Political Economy* 105: 211–48.

Leybourne, Stephen, Paul Newbold, and Dimitrios Vougas. 1998. Unit roots and smooth transitions. *Journal of Time Series Analysis* 19: 83–97.

Lorenzoni, Guido. 2008. Inefficient credit booms. *Review of Economic Studies* 78: 809–33.

Meier, Andre, and Gernot J. Müller. 2006. Fleshing out the monetary transmission mechanism: Output composition and the role of financial frictions. *Journal of Money, Credit, and Banking* 38: 2099–133.

Mian, Atif, and Amir Sufi. 2010. The great recession: Lessons from microeconomic data. *American Economic Review* 100: 1–10.

Miller, Marcus, and Joseph E. Stiglitz. 2010. Leverage and asset bubbles: Averting armageddon with chapter 11? *The Economic Journal* 120: 500–18.

Nelson, Charles R., Jeremy Piger, and Eric Zivot. 2001. Markov regime switching and unit-root tests. *Journal of Business & Economic Statistics* 19: 404–15.

Repullo, Rafael, Jesus Saurina, and Carlos Trucharte. 2010. Mitigating the pro-cyclicality of Basel II. *Economic Policy* 25: 659–702.

Ruckes, Martin. 2004. Bank competition and credit standards. *The Review of Financial Studies* 17: 1073–102.

Saikkonen, Pentti, and In Choi. 2004. Cointegration smooth transition regressions. *Econometric Theory* 20: 301–40.

Saikkonen, Pentti, and In Choi. 2010. Tests for nonlinear cointegration. *Econometric Theory* 26: 682–709.

Stein, Jerome L. 2006. *Stochastic Optimal Control, International Finance, and Debt Crises*. Oxford: Oxford University Press.

Stohs, Mark Hoven, and David C. Mauer. 1996. The determinants of corporate debt maturity structure. *The Journal of Business* 69: 279–312.

Van Dijk, Dick, Timo Teräsvirta, and Philip Hans Franses. 2002. Smooth transition autoregressive models—A survey of recent developments. *Econometric Reviews* 21: 1–47.

econometrics

MDPI

Article

Improved Inference on Cointegrating Vectors in the Presence of a near Unit Root Using Adjusted Quantiles

Massimo Franchi [1] **and Søren Johansen** [2,3,*]

[1] Department of Statistical Sciences, Sapienza University of Rome, P.le A. Moro 5, 00198 Rome, Italy; massimo.franchi@uniroma1.it

[2] Department of Economics, University of Copenhagen, Øster Farimagsgade 5 Building 26, 1353 Copenhagen K, Denmark

[3] CREATES, Department of Economics and Business, Aarhus University, Building 1322, DK-8000 Aarhus C, Denmark

* Correspondence: soren.johansen@econ.ku.dk; Tel.: +45-35-323-071

Academic Editor: Katarina Juselius

Received: 20 April 2017; Accepted: 7 June 2017; Published: 14 June 2017

Abstract: It is well known that inference on the cointegrating relations in a vector autoregression (CVAR) is difficult in the presence of a near unit root. The test for a given cointegration vector can have rejection probabilities under the null, which vary from the nominal size to more than 90%. This paper formulates a CVAR model allowing for multiple near unit roots and analyses the asymptotic properties of the Gaussian maximum likelihood estimator. Then two critical value adjustments suggested by McCloskey (2017) for the test on the cointegrating relations are implemented for the model with a single near unit root, and it is found by simulation that they eliminate the serious size distortions, with a reasonable power for moderate values of the near unit root parameter. The findings are illustrated with an analysis of a number of different bivariate DGPs.

Keywords: long-run inference; test on cointegrating relations; likelihood inference; vector autoregressive model; near unit roots; Bonferroni type adjusted quantiles

JEL Classification: C32

---

1. Introduction

Elliott (1998) and Cavanagh et al. (1995) investigated the test on a coefficient of a cointegrating relation in the presence of a near unit root in a bivariate cointegrating regression. They show convincingly that when inference on the coefficient is performed as if the process has a unit root, then the size distortion is serious, see top panel of Figure A1 for a reproduction of their results. This paper analyses the p-dimensional cointegrated VAR model with r cointegrating relations under local alternatives

$$\Delta y_t = (\alpha\beta' + T^{-1}\alpha_1 c\beta_1')y_{t-1} + \varepsilon_t, \qquad t = 1, \ldots, T, \tag{1}$$

where α, β are $p \times r$ and ε_t is i.i.d. $N_p(0, \Omega)$. It is assumed that α_1 and β_1 are known $p \times (p-r)$ matrices of rank $p-r$, and c is $(p-r) \times (p-r)$ and an unknown parameter, such that the model allows for a whole matrix, c, of near unit roots. We consider below the likelihood ratio test, Q_β, for a given value of β, calculated as if $c = 0$, that is, as if we have a CVAR with rank r. The properties of the test Q_β can be very bad, when the actual data generating process (DGP) is a slight perturbation of the process generated by the model specified by $\alpha\beta'$. The matrix $\alpha\beta'$ describes a surface in the space of $p \times p$ matrices of dimension $p^2 - (p-r)^2$. Therefore a model is formulated that in some particular "directions", given by the matrix $\alpha_1 c\beta_1'$, has a small perturbation of the order of T^{-1} and $(p-r)^2$ extra parameters, c, that are used to describe the near unit roots.

A similar model could be suggested for near unit roots in the $I(2)$ model, see Di Iorio et al. (2016), but this will not be attempted here.

The model (1) contains as a special case the DGP used for the simulations in Elliott (1998), whe the errors are i.i.d. Gaussian and no deterministic components are present. The likelihood ratio test, Q_β, for β equal to a given value, is derived assuming that $c = 0$ and analyzed when in fact near unit roots are present, $c \neq 0$. The parameters α, β, and Ω can be estimated consistently, but c cannot, and this is what causes the bad behaviour of Q_β.

The matrix $\Pi(\alpha, \beta, c) = \alpha\beta' + T^{-1}\alpha_1 c\beta_1'$ is an invertible function of the p^2 parameters (α, β, c), see Lemma 1, so that the Gaussian maximum likelihood estimator in model (1) is least squares, and their limit distributions are found in Theorem 2. The main contribution of this paper, however, is a simulation study for the bivariate VAR with $p = 2$, $r = 1$. It is shown that two of the methods introduced by McCloskey (2017, Theorems Bonf and Bonf -Adj), for allowing the critical value for Q_β to depend on the estimator of c, give a much better solution to inference on β, in the case of a near unit root. The results of McCloskey (2017) also allow for multivariate parameters and for more complex adjustments, but in the present paper we focus for the simulations on the case with $p = 2$ and $r = 1$, so there is only one parameter in c. In case $r = 1$, the matrix $I_p + \Pi$ is linear in $c \in \mathbb{R}$, and for $c = 0$, it has an extra unit root. Therefore there is a near unit root for $c \neq 0$, and we choose the vector α_1 such $c \geq 0$ corresponds to the non-explosive near unit roots of interest.

The assumption that α_1 and β_1 are known is satisfied under the null, in the DGP analyzed by Elliott, see (15) and (16). This is of course convenient, because α_1, β_1 as free parameters, are not estimable.

Let θ denote the parameters α, β and Ω and let $\hat{\theta}$ and $\hat{c}$ denote the maximum likelihood estimators in model (1). For a given η (here 5% or 10%), the quantile $c_{\theta,\eta}(c)$ is defined by $P_{c,\theta}\{\hat{c} \leq c_{\theta,\eta}(c)\} = \eta$. Simulations show that the quantile is increasing in c, and solving the inequality for c, a $1-\eta$ confidence interval, $[0, c_{\theta,\eta}^{-1}(\hat{c})]$, is defined for c. For given ξ (here 90% or 95%) the quantile $q_{\theta,\xi}(c)$ is defined by $P_{c,\theta}\{Q_\beta \leq q_{\theta,\xi}(c)\} = \xi$, and McCloskey (2017) suggests replacing the critical value $q_{\theta,\xi}(c)$, by the stochastic critical value $q_{\theta,\xi}(c_{\theta,\eta}^{-1}(\hat{c}))$, or introducing the optimal ξ by solving the equation

$$\max_{0 \leq c \leq \infty} P_{c,\theta}\left\{Q_\beta \leq q_{\theta,\xi}\left(c_{\theta,\eta}^{-1}(\hat{c})\right)\right\} = v,$$

for a given nominal size v (here 10%).

These methods are explained and implemented by a simulation study, and it is shown that they offer a solution to the problem of inference on β in the presence of a near unit root.

2. The Vector Autoregressive Model with near Unit Roots

2.1. The Model

The model is given by (1) and the following standard $I(1)$ assumptions are made.

Assumption 1. *It is assumed that $r < p$, c is $(p-r) \times (p-r)$, and that the equation*

$$\det\left(I_p(1-z) - \alpha\beta' z\right) = 0$$

has $p-r$ roots equal to one, and the remaining roots are outside the unit circle, such that $|eigen(I_r + \beta'\alpha)| < 1$. Moreover $\Pi = \alpha\beta' + T^{-1}\alpha_1 c\beta_1'$ has rank p and

$$\det\left(I_p(1-z) - \alpha\beta' z - T^{-1}\alpha_1 c\beta_1' z\right) = 0, \tag{2}$$

has all roots outside the unit circle for all $T \geq T_0$.

For the asymptotic analysis we need condition (2) to hold for T tending to ∞, and for the simulations, we need it to hold for $T = 100$. In model (1) with cointegrating rank r and α_1 and β_1 known, the number of free parameters in α and β is $2pr - r^2 = p^2 - (p-r)^2$. The next result shows how the parameters α, β, c are calculated from Π. For any $p \times m$ matrix of rank $m < p$, we use the notation $a_\perp$ to indicate a $p \times (p-m)$ matrix of rank $p - m$, for which $a'_\perp a = 0$, and the notation $\bar{a} = a(a'a)^{-1}$.

Lemma 1. *Let $\Pi = \alpha\beta' + T^{-1}\alpha_1 c\beta_1'$ and let Assumption 1 be satisfied. Then, for β normalized as $\beta'b = I_r$,*

$$\alpha = \Pi\beta_{1\perp}(\alpha'_{1\perp}\Pi\beta_{1\perp})^{-1}\alpha'_{1\perp}\Pi b, \tag{3}$$
$$\beta' = (\alpha'_{1\perp}\Pi b)^{-1}\alpha'_{1\perp}\Pi, \tag{4}$$
$$c = T(\beta_1'\Pi^{-1}\alpha_1)^{-1}. \tag{5}$$

To discuss the estimation we introduce the product moments of Δy_t and y_{t-1}

$$S_{00} = T^{-1}\sum_{t=1}^{T}\Delta y_t \Delta y_t', \qquad S_{11} = T^{-1}\sum_{t=1}^{T} y_{t-1}y_{t-1}', \qquad S_{10} = S_{01}' = T^{-1}\sum_{t=1}^{T} y_{t-1}\Delta y_t'.$$

Theorem 2. *In model (1) with α_1 and β_1 known, the Gaussian maximum likelihood estimator of $\Pi = \alpha\beta' + T^{-1}\alpha_1 c\beta_1'$ is the coefficient in a least squares regression of Δy_t on y_{t-1}. For β normalized on some $p \times r$ matrix b, $\beta'b = I_r$, the maximum likelihood estimators (α, β, c) are given in (3)–(5) by inserting $\hat{\Pi}$.*

For $c = 0$, such that the rank of Π is r, the likelihood ratio test for a given value of β is

$$Q_\beta = T \log \frac{\det\left(S_{00} - S_{01}\beta(\beta' S_{11}^{-1}\beta)\beta' S_{10}\right)}{\det\left(S_{00} - S_{01}\breve{\beta}(\breve{\beta}' S_{11}^{-1}\breve{\beta})\breve{\beta}' S_{10}\right)}, \tag{6}$$

where the maximum likelihood estimator $\breve{\beta}$ is determined by reduced rank regression assuming the rank is r.

2.2. Asymptotic Distributions

The basic asymptotic result for the analysis of the estimators and the test statistic is that $\alpha'_\perp y_t$ converges to an Ornstein-Uhlenbeck process. This technique was developed by Phillips (1988), and Johansen (1996, chp. 14) is used as a reference for details related to the CVAR. The results for the test statistic can be found in Elliott (1998).

Under Assumption 1, the process given by (1) satisfies

$$T^{-1/2}\alpha'_\perp y_{[Tu]} \overset{D}{\to} K(u),$$

where K is the Ornstein-Uhlenbeck process

$$K(u) = \alpha'_\perp \int_0^u \exp\left\{\alpha_1 c\beta_1' C(u-s)\right\} dW_\varepsilon(s),$$

$C = \beta_\perp(\alpha'_\perp\beta_\perp)^{-1}\alpha'_\perp$ and W_ε is Brownian motion generated by the cumulated ε_t.

Theorem 3. *The test Q_β for a given value of β, derived assuming $c = 0$, see (6), satisfies*

$$Q_\beta \overset{D}{\to} \chi^2_{(p-r)r} + B, \tag{7}$$

where the stochastic noncentrality parameter

$$B = tr\left\{\beta_1 c'\zeta c\beta_1'\beta_\perp(\alpha_\perp'\beta_\perp)^{-1}\left(\int_0^1 KK'du\right)(\beta_\perp'\alpha_\perp)^{-1}\beta_\perp'\right\}, \tag{8}$$

is independent of the χ^2 *distribution and has expectation*

$$E(B) = tr\left\{\beta_1 c'\zeta c\beta_1' C\left(\int_0^1 (1-v)\exp(v\tau C)\Omega\exp(vC'\tau')dv\right)C'\right\}. \tag{9}$$

Here $\zeta = \alpha_1'\Omega^{-1}\alpha(\alpha'\Omega^{-1}\alpha)^{-1}\alpha'\Omega^{-1}\alpha_1$ *and* $\tau = \alpha_1 c\beta_1'$, *so it follows that* $E(B) = 0$ *if and only if* $\alpha_1'\Omega^{-1}\alpha = 0$, *in which case* $Q_\beta \xrightarrow{D} \chi^2_{(p-r)r}$.

Let β *be normalized as* $\beta'\beta_{1\perp} = I_r$. *The asymptotic distribution of the estimators,* $\hat{\alpha}$, $\hat{\beta}$, $\hat{c}$, *see (3)–(5), are given as*

$$T^{1/2}(\hat{\alpha}-\alpha) \xrightarrow{D} N_{p\times r}(0, \Sigma_{\beta\beta}^{-1}\otimes\Omega), \tag{10}$$

$$T(\hat{\beta}-\beta)'\beta_\perp \xrightarrow{D} (\alpha_{1\perp}'\alpha)^{-1}\alpha_{1\perp}'\int_0^1 (dW_\varepsilon)K'\left(\int_0^1 KK'du\right)^{-1}\alpha_\perp'\beta_\perp, \tag{11}$$

$$\hat{c}-c \xrightarrow{D} (\alpha_\perp'\alpha_1)^{-1}\alpha_\perp'\int_0^1 (dW_\varepsilon)K'\left(\int_0^1 KK'du\right)^{-1}\alpha_\perp'\beta_\perp(\beta_1'\beta_\perp)^{-1}. \tag{12}$$

Note that the asymptotic distributions of $\hat{\beta}$ and $\hat{c}$ given in (11) and (12) are not mixed Gaussian, because $\alpha_{1\perp}'W_\varepsilon(u)$ and $\alpha_\perp'W_\varepsilon(u)$ are not independent of $K(u)$, which is generated by $\alpha_\perp'\varepsilon_t$.

Corollary 1. *In the special case where* $r = p-1$, *we choose* α_1 *so that* $c \geq 0$, *and find*

$$E(B) = \frac{e^{2\delta c}-1-2\delta c}{(2\delta)^2}\kappa\zeta, \tag{13}$$

where

$$\delta = \beta_1'C\alpha_1, \quad \kappa = \beta_1'C\Omega C'\beta_1, \quad \zeta = \alpha_1'\Omega^{-1}\alpha(\alpha'\Omega^{-1}\alpha)^{-1}\alpha'\Omega^{-1}\alpha_1.$$

3. Critical Value Adjustment for Test on β in the CVAR with near Unit Roots

3.1. Bonferroni Bounds

In this section the method of McCloskey (2017, Theorem Bonf) is illustrated by a number of simulation experiments. The simulations are performed with data generated by a bivariate model (1), where $p = 2$ and $r = 1$. The direction α_1 is chosen such that $c \geq 0$. The test Q_β for a given value of β, is calculated assuming $c = 0$, see (6). The simulations of Elliott (1998), see Section 3.3, show that there may be serious size distortions of the test, depending on the value of c and ρ, if the test is based on the quantiles from the asymptotic $\chi^2(1)$ distribution.

The methods of McCloskey (2017) consists in this case of replacing the $\chi^2(1)$ critical value with a stochastic critical value depending on $\hat{c}$, in order to control the rejection probability under the null hypothesis.

Let $\theta = (\alpha, \beta, \Omega)$ and let $P_{c,\theta}$ denote the probability measure corresponding to the parameters c, θ. The method consists of finding the η quantile of $\hat{c}$, see (5) with Π replaced by $\hat{\Pi}$, as defined by

$$P_{c,\theta}\left(\hat{c} \leq c_{\theta,\eta}(c)\right) = \eta,$$

for $\eta = 5\%$ or 10%, say, and the ξ quantile $q_{\theta,\xi}(c)$ of Q_β as defined by

$$P_{c,\theta}\Big(Q_\beta \leq q_{\theta,\xi}(c)\Big) = \xi,$$

for $\xi = 90\%$ or 95%, say.

By simulation for given θ and a grid of given of values $c \in (c_1, \ldots, c_n)$, the quantiles $c_{\theta,\eta}(c_i)$ and $q_{\theta,\xi}(c_i)$ are determined. It turns out, that both $c_{\theta,\eta}(c)$ and $q_{\theta,\xi}(c)$ are increasing in c, see Figure A2. Therefore, a solution $c_{\theta,\eta}^{-1}(\hat{c})$ can be found such that

$$P_{c,\theta}\Big\{\hat{c} > c_{\theta,\eta}(c)\Big\} = P_{c,\theta}\Big\{c \leq c_{\theta,\eta}^{-1}(\hat{c})\Big\} = 1 - \eta. \tag{14}$$

This gives a $1 - \eta$ confidence interval $[0, c_{\theta,\eta}^{-1}(\hat{c})]$ for c, based on the estimator $\hat{c}$. Note that for $c \leq c_{\theta,\eta}^{-1}(\hat{c})$ it holds by monotonicity of $q_{\theta,\xi}(\cdot)$ that $q_{\theta,\xi}(c) \leq q_{\theta,\xi}(c_{\theta,\eta}^{-1}(\hat{c}))$, such that

$$P_{c,\theta}\left[Q_\beta > q_{\theta,\xi}\Big\{c_{\theta,\eta}^{-1}(\hat{c})\Big\} \text{ and } c \leq c_{\theta,\eta}^{-1}(\hat{c})\right] \leq P_{c,\theta}\Big\{Q_\beta > q_{\theta,\xi}(c)\Big\} \leq 1 - \xi,$$

but we also have

$$P_{c,\theta}\left[Q_\beta > q_{\theta,\xi}\Big\{c_{\theta,\eta}^{-1}(\hat{c})\Big\} \text{ and } c > c_{\theta,\eta}^{-1}(\hat{c})\right] \leq P_{c,\theta}\left[c > c_{\theta,\eta}^{-1}(\hat{c})\right] = \eta,$$

such that

$$P_{c,\theta}\left[Q_\beta > q_{\theta,\xi}\Big\{c_{\theta,\eta}^{-1}(\hat{c})\Big\}\right\} \leq 1 - \xi + \eta.$$

In the paper from McCloskey (2017) it is proved under suitable conditions that we have the much stronger result

$$1 - \xi \leq \limsup_{T\to\infty} \sup_{0\leq c<\infty} P_{c,\theta}\left[Q_\beta > q_{\hat{\theta},\xi}\Big\{c_{\hat{\theta},\eta}^{-1}(\hat{c})\Big\}\right] \leq 1 - \xi + \eta.$$

Thus, the limiting rejection probability, for given θ, of the test on β, calculated as if $c = 0$, but replacing the $\chi_\xi^2(1)$ quantile by the estimated stochastic quantile $q_{\hat{\theta},\xi}(c_{\hat{\theta},\eta}^{-1}(\hat{c}))$, lies between $1 - \xi$ and $1 - \xi + \eta$. In the simulations we set $\eta = 0.05$ and $\xi = 0.95$, so that the limiting rejection probability is bounded by 10%.

Note that θ is replaced by the consistent estimator $\hat{\theta}$. It obviously simplifies matters that in all the examples we simulate, it turns out that $c_{\theta,\eta}(c)$ is approximately linear and increasing in c, and $q_{\theta,\xi}(c)$ is approximately quadratic and increasing in c for the relevant values of c, see Figure A2.

3.2. *Adjusted Bonferroni Bounds*

McCloskey (2017, Theorem Bonf-Adj) suggests determining by simulation on a grid of values of c and ξ, the quantitity

$$\bar{P}_{\theta,\eta}(\xi) = \max_{0\leq c\leq\infty} P_{c,\theta}\Big(Q_\beta > q_{\theta,\xi}(c_{\theta,\eta}^{-1}(\hat{c})\Big).$$

It turns out that $\bar{P}_{\theta,\eta}(\xi)$ is monotone in ξ, and we can determine for a given nominal size v (here 10%)

$$\xi_{opt} = \bar{P}_{\theta,\eta}^{-1}(v).$$

The Adjusted Bonferroni quantile is then

$$q_{\theta,\xi_{opt}}\Big(c_{\theta,\eta}^{-1}(\hat{c})\Big),$$

and we find

$$P_{c,\theta}\left(Q_\beta > q_{\theta,\xi_{opt}}(c_{\theta,\eta}^{-1}(\hat{c})\right) \leq v.$$

The result of McCloskey (2017, Theorem Bonf-Adj) is that under suitable assumptions

$$\limsup_{T\to\infty} \sup_{0\leq c<\infty} P_{c,\theta}\left[Q_\beta > q_{\hat{\theta},\xi_{opt}}\left\{c_{\hat{\theta},\eta}^{-1}(\hat{c})\right\}\right] = v,$$

where we illustrate the upper bound.

3.3. The Simulation Study of Elliott (1998)

The DGP is defined by the equations,

$$y_{1t} = \left(1 - \frac{c}{T}\right) y_{1t-1} + u_{1t}, \tag{15}$$

$$y_{2t} = \gamma y_{1t} + u_{2t}. \tag{16}$$

It is assumed that $u_t = (u_{1t}, u_{2t})'$ are i.i.d. $N_2(0, \Omega_u)$ with

$$\Omega_u = \begin{pmatrix} 1 & \rho \\ \rho & 1 \end{pmatrix},$$

and the initial values are $y_{10} = y_{20} = 0$. The data $y_1, \ldots, y_T$ are generated from (15) and (16), and the test statistic Q_β for the hypothesis $\gamma = 0$, is calculated using (6).

The DGP defined by (15) and (16) is contained in model (1) for $p = 2$. Note that $y_{2t} = \gamma(1 - c/T)y_{1t-1} + \gamma u_{1t} + u_{2t}$ such that

$$\alpha = \begin{pmatrix} 0 \\ 1 \end{pmatrix}, \beta = \begin{pmatrix} \gamma \\ -1 \end{pmatrix}, \alpha_1 = \begin{pmatrix} -1 \\ -\gamma \end{pmatrix}, \beta_1 = \begin{pmatrix} 1 \\ 0 \end{pmatrix}, \tag{17}$$

where the sign on α_1 has been chosen such that $c \geq 0$. Finally $\varepsilon_{1t} = u_{1t}$ and $\varepsilon_{2t} = u_{2t} + \gamma u_{1t}$, and therefore

$$\Omega = \begin{pmatrix} 1 & \rho + \gamma \\ \rho + \gamma & 1 + \gamma^2 + 2\gamma\rho \end{pmatrix}.$$

For $c = 0$, the process $y_t = (y_{1t}, y_{2t})'$ is $I(1)$ and $\gamma y_{1t} - y_{2t}$ is stationary, and if c/T is close to zero, y_t has a near unit root.

Applying Corollary 1 to the DGP (15) and (16), the expectation of the test statistic Q_β is found to be

$$E(Q_\beta) = p - 1 + \frac{e^{-2c} - 1 + 2c}{4} \frac{\rho^2}{1 - \rho^2}, \tag{18}$$

which increases approximately linearly in c.

Based on $N = 1000$ simulations of errors $u_1, \ldots, u_T$, $T = 100$, the data $y_1, \ldots, y_T$, are constructed from the DGP for each combination of the parameters

$$(\gamma, c, \rho) \in [-0.5 : (0.01) : 0.5] \times [1 : (1) : 20] \times [-0.9 : (0.1) : 0.9],$$

where $[a : (b) : c]$ indicates the interval from a to c with step b. Based on each simulation, $\hat{c}$ and the test Q_β for $\gamma = 0$ are calculated.

Top panel of Figure A1 shows the rejection probabilities of the test Q_β as a function of (c, ρ), using the asymptotic critical value, $\chi^2_{0.90}(1) = 2.71$, for a nominal rejection probability of 10%. The rejection probability increases with $|\rho|$ and with c. When $c = 10$ (corresponding to an autoregressive coefficient of $c/T = 0.9$) and $|\rho| = 0.7$, the size of the test Q_β is around 50%, as found in Elliott (1998). The results are analogous across models with an unrestricted constant term, or with a constant restricted to the cointegrating space. In the paper by Elliott (1998) a number of tests are analyzed, and it was found that they were quite similar in their performance and similar to the above likelihood ratio test Q_β from the CVAR with rank equal to 1.

3.4. Results with Bonferroni Quantiles and Adjusted Bonferroni Quantiles for Q_β

Data are simulated as above and first the rank test statistic, Q_r, see Johansen (1996, chp. 11) for rank equal to 1, is calculated. The rejection probabilities for a 5% test using Q_r are given in the bottom panel of Figure A1 and they show that for $c = 20$, the hypothesis that the rank is 1, is practically certain to be rejected. If $c = 8$, the probability of rejecting that the rank is 1 is around 50%, so that plotting the rejection probabilities for $0 \leq c \leq 10$, covers the relevant values, see Figure A3.

For $\eta = 5\%$ and 10%, the quantiles $c_\eta(c)$ of $\hat{c}$ are reported in Figure A2 as a function of c. The quantiles $c_\eta(c)$ are nearly linear in c, and they are approximated by

$$\tilde{c}_\eta(c) = a_\eta + b_\eta c,$$

where the coefficients (a_η, b_η) depend on η, which is used to construct the upper confidence limit in (14) as

$$\tilde{c}_\eta^{-1}(\hat{c}) = (\hat{c} - a_\eta) b_\eta^{-1}.$$

For $\xi = 90\%$ and 95%, the quantiles $q_{\rho,\xi}(c)$ of Q_β are reported in Figure A2 as function of c for four values of ρ. It is seen that for given ρ, the quantiles $q_{\rho,\xi}(c)$ are monotone and quadratic in c, for relevant values of c, and hence they can be approximated by

$$\tilde{q}_{\rho,\xi}(c) = f_{\rho,\xi} + g_{\rho,\xi} c + h_{\rho,\xi} c^2, \tag{19}$$

where the coefficients $(f_{\rho,\xi}, g_{\rho,\xi}, h_{\rho,\xi})$ depend on ρ and ξ. The modified critical value is then constructed replacing (c, ρ) by $(\tilde{c}_\eta^{-1}(\hat{c}), \hat{\rho})$ in (19), and thus one finds the adjusted critical value

$$\tilde{q}_{\hat{\rho},\xi,\eta}(\hat{c}) = f_{\hat{\rho},\xi} + g_{\hat{\rho},\xi}(\hat{c} - a_\eta) b_\eta^{-1} + h_{\rho,\xi}\left((\hat{c} - a_\eta) b_\eta^{-1}\right)^2 \tag{20}$$

which depends on estimated values, $\hat{c}$ and $\hat{\rho}$, and on discretionary values, ξ and η.

The adjusted Bonferroni quantile is explained in Section 3.2. Simulations show that $\bar{P}_{\theta,\eta}(\xi)$ is linear in ξ and the solution of the equation

$$\bar{P}_{\theta,\eta}(\xi) = v,$$

where $v = 0.10$ is the nominal size of the test, determines ξ_{opt}; the adjusted Bonferroni q-quantile is then found like (20) as

$$\tilde{q}_{\hat{\rho},\xi_{opt},\eta}(\hat{c}) = f_{\hat{\rho},\xi_{opt}} + g_{\hat{\rho},\xi_{opt}}(\hat{c} - a_\eta) b_\eta^{-1} + h_{\rho,\xi_{opt}}\left((\hat{c} - a_\eta) b_\eta^{-1}\right)^2, \tag{21}$$

where $\eta = 0.05$.

The rejection frequency of Q_β, the test for $\gamma = 0$, calculated using the $\chi^2(1)_{0.90}$ quantile, the Bonferroni quantile in (20) for $\xi = 95\%$ and $\eta = 5\%$ and the adjusted Bonferroni quantile in (21) for $\eta = 5\%$ is reported as a function of c for four values of ρ in Figure A3. For both corrections the rejection frequency is below the nominal size of 10%; hence both procedures are able to eliminate the serious size-distortions of the χ^2 test. While the Bonferroni adjustment leads to rather conservative test with rejection frequency well below the nominal size, the adjusted Bonferroni procedure is closer to the nominal value. The power of the two procedures is shown in Figures A4 and A5 for values of $|\gamma| \leq 1/2$. It is seen that the better rejection probabilities in Figure A3 are achieved together with a reasonable power for $c \leq 5$, where the probability of rejecting the hypothesis of $r = 1$ is around 30%, see bottom panel of Figure A1. Notice that both tests become slightly biased, that is, the power functions are not flat around the null $\gamma = 0$.

In conclusion, the simulations indicate that the adjusted Bonferroni procedure works better than the simple Bonferroni, the reason being that the former relies on the joint distribution of Q_β and $\hat{c}$.

3.5. A Few Examples of Other DGPs

Four other data generating processes are defined in Table 1, to investigate the role of different choices of α_1 and β_1 for the results on improving the rejection probabilities for test on β under the null and alternative. The DGPs all have $\alpha = -\beta = (-1,1)'/2$. The vectors α_1 and β_1 are chosen to investigate different positions of the near unit root in the DGP.

The choice of DGP turns out to be important also for the test, Q_r, for $r = 1$. In fact the probability of rejecting $r = 1$ is around 50% for DGP 1 if $c = 4$, for DGP 2 if $c = 20$, whereas for DGP 3 and 4 the 50% value value is 8.

The rejection probabilities in Figure A6 are plotted for $0 \leq c \leq 10$, to cover the most relevant values.

The results are summarized in Figures A6–A8. It is seen that the conclusions from the study of the DGP analyzed by Elliott seem to be valid also for other DGPs. For moderate values of c, using the Bonferroni quantiles gives a rather conservative test while the adjusted Bonferroni procedure is closer to the nominal size and the power curves look reasonable for $c \leq 5$, although the tests are slightly biased, except for DGP 1. For this DGP, $\alpha_1 = \beta_1 = (1,1)'$, $\Omega = I_2$, such that $\alpha_1'\Omega^{-1}\alpha = 0$, which means that the asymptotic distribution of Q_β is $\chi^2(1)$, see Theorem 3, despite the near unit root. It is seen from Figure A6, there is only moderate distortion of the rejection probability in this case and in Figures A7 and A8, the power curves are symmetric around $\gamma = 0$, so the tests are approximately unbiased.

Table 1. The matrix Π for four different DGPs given by $\alpha = -\beta = (-1,1)'/2$ which are the basis for the simulations of rejection probabilities for the adjusted test for $\beta = (1,-1)'/2$. The positions of c/T give the different α_1 and β_1.

Four DGPs Allowing for near Unit Roots, $\Omega = I_2$			
1:	$\begin{pmatrix} -\frac{1}{4} - c/T & \frac{1}{4} - c/T \\ \frac{1}{4} - c/T & -\frac{1}{4} - c/T \end{pmatrix}$	2:	$\begin{pmatrix} -\frac{1}{4} & \frac{1}{4} \\ \frac{1}{4} & -\frac{1}{4} - c/T \end{pmatrix}$
3:	$\begin{pmatrix} -\frac{1}{4} & \frac{1}{4} \\ \frac{1}{4} - c/T & -\frac{1}{4} - c/T \end{pmatrix}$	4:	$\begin{pmatrix} -\frac{1}{4} - c/T & \frac{1}{4} - c/T \\ \frac{1}{4} & -\frac{1}{4} \end{pmatrix}$

4. Conclusions

It has been demonstrated that for the DGP analyzed by Elliott (1998), it is possible to apply the methods of McCloskey (2017) to adjust the critical value in such a way that the rejection probabilities of the test for β are very close to the nominal values. By simulating the power of the test for β, it is seen that for $c \leq 5$, the test has a reasonable power. Some other DGPs have been investigated and similar results have been found.

Acknowledgments: The first author gratefully acknowledges partial financial support from MIUR PRIN grant 2010J3LZEN and Stefano Fachin for discussions. The second author is grateful to CREATES - Center for Research in Econometric Analysis of Time Series (DNRF78), funded by the Danish National Research Foundation, and to Peter Boswijk and Adam McCloskey for discussions.

Author Contributions: Both authors contributed equally to the paper.

Conflicts of Interest: The authors declare no conflict of interest.

Appendix A. Proofs

Proof of Lemma 1. Multiplying $\Pi = \alpha\beta' + T^{-1}\alpha_1 c\beta_1'$ by $\beta_{1\perp}$, we find

$$\Pi\beta_{1\perp} = \alpha\beta'\beta_{1\perp}. \tag{A1}$$

Multiplying Π by $\alpha_{1\perp}'$ we find

$$\alpha_{1\perp}'\Pi = \alpha_{1\perp}'\alpha\beta' = \alpha_{1\perp}'\Pi\beta_{1\perp}(\beta'\beta_{1\perp})^{-1}\beta'. \tag{A2}$$

Multiplying by b we find

$$(\beta'\beta_{1\perp})^{-1} = (\alpha_{1\perp}'\Pi\beta_{1\perp})^{-1}\alpha_{1\perp}'\Pi b.$$

It follows that from (A2)

$$\beta' = \beta'\beta_{1\perp}(\alpha_{1\perp}'\Pi\beta_{1\perp})^{-1}\alpha_{1\perp}'\Pi = (\alpha_{1\perp}'\Pi b)^{-1}\alpha_{1\perp}'\Pi$$

and from (A1)

$$\alpha = \Pi\beta_{1\perp}(\beta'\beta_{1\perp})^{-1} = \Pi\beta_{1\perp}(\alpha_{1\perp}'\Pi\beta_{1\perp})^{-1}\alpha_{1\perp}'\Pi b,$$

which proves (3) and (4).

Inserting these results in the expression for Π, we find using $\alpha_{1\perp}'\Pi b\beta' = \alpha_{1\perp}'\alpha\beta' b\beta' = \alpha_{1\perp}\Pi$

$$\Pi = \alpha\beta' + T^{-1}\alpha_1 c\beta_1' = \Pi\beta_{1\perp}(\alpha_{1\perp}'\Pi\beta_{1\perp})^{-1}\alpha_{1\perp}'\Pi + T^{-1}\alpha_1 c\beta_1'. \tag{A3}$$

Next Π is decomposed using

$$\Pi = \Pi\beta_{1\perp}(\alpha_{1\perp}'\Pi\beta_{1\perp})^{-1}\alpha_{1\perp}'\Pi + \alpha_1(\beta_1'\Pi^{-1}\alpha_1)^{-1}\beta_1', \tag{A4}$$

which is proved by premultiplying (A4) by $\alpha_{1\perp}'$ and $\beta_1'\Pi^{-1}$. Subtracting (A3) and (A4) and multiplying by $\bar{\alpha}_1'$ and $\bar{\beta}_1$, it is seen that

$$(\beta_1'\Pi^{-1}\alpha_1)^{-1} = c/T.$$

□

Proof of Theorem 2. The unrestricted maximum likelihood estimator of Π is $\hat{\Pi} = S_{01}S_{11}^{-1}$, and $\hat{\Omega} = S_{00} - S_{01}S_{11}^{-1}S_{10}$, and the results for $\hat{\alpha}, \hat{\beta}, \hat{c}$ follow from Lemma 1. If $c = 0$, the maximum likelihood estimator $\breve{\beta}$ can be determined by reduced rank regression, see (Johansen (1996, chp. 6)). □

Proof of Theorem 3. Proof of (7) and (8): The limit results for the product moments are given first, using the normalization matrix $C_T = (\beta, T^{-1/2}\alpha_\perp)$ and the notation $S_{1\varepsilon} = T^{-1}\sum_{t=1}^T y_{t-1}\varepsilon_t'$,

$$C_T'S_{11}C_T = \begin{pmatrix} \beta'S_{11}\beta & T^{-1/2}\beta'S_{11}\alpha_\perp \\ T^{-1/2}\alpha_\perp'S_{11}\beta & T^{-1}\alpha_\perp'S_{11}\alpha_\perp \end{pmatrix} \overset{D}{\to} \begin{pmatrix} \Sigma_{\beta\beta} & 0 \\ 0 & \int_0^1 KK'du \end{pmatrix}, \tag{A5}$$

$$T^{1/2}C_T'S_{1\varepsilon} = \begin{pmatrix} T^{1/2}\beta'S_{1\varepsilon} \\ T^{-1}\alpha_\perp'S_{1\varepsilon} \end{pmatrix} \overset{D}{\to} \begin{pmatrix} N_{r\times p}(0, \Omega\otimes\Sigma_{\beta\beta}) \\ \int_0^1 K(dW_\varepsilon)' \end{pmatrix}. \tag{A6}$$

The test for a known value of β is given in (6). It is convenient for the derivation of the limit distribution of Q_β, to normalize $\check{\beta}$ on the matrix $\alpha(\beta'\alpha)^{-1}$, such that $\check{\beta}'\alpha(\beta'\alpha)^{-1} = I_r$, and define $\check{\theta} = (\beta_\perp'\alpha_\perp)^{-1}\beta_\perp'(\check{\beta} - \beta)$. This gives the representation

$$\check{\beta} - \beta = \alpha_\perp(\beta_\perp'\alpha_\perp)^{-1}\beta_\perp'(\check{\beta} - \beta) + \beta(\alpha'\beta)^{-1}\alpha'(\check{\beta} - \beta) = \alpha_\perp\check{\theta}.$$

The proof under much weaker conditions can be found in Elliott (1998), and is just sketched here. The estimator for θ for known α, Ω and $c = 0$, is given by the equation

$$T\check{\theta} = (\alpha_\perp' T^{-1} S_{11}\alpha_\perp)^{-1}(\alpha_\perp' S_{1\varepsilon} + \alpha_\perp' T^{-1} S_{11}\beta_1 c\alpha_1')\alpha_\Omega,$$

where $\alpha_\Omega = \Omega^{-1}\alpha(\alpha'\Omega^{-1}\alpha)^{-1}$. The limit distribution of $T\check{\theta}$ follows from (A5) and (A6) as follows. Because $T^{-1}\alpha_\perp' S_{11}\beta \overset{\mathrm{P}}{\to} 0$ it follows that

$$\begin{aligned}\alpha_\perp' T^{-1} S_{11}\beta_1 c\alpha_1' &= \alpha_\perp' T^{-1} S_{11}\left(\alpha_\perp(\beta_\perp'\alpha_\perp)^{-1}\beta_\perp' + \beta(\alpha'\beta)^{-1}\alpha'\right)\beta_1 c\alpha_1' \\ &\overset{\mathrm{D}}{\to} \left(\int_0^1 KK'du\right)(\beta_\perp'\alpha_\perp)^{-1}\beta_\perp'\beta_1 c\alpha_1',\end{aligned}$$

and from $\alpha_\perp' S_{1\varepsilon} \overset{\mathrm{D}}{\to} \int_0^1 K(dW_\varepsilon)$, it is seen that

$$T\check{\theta} \overset{\mathrm{D}}{\to} \left(\int_0^1 KK'du\right)^{-1}\left(\int_0^1 K(dW_\varepsilon) + \left(\int_0^1 KK'du\right)(\beta_\perp'\alpha_\perp)^{-1}\beta_\perp'\beta_1 c\alpha_1'\right)\alpha_\Omega = U,$$

say. Conditional on K, the distribution of U is Gaussian with variance $(\alpha'\Omega^{-1}\alpha)^{-1} \otimes (\int_0^1 KK'du)^{-1}$ and mean $(\beta_\perp'\alpha_\perp)^{-1}\beta_\perp'\beta_1 c\alpha_1'\alpha_\Omega$. The information about θ satisfies

$$T^{-2} I_{\theta\theta} = tr\left\{\Omega^{-1}\alpha(d\theta)'\alpha_\perp' S_{11}\alpha_\perp(d\theta)\alpha'\right\} \overset{\mathrm{D}}{\to} tr\left\{\alpha'\Omega^{-1}\alpha(d\theta)'\int_0^1 KK'du(d\theta)\right\},$$

and inserting U for $(d\theta)$ determines the asymptotic distribution of Q_β. Conditional on K, this has a noncentral $\chi^2((p-r)r)$ distribution with noncentrality parameter

$$B = tr\left\{(\beta_\perp'\alpha_\perp)^{-1}\beta_\perp'\beta_1 c'\zeta c\beta_1'\beta_\perp(\alpha_\perp'\beta_\perp)^{-1}\int_0^1 KK'du\right\},$$

where $\zeta = \alpha_1'\Omega^{-1}\alpha(\alpha'\Omega^{-1}\alpha)^{-1}\alpha'\Omega^{-1}\alpha_1$, which proves (8). The marginal distribution is therefore a noncentral χ^2 distribution with a stochastic noncentrality parameter, which is independent of the χ^2 distribution, as shown by Elliott (1998).

Proof of (9): For $\tau = \alpha_1 c\beta_1'$ it is seen that

$$\begin{aligned}&Etr\left\{(\beta_\perp'\alpha_\perp)^{-1}\beta_\perp'\beta_1 c'\zeta c\beta_1'\beta_\perp(\alpha_\perp'\beta_\perp)^{-1}\int_0^1 KK'du\right\} \\ &= Etr\left\{\beta_1 c'\zeta c\beta_1' C\int_0^1\left(\int_0^u \exp\left(\tau C(u-s)\right)dW(s)\right)\left(\int_0^u dW(t)'\exp\left(C'\tau'(u-t)\right)\right)duC'\right\} \\ &= tr\left\{\beta_1 c'\zeta c\beta_1' C\int_0^1\left(\int_0^u \exp\left(\tau C(u-s)\right)\Omega\exp(C'\tau'(u-s)\right)ds\right)duC'\right\} \\ &= tr\left\{\beta_1 c'\zeta c\beta_1' C\left(\int_0^1 (1-v)\exp(v\tau C)\Omega\exp(vC'\tau')dv\right)C'\right\},\end{aligned}$$

which proves (9). Note that this expression is zero if and only if $\zeta = 0$, or $\alpha_1'\Omega^{-1}\alpha = 0$, in which case the asymptotic distribution of Q_β is χ^2.

Proof of (10) and (11):

It follows that $\hat{\Pi} = S_{01}S_{11}^{-1}$ can be expressed as

$$\begin{aligned}\hat{\Pi} &= \alpha\beta' + T^{-1}\alpha_1 c\beta_1' + S_{\varepsilon 1}S_{11}^{-1} \\ &= \alpha\beta' + T^{-1}\alpha_1 c\beta_1' + T^{-1/2}(T^{1/2}S_{\varepsilon 1}C_T)(C_T'S_{11}C_T)^{-1}\left(\beta, T^{-1/2}\alpha_\perp\right)' \\ &= \alpha\beta' + T^{-1}\alpha_1 c\beta_1' + T^{-1/2}M_{1T}\beta' + T^{-1}M_{2T}\alpha_\perp',\end{aligned} \tag{A7}$$

where, using (A5) and (A6),

$$M_{1T} \overset{D}{\rightarrow} M_1 = N_{p\times r}(0, \Sigma_{\beta\beta}^{-1} \otimes \Omega), \tag{A8}$$

$$M_{2T} \overset{D}{\rightarrow} M_2 = \int_0^1 dW_\varepsilon K' \left(\int_0^1 KK'du\right)^{-1}. \tag{A9}$$

From $\hat{\beta}' = (\alpha_{1\perp}'\hat{\Pi}b)^{-1}\alpha_{1\perp}'\hat{\Pi}$, it follows that

$$\begin{aligned}T(\hat{\beta} - \beta)'\beta_\perp &= T(\alpha_{1\perp}'\hat{\Pi}b)^{-1}\alpha_{1\perp}'(\hat{\Pi} - \alpha\beta')\beta_\perp \\ &= (\alpha_{1\perp}'\hat{\Pi}b)^{-1}\alpha_{1\perp}'(T^{1/2}M_{1T}\beta' + M_{2T}\alpha_\perp')\beta_\perp \\ &\overset{D}{\rightarrow} (\alpha_{1\perp}'\alpha\beta'b)^{-1}\alpha_{1\perp}'M_2\alpha_\perp'\beta_\perp = (\alpha_{1\perp}'\alpha)^{-1}\alpha_{1\perp}'M_2\alpha_\perp'\beta_\perp,\end{aligned}$$

where $T^{1/2}M_{1T}\beta'\beta_\perp = 0$, $\alpha_{1\perp}'\alpha_1 c\beta_1' = 0$ and $\beta'b = I_r$. This proves (11).

From the normalization $\hat{\beta}'b = I_r$ we find, replacing $\hat{\beta}$ by β

$$\begin{aligned}T^{1/2}(\hat{\alpha} - \alpha) &= T^{1/2}(\hat{\Pi}\beta_{1\perp}(\beta'\beta_{1\perp})^{-1} - \Pi\beta_{1\perp}(\beta'\beta_{1\perp})^{-1}) \\ &= T^{1/2}(T^{-1/2}M_{1T} + T^{-1}M_{2T}\alpha_\perp'\beta_{1\perp}(\beta'\beta_{1\perp})^{-1}) + o_P(1) \\ &= M_{1T} + T^{-1/2}M_{2T}\alpha_\perp'\beta_{1\perp}(\beta'\beta_{1\perp})^{-1} + o_P(1) \overset{D}{\rightarrow} M_1,\end{aligned}$$

which proves (10).

Proof of (12): To analyse the limit distribution of $\hat{c}$, define

$$A_T = (T^{-1/2}\bar{\alpha}, \alpha_\perp) \text{ and } B_T = (T^{-1/2}\bar{\beta}, \beta_\perp),$$

and write

$$\hat{c} = T(\beta_1'\hat{\Pi}^{-1}\alpha_1)^{-1} = (\beta_1'B_T(A_T'T\hat{\Pi}B_T)^{-1}A_T'\alpha_1)^{-1}.$$

The expansion (A7), and the limits (A8) and (A9) are then applied to give the limit results

$$\begin{aligned}T^{-1/2}\bar{\alpha}'(T\hat{\Pi})T^{-1/2}\bar{\beta} &= I_r + O(T^{-1}) + O_P(T^{-1}), \\ T^{-1/2}\bar{\alpha}'(T\hat{\Pi})\beta_\perp &= 0 + O(T^{-1/2}) + O_P(T^{-1/2}), \\ \alpha_\perp'(T\hat{\Pi})\bar{\beta}T^{-1/2} &= 0 + O(T^{-1/2}) + \alpha_\perp'M_{1T}, \\ \alpha_\perp'(T\hat{\Pi})\beta_\perp &= 0 + \alpha_\perp'\alpha_1 c\beta_1'\beta_\perp + \alpha_\perp'M_{2T}\alpha_\perp'\beta_\perp.\end{aligned}$$

Thus

$$A'_T(T\hat{\Pi})B_T \overset{D}{\to} \begin{pmatrix} I_r & 0 \\ \alpha'_\perp M_1 & \alpha'_\perp \alpha_1 c \beta'_1 \beta_\perp + \alpha'_\perp M_2 \alpha'_\perp \beta_\perp \end{pmatrix},$$

$$B_T(A'_T(T\hat{\Pi})B_T)^{-1}A'_T \overset{D}{\to} (0,\beta_\perp) \begin{pmatrix} I_r & 0 \\ \alpha'_\perp M_1 & \alpha'_\perp \alpha_1 c \beta'_1 \beta_\perp + \alpha'_\perp M_2 \alpha'_\perp \beta_\perp \end{pmatrix}^{-1} (0,\alpha_\perp)'$$

$$= \beta_\perp(\alpha'_\perp \alpha_1 c \beta'_1 \beta_\perp + \alpha'_\perp M_2 \alpha'_\perp \beta_\perp)^{-1}\alpha'_\perp.$$

Multiplying by β'_1 and α_1 and inverting, it is seen that because $\beta'_1\beta_\perp$ and $\alpha'_1\alpha_\perp$ are $(p-r)\times(p-r)$ of full rank,

$$\begin{aligned} \hat{c} = (\beta'_1 B_T(A'_T T\hat{\Pi} B_T)^{-1}A'_T\alpha_1)^{-1} &\overset{D}{\to} [\beta'_1\beta_\perp(\alpha'_\perp \alpha_1 c \beta'_1 \beta_\perp + \alpha'_\perp M_2 \alpha'_\perp \beta_\perp)^{-1}\alpha'_\perp\alpha_1]^{-1} \\ &= (\alpha'_\perp\alpha_1)^{-1}(\alpha'_\perp \alpha_1 c \beta'_1 \beta_\perp + \alpha'_\perp M_2 \alpha'_\perp \beta_\perp)(\beta'_1\beta_\perp)^{-1} \\ &= c + (\alpha'_\perp\alpha_1)^{-1}\alpha'_\perp M_2 \alpha'_\perp \beta_\perp(\beta'_1\beta_\perp)^{-1}, \end{aligned}$$

which proves (12). □

Proof of Corollary 1. *Proof of (13):* If $r = p-1$, the expression (9) can be reduced as follows. For $\tau = \alpha_1 c \beta'_1$

$$(\tau C)^2 = c\alpha_1 c(\beta'_1 C\alpha_1)\beta'_1 C = c(\beta'_1 C\alpha_1)\alpha_1 c\beta'_1 C = c\delta\tau C,$$

for $\delta = \beta'_1 C\alpha_1$, and in general for $n \geq 0$, it is seen that

$$(\tau C)^{n+1} = (c\delta)^n \tau C.$$

Therefore, using $\beta_1 c'\zeta c\beta'_1 = \beta_1 c'\tau\Omega^{-1}\alpha(\alpha'\Omega^{-1}\alpha)^{-1}\alpha'\Omega^{-1}\tau'$,

$$E(B) = tr\{\Omega^{-1}\alpha(\alpha'\Omega^{-1}\alpha)^{-1}\alpha'\Omega^{-1}\tau C\left(\int_0^1 (1-v)\exp(v\tau C)\Omega\exp(vC'\tau')dv\right)C'\tau'\}.$$

The integral can be calculated by the expansion

$$\tau C\exp(v\tau C)\Omega\exp(vC'\tau')C'\tau' = \sum_{n,m=0}^{\infty}\frac{v^n}{n!}(\tau C)^{n+1}\Omega(C'\tau')^{m+1}\frac{v^m}{m!}$$

$$= \sum_{n,m=0}^{\infty}\frac{(vc\delta)^{n+m}}{n!m!}\tau C\Omega C'\tau' = \exp(2vc\delta)c^2\kappa\alpha_1\alpha'_1,$$

where $\kappa = \beta'_1 C\Omega C'\beta_1$. This allows the integral to be calculated

$$\tau C\left(\int_0^1 (1-v)\exp(v\tau C)\Omega\exp(vC'\tau')dv\right)C'\tau'$$

$$= \left(\int_0^1 (1-v)\exp(2vc\delta)dv\right)c^2\kappa\alpha_1\alpha'_1 = \frac{e^{2\delta c} - 1 - 2c\delta}{(2\delta c)^2}c^2\kappa\alpha_1\alpha'_1.$$

Therefore

$$E(B) = \frac{e^{2c\delta} - 1 - 2c\delta}{(2\delta)^2}\kappa\alpha'_1\Omega^{-1}\alpha(\alpha'\Omega^{-1}\alpha)^{-1}\alpha'\Omega^{-1}\alpha_1 = (e^{2c\delta} - 1 - 2c\delta)\frac{\kappa\zeta}{(2\delta)^2},$$

where $\zeta = \alpha'_1\Omega^{-1}\alpha(\alpha'\Omega^{-1}\alpha)^{-1}\alpha'\Omega^{-1}\alpha_1$. □

Appendix B. Figures

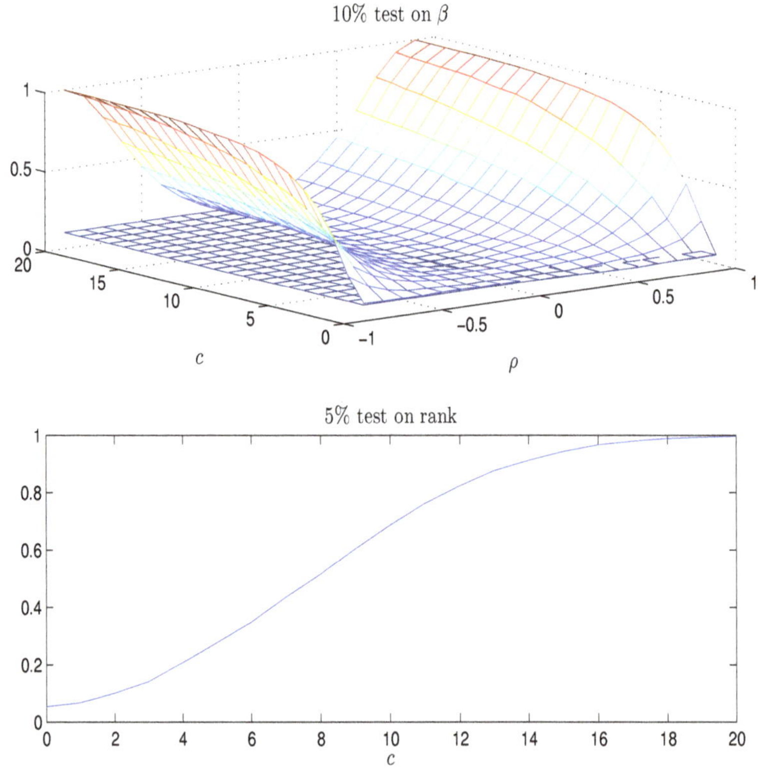

Figure A1. Top panel: Rejection frequency of the test Q_β for $\gamma = 0$ using the $\chi^2(1)_{0.90}$ quantile as a function of c and ρ. Bottom panel: Rejection frequency of the 5% test Q_r for $r = 1$ using Table 15.1 in Johansen (1996) as a function of c. $N = 1000$ simulations of $T = 100$ observations from the DGP (15) and (16).

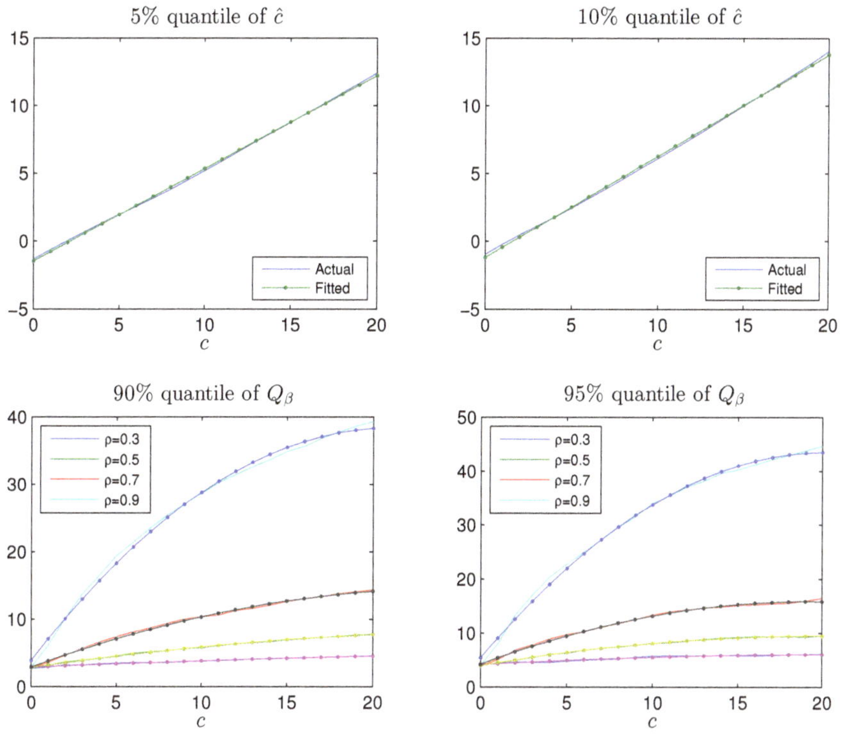

Figure A2. Quantiles and fitted values in the distributions of $\hat{c}$ and Q_β as a function of c for different values of ρ; $N = 1000$ simulations of $T = 100$ observations from the DGP (15) and (16).

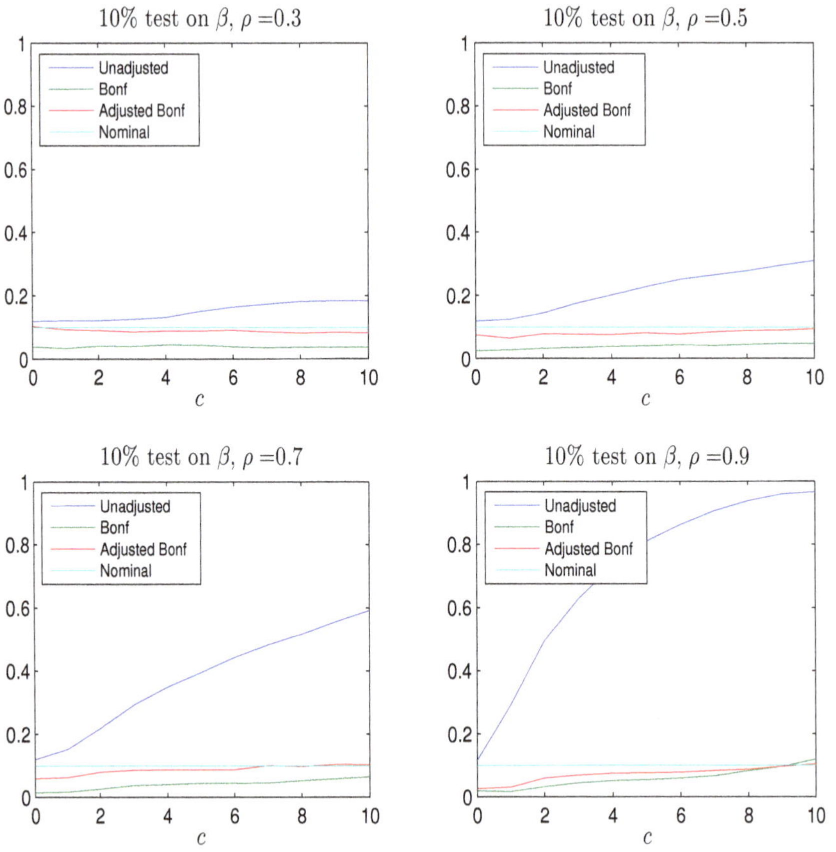

Figure A3. Rejection frequency of the test Q_β for $\gamma = 0$ using the $\chi^2(1)_{0.90}$ quantile (Unadjusted), the Bonferroni quantile in (20) for $\xi = 95\%$ and $\eta = 5\%$ (Bonf) and the adjusted Bonferroni quantile in (21) for $\eta = 5\%$ (Adjusted Bonf) as a function of c for different values of ρ; $N = 1000$ simulations of $T = 100$ observations from the DGP (15) and (16).

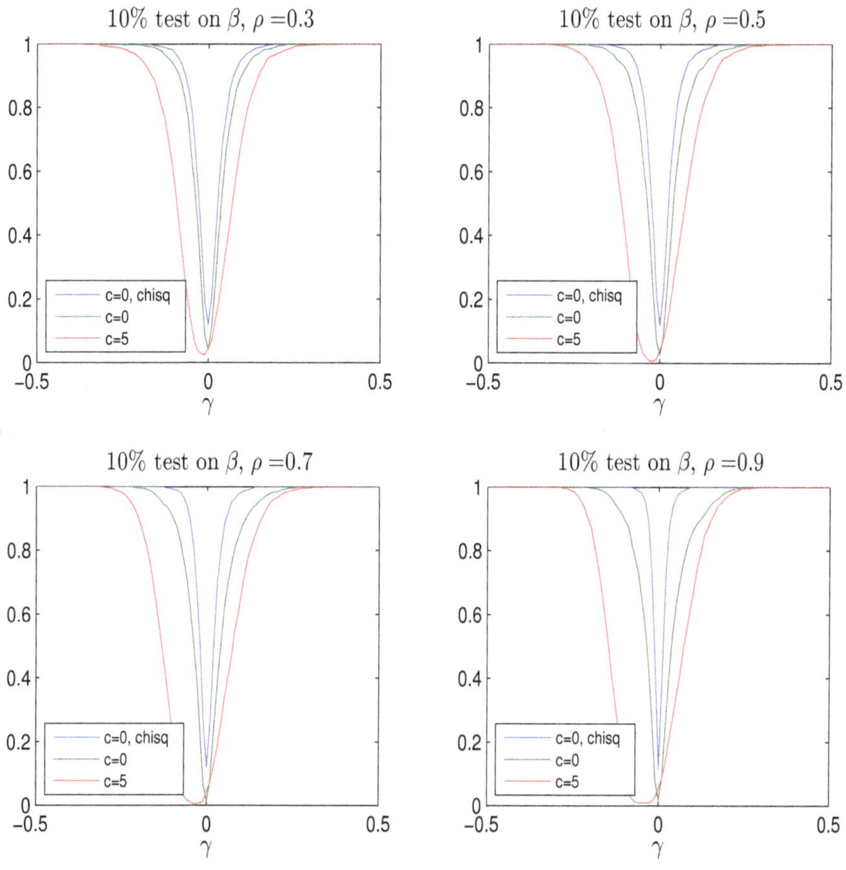

Figure A4. Rejection frequency of the test Q_β for $\gamma = 0$ using the $\chi^2(1)_{0.90}$ quantile (c = 0, chisq) and the Bonferroni quantile in (20) for $\xi = 95\%$ and $\eta = 5\%$, as a function of γ for different values of c and ρ; $N = 1000$ simulations of $T = 100$ observations from the DGP (15) and (16).

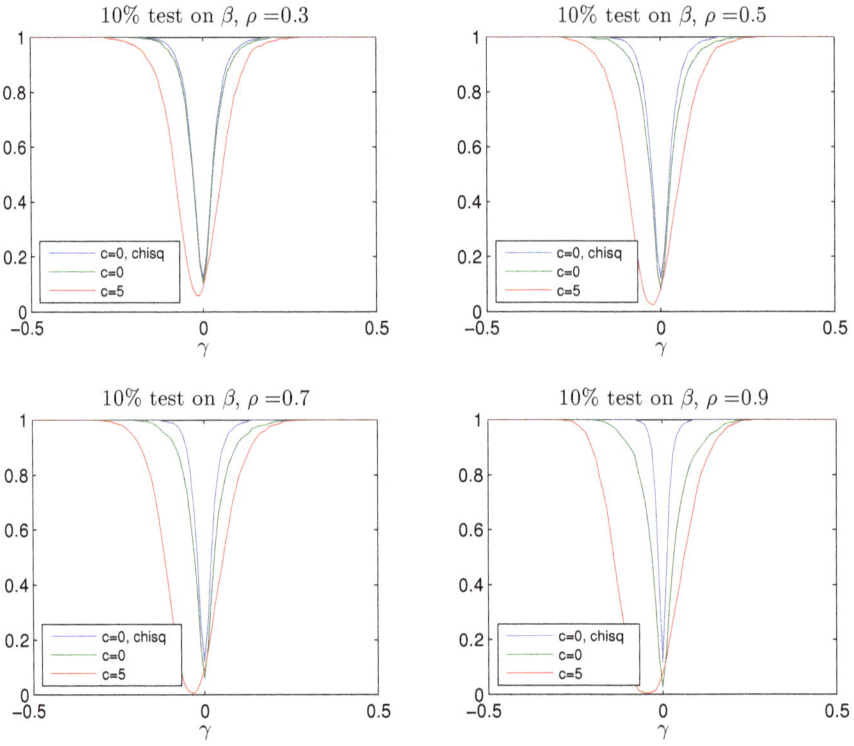

Figure A5. Rejection frequency of the test Q_β for $\gamma = 0$ using the $\chi^2(1)_{0.90}$ quantile (c=0, chisq) and the adjusted Bonferroni quantile in (21) for $\eta = 5\%$ as a function of γ for different values of c and ρ; $N = 1000$ simulations of $T = 100$ observations from the DGP (15) and (16).

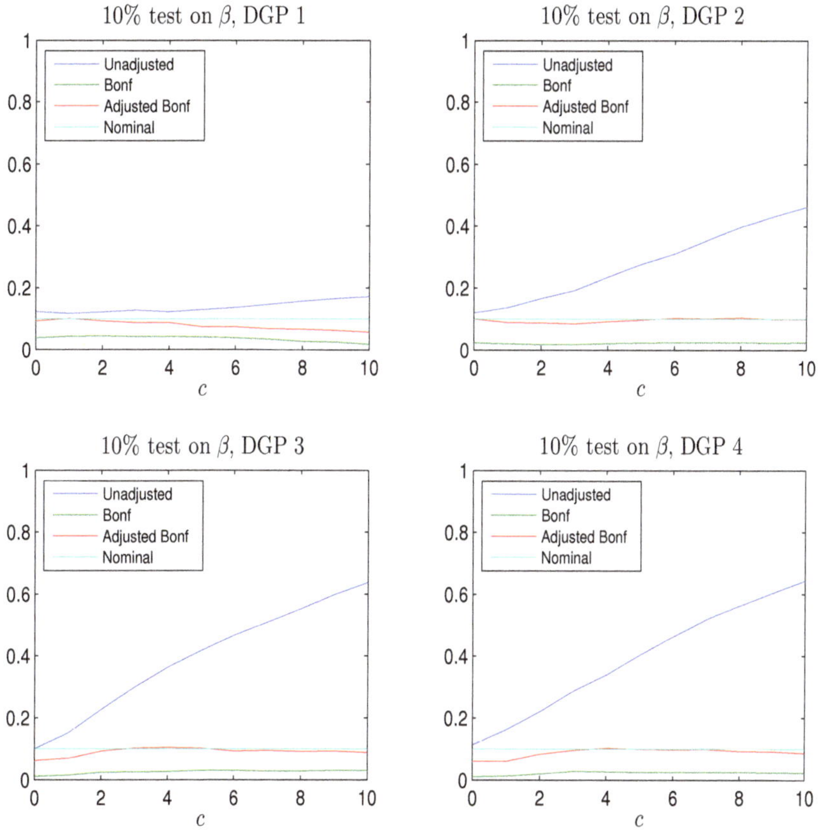

Figure A6. Rejection frequency of the test Q_β for $\gamma = 0$ using the $\chi^2(1)_{0.90}$ quantile (Unadjusted), the Bonferroni quantile in (20) for $\xi = 95\%$ and $\eta = 5\%$ (Bonf) and the adjusted Bonferroni quantile in (21) for $\eta = 5\%$ (Adjusted Bonf) as a function of c; $N = 1000$ simulations of $T = 100$ observations from the DGPs in Table 1.

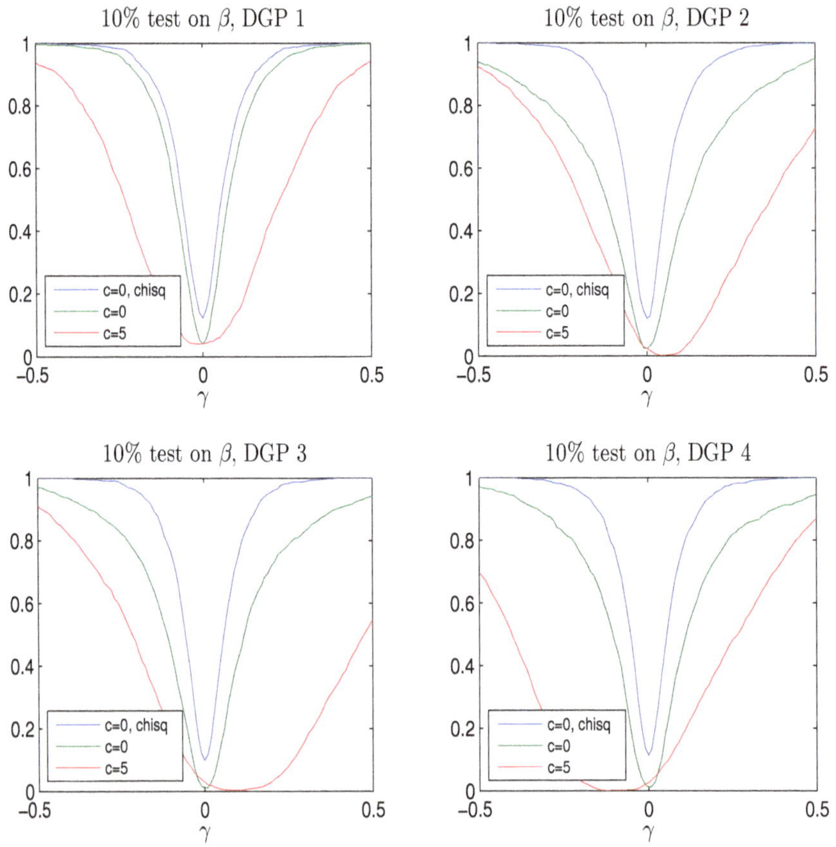

Figure A7. Rejection frequency of the test Q_β for $\gamma = 0$ using the $\chi^2(1)_{0.90}$ quantile (c = 0, chisq) and the Bonferroni quantile in (20) for $\xi = 95\%$ and $\eta = 5\%$, as a function of γ for different values of c; $N = 1000$ simulations of $T = 100$ observations from the DGPs in Table 1.

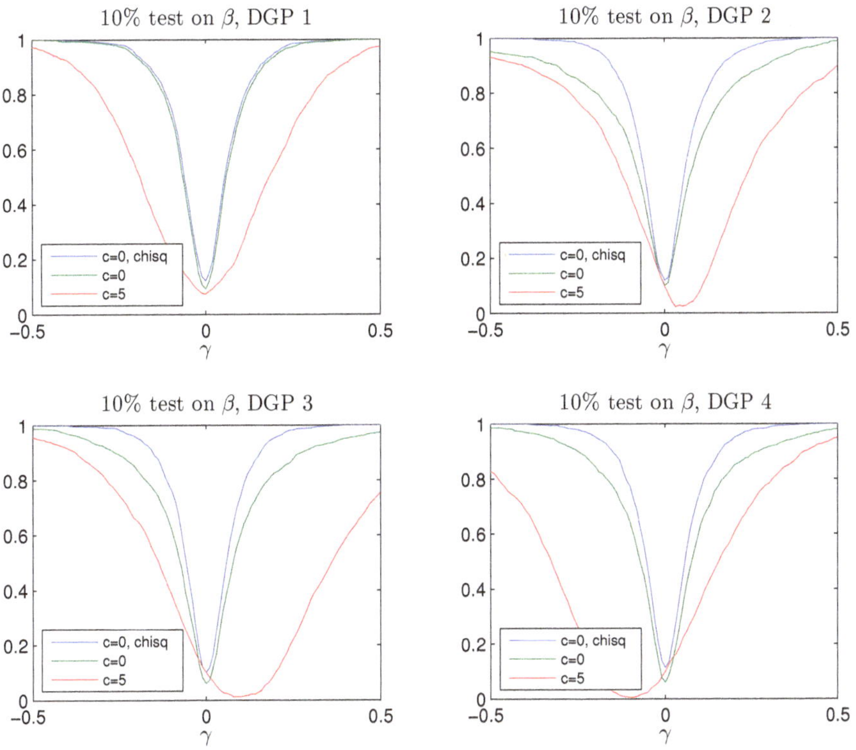

Figure A8. Rejection frequency of the test Q_β for $\gamma = 0$ using the $\chi^2(1)_{0.90}$ quantile (c = 0, chisq) and the adjusted Bonferroni quantile in (21) for $\eta = 5\%$ as a function of γ for different values of c; $N = 1000$ simulations of $T = 100$ observations from the DGPs in Table 1.

References

Cavanagh, Christopher L., Graham Elliott, and James H. Stock. 1995. Inference in Models with Nearly Integrated Regressors. *Econometric Theory* 11: 1131–47.

Di Iorio, Francesca, Stefano Fachin, and Riccardo Lucchetti. 2016. Can you do the wrong thing and still be right? Hypothesis testing in I(2) and near-I(2) cointegrated VARs. *Applied Economics* 48: 3665–78. doi:10.1080/00036846.2016.1142660.

Elliott, Graham. 1998. On the robustness of cointegration methods when regressors almost have unit roots. *Econometrica* 66: 149–58.

Johansen, Søren. 1996. *Likelihood-Based Inference in Cointegrated Vector Autoregressive Models*. Oxford: Oxford University Press.

McCloskey, Adam. 2017. Bonferroni-based size-correction for nonstandard testing problems. *Journal of Econometrics* in press. Available online: http://www.sciencedirect.com/science/article/pii/S0304407617300556 (accessed on 12 June 2017).

Phillips, Peter C. B. 1988. Regression theory for near integrated time series. *Econometrica* 56: 1021–44.

econometrics

MDPI

Article

Cointegration between Trends and Their Estimators in State Space Models and Cointegrated Vector Autoregressive Models

Søren Johansen * and Morten Nyboe Tabor

Department of Economics, University of Copenhagen, Øster Farimagsgade 5, Building 26, 1353 Copenhagen K, Denmark; morten.nyboe.tabor@econ.ku.dk

* Correspondence: soren.johansen@econ.ku.dk; Tel.: +45-35-323-071

Academic Editors: Katarina Juselius and Marc S. Paolella

Received: 1 March 2017; Accepted: 17 August 2017; Published: 22 August 2017

Abstract: A state space model with an unobserved multivariate random walk and a linear observation equation is studied. The purpose is to find out when the extracted trend cointegrates with its estimator, in the sense that a linear combination is asymptotically stationary. It is found that this result holds for the linear combination of the trend that appears in the observation equation. If identifying restrictions are imposed on either the trend or its coefficients in the linear observation equation, it is shown that there is cointegration between the identified trend and its estimator, if and only if the estimators of the coefficients in the observation equations are consistent at a faster rate than the square root of sample size. The same results are found if the observations from the state space model are analysed using a cointegrated vector autoregressive model. The findings are illustrated by a small simulation study.

Keywords: cointegration of trends; state space models; cointegrated vector autoregressive models

JEL Classification: C32

---

1. Introduction and Summary

This paper is inspired by a study on long-run causality, see Hoover et al. (2014). Causality is usually studied for a sequence of multivariate i.i.d. variables using conditional independence, see Spirtes et al. (2000) or Pearl (2009). For stationary autoregressive processes, causality is discussed in terms of the variance of the shocks, that is, the variance of the i.i.d. error term. For nonstationary cointegrated variables, the common trends play an important role for long-run causality. In Hoover et al. (2014), the concept is formulated in terms of independent common trends and their causal impact coefficients on the nonstationary observations. Thus, the emphasis is on independent trends, and how they enter the observation equations, rather than on the variance of the measurement errors.

The trend is modelled as an $m-$dimensional Gaussian random walk, starting at T_0,

$$T_{t+1} = T_t + \eta_{t+1}, t = 0, \dots, n-1, \tag{1}$$

where η_t are i.i.d. $N_m(0, \Omega_\eta)$, that is, Gaussian in m dimensions with mean zero and $m \times m$ variance $\Omega_\eta > 0$. This trend has an impact on future values of the $p-$dimensional observation y_t modelled by

$$y_{t+1} = BT_t + \varepsilon_{t+1}, t = 0, \dots, n-1, \tag{2}$$

where ε_t are i.i.d. $N_p(0, \Omega_\varepsilon)$ and $\Omega_\varepsilon > 0$. It is also assumed that the ε_s and η_t are independent for all s and t. In the following the joint distribution of $T_1, \dots, T_n, y_1, \dots, y_n$ conditional on a given value of T_0 is considered.

The observations are collected in the matrices Y_n, $p \times n$, and ΔY_n, $p \times (n-1)$, which are defined as

$$Y_n = (y_1, \ldots, y_n), \text{ and } \Delta Y_n = (y_2 - y_1, \ldots, y_n - y_{n-1}).$$

The processes y_t and T_t are obviously nonstationary, but the conditional distribution of Y_n given T_0 is well defined. We define

$$\begin{aligned} E_t T_t &= E(T_t | Y_t, T_0), \\ V_t &= Var_t(T_t) = Var(T_t | Y_t, T_0). \end{aligned}$$

Then the density of Y_n conditional on T_0 is given by the prediction error decomposition

$$p(Y_n | T_0) = p(y_1 | T_0) \prod_{t=1}^{n-1} p(y_{t+1} | Y_t, T_0),$$

where y_{t+1} given (Y_t, T_0) is p dimensional Gaussian with mean and variance

$$\begin{aligned} E_t y_{t+1} &= B E_t T_t, \\ Var_t(y_{t+1}) &= B V_t B' + \Omega_\varepsilon. \end{aligned}$$

In this model it is clear that y_t and T_t cointegrate, that is, $y_{t+1} - BT_{t+1} = \varepsilon_{t+1} - B\eta_{t+1}$ is stationary, and the same holds for T_t and the extracted trend $E_t T_t = E(T_t | y_1, \ldots, y_t, T_0)$. Note that in the statistical model defined by (1) and (2) with parameters B, Ω_η, and Ω_ε, only the matrices $B\Omega_\eta B'$ and Ω_ε are identified because for any $m \times m$ matrix ξ of full rank, $B\xi^{-1}$ and $\xi \Omega_\eta \xi'$ give the same likelihood, by redefining the trend as ξT_t.

Let $\hat{E}_t T_t$ be an estimator of $E_t T_t$. The paper investigates whether there is cointegration between $E_t T_t$ and $\hat{E}_t T_t$ given two different estimation methods: A simple cointegrating regression and the maximum likelihood estimator in an autoregressive representation of the state space model.

Section 2, on the probability analysis of the data generating process, formulates the model as a common trend state space model, and summarizes some results in three Lemmas. Lemma 1 contains the Kalman filter equations and the convergence of $Var(T_t | y_1, \ldots, y_t, T_0)$, see Durbin and Koopman (2012), and shows how its limit can be calculated by solving an eigenvalue problem. Lemma 1 also shows how y_t can be represented in terms of its prediction errors $v_j = y_j - E_{j-1} y_j$, $j = 1, \ldots, t$. This result is used in Lemma 2 to represent y_t in steady state as an infinite order cointegrated vector autoregressive model, see (Harvey 2006, p. 373). Section 3 discusses the statistical analysis of the data and the identification of the trends and their loadings. Two examples are discussed. In the first example, only B is restricted and the trends are allowed to be correlated. In the second example, B is restricted but the trends are uncorrelated, so that also the variance matrix is restricted. Lemma 3 analyses the data from (1) and (2) using a simple cointegrating regression, see Harvey and Koopman (1997), and shows that the estimator of the coefficient B suitably normalized is n-consistent.

Section 4 shows in Theorem 1 that the spread between $BE_t T_t$ and its estimator $\hat{B}\hat{E}_t T_t$ is asymptotically stationary irrespective of the identification of B and T_t. Then Theorem 2 shows that the spread between $E_t T_t$ and its estimator $\hat{E}_t T_t$ is asymptotically stationary if and only if B has been identified so that the estimator of B is superconsistent, that is, consistent at a rate faster than $n^{1/2}$.

The findings are illustrated with a small simulation study in Section 5. Data are generated from (1) and (2) with $T_0 = 0$, and the observations are analysed using the cointegrating regression discussed in Lemma 3. If the trends and their coefficients are identified by the trends being independent, the trend extracted by the state space model does not cointegrate with its estimator. If, however, the trends are identified by restrictions on the coefficients alone, they do cointegrate

2. Probability Analysis of the Data Generating Model

This section contains first two examples, which illustrate the problem to be solved. Then a special parametrization of the common trends model is defined and some, mostly known, results are given in Lemmas 1 concerning the Kalman filter recursions. Lemma 2 is about the representation of the steady state solution as an autoregressive process. All proofs are given in the Appendix.

2.1. *Two Examples*

Two examples are given which illustrate the problem investigated. The examples are analysed further by a simulation study in Section 5.

Example 1. In the first example the two random walks T_{1t} and T_{2t} are allowed to be dependent, so Ω_η is unrestricted, and identifying restrictions are imposed only on their coefficients B. The equations are

$$\begin{aligned} y_{1,t+1} &= T_{1t} + \varepsilon_{1,t+1}, \\ y_{2,t+1} &= T_{2t} + \varepsilon_{2,t+1}, \\ y_{3,t+1} &= b_{31}T_{1t} + b_{32}T_{2t} + \varepsilon_{3,t+1}. \end{aligned} \tag{3}$$

for $t = 0, \ldots, n-1$. Thus, $y_t = (y_{1t}, y_{2t}, y_{3t})'$, $T_t = (T_{1t}, T_{2t})'$, and

$$B = \begin{pmatrix} 1 & 0 \\ 0 & 1 \\ b_{31} & b_{32} \end{pmatrix}. \tag{4}$$

Moreover, $\Omega_\eta > 0$ is 2×2, $\Omega_\varepsilon > 0$ is 3×3, and both are unrestricted positive definite. Simulations indicate that $E_t y_{t+1} - \hat{E}_t y_{t+1} = BE_t T_t - \hat{B}\hat{E}_t T_t$ is stationary, and this obviously implies that the same holds for the first two coordinates $E_t T_{1t} - \hat{E}_t T_{1t}$ and $E_t T_{2t} - \hat{E}_t T_{2t}$. ∎

Example 2. The second example concerns two independent random walks T_{1t} and T_{2t}, and the three observation equations

$$\begin{aligned} y_{1,t+1} &= T_{1t} + \varepsilon_{1,t+1}, \\ y_{2,t+1} &= b_{21}T_{1t} + T_{2t} + \varepsilon_{2,t+1}, \\ y_{3,t+1} &= b_{31}T_{1t} + b_{32}T_{2t} + \varepsilon_{3,t+1}. \end{aligned} \tag{5}$$

In this example

$$B = \begin{pmatrix} 1 & 0 \\ b_{21} & 1 \\ b_{31} & b_{32} \end{pmatrix}, \Omega_\eta = diag(\sigma_1^2, \sigma_2^2), \tag{6}$$

and $\Omega_\varepsilon > 0$ is 3×3 and unrestricted positive definite. Thus the nonstationarity is caused by two independent trends. The first, T_{1t}, is the cause of the nonstationarity of y_{1t}, whereas both trends are causes of the nonstationarity of (y_{2t}, y_{3t}). From the first equation it is seen that y_{1t} and T_{1t} cointegrate. It is to be expected that also the extracted trend $E_t T_{1t}$ cointegrates with T_{1t}, and also that $E_t T_{1t}$ cointegrates with its estimator $\hat{E}_t T_{1t}$. This is all supported by the simulations. Similarly, it turns out that

$$E_t y_{2,t+1} - \hat{E}_t y_{2,t+1} = b_{21}E_t T_{1t} - \hat{b}_{21}\hat{E}_t T_{1t} + E_t T_{2t} - \hat{E}_t T_{2t},$$

is asymptotically stationary. In this case, however, $E_t T_{2t} - \hat{E}_t T_{2t}$ is not asymptotically stationary, and the paper provides an answer to why this is the case. ∎

The problem to be solved is why in the first example cointegration was found between the extracted trends and their estimators, and in the second example they do not cointegrate. The solution to the problem is that it depends on the way the trends and their coefficients are identified. For some identification schemes the estimator of B is n-consistent, and then stationarity of $E_tT_t - \hat{E}_tT_t$ can be proved. But if identification is achieved by imposing restrictions also on the covariance of the trends, as in Example 2, then the estimator for B is only $n^{1/2}$-consistent, and that is not enough to get asymptotic stationarity of $E_tT_t - \hat{E}_tT_t$.

2.2. Formulation of the Model as a Common Trend State Space Model

The common trend state space model with constant coefficients is defined by

$$\begin{aligned} \alpha_{t+1} &= \alpha_t + \eta_t, \\ y_t &= B\alpha_t + \varepsilon_t, \end{aligned} \tag{7}$$

$t = 1, \ldots, n$, see Durbin and Koopman (2012) or Harvey (1989), with initial state α_1. Here α_t is the unobserved $m-$dimensional state variable and y_t the $p-$dimensional observation and B is $p \times m$ of rank $m < p$. The errors ε_t and η_t are as specified in the discussion of the model given by (1) and (2).

Defining $T_t = \alpha_{t+1}, t = 0, \ldots, n$, gives the model (1) and (2). Note that in this notation $E_tT_t = E_t\alpha_{t+1}$ is the predicted value of the trend α_{t+1}, which means that it is easy to formulate the Kalman filter.

The Kalman filter calculates the prediction $a_{t+1} = E_t\alpha_{t+1}$ and its conditional variance $P_{t+1} = Var_t(\alpha_{t+1})$ by the equations

$$a_{t+1} = a_t + P_tB'(BP_tB' + \Omega_\varepsilon)^{-1}(y_t - E_{t-1}(y_t)), \tag{8}$$

$$P_{t+1} = P_t + \Omega_\eta - P_tB'(BP_tB' + \Omega_\varepsilon)^{-1}BP_t, \tag{9}$$

starting with $a_1 = \alpha_1$ and $P_1 = 0$.

The recursions (8) and (9) become

$$E_{t+1}T_{t+1} = E_tT_t + K_t'(y_{t+1} - E_ty_{t+1}), \tag{10}$$

$$V_{t+1} = \Omega_\eta + V_t - K_t'BV_t, \tag{11}$$

$t = 0, \ldots, n-1$ starting with $E_1T_1 = T_0$ and $V_1 = \Omega_\eta$, and defining the Kalman gain

$$K_t' = V_tB'(BV_tB' + \Omega_\varepsilon)^{-1}. \tag{12}$$

Lemma 1 contains the result that V_{t+1} converges for $t \to \infty$ to a finite limit V, which can be calculated by solving an eigenvalue problem. Equation (11) is an algebraic Ricatti equation, see Chan et al. (1984), where the convergence result can be found. The recursion (10) is used to represent y_{t+1} in terms of its cumulated prediction errors $v_{t+1} = y_{t+1} - E_ty_{t+1}$, as noted by Harvey (2006, Section 7.3.2).

Lemma 1. *Let $V_t = Var(T_t|Y_t)$ and $E_tT_t = E(T_t|Y_t)$.*

(a) The recursion for V_t, (11), can be expressed as

$$V_{t+1} = \Omega_\eta + V_t - V_t(V_t + \Omega_B)^{-1}V_t \to V, t \to \infty, \tag{13}$$

where $\Omega_B = Var(\bar{B}'\varepsilon_t|B_\perp'\varepsilon_t)$ for $\bar{B} = B(B'B)^{-1}$. Moreover,

$$I_m - K_t'B = I_m - V_tB'(BV_tB' + \Omega_\varepsilon)^{-1}B \to I_m - K'B = \Omega_B(V + \Omega_B)^{-1}, t \to \infty, \tag{14}$$

which has positive eigenvalues less than one, such that $I_m - K'B$ is a contraction, that is, $(I_m - K'B)^n \to 0$, $n \to \infty$.

(b) The limit of V_t can be found by solving the eigenvalue problem

$$|\lambda\Omega_B - \Omega_\eta| = 0,$$

for eigenvectors W and eigenvalues $(\lambda_1, \ldots, \lambda_m)$*, such that* $W'\Omega_B W = I_m$ *and* $W'\Omega_\eta W = diag(\lambda_1, \ldots, \lambda_m)$*. Hence,* $W'VW = diag(\tau_1, \ldots, \tau_m)$ *for*

$$\tau_i = \frac{1}{2}\{\lambda_i + (\lambda_i^2 + 4\lambda_i)^{1/2}\}. \tag{15}$$

(c) Finally, using the prediction error, $v_{t+1} = y_{t+1} - E_t y_{t+1}$*, it is found from (10) that*

$$E_t T_t = T_0 + \sum_{j=1}^{t} K'_{j-1} v_j, \text{ and } y_{t+1} = v_{t+1} + B(T_0 + \sum_{j=1}^{t} K'_{j-1} v_j). \tag{16}$$

The prediction errors are independent Gaussian with mean zero and variances

$$Var(v_{t+1}) = Var_t(y_{t+1}) = Var_t(BT_t + \varepsilon_{t+1}) = BV_t B' + \Omega_\varepsilon \to BVB' + \Omega_\varepsilon, t \to \infty,$$

such that in steady state the prediction errors are i.i.d. $N_p(0, BVB' + \Omega_\varepsilon)$, and (16) shows that y_t is approximately an $AR(\infty)$ process, for which the reduced form autoregressive representation can be found, see (Harvey 2006, Section 7.3.2).

Lemma 2. *If the system (7) is in steady state, prediction errors* v_t *are i.i.d.* $N(0, BVB' + \Omega_\varepsilon)$ *and*

$$\Delta y_t = \Delta v_t + BK' v_{t-1}. \tag{17}$$

Applying the Granger Representation Theorem, y_t *is given by*

$$\Delta y_t = \alpha\beta' y_{t-1} + \sum_{i=1}^{\infty} \Gamma_i \Delta y_{t-i} + v_t. \tag{18}$$

Here $\alpha = -K_\perp (B'_\perp K_\perp)^{-1}$ *and* $\beta = B_\perp$*.*

2.3. Cointegration among the Observations and Trends

In model (1) and (2), the equation $y_{t+1} = BT_t + \varepsilon_{t+1}$ shows that y_t and T_t are cointegrated. It also holds that $T_t - E_t T_t$ is asymptotically stationary because

$$v_{t+1} = y_{t+1} - E_t y_{t+1} = BT_t + \varepsilon_{t+1} - BE_t T_t,$$

which shows that $B(T_t - E_t T_t) = v_{t+1} - \varepsilon_{t+1}$ is asymptotically stationary. Multiplying by $\bar{B}' = (B'B)^{-1}B'$, the same holds for $T_t - E_t T_t$.

In model (18) the extracted trend is

$$T_t^* = \alpha'_\perp \sum_{i=1}^{t} v_i = K' \sum_{i=1}^{t} v_i,$$

and (16) shows that in steady state, $y_{t+1} - BT_t^* = v_{t+1} + BT_0$ is stationary, so that y_t cointegrates with T_t^*. Thus, the process y_t and the trends T_t, T_t^*, and $E_t T_t$ all cointegrate, in the sense that suitable linear combinations are asymptotically stationary. The next section investigates when similar results hold for the estimated trends.

3. Statistical Analysis of the Data

In this section it is shown how the parameters of (7) can be estimated from the CVAR (18) using results of Saikkonen (1992) and Saikkonen and Lutkepohl (1996), or using a simple cointegrating regression, see (Harvey and Koopman 1997, p. 276) as discussed in Lemma 3. For both the state space model (1)–(2) and for the CVAR in (18) there is an identification problem between T_t and its coefficient B, or between $\beta_\perp$ and T_t^*, because for any $m \times m$ matrix ξ of full rank, one can use $B\xi^{-1}$ as parameter and ξT_t as trend and $\xi\Omega_\eta\xi'$ as variance, and similarly for $\beta_\perp$ and T_t^*. In order to estimate B, T, and Ω_η, it is therefore necessary to impose identifying restrictions. Examples of such identification are given next.

Identification 1. Because B has rank m, the rows can be permuted such that $B' = (B_1', B_2')$, where B_1 is $m \times m$ and has full rank. Then the parameters and trend are redefined as

$$B^\dagger = \begin{pmatrix} I_m \\ B_2 B_1^{-1} \end{pmatrix} = \begin{pmatrix} I_m \\ \gamma' \end{pmatrix}, \Omega_\eta^\dagger = B_1 \Omega_\eta B_1', \ T_t^\dagger = B_1 T_t. \tag{19}$$

Note that $B^\dagger T_t^\dagger = BT_t$ and $B^\dagger \Omega_\eta^\dagger B^{\dagger\prime} = B\Omega_\eta B'$. This parametrization is the simplest which separates parameters that are n-consistently estimated, γ, from those that are $n^{1/2}$-consistently estimated, $(\Omega_\eta, \Omega_\varepsilon)$, see Lemma 3. Note that the (correlated) trends are redefined by choosing T_{1t} as the trend in y_{1t}, then T_{2t} as the trend in y_{2t}, as in Example 1.

A more general parametrization, which also gives n-consistency, is defined, as in simultaneous equations, by imposing linear restrictions on each of the m columns and require the identification condition to hold, see Fisher (1966). ■

Identification 2. The normalization with diagonality of $\Omega_\eta^\dagger$ is part of the next identification, because this is the assumption in the discussion of long-run causality. Let $\Omega_\eta^\dagger = C_\eta diag(\sigma_1^2, \ldots, \sigma_m^2) C_\eta'$ be a Cholesky decomposition of Ω_η. That is, C_η is lower-triangular with one in the diagonal, corresponding to an ordering of the variables. Using this decomposition the new parameters and the trend are

$$B^\# = \begin{pmatrix} C_\eta \\ \gamma' C_\eta \end{pmatrix}, \Omega_\eta^\# = diag(\sigma_1^2, \ldots, \sigma_m^2), \ T_t^\# = C_\eta^{-1} T_t^\#, \tag{20}$$

such that $B^\# T_t^\# = B^\dagger T_t^\dagger = BT_t$ and $B^\# \Omega_\eta^\# B^{\#\prime} = B^\dagger \Omega_\eta^\dagger B^{\dagger\prime} = B\Omega_\eta B'$.

Identification of the trends is achieved in this case by defining the trends to be independent and constrain how they load into the observations. In Example 2, T_{1t} was defined as the trend in y_{1t}, and T_{2t} as the trend in y_{2t}, but orthogonalized on T_{1t}, such that the trend in y_{2t} is a combination of T_{1t} and T_{2t}. ■

3.1. The Vector Autoregressive Model

When the process is in steady state, the infinite order CVAR representation is given in (18). The model is approximated by a sequence of finite lag models, depending on sample size n,

$$\Delta y_t = \alpha\beta' y_{t-1} + \sum_{i=1}^{k_n} \Gamma_i \Delta y_{t-i} + v_t,$$

where the lag length k_n is chosen to depend on n such that k_n increases to infinity with n, but so slowly that k_n^3/n converges to zero. Thus one can choose for instance $k_n = n^{1/3}/\log n$ or $k_n = n^{1/3-\epsilon}$, for some $\epsilon > 0$. With this choice of asymptotics, the parameters α, β, $\Gamma = I_p - \sum_{i=1}^{\infty} \Gamma_i$, $\Sigma = Var(v_t)$, and the residuals, v_t, can be estimated consistently, see Johansen and Juselius (2014) for this application of the results of Saikkonen and Lutkepohl (1996).

This defines for each sample size consistent estimators $\breve{\alpha}$, $\breve{\beta}$, $\breve{\Gamma}$ and $\breve{\Sigma}$, as well residuals $\breve{v}_t$. In particular the estimator of the common trend is $\breve{T}_t^* = \breve{\alpha}_\perp' \sum_{i=1}^t \breve{v}_i$. Thus, $\breve{\alpha}\breve{\beta}' \xrightarrow{P} \alpha\beta'$,

$\check{C} = \check{\beta}_\perp(\check{\alpha}'_\perp \check{\Gamma}\check{\beta}_\perp)^{-1}_\perp \check{\alpha}'_\perp \overset{P}{\to} C = BK'$ and $\check{\Sigma} \overset{P}{\to} \Sigma = BVB' + \Omega_\varepsilon$. If $\beta_\perp$ is identified as $(I_m, \gamma)'$, then $\check{B} = \check{\beta}_\perp \overset{P}{\to} \beta_\perp$. In steady state, the relations

$$\Omega_\eta = VB'(BVB' + \Omega_\varepsilon)^{-1}B'V = VB'\Sigma^{-1}B'V,$$
$$C = BK' = BVB'(BVB' + \Omega_\varepsilon)^{-1} = BVB'\Sigma^{-1},$$

hold, see (11) and Lemma 2. It follows that

$$\check{B}\check{\Omega}_\eta \check{B}' = \check{C}\check{\Sigma}\check{C}' \overset{P}{\to} B\Omega_\eta B', \text{ and } \check{\Omega}_\eta = (\check{B}'\check{B})^{-1}\check{B}'\check{C}\check{\Sigma}\check{C}'\check{B}(\check{B}'\check{B})^{-1} \overset{P}{\to} \Omega_\eta.$$

Finally, an estimator for Ω_ε can be found as

$$\check{\Omega}_\varepsilon = \check{\Sigma} - \frac{1}{2}(\check{C}\check{\Sigma} + \check{\Sigma}\check{C}') \overset{P}{\to} BVB' + \Omega_\varepsilon - \frac{1}{2}(BVB' + BVB') = \Omega_\varepsilon.$$

Note that $C\Sigma$ is not a symmetric matrix in model (18), but its estimator converges in probability towards the symmetric matrix BVB'.

3.2. The State Space Model

The state space model is defined by (1) and (2). It can be analysed using the Kalman filter to calculate the diffuse likelihood function, see Durbin and Koopman (2012), and an optimizing algorithm can be used to find the maximum likelihood estimator for the parameters Ω_η, Ω_ε, and B, once B is identified.

In this paper, an estimator is used which is simpler to analyse and which gives an n-consistent estimator for B suitably normalized, see (Harvey and Koopman 1997, p. 276).

The estimators are functions of ΔY_n and $B'_\perp Y_n$, and therefore do not involve the initial value T_0. Irrespective of the identification, the relations

$$Var(\Delta y_t) = B\Omega_\eta B' + 2\Omega_\varepsilon, \tag{21}$$
$$Cov(\Delta y_t, \Delta y_{t+1}) = -\Omega_\varepsilon, \tag{22}$$

hold, and they gives rise to two moment estimators, which determine Ω_η and Ω_ε, once B has been identified and estimated.

Consider the identified parametrization (19), where $B = (I_m, \gamma)'$, and take $B_\perp = (\gamma', -I_{p-m})'$. Then define $z_{1t} = (y_{1t}, \ldots, y_{mt})'$ and $z_{2t} = (y_{m+1,t}, \ldots, y_{pt})'$, such that $y_t = (z'_{1t}, z'_{2t})'$ and $B'_\perp y_t = \gamma' z_{1t} - z_{2t} = B'_\perp \varepsilon_t$, that is,

$$z_{2t} = \gamma' z_{1t} - B'_\perp \varepsilon_t. \tag{23}$$

This equation defines the regression estimator $\hat{\gamma}_{reg}$:

$$\hat{\gamma}_{reg} = (\sum_{t=0}^{n-1} z_{1t}z'_{1t})^{-1} \sum_{t=0}^{n-1} z_{1t}z'_{2t} = \gamma - (\sum_{t=0}^{n-1} z_{1t}z'_{1t})^{-1} \sum_{t=0}^{n-1} z_{1t}\varepsilon'_t B_\perp. \tag{24}$$

To describe the asymptotic properties of $\hat{\gamma}_{reg}$, two Brownian motions are introduced

$$n^{-1/2}\sum_{t=1}^{[nu]} \varepsilon_t \overset{D}{\to} W_\varepsilon(u) \text{ and } n^{-1/2}\sum_{t=1}^{[nu]} \eta_t \overset{D}{\to} W_\eta(u). \tag{25}$$

Lemma 3. *Let the data be generated by the state space model (1) and (2).*
(a) From (21) and (22) it follows that

$$S_{n1} = n^{-1}\textstyle\sum_{i=1}^{n} \Delta y_t \Delta y'_t \overset{P}{\to} B\Omega_\eta B' + 2\Omega_\varepsilon,$$
$$S_{n2} = n^{-1}\textstyle\sum_{i=2}^{n}(\Delta y_t \Delta y'_{t-1} + \Delta y_{t-1}\Delta y'_t) \overset{P}{\to} -2\Omega_\varepsilon, \tag{26}$$

define $n^{1/2}$-consistent asymptotically Gaussian estimators for $B\Omega_\eta B'$ and Ω_ε, irrespective of the identification of B.

(b) If B and $B_\perp$ are identified as $B = (I_m, \gamma)'$, $B'_\perp = (\gamma', -I_{p-m})$, and Ω_η is adjusted accordingly, then $\hat{\gamma}_{reg}$ in (24) is n-consistent with asymptotic Mixed Gaussian distribution

$$n(\hat{\gamma}_{reg} - \gamma) = -n(\hat{B} - B)'B_\perp = nB'(\hat{B}_\perp - B_\perp) \quad (27)$$
$$\xrightarrow{D} -(\int_0^1 W_\eta W'_\eta du)^{-1} \int_0^1 W_\eta (dW_\varepsilon)'B_\perp.$$

(c) If B is identified as $B = (C'_\eta, C'_\eta \gamma)'$, $B'_\perp = (\gamma', -I_{p-m})$, and $\Omega_\eta = diag(\sigma_1^2, \ldots, \sigma_m^2)$, then $\hat{B} - B = O_P(n^{-1/2})$, but (27) still holds for $-n(\hat{B} - B)'B_\perp = \hat{C}'_\eta(\hat{\gamma}_{reg} - \gamma)$, so that some linear combinations of $\hat{B}$ are $n-$consistent.

Note that the parameters $B = (I_m, \gamma)'$, Ω_η, and Ω_ε can be estimated consistently from (24) and (26) by

$$\hat{B} = \begin{pmatrix} I_m \\ \hat{\gamma}'_{reg} \end{pmatrix}, \hat{\Omega}_\varepsilon = -\frac{1}{2} S_{n2}, \text{ and } \hat{\Omega}_\eta = (\hat{B}'\hat{B})^{-1}\hat{B}'(S_{n1} + S_{n2})\hat{B}(\hat{B}'\hat{B})^{-1}. \quad (28)$$

In the simulations of Examples 1 and 2 the initial value is $T_0 = 0$, so the Kalman filter with $T_0 = 0$ is used to calculate the extracted trend $E_t T_t$ using observations and known parameters. Similarly the estimator of the extracted trend $\hat{E}_t T_t$ is calculated using observations and estimated parameters based on Lemma 3. The next section investigates to what extent these estimated trends cointegrate with the extracted trends, and if they cointegrate with each other.

4. Cointegration between Trends and Their Estimators

This section gives the main results in two theorems with proofs in the Appendix. In Theorem 1 it is shown, using the state space model to extract the trends and the estimator from Lemma 3, that $BE_tT_t - \hat{B}\hat{E}_tT_t$ is asymptotically stationary. For the CVAR model it holds that $BT_t^* - \check{B}\check{T}_t^* \xrightarrow{P} 0$, such that this spread is asymptotically stationary. Finally, the estimated trends in the two models are compared, and it is shown that $\hat{B}\hat{E}_tT_t - \check{B}\check{T}_t^*$ is asymptotically stationary. The conclusion is that in terms of cointegration of the trends and their estimators, it does not matter which model is used to extract the trends, as long as the focus is on the identified trends BT_t and BT_t^*.

Theorem 1. *Let y_t and T_t be generated by the DGP given in (1) and (2).*

(a) If the state space model is used to extract the trends, and Lemma 3 is used for estimation, then $BE_tT_t - \hat{B}\hat{E}_tT_t$ is asymptotically stationary.

(b) If the vector autoregressive model is used to extract the trends and for estimation, then $BT_t^* - \check{B}\check{T}_t^* \xrightarrow{P} 0$.

(c) Under assumptions of (a) and (b), it holds that $\hat{B}\hat{E}_tT_t - \check{B}\check{T}_t^*$ is asymptotically stationary.

In Theorem 2 a necessary and sufficient condition for asymptotic stationarity of $T_t^* - \check{T}_t^*$, $E_tT_t - \hat{E}_tT_t$, and $\hat{E}_tT_t - \check{T}_t^*$ is given.

Theorem 2. *In the notation of Theorem 1, any of the spreads $T_t^* - \check{T}_t^*$, $E_tT_t - \hat{E}_tT_t$ or $\hat{E}_tT_t - \check{T}_t^*$ is asymptotically stationary if and only if B and the trend are identified such that the corresponding estimator for B satisfies $n^{1/2}(\hat{B} - B) = o_P(1)$ and $n^{1/2}(\check{B} - B) = o_P(1)$.*

The missing cointegration between E_tT_t and $\hat{E}_tT_t$, say, can be explained in terms of the identity

$$B(E_tT_t - \hat{E}_tT_t) = (\hat{B} - B)E_tT_t + (BE_tT_t - \hat{B}\hat{E}_tT_t).$$

Here the second term, $BE_tT_t - \hat{B}\hat{E}_tT_t$, is asymptotically stationary by Theorem $1(a)$. But the first term, $(\hat{B} - B)T_t$, is not necessarily asymptotically stationary, because in general, that is, depending on the identification of the trend and B, it holds that $\hat{B} - B = O_P(n^{-1/2})$ and $E_tT_t = O_P(n^{1/2})$, see (16).

The parametrization $B = (I_m, \gamma)'$ ensures n-consistency of $\hat{B}$, so there is asymptotic stationarity of $T_t^* - \check{T}_t^*$, $E_tT_t - \hat{E}_tT_t$, and $\hat{E}_tT_t - \check{T}_t^*$ in this case. This is not so surprising because

$$BE_tT_t - \hat{B}\hat{E}_tT_t = \begin{pmatrix} E_tT_t - \hat{E}_tT_t \\ \gamma' E_tT_t - \hat{\gamma}'\hat{E}_tT_t \end{pmatrix},$$

is stationary. Another situation where the estimator for B is n-consistent is if $B = (B_1, \ldots, B_m)$ satisfies linear restriction of the columns, $R_i'B_i = 0$, or equivalently $B_i = R_{i\perp}\phi_i$ for some ϕ_i, and the condition for identification is satisfied

$$rank\{R_i'(R_{1\perp}\phi_1, \ldots, R_{m\perp}\phi_m)\} = r - 1, \text{ for } i = 1, \ldots, m, \tag{29}$$

see Fisher (1966). For a just-identified system, one can still use $\hat{\gamma}_{reg}$, and then solve for the identified parameters. For overidentified systems, the parameters can be estimated by a nonlinear regression of z_{2t} on z_{1t} reflecting the overidentified parametrization. In either case the estimator is n-consistent such that $T_t^* - \check{T}_t^*$, $E_tT_t - \hat{E}_tT_t$, and $\hat{E}_tT_t - \check{T}_t^*$ are asymptotically stationary.

If the identification involves the variance Ω_η, however, the estimator of B is only $n^{1/2}$-consistent, and hence no cointegration is found between the trend and estimated trend.

The analogy with the results for the CVAR, where β and α need to be identified, is that if β is identified using linear restrictions (29) then $\hat{\beta}$ is n-consistent, whereas if β is identified by restrictions on α then β is $n^{1/2}$-consistent. An example of the latter is if β is identified as the first m rows of the matrix $\Pi = \alpha\beta'$, corresponding to $\alpha = (I_m, \phi)'$, then $\hat{\beta}$ is $n^{1/2}$-consistent and asymptotically Gaussian, see (Johansen 2010, Section 4.3).

5. A Small Simulation Study

The two examples introduced in Section 2.1 are analysed by simulation. The equations are given in (5) and (3). Both examples have $p = 3$ and $m = 2$. The parameters B and Ω_η contain $6 + 3$ parameters, but the 3×3 matrix $B\Omega_\eta B'$ is of rank 2 and has only 5 estimable parameters. Thus, 4 restrictions must be imposed to identify the parameters. In both examples the Kalman filter with $T_0 = 0$ is used to extract the trends, and the cointegrating regression in Lemma 3 is used to estimate the parameters.

Example 1 continued. The parameter B is given in (4), and the parameters are just-identified. Now

$$E_tBT_{1t} - \hat{E}_t\hat{B}T_{1t} = \begin{pmatrix} E_tT_{1t} - \hat{E}_tT_{1t} \\ E_tT_{2t} - \hat{E}_tT_{2t} \\ b_{31}E_tT_{1t} + b_{32}E_tT_{2t} - \hat{b}_{31}\hat{E}_tT_{1t} - \hat{b}_{32}\hat{E}_tT_{2t} \end{pmatrix}. \tag{30}$$

As $E_tT_{1t} - \hat{E}_tT_{1t}$ and $E_tT_{2t} - \hat{E}_tT_{2t}$ are the first two rows of $E_tBT_{1t} - \hat{E}_t\hat{B}T_{1t}$ in (30), they are both asymptotically stationary by Theorem 1(a).

To illustrate the results, data are simulated with $n = 100$ observations starting with $T_0 = 0$ and parameter values $b_{31} = b_{32} = 0.5$, $\sigma_1^2 = \sigma_2^2 = 1$, and $\sigma_{12} = 0$, such that

$$B = \begin{pmatrix} 1 & 0 \\ 0 & 1 \\ 0.5 & 0.5 \end{pmatrix}, \Omega_\eta = \begin{pmatrix} 1 & 0 \\ 0 & 1 \end{pmatrix}. \tag{31}$$

The parameters are estimated by (28) and the estimates become $\hat{b}_{31} = 0.48$, $\hat{b}_{32} = 0.41$, $\hat{\sigma}_1^2 = 0.93$, $\hat{\sigma}_{12} = 0.26$, and $\hat{\sigma}_2^2 = 1.63$. The extracted and estimated trends are plotted in Figure 1. Panels *a* and b show plots of $(E_t T_{1t}, \hat{E}_t T_{1t})$ and $(E_t T_{2t}, \hat{E}_t T_{2t})$, respectively, and it is seen that they co-move. In panels c and d the differences $\hat{E}_t T_{1t} - E_t T_{1t}$ and $\hat{E}_t T_{2t} - E_t T_{2t}$ both appear to be stationary in this parametrization of the model. ∎

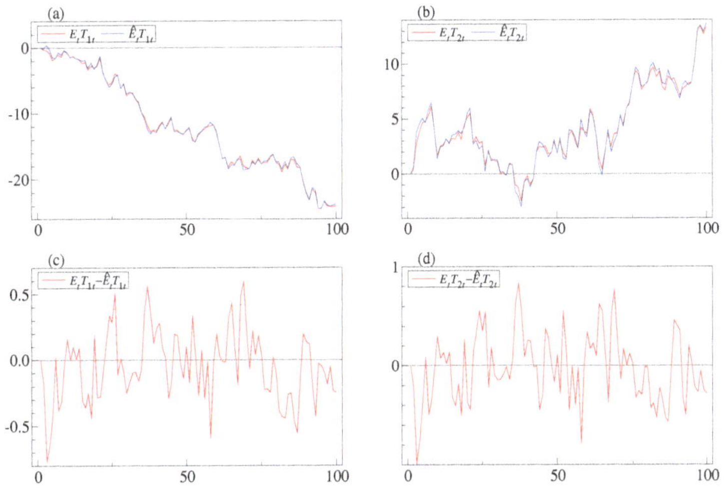

Figure 1. The figure shows the extracted and estimated trends for the simulated data in Example 1 with the identification in (19). Panels a and b show plots of $E_t T_{1t}$ and $\hat{E}_t T_{1t}$, and $E_t T_{2t}$ and $\hat{E}_t T_{2t}$, respectively. Note that in both cases, the processes seem to co-move. In panels c and d, $E_t T_{1t} - \hat{E}_t T_{1t}$ and $E_t T_{2t} - \hat{E}_t T_{2t}$ are plotted and appear stationary, because they are both recovered from $BE_t T_t - \hat{B}\hat{E}_t T_t$ as the first two coordinates, see (19).

Example 2 continued. The parameter B in this example is given in (6) such that

$$E_t BT_t - \hat{E}_t \hat{B} T_t = \begin{pmatrix} E_t T_{1t} - \hat{E}_t T_{1t} \\ b_{21} E_t T_{1t} + E_t T_{2t} - \hat{b}_{21} \hat{E}_t T_{1t} - \hat{E}_t T_{2t} \\ b_{31} E_t T_{1t} + b_{32} E_t T_{2t} - \hat{b}_{31} \hat{E}_t T_{1t} - \hat{b}_{32} \hat{E}_t T_{2t} \end{pmatrix}. \tag{32}$$

By the results in Theorem 1(a), all three rows are asymptotically stationary, in particular $E_t T_{1t} - \hat{E}_t T_{1t}$. Moreover, the second row of (32), $(b_{21} E_t T_{1t} - \hat{b}_{21} \hat{E}_t T_{1t}) + (E_t T_{2t} - \hat{E}_t T_{2t})$, is asymptotically stationary. Thus, asymptotic stationarity of $E_t T_{2t} - \hat{E}_t T_{2t}$ requires asymptotic stationary of the term

$$b_{21} E_t T_{1t} - \hat{b}_{21} \hat{E}_t T_{1t} = (b_{21} - \hat{b}_{21}) E_t T_{1t} + \hat{b}_{21} (E_t T_{1t} - \hat{E}_t T_{1t}). \tag{33}$$

Here, the second term, $\hat{b}_{21}(E_t T_{1t} - \hat{E}_t T_{1t})$, is asymptotically stationary because $E_t T_{1t} - \hat{E}_t T_{1t}$ is. However, the first term, $(b_{21} - \hat{b}_{21}) E_t T_{1t}$, is not asymptotically stationary because $\hat{b}_{21}$ is $n^{1/2}$-consistent. In this case $n^{1/2}(b_{21} - \hat{b}_{21}) \xrightarrow{D} Z$, which has a Gaussian distribution, and $n^{-1/2} E_{[nu]} T_{1[nu]} \xrightarrow{D} W_{\eta_1}(u)$, where W_{η_1} is the Brownian motion generated by the sum of η_{1t}. It follows that their product

$$(b_{21} - \hat{b}_{21}) E_{[nu]} T_{1[nu]} = \{n^{1/2}(b_{21} - \hat{b}_{21})\}\{n^{-1/2} E_{[nu]} T_{1[nu]}\}$$

converges in distribution to the product of Z and $W_{\eta_1}(u)$, $n \to \infty$, and this limit is nonstationary. It follows that $E_t T_{2t} - \hat{E}_t T_{2t}$ is not asymptotically stationary for the identification in this example. This argument is a special case of the proof of Theorem 2.

To illustrate the results, data are simulated from the model with $n = 100$ observations starting with $T_0 = 0$ and parameter values $b_{21} = 0.0$, $b_{31} = b_{32} = 0.5$, and $\sigma_1^2 = \sigma_2^2 = 1$, which is identical to (31). The model is written in the form (19) with a transformed B and Ω_η, as

$$B^\dagger = \begin{pmatrix} 1 & 0 \\ 0 & 1 \\ b_{31} - b_{32}b_{21} & b_{32} \end{pmatrix}, \; \Omega_\eta^\dagger = \begin{pmatrix} \sigma_1^2 & b_{21}\sigma_1^2 \\ b_{21}\sigma_1^2 & \sigma_2^2 + b_{21}^2\sigma_1^2 \end{pmatrix}.$$

The parameters are estimed as in Example 1 and we find $\hat{b}_{31} - \hat{b}_{32}\hat{b}_{21} = 0.48$, $\hat{b}_{32} = 0.41$, $\hat{\sigma}_1^2 = 0.93$, $\hat{b}_{21}\hat{\sigma}_{12} = 0.26$, and $\hat{\sigma}_2^2 + \hat{b}_{21}^2\hat{\sigma}_1^2 = 1.63$, which are solved for $\hat{b}_{21} = 0.28$, $\hat{b}_{31} = 0.59$, $\hat{b}_{32} = 0.41$, $\hat{\sigma}_1^2 = 0.93$, and $\hat{\sigma}_2^2 = 1.56$. The extracted and estimated trends are plotted in Figure 2. The panels a and b show plots of $(E_tT_{1t}, \hat{E}_tT_{1t})$ and $(E_tT_{2t}, \hat{E}_tT_{2t})$, respectively. It is seen that E_tT_{1t} and $\hat{E}_tT_{1t}$ co-move, whereas E_tT_{2t} and $\hat{E}_tT_{2t}$ do not co-move. In panels c and d, the differences $E_tT_{1t} - \hat{E}_tT_{1t}$ and $E_tT_{2t} - \hat{E}_tT_{2t}$ are plotted. Note that the first looks stationary, whereas the second is clearly nonstationary. When comparing with the plot of E_tT_{1t} in panel a, it appears that the process $\hat{E}_tT_{1t}$ can explain the nonstationarity of $E_tT_{2t} - \hat{E}_tT_{2t}$. This is consistent with Equation (33) with $b_{21} = 0$ and $\hat{b}_{21} = 0.28$. In panel d, $E_tT_{2t} - \hat{E}_tT_{2t} - 0.28\hat{E}_tT_{1t}$ is plotted and it is indeed stationary. ■

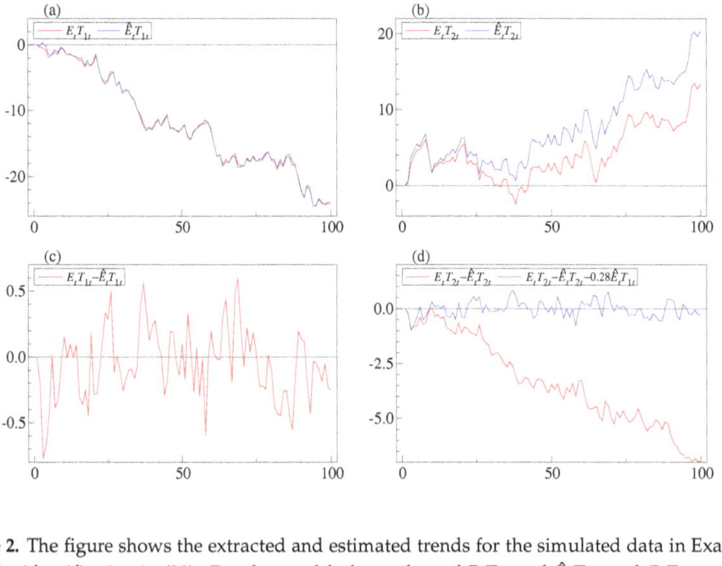

Figure 2. The figure shows the extracted and estimated trends for the simulated data in Example 2 with the identification in (20). Panels a and b show plots of E_tT_{1t} and $\hat{E}_tT_{1t}$, and E_tT_{2t} and $\hat{E}_tT_{2t}$, respectively. Note that E_tT_{1t} and $\hat{E}_tT_{1t}$ seem to co-move, whereas E_tT_{2t} and $\hat{E}_tT_{2t}$ do not. In panel c, $E_tT_{1t} - \hat{E}_tT_{1t}$ is plotted and appears stationary, but in panel d the spread $E_tT_{2t} - \hat{E}_tT_{2t}$ is nonstationary, whereas $E_tT_{2t} - \hat{E}_tT_{2t} - 0.28\hat{E}_tT_{1t}$ is stationary.

6. Conclusions

The paper analyses a sample of n observations from a common trend model, where the state is an unobserved multivariate random walk and the observation is a linear combination of the lagged state variable and a noise term. For such a model, the trends and their coefficients in the observation equation need to be identified before they can be estimated separately. The model leads naturally to cointegration between observations, trends, and the extracted trends. Using simulations it was discovered, that the extracted trends do not necessarily cointegrate with their estimators. This problem is investigated, and it is found to be related to the identification of the trends and their coefficients in the observation equation. It is shown in Theorem 1, that provided only the linear combinations of the trends from the observation equation are considered, there is always cointegration between extracted trends and their estimators. If the trends and their coefficients are defined by identifying restrictions, the same result holds if and only if the estimated identified coefficients in the observation equation are consistent at a rate faster than $n^{1/2}$. For the causality study mentioned in the introduction, where the components of the unobserved trend are assumed independent, the result has the following implication: For the individual extracted trends to cointegrate with their estimators, overidentifying restrictions must be imposed on the trend's causal impact coefficients on the observations, such that the estimators of these become super-consistent.

Acknowledgments: S.J. is grateful to CREATES—Center for Research in Econometric Analysis of Time Series (DNRF78), funded by the Danish National Research Foundation. M.N.T. is grateful to the Carlsberg Foundation (grant reference 2013_01_0972). We have benefitted from discussions with Siem Jan Koopman and Eric Hillebrand on state space models and thankfully acknowledge the insightful comments from two anonymous referees.

Author Contributions: S.J. has contributed most of the mathematical derivations. M.N.T. has performed the simulations and posed the problem to be solved.

Conflicts of Interest: The authors declare no conflict of interest.

Appendix A

Proof of Lemma 1 *Proof of (a):* Let $N=(\bar{B}, B_\perp)$, $\bar{B} = B(B'B)^{-1}$, such that

$$K_t'B = V_tB'[BV_tB' + \Omega_\varepsilon]^{-1}B = V_tB'N[(N'BV_tB'N + N'\Omega_\varepsilon N)]^{-1}N'B$$
$$= V_t \begin{pmatrix} I_m \\ 0 \end{pmatrix}' \begin{pmatrix} V_t + \bar{B}'\Omega_\varepsilon\bar{B} & \bar{B}'\Omega_\varepsilon B_\perp \\ B_\perp'\Omega_\varepsilon\bar{B} & B_\perp'\Omega_\varepsilon B_\perp \end{pmatrix}^{-1} \begin{pmatrix} I_m \\ 0 \end{pmatrix} = V_t(V_t + \Omega_B)^{-1},$$

where

$$\Omega_B = \bar{B}'[\Omega_\varepsilon - \Omega_\varepsilon B_\perp(B_\perp'\Omega_\varepsilon B_\perp)^{-1}B_\perp'\Omega_\varepsilon]\bar{B} = Var(\bar{B}'\varepsilon_t|B_\perp'\varepsilon_t).$$

This proves (13) and (14).

Proof of (b): If the recursion starts with $V_1 = \Omega_\eta$, then V_t can be diagonalized by W for all t and the limit satisfies $W'VW = diag(\tau_1, \ldots, \tau_m)$, where

$$\tau_i = \lambda_i + \tau_i - \frac{\tau_i^2}{1+\tau_i}.$$

This has solution given in (15).

Proof of (c): The first result follows by summation from the recursion for E_tT_t in (10), and the second from $y_{t+1} = v_{t+1} + BE_tT_t$. ∎

Proof of Lemma 2 The polynomial $\Phi(z) = I_p - z(I_p - BK')$ describes (17) as

$$(1-L)y_t = \Phi(L)v_t.$$

Note that $\Phi(1) = BK'$ is singular and $d\Phi(z)/dz|_{z=1} = BK' - I_p = BVB'(BVB' + \Omega_\varepsilon)^{-1} - I_p$, satisfies $B_\perp'(BK' - I_p)K_\perp = B_\perp'\Omega_\varepsilon B_\perp$ is nonsingular, where $K_\perp = (BVB' + \Omega_\varepsilon)B_\perp$. This means that the Granger Representation Theorem (Johansen 1996, Theorem 4.5) can be applied and gives the expansion (18) for $\alpha = -K_\perp(B_\perp'K_\perp)^{-1}$ and $\beta = B_\perp'$. ∎

Proof of Lemma 3 *Proof of (a):* Consider first the product moments (21) and (22). The result (26) follows from the Law of Large Numbers and the asymptotic Gaussian distribution of $\hat{\Omega}_c = -\frac{1}{2}S_{n2}$ and $\hat{\Omega}_\eta = \hat{\bar{B}}'(S_{1n} + S_{n2})\hat{\bar{B}}$ follows from the Central Limit Theorem.

Proof of (b): It follows from (23), (24), and (25) that the least squares estimator $\hat{\gamma}_{reg}$ satisfies (27). Let $B_\perp = (\gamma', -I_{p-m})'$, then

$$-(\hat{B} - B)'B_\perp = \hat{\gamma}_{reg} - \gamma = B'(\hat{B}_\perp - B_\perp).$$

Proof of (c): Note that for the other parametrization, (20), where $B = (C_\eta', C_\eta'\gamma)'$, it holds that $B_\perp = (\gamma', -I_{p-m})'$, such that for both parametrizations (27) holds. The estimator of B, in the parametrization (20), is $\hat{B}' = (\hat{C}_\eta', \hat{C}_\eta'\hat{\gamma})$, where $\hat{C}_\eta$ is derived from the $n^{1/2}$-consistent estimator of Ω_η, such that for this parametrization, estimation of B is not n-consistent, but only $n^{1/2}$-consistent and $\hat{B} - B = O_P(n^{-1/2})$. ∎

Proof of Theorem 1. *Proof of (a):* Let $w_t = BT_t - \hat{B}\hat{E}_tT_t$, then

$$BE_tT_t - \hat{B}\hat{E}_tT_t = B(E_tT_t - T_t) + (BT_t - \hat{B}\hat{E}_tT_t) = B(E_tT_t - T_t) + w_t. \tag{A1}$$

Here $B(E_tT_t - T_t)$ is stationary, so that it is enough to show that w_t is asymptotically stationary. From the definition of T_{t+1} and the Kalman filter recursion (10) calculated for $T_0 = 0$ and for the estimated parameters, it holds that

$$\begin{aligned} BT_{t+1} &= BT_t + B\eta_{t+1}, \\ \hat{B}\hat{E}_{t+1}T_{t+1} &= \hat{B}\hat{E}_tT_t - \hat{B}\hat{K}_t'(y_{t+1} - \hat{B}\hat{E}_tT_t). \end{aligned}$$

Subtracting the expressions gives

$$\begin{aligned} BT_{t+1} - \hat{B}\hat{E}_{t+1}T_{t+1} &= BT_t + B\eta_{t+1} - \hat{B}\hat{E}_tT_t - \hat{B}\hat{K}_t'(y_{t+1} - B\hat{E}_tT_t) \\ &= BT_t - \hat{B}\hat{E}_tT_t - \hat{B}\hat{K}_t'(BT_t + \varepsilon_{t+1} - \hat{B}\hat{E}_tT_t) + B\eta_{t+1}, \end{aligned}$$

which gives the recursion

$$w_{t+1} = (I_p - \hat{B}\hat{K}_t')w_t - \hat{B}\hat{K}_t'\varepsilon_{t+1} + B\eta_{t+1}. \tag{A2}$$

Note that $(I_p - \hat{B}\hat{K}_t')$ is not a contraction, because $p - m$ eigenvalues are one. Hence it is first proved that $\hat{B}_\perp' w_t$ is small and then a contraction is found for $\hat{B}'w_t$. From the definition of w_t, it follows from (27), that

$$\hat{B}_\perp' w_t = \hat{B}_\perp' BT_t = \hat{B}_\perp'(B - \hat{B})T_t = -(B_\perp - \hat{B}_\perp)'\hat{B}T_t = O_P(n^{-1})O_P(n^{1/2}) = O_P(n^{-1/2}).$$

Next define $\overline{\hat{B}} = \hat{B}(\hat{B}'\hat{B})^{-1}$and $\overline{\hat{B}}_\perp = \hat{B}_\perp(\hat{B}_\perp'\hat{B}_\perp)^{-1}$, such that $I_p = \hat{B}\overline{\hat{B}}' + \hat{B}_\perp\overline{\hat{B}}_\perp'$. From (A2) it follows by multiplying by $\overline{\hat{B}}'$ and using $\overline{\hat{B}}'B = \overline{\hat{B}}'(B - \hat{B}) + I_m = I_m + O_P(n^{-1/2})$, that

$$\begin{aligned} \overline{\hat{B}}' w_{t+1} &= (\overline{\hat{B}} - \hat{K}_t)'w_t - \hat{K}_t'\varepsilon_{t+1} + \overline{\hat{B}}' B\eta_{t+1} \\ &= (\overline{\hat{B}} - \hat{K}_t)'(\hat{B}\overline{\hat{B}}' + \hat{B}_\perp\overline{\hat{B}}_\perp')w_t - \hat{K}_t'\varepsilon_{t+1} + \eta_{t+1} + \overline{\hat{B}}'(B - \hat{B})\eta_{t+1} \\ &= (I_m - \hat{K}_t'\hat{B})\overline{\hat{B}}' w_t - \hat{K}_t'\varepsilon_{t+1} + \eta_{t+1} + O_P(n^{-1/2}), \end{aligned}$$

because $\overline{\hat{B}}'(B - \hat{B})\eta_{t+1} = O_P(n^{-1/2})$ and $(\overline{\hat{B}} - \hat{K}_t)'\hat{B}_\perp\overline{\hat{B}}_\perp' w_t = -\hat{K}_t'\hat{B}_\perp\overline{\hat{B}}_\perp' w_t = O_P(n^{-1/2})$.

From (14) it is seen that $I_m - \hat{K}_t'\hat{B} \overset{P}{\to} \Omega_B(V + \Omega_B)^{-1}$ and $(I_m - K'B)^n \to 0, n \to \infty$. This shows that $\overline{\hat{B}}' w_t$ and hence w_t is asymptotically a stationary $AR(1)$ process.

Proof of (b): The CVAR (18) is expressed as $\Pi(L)y_t = v_t$, and the parameters are estimated using maximum likelihood with lag length $k_n \to \infty$ and $k_n^3/n \to 0$. This gives estimators $(\check{\alpha}, \check{\beta}, \check{\Gamma}, \check{C}, \check{\Sigma})$ and residuals $\check{v}_t$. The representation of y_t in terms of v_t is given by

$$y_t = C\sum_{i=1}^{t} v_i + \sum_{i=0}^{\infty} C_i v_{t-i} + A,$$

where $\beta' A = 0$. This relation also holds for the estimated parameters and residuals, and subtracting one finds

$$BT_t^* \sum_{i=1}^{t} v_i - \check{B}\check{T}_t^* \sum_{i=1}^{t} \check{v}_i = \sum_{i=0}^{\infty} \check{C}_i \check{v}_{t-i} - \sum_{i=0}^{\infty} C_i v_{t-i} - A + \check{A}.$$

It is seen that the right hand side is $o_P(1)$ and hence asymptotically stationary.

Proof of (c): Each estimated trend is compared with the corresponding trend which gives

$$\hat{B}\hat{E}_t T_t - \check{B}\check{T}_t^* = (\hat{B}\hat{E}_t T_t - BT_t) + (BT_t - BT_t^*) + (BT_t^* - \check{B}\check{T}_t^*).$$

Here the first term is asymptotically stationary using Theorem 2(a), the middle term is asymptotically stationary, and the last is $o_P(1)$ by Theorem 1(b). ■

Proof of Theorem 2. The proof is the same for all the spreads, so consider $E_t T_t - \hat{E}_t T_t$, and the identity

$$\hat{B}'(BE_t T_t - \hat{B}\hat{E}_t T_t) = \hat{B}'(B - \hat{B})E_t T_t + \hat{B}'\hat{B}(E_t T_t - \hat{E}_t T_t).$$

The left hand side is asymptotically stationary by Theorem 1(a) and therefore $E_t T_t - \hat{E}_t T_t$ is asymptotically stationary if and only

$$\hat{B}'(B - \hat{B})E_t T_t = [n^{1/2}\hat{B}'(B - \hat{B})][n^{-1/2}E_t T_t],$$

is asymptotically stationary. Here the second factor converges to a nonstationary process,

$$n^{-1/2}E_{[nu]}T_{[nu]} = n^{-1/2}E_0 T_0 + n^{-1/2}\sum_{j=2}^{[nu]} K_{j-1}' v_j \xrightarrow{D} W_v(u),$$

see (16), so for the term $[n^{1/2}\hat{B}'(B - \hat{B})][n^{-1/2}E_t T_t]$ to be asymptotically stationary it is necessary and sufficient that $n^{1/2}\hat{B}'(B - \hat{B}) \xrightarrow{P} 0$. ■

References

Chan, Siew Wah, Graham Clifford Goodwin, and Kwai Sang Sin. 1984. Convergence properties of the Ricatti difference equation in optimal filtering of nonstabilizable systems. *IEEE Transaction on Automatic Control* 29: 110–18.

Durbin, Jim, and Siem Jan Koopman. 2012. *Time Series Analysis by State Space Methods*, 2nd ed. Oxford: Oxford University Press.

Fisher Frank, M. 1966. *The Identification Problem in Econometrics*. New York: McGraw-Hill.

Harvey, Andrew. 1989. *Forecasting, Structural Time Series Models and the Kalman Filter*. Cambridge: Cambridge University Press.

Harvey, Andrew C. 2006. Forecasting with Unobserved Components Time Series Models. In *Handbook of Economic Forecasting*. Edited by G. Elliot, C. Granger and A. Timmermann. Amsterdam: North Holland, pp. 327–412.

Harvey, Andrew C., and Siem Jan Koopman. 1997. Multivariate structural time series models. In *System Dynamics in Economics and Financial Models*. Edited by C. Heij, J. M. Schumacher, B. Hanzon and C. Praagman. New York: John Wiley and Sons.

Hoover, Kevin D., Søren Johansen, Katarina Juselius, and Morten Nyboe Tabor. 2014. Long-run Causal Order: A Progress Report. Unpublished manuscript.

Johansen, Søren. 1996. *Likelihood-Based Inference in Cointegrated Vector Autoregressive Models*, 2nd ed. Oxford: Oxford University Press.

Johansen, Søren. 2010. Some identification problems in the cointegrated vector autoregressive model. *Journal of Economietrics* 158: 262–73.

Johansen, Søren, and Katarina Juselius. 2014. An asymptotic invariance property of the common trends under linear transformations of the data. *Journal of Econometrics* 178: 310–15.

Pearl, Judea. 2009. *Causality: Models, Reasoning and Inference*, 2nd ed. Cambridge: Cambridge University Press.

Saikkonen, Pentti. 1992. Estimation and testing of cointegrated systems by an autoregressive approximation. *Econometric Theory* 8: 1–27.

Saikkonen, Pentti, and Helmut Lütkepohl. 1996. Infinite order cointegrated vector autoregressive processes. Estimation and Inference. *Econometric Theory* 12: 814–44.

Spirtes, Peter, Clark Glymour, and Richard Scheines. 2000. *Causation, Prediction, and Search*, 2nd ed. Cambridge: MIT Press.

econometrics

MDPI

Article

Panel Cointegration Testing in the Presence of Linear Time Trends

Uwe Hassler * and Mehdi Hosseinkouchack

Department of Business and Economics, Goethe University Frankfurt, Theodor-W.-Adorno-Platz 4, 60323 Frankfurt, Germany; hosseinkouchack@wiwi.uni-frankfurt.de

* Correspondence: hassler@wiwi.uni-frankfurt.de; Tel.: +49-69-798-34762

Academic Editor: Katarina Juselius

Received: 15 May 2016; Accepted: 20 October 2016; Published: 1 November 2016

Abstract: We consider a class of panel tests of the null hypothesis of no cointegration and cointegration. All tests under investigation rely on single-equations estimated by least squares, and they may be residual-based or not. We focus on test statistics computed from regressions with intercept only (i.e., without detrending) and with at least one of the regressors (integrated of order 1) being dominated by a linear time trend. In such a setting, often encountered in practice, the limiting distributions and critical values provided for and applied with the situation "with intercept only" are not correct. It is demonstrated that their usage results in size distortions growing with the panel size N. Moreover, we show which are the appropriate distributions, and how correct critical values can be obtained from the literature.

Keywords: single-equations; large N asymptotics; integrated series with drift

JEL Classification: C22; C23

1. Introduction

Most panel tests for the null hypothesis of (no) cointegration rely on single-equations, notable exceptions being Larsson et al. [1], Groen and Kleibergen [2], Breitung [3] and Karaman Örsal and Droge [4] who proposed panel system approaches. In particular, the more recent paper by Miller [5], building on nonlinear instrumental variable likelihood-based rank tests, allows for cross-correlation between the units. Similarly, recent single-equation tests by Chang and Nguyen [6] or Demetrescu et al. [7] also rely on nonlinear instrumental variable estimation, while the vast majority of such panel tests builds on ordinary or fully modified or dynamic least squares (LS). Here, we study exactly this class of LS-based single-equation panel tests for the null of either cointegration or no cointegration.

We focus on the situation where the test statistics are computed from regressions with an intercept only, and with at least one of the integrated regressors displaying a linear time trend on top of the stochastic trend. Such a constellation is often met in practical applications, see for instance Coe and Helpman [8] and Westerlund [9] on R&D spillovers (total factor productivity and capital stock), Larsson et al. [1] on log real consumption and income (per capita), or Hanck [10] on prices and exchange rate series testing the weak purchasing power parity (PPP). The relevance of a linear trend in panel data has been addressed in Hansen and King [11] when commenting on the link between health care expenditure and GDP, see McCoskey and Selden [12]; consequently, Blomqvist and Carter [13], Gerdtham and Löthgren [14] or Westerlund [15] worked (partly) with detrended series, i.e., they included time as an explanatory variable in their panel tregressions. Hansen ([16], p. 103), however, argue that "it seems reasonable that excess detrending will reduce the test's power". Therefore, we study the empirically relevant case where test statistics are computed from regressions with intercept only (i.e., without detrending) when at least one of the I(1) regressors displays a linear time trend.

Before becoming more technical, we want to outline our findings as a rule for empirical applications. Let $\bar{Z}^{(m)}$ denote a generic panel cointegration statistic computed from a regression with intercept only involving $m = k + 1$ I(1) variables. The least squares regression may be static in levels,

$$y_{i,t} = \bar{\alpha}_i + \bar{\beta}_{i,1} x_{i,1,t} + \cdots + \bar{\beta}_{i,k} x_{i,k,t} + \bar{u}_{i,t}, \quad t = 1, \ldots, T, \; i = 1, \ldots, N,$$

where $\{u_{i,t}\}$ is assumed to be I(1) in the case of no cointegration, or I(0) under the null hypothesis of cointegration, see Remarks 1 and 3 below, respectively. Alternatively, $\bar{Z}^{(m)}$ may be from the error-correction regression[1],

$$\Delta y_{i,t} = \bar{\kappa}_i + \bar{\gamma}_i y_{i,t-1} + \bar{\theta}_{i,1} x_{i,1,t-1} + \cdots + \bar{\theta}_{i,k} x_{i,k,t-1} + \bar{\varepsilon}_{i,t}, \quad t = 1, \ldots, T, \; i = 1, \ldots, N,$$

where contemporaneous differences $\Delta x_{i,t}$ or additional lags of differences may be required as additional regressors to render $\bar{\varepsilon}_{i,t}$ free of serial correlation, see Remark 2 below. The test statistic may be constructed from pooling the data or from averaging individual statistics, see e.g., Pedroni [18,19] or Westerlund [15]. Much of the nonstationary panel literature relies on sequential limit theory where $T \to \infty$ is followed by $N \to \infty$, such that limiting normality can be established under the assumption that none of the I(1) regressors follows a deterministic time trend:

$$\sqrt{N}\left(\bar{Z}^{(m)} - \bar{\mu}_m\right) / \bar{\sigma}_m \sim \mathcal{N}(0,1).$$

The constants $\bar{\mu}_m$ and $\bar{\sigma}_m$ required for appropriate normalization are typically tabulated for a selected number of values of m, see again Remarks 1 through 3. A different set of such moments $\tilde{\mu}_m$ and $\tilde{\sigma}_m$ is also typically given for detrended regressions, where the test statistic $\widetilde{Z}^{(m)}$ stems from regressions of the type ($m = k + 1$)

$$y_{i,t} = \widetilde{\alpha}_i + \widetilde{\delta}_i t + \widetilde{\beta}_{i,1} x_{i,1,t} + \cdots + \widetilde{\beta}_{i,k} x_{i,k,t} + \widetilde{u}_{i,t},$$

or

$$\Delta y_{i,t} = \widetilde{\kappa}_i + \widetilde{\psi}_i t + \widetilde{\gamma}_i y_{i,t-1} + \widetilde{\theta}_{i,1} x_{i,1,t-1} + \cdots + \widetilde{\theta}_{i,k} x_{i,k,t-1} + \widetilde{\varepsilon}_{i,t}.$$

We call such regressions "detrended" because, in a single-equation framework, the resulting parameter estimators are equivalent to what one obtains from a two-step procedure: first, regress all variables on a linear time trend, and, second, regress the individually detrended residuals on each other. This equivalence is sometimes called Frisch-Waugh-Lovell Theorem, see e.g., Greene ([20], Theorem 3.2). For generic $\widetilde{Z}^{(m)}$ from, e.g., the tests mentioned in Remarks 1 through 3, it holds, irrespective of an eventual linear trend in the data, that

$$\sqrt{N}\left(\widetilde{Z}^{(m)} - \widetilde{\mu}_m\right) / \widetilde{\sigma}_m \sim \mathcal{N}(0,1).$$

Our main contribution is twofold for the case that at least one of the I(1) regressors has a linear time trend and the regressions are run with intercept only (without detrending). First, it is shown that the normalization with $\bar{\mu}_m$ and $\bar{\sigma}_m$ and the resulting critical values for $\bar{Z}^{(m)}$ from the regression "with intercept only" are not correct in the presence of linear time trends in the data. It is analytically (Proposition 1) and numerically demonstrated that their usage results in size distortions growing with the panel size N. Second, we characterize the appropriate limiting distributions by showing

---

[1] Under the alternative of cointegration, the intercept κ from the error correction form can be decomposed in a rather complicated way, see Juselius ([17], Section 6.2)); below; however, we will maintain the assumption of no cointegration.

that normalization of $\bar{Z}^{(m)}$ with $\widetilde{\mu}_{m-1}$ and $\widetilde{\sigma}_{m-1}$ results in a standard normal limit, such that the size of the tests can be controlled (Theorem 1). Put differently, Theorem 1 means in non-technical terms: The limiting distribution arising from a regression on k I(1) variables with drift and an intercept amounts to the limiting distribution in the case of a regression on $k-1$ I(1) variables and an intercept plus a linear time trend. Such a rule is known in a pure time series context for the special case of the residual-based Phillips-Ouliaris test for no cointegration from Hansen ([16], p. 103): "[...] deterministic trends in the data affect the limiting distribution of the test statistics *whether or not we detrend the data*"; see also the expositions in Hamilton ([21], p. 596, 597) and Hassler ([22], Proposition 16.6). It is even more relevant in our panel framework since we illustrate numerically and analytically that the size distortions of an inappropriate normalization grow with the panel size N (either to zero or one, depending on the specific test). Moreover, we compare our proposal to account for linear trends in the data with the more traditional method of detrending the regression. By simulation, we show that power gains of our new strategy according to Theorem 1 over detrending may be considerable. We hence recommend this strategy as being superior to detrending.

The rest of the paper is organized as follows. The next section sets some notation and assumptions. Section 3 establishes and discusses our asymptotic results and illustrates them with numerical evidence. It also compares our suggestion to account for linear trends with the conventional method of detrending. The last section discusses consequences for applied work. Mathematical proofs are relegated to the Appendix A.

2. Notation and Assumptions

Restricting our attention to the single-equation framework we partition the m-vector $z_{i,t}$ of observables into a scalar $y_{i,t}$ and a k-element vector $x_{i,t}$, $z'_{i,t} = (y_{i,t}, x'_{i,t})$, $m = k+1$. As usual, the index i stands for the cross-section, $i = 1, \ldots, N$, while t denotes time, $t = 1, \ldots, T$. Each sequence $\{z_{i,t}\}$, $t = 1, \ldots, T$, is assumed to be integrated of order 1, I(1), where we allow for a non-zero drift, and assume for simplicity a negligible starting value, $z_{i,0} = 0$. While $\{z_{i,t}\}$ may be cointegrated or not, depending on the respective null hypothesis, we rule out cointegration among $\{x_{i,t}\}$. Technically, these assumptions translate as follows, where $W_{i,m}(\cdot)$ denotes an m-dimensional standard Wiener process, $\lfloor x \rfloor$ stands for the integer part of a number x, and $\Rightarrow$ is the symbol for weak convergence.

Assumption 1. *With obvious partitioning according to $(y_{i,t}, x'_{i,t})'$, we assume $(i = 1, \ldots, N)$*

$$z_{i,t} = \mu_{i,z}\, t + \sum_{j=1}^{t} e_{i,j} = \begin{pmatrix} \mu_{i,y} \\ \mu_{i,x} \end{pmatrix} t + \sum_{j=1}^{t} \begin{pmatrix} e_{i,y,j} \\ e_{i,x,j} \end{pmatrix}, \quad t = 1, \ldots, T.$$

The stochastic zero mean process $\{e_{i,t}\}$ is integrated of order 0 in that it satisfies

$$T^{-0.5} \sum_{t=1}^{\lfloor rT \rfloor} e_{i,t} \Rightarrow \Omega_i^{0.5} W_{i,m}(r) = \Omega_i^{0.5} \begin{pmatrix} W_{i,y}(r) \\ W_{i,x}(r) \end{pmatrix}, \quad r \in [0,1],$$

with

$$\Omega_i = \begin{pmatrix} \omega_{i,yy}^2 & \omega'_{i,xy} \\ \omega_{i,xy} & \Omega_{i,xx} \end{pmatrix},$$

where $\omega_{i,yy}^2 > 0$ and $\Omega_{i,xx}$ is positive definite.

Now, we turn to assumptions with respect to the tests. Let $\bar{S}_i^{(m)}$ and $\widetilde{S}_i^{(m)}$ stand again for generic test statistics computed from individual single-equation least squares regressions with "intercept only" and "intercept plus linear trend", respectively. The superscript (m) stands for the dimension of the I(1) vector entering the equations. One route to panel testing relies on so-called group statistics averaging individual statistics. We denote them as follows:

$$\bar{G}^{(m)} = \frac{1}{N}\sum_{i=1}^{N} \bar{S}_i^{(m)} \quad \text{or} \quad \tilde{G}^{(m)} = \frac{1}{N}\sum_{i=1}^{N} \tilde{S}_i^{(m)}.$$

Similarly, panel statistics rely on pooling the data across the dimension within, i.e., summing over terms showing up in the numerator and denominator separately,

$$\bar{P}^{(m)} = g\left(\sum_{i=1}^{N} \bar{N}_{i,T}^{(m)}, \sum_{i=1}^{N} \bar{D}_{i,T}^{(m)}\right) \quad \text{or} \quad \tilde{P}^{(m)} = g\left(\sum_{i=1}^{N} \tilde{N}_{i,T}^{(m)}, \sum_{i=1}^{N} \tilde{D}_{i,T}^{(m)}\right).$$

A typical example for the mapping g is $g(x, y) = x/\sqrt{y}$ in the case of t-type statistics. Here, it is assumed that the generic $\bar{N}_{i,T}^{(m)}$ and $\bar{D}_{i,T}^{(m)}$ or $\tilde{N}_{i,T}^{(m)}$ and $\tilde{D}_{i,T}^{(m)}$ are computed from individually demeaned or detrended regressions, respectively. We allow for group and panel statistics by introducing the generic notation $\bar{Z}^{(m)}$ and $\tilde{Z}^{(m)}$, and maintain for the panel the joint null hypothesis

$$H_0 = \bigcap_{i=1}^{N} H_{i,0}. \tag{1}$$

A distinction between the individual null hypotheses $H_{i,0}$ of cointegration or absence of cointegration is not required, and both cases are treated in the generic assumption as follows.

Assumption 2. *Consider linear single-equation least squares regressions ($i = 1, \ldots, N$, $t = 1, \ldots, T$)*

$$y_{i,t} = \bar{\alpha}_i + \bar{\beta}_i' x_{i,t} + \bar{u}_{i,t} \quad \textit{and} \quad y_{i,t} = \tilde{\alpha}_i + \tilde{\delta}_i t + \tilde{\beta}_i' x_{i,t} + \tilde{u}_{i,t}, \tag{2}$$

or

$$\Delta y_{i,t} = \bar{\kappa}_i + \bar{\gamma}_i y_{i,t-1} + \bar{\theta}_i' x_{i,t-1} + \bar{\varepsilon}_{i,t} \quad \textit{and} \quad \Delta y_{i,t} = \tilde{\kappa}_i + \tilde{\psi}_i t + \tilde{\gamma}_i y_{i,t-1} + \tilde{\theta}_i' x_{i,t-1} + \tilde{\varepsilon}_{i,t}, \tag{3}$$

where contemporaneous differences $\Delta x_{i,t}$ or lags of $\Delta z_{i,t-j}$, $j > 0$, may be required as additional regressors in (3) to ensure residuals free of serial correlation. Let $\bar{Z}^{(m)}$ and $\tilde{Z}^{(m)}$ stand for group statistics $\bar{G}^{(m)}$ and $\tilde{G}^{(m)}$ or for panel statistics $\bar{P}^{(m)}$ and $\tilde{P}^{(m)}$ computed from regressions with "intercept only" and "intercept plus linear trend", respectively. We assume under the null hypothesis (1) that

$$\begin{aligned} \sqrt{N}\left(\bar{Z}^{(m)} - \bar{\mu}_m\right) &\Rightarrow \mathcal{N}(0, \bar{\sigma}_m^2) \quad \textit{if } \mu_{i,z} = 0 \textit{ for all } i = 1, \ldots, N, \\ \sqrt{N}\left(\tilde{Z}^{(m)} - \tilde{\mu}_m\right) &\Rightarrow \mathcal{N}(0, \tilde{\sigma}_m^2) \quad \textit{for } \mu_{i,z} \textit{ unrestricted}, \end{aligned}$$

as $T \to \infty$ followed by $N \to \infty$.

Tests, e.g., by Kao [23], Pedroni [18,19], Westerlund [9,24] or Westerlund [15] meet Assumption 2 under different sets of restrictions, and they will be considered in the next section, see Remarks 1 through 3. In particular, these authors tabulate values of $(\bar{\mu}_m, \bar{\sigma}_m)$ and $(\tilde{\mu}_m, \tilde{\sigma}_m)$, $m \geq 2$. Our assumption of a single equation approach is motivated by the fact that much of applied work relies on this. However, such an assumption comes at a price: In (2), we have to assume that the regressors $x_{i,t}$ alone are not cointegrated ($\Omega_{i,xx}$ is positive definite according to Assumption 2), and, in (3), we have to assume under the alternative of cointegration that $\Delta y_{i,t}$ adjust to deviations from the long-run equilibrium, and not $\Delta x_{i,t}$.

Much of the earlier panel cointegration literature assumed independent units invoking a central limit theorem to establish Assumption 2, see e.g., Pedroni [18,19] and Kao [23]. Cross-sectional independence, however, is not maintained in our Assumption 2. Westerlund [15,24] e.g., allows for cross-correlation driven by a common factor. To account for this, he suggests replacing $x_{i,t}$ and $y_{i,t}$ by the cross-sectionally demeaned time series,

$$x_{i,t} - \bar{x}_t \text{ and } y_{i,t} - \bar{y}_t\,, \quad \text{where } \bar{x}_t = \frac{1}{N}\sum_{i=1}^{N} x_{i,t}\,,\ \bar{y}_t = \frac{1}{N}\sum_{i=1}^{N} y_{i,t}\,.$$

This way, he establishes that the limiting results maintained under Assumption 2 are met under cross-sectional correlation (subject to some restrictions).

3. Results

3.1. Asymptotic Theory

The first paper allowing for linear time trends in a panel cointegration context was by Kao [23]. He considers a residual-based unit root test for the null hypothesis of no cointegration in the tradition of Phillips and Ouliaris [25]. His test builds on pooling the data while allowing for a individual-specific intercept. Kao [23] does not consider regressions containing a linear time trend as additional regressors, but allows for a linear drift in the data when performing a regression with a fixed effect intercept. In the case of the $k = 1$ regressor (i.e., $m = 2$), Kao ([23], Equation (15)) observed that the linear time trend dominates the I(1) component; hence, the limiting distribution amounts to that of the panel unit root test by Levin et al. [26] upon detrending. To be precise: let $\widetilde{\mu}_1$ and $\widetilde{\sigma}_1$ denote the normalizing constants provided by Levin et al. [26] for detrended panel unit root tests; then, one should use them for the pooled residual-based panel cointegration statistic $\bar{P}^{(2)}$ in a bivariate regression if the regressor is I(1) with drift, see Kao ([23], Theorem 4):

$$\sqrt{N}\left(\bar{P}^{(2)} - \widetilde{\mu}_1\right) \Rightarrow \mathcal{N}(0, \widetilde{\sigma}_1^2) \quad \text{under } \mu_{i,x} \neq 0\,. \tag{4}$$

In Theorem 1, we extend Kao's result for any panel or group statistics from static or dynamic regressions with $m \geq 2$ computed from regressions with intercept only in the presence of linear time trends.

Theorem 1. *Let the data satisfy Assumption 1, and the generic test statistic $\bar{Z}^{(m)}$ meets Assumption 2 for $m \geq 2$. Furthermore, assume that $\mu_{i,x} \neq 0$ for all $i = 1, \ldots, N$. Under the null hypothesis (1), it then holds true that*

$$\sqrt{N}\left(\bar{Z}^{(m)} - \widetilde{\mu}_{m-1}\right) \Rightarrow \mathcal{N}(0, \widetilde{\sigma}_{m-1}^2)$$

as $N \to \infty$, where $(\widetilde{\mu}_{m-1}, \widetilde{\sigma}_{m-1})$ are from Assumption 2.

For proof, see Appendix A.

Note that Assumption 2 does not impose any restriction on $\mu_{i,y}$. As is shown in the proof, Theorem 1 holds irrespective of whether $\{y_{i,t}\}$ displays a linear trend or not ($\mu_{i,y} \neq 0$ or $\mu_{i,y} = 0$).

Two research strategies can be employed in the presence of linear time trends when dealing with statistics resulting from regressions with intercept only. The first one simply ignores the linear time trends in the data and standardizes $\bar{Z}^{(m)}$ with $\bar{\mu}_m$ and $\bar{\sigma}_m$. The second strategy accounts for the drift in the data according to Theorem 1; in other words, it applies $\bar{Z}^{(m)}$ upon standardizing with $\widetilde{\mu}_{m-1}$ and $\widetilde{\sigma}_{m-1}$. We summarize as follows:

Strategy S_I: When $\bar{Z}^{(m)}$ is computed from panel regressions without detrending, then compare $\sqrt{N}\left(\bar{Z}^{(m)} - \bar{\mu}_m\right)/\bar{\sigma}_m$ with quantiles from the standard normal distribution, i.e., ignore the presence of linear trends in the data.

Strategy S_A: When $\bar{Z}^{(m)}$ is computed from panel regressions without detrending, then compare $\sqrt{N}\left(\bar{Z}^{(m)} - \widetilde{\mu}_{m-1}\right)/\widetilde{\sigma}_{m-1}$ with quantiles from the standard normal distribution, i.e., account for the presence of linear trends in the data.

For the rest of the paper, we assume that an applied econometrician is able to distinguish between the two cases, whether a linear time trend underlies the variables (e.g., log income or log prices) or not (e.g., interest or inflation rates). Hence, we maintain the assumption behind Theorem 1: the researcher knows that at least one regressor is I(1) with drift ($\mu_{i,x} \neq 0$). We assume that strategy S_A is only employed when linear trends are truly present and thus refrain from the discussion of misspecification: what happens if there are no linear time trends in the data, but one erroneously accounts for trends.

The situation analyzed in Theorem 1 has not been considered in the previous panel cointegration literature, with the notable exception of Kao [23]. Consequently, all applied papers that we are aware of standardize $\bar{Z}^{(m)}$, with $\bar{\mu}_m$ and $\bar{\sigma}_m$ ignoring the effect of deterministic trends in the series, which amounts to strategy S_I. The effect of strategy S_I under linear time trends is discussed for growing N in the following proposition. The resulting size distortions depend on whether the test is right-tailed or left-tailed (null hypothesis is rejected for too large or too small values, respectively).

Proposition 1. *Let the assumptions from Theorem 1 hold true. Furthermore, assume*

$$\widetilde{\mu}_{m-1} < \bar{\mu}_m \,. \tag{5}$$

Under the null hypothesis, one has the following results for strategy S_I:

(a) For a left-tailed test, the probability to reject according to strategy S_I increases with growing N to 1;
(b) for a right-tailed test, the probability to reject according to strategy S_I decreases with growing N to 0.

For proof, see Appendix A.

We now discuss a couple of panel tests satisfying Assumption 2 and (5), such that Theorem 1 and Proposition 1 apply.

Remark 1. *The residual-based unit root tests for the null hypothesis of no cointegration proposed by Pedroni [18,19] build on static regressions as in (2). The null hypothesis (1) is rejected for too negative values of the test statistic (of $\bar{Z}^{(m)}$ in our generic notation). The expected values and standard deviations $(\bar{\mu}_m, \bar{\sigma}_m)$ and $(\widetilde{\mu}_m, \widetilde{\sigma}_m)$ showing up in Assumption 2 are available from Pedroni ([18], Table 2) for $m > 2$ and from Pedroni ([19], Corollary 1) for $m = 2$. In order to apply Theorem 1 (strategy S_A) for $m = 2$, one requires $\widetilde{\mu}_1$ and $\widetilde{\sigma}_1$. These values stem from the detrended Dickey-Fuller distribution in the case of group statistics and have been tabulated by Nabeya ([27], Table 4): $\widetilde{\mu}_1 = -2.18136$ and $\widetilde{\sigma}_1 = 0.74991$. Throughout this, we observe $\widetilde{\mu}_{m-1} < \bar{\mu}_m < 0$. Hence, Proposition 1(a) applies. If strategy S_I is employed under linear trends, and then the probability to reject the true null hypothesis converges into one with growing panel size N. Alternatively, Westerlund [24] suggested group and panel variance ratio type tests along the lines of Breitung [28]. The null hypothesis of no cointegration is rejected again for too small values of the variance ratio statistic, and $(\bar{\mu}_m, \bar{\sigma}_m)$ and $(\widetilde{\mu}_m, \widetilde{\sigma}_m)$ showing up in Assumption 2 are given in Westerlund ([24], Table 1) for $m \geq 2$. To apply Theorem 1 with $m = 2$, we need $\widetilde{\mu}_1$ and $\widetilde{\sigma}_1$. For the detrended Breitung distribution we obtain by simulation $\widetilde{\mu}_1 = 0.0110$ and $\widetilde{\sigma}_1 = 0.005197$, which are the values corresponding to the case of group statistics. Again, we observe $0 < \widetilde{\mu}_{m-1} < \bar{\mu}_m$, so that (5) holds. Consequently, Proposition 1(a) applies, and the probability to reject the true null hypothesis under strategy S_I grows with N as long as there is a linear trend in the data. To sum up: in the case of residual-based tests for no cointegration, strategy S_I results in massive size distortions; numerical evidence for finite N is given in Table 1 below.*

Remark 2. *The error-correction tests by Westerlund [15] relies on regressions of type (3). It is again a left-tailed test: The null hypothesis of no cointegration is rejected for too negative t-values associated with γ. Values of $(\bar{\mu}_m, \bar{\sigma}_m)$ and $(\widetilde{\mu}_m, \widetilde{\sigma}_m)$ are tabulated in Westerlund ([15], Table 1) for $m \geq 2$. In case of $m = 1$ (i.e., no $x_{i,t}$ on the right-hand side), the limiting distributions are of the usual Dickey-Fuller type. Hence, $\widetilde{\mu}_1$ and $\widetilde{\sigma}_1$ for group statistics are again from detrended Dickey-Fuller-type distributions and given in Nabeya ([27], Table 4) (see above). Comparing $\bar{\mu}_m$ with $\widetilde{\mu}_m$, we find $\widetilde{\mu}_{m-1} < \bar{\mu}_m < 0$ meeting (5) again. Consequently, strategy S_I is increasingly liberal in the presence of linear time trends, and the probability to reject the true null* *hypothesis approaches 1 in the limit as long as the series display a linear time trend. For numerical evidence, see Table 2 below.*

Remark 3. *We now flip the null and the alternative hypotheses. Westerlund [9] suggested testing the null hypothesis of cointegration. He proposed a CUSUM group test statistic for this null hypothesis to be applied with tabulated values* $(\bar{\mu}_m, \bar{\sigma}_m)$ *and* $(\tilde{\mu}_m, \tilde{\sigma}_m)$, $m \geq 2$. *To apply Theorem 1 for* $m = 2$, *we provide as moments of the univariate, detrended distribution by simulation:* $\tilde{\mu}_1 = 0.6367$ *and* $\tilde{\sigma}_1 = 0.14595$[2]. *This test is right-tailed and in accordance with Westerlund ([9], Table 1)* $0 < \tilde{\mu}_{m-1} < \bar{\mu}_m$. *Thus, this time Proposition 1(b) comes in. Under strategy* S_I *in the presence of linear trends, the test is increasingly undersized with growing N. Such a conservative behaviour implies low power under the alternative hypothesis.*

3.2. Numerical Evidence

The statements obtained from Proposition 1 may be quantified more precisely by means of Equations (A2) and (A3) given in the Appendix. These rejection probabilities apply approximately (for large N) under the null hypothesis at nominal significance level α. We report results for the group t-tests by Pedroni [18,19] and by Westerlund [15] in Tables 1 and 2.

Table 1. Approximate effective size of the group t-test by Pedroni [18,19] computed from (A2) at nominal level α under strategy S_I for $\mu_{i,x} \neq 0$.

	$N =$	10	20	30	40	50
	$\alpha = 0.01$	0.030	0.053	0.079	0.107	0.137
$k = 1$	$\alpha = 0.05$	0.126	0.190	0.249	0.307	0.361
	$\alpha = 0.10$	0.227	0.314	0.389	0.455	0.515
	$\alpha = 0.01$	0.017	0.024	0.030	0.036	0.043
$k = 2$	$\alpha = 0.05$	0.080	0.102	0.122	0.141	0.159
	$\alpha = 0.10$	0.154	0.188	0.217	0.243	0.268
	$\alpha = 0.01$	0.014	0.017	0.020	0.022	0.025
$k = 3$	$\alpha = 0.05$	0.067	0.078	0.087	0.096	0.104
	$\alpha = 0.10$	0.130	0.148	0.162	0.175	0.187

Table 2. Approximate effective size of the group t-test by Westerlund [15] computed from (A2) at nominal level α under strategy S_I for $\mu_{i,x} \neq 0$

	$N =$	10	20	30	40	50
	$\alpha = 0.01$	0.139	0.352	0.564	0.732	0.846
$k = 1$	$\alpha = 0.05$	0.394	0.669	0.836	0.924	0.967
	$\alpha = 0.10$	0.566	0.808	0.921	0.969	0.988
	$\alpha = 0.01$	0.089	0.208	0.344	0.478	0.598
$k = 2$	$\alpha = 0.05$	0.283	0.484	0.644	0.763	0.846
	$\alpha = 0.10$	0.436	0.645	0.783	0.870	0.924
	$\alpha = 0.01$	0.067	0.150	0.247	0.349	0.450
$k = 3$	$\alpha = 0.05$	0.232	0.392	0.531	0.647	0.738
	$\alpha = 0.10$	0.372	0.553	0.687	0.783	0.852

Generally, the size distortions in Tables 1 and 2 grow with N, while decreasing with $m = k + 1$ at the same time. The fact that S_I is too liberal is characteristic for these tests where we reject for too negative values (of $\sqrt{N}(\bar{Z}^{(m)} - \bar{\mu}_m)/\bar{\sigma}_m$ in our generic notation). Overrejection is not the general case,

[2] The univariate distribution is the supremum over the absolute value of a so-called second-level Brownian bridge, which shows up with the detrended KPSS test, too; see Kwiatkowski et al. [29].

however, as we see when reversing the null and alternative hypotheses. To quantify distortions for the CUSUM test discussed in Remark 3, we use Equation (A3) from the Appendix. When evaluating S_I under $\mu_{i,x} \neq 0$, we observe rejection probabilities equal to zero up to three digits for $N = 10, 20, \ldots$; this strongly supports the limiting result from Proposition 1 (b).

3.3. Regressions with a Linear Time Trend

For regressions with intercept only, strategy S_I has been used in the literature and applied with the tests mentioned in the remarks above. We have illustrated its failure to control size under the null hypothesis in the presence of a linear time trend. In practice, one may use two strategies to account for linear time trends. The first one is the new S_A according to Theorem 1 from regressions without detrending. The second one consists of detrending the series, or equivalently running detrended regressions, i.e., including $\widetilde{\delta}_i t$ and $\widetilde{\psi}_i t$ in (2) and (3), respectively. The empirical strategy then becomes the following:

Strategy S_D: Compute $\widetilde{Z}^{(m)}$ from detrended panel regressions and compare the normalization $\sqrt{N}\left(\widetilde{Z}^{(m)} - \widetilde{\mu}_m\right)/\widetilde{\sigma}_m$ with quantiles from the standard normal distribution.

By Assumption 2, this strategy will provide asymptotically correct size. However, tests from detrended regressions will be prone to power losses relative to strategy S_A, which is more parsimonious. For this reason, we next investigate the price of strategy S_D relative to S_A in terms of power.

In Monte Carlo experiments, we study in particular the error-correction test (group t-statistic) by Westerlund [15]. Before turning to a power analysis, we make sure that size is under control. For the data-generating process (DGP), we consider hence the null hypothesis of no cointegration under linear time trends:

$$y_{i,t} = \delta_i t + x_{i,1,t} + x_{i,2,t} + \cdots + x_{i,k,t} + r_{i,0,t}\,, \quad (6)$$

$$t = 1, 2, \ldots, T, \quad i = 1, 2, \ldots, N,$$

$$x_{i,j,t} = \mu_{i,j,x} + x_{i,j,t-1} + v_{i,j,t}\,, \quad j = 1, 2, ..., k, \quad (7)$$

where $\{v_{i,j,t}\}$ are normal iid sequences, $\mathcal{N}(0, \sigma^2_{i,j})$, independent of each other. Finally, $r_{i,0,t} = r_{i,0,t-1} + v_{i,0,t}$ is an independent random walk entering (6). The DGP under the alternative of cointegration becomes

$$\Delta y_{i,t} = -0.02\left(y_{i,t-1} - \delta_i(t-1) - x_{i,1,t-1} - x_{i,2,t-1} - \cdots - x_{i,k,t-1}\right) + v_{i,0,t}\,, \quad (8)$$

where $x_{i,j,t}$ and $v_{i,0,t}$ are generated as before. Using the regression

$$\Delta y_{i,t} = \bar{\kappa}_i + \bar{\gamma}_i y_{i,t-1} + \bar{\theta}_i' x_{i,t-1} + \bar{\phi}_i' \Delta x_{i,t} + \bar{\varepsilon}_{i,t}\,, \quad (9)$$

we computed the group t-statistic proposed by Westerlund [15]. Strategy S_D is employed with

$$\Delta y_{i,t} = \widetilde{\kappa}_i + \widetilde{\psi}_i t + \widetilde{\gamma}_i y_{i,t-1} + \widetilde{\theta}_i' x_{i,t-1} + \widetilde{\phi}_i' \Delta x_{i,t} + \widetilde{\varepsilon}_{i,t}\,. \quad (10)$$

All reported rejection frequencies rely on 10,000 replications.

The leading case consists of the following parameterization, where only the first component of the regressors $\{x_{i,t}\}$ is driven by a linear time trend:

$$T = 250\,, \quad \mu_{i,x}' = (1, 0, \ldots, 0)\,, \quad \sigma^2_{i,0} = \sigma^2_{i,1} = \cdots = \sigma^2_{i,k} = 1\,. \quad (11)$$

This mimics with $k = 2$ or $k = 3$ a typical macro panel with monthly data and e.g., income, interest rates and inflation rates as regressors. Table 3 reports the frequencies of rejection for different values of δ_i from (6), and rejection is based on strategy S_A according to Theorem 1. It illustrates how well the rule of Theorem 1 works: the experimental sizes are close to the nominal ones. This is particularly true for $\delta_i = 1$, while the test is mildly conservative for $\delta_i = 0.1$, and a bit more conservative for

$\delta_i = 0$, in particular for N large relative to $T = 250$. Next, we consider strategy S_D with the same data. The rejection frequencies are given in Table 4. We observe that the experimental size from detrended regressions is close to the nominal one under the null hypothesis of no cointegration, irrespective of δ_i.

Since strategies S_A and S_D both hold the nominal size, the question of which one is more powerful naturally arises. The results contained in Table 5 are very clear: first, the power increases with δ_i; second, strategy S_A always outperforms S_D considerably, and has, e.g., rejection frequencies more than twice as large for $N = 10$ or $k = 3$. In particular, detrending becomes all the more costly; relative to strategy S_A, the larger N is, which is intuitively clear: including a linear time trend in a regression requires the estimation of an additional parameter; in a panel of N units, detrending thus involves the estimation of N additional parameters compared to strategy S_A. At the same time, these estimated trends can be spuriously correlated with the stochastic trends in the data, and, therefore, incorrectly lead to support for cointegration, in particular when the time dimension is relatively short.

Table 3. Experimental size at nominal level α under S_A according to Theorem 1 for (11); data-generating process (DGP): (6) and (7).

	$N =$	10	20	30	40	50
				$\delta_i = 0$		
	$\alpha = 0.01$	0.010	0.009	0.008	0.008	0.008
$k = 1$	$\alpha = 0.05$	0.048	0.048	0.043	0.040	0.041
	$\alpha = 0.10$	0.093	0.095	0.087	0.080	0.083
	$\alpha = 0.01$	0.008	0.009	0.007	0.009	0.006
$k = 2$	$\alpha = 0.05$	0.046	0.040	0.039	0.040	0.034
	$\alpha = 0.10$	0.093	0.082	0.083	0.082	0.073
	$\alpha = 0.01$	0.010	0.010	0.012	0.010	0.011
$k = 3$	$\alpha = 0.05$	0.051	0.052	0.052	0.049	0.052
	$\alpha = 0.10$	0.101	0.101	0.102	0.098	0.098
				$\delta_i = 0.1$		
	$\alpha = 0.01$	0.009	0.010	0.009	0.008	0.008
$k = 1$	$\alpha = 0.05$	0.050	0.048	0.048	0.044	0.043
	$\alpha = 0.10$	0.096	0.095	0.096	0.089	0.088
	$\alpha = 0.01$	0.009	0.009	0.008	0.009	0.007
$k = 2$	$\alpha = 0.05$	0.044	0.047	0.045	0.046	0.040
	$\alpha = 0.10$	0.093	0.094	0.090	0.092	0.085
	$\alpha = 0.01$	0.013	0.013	0.013	0.013	0.011
$k = 3$	$\alpha = 0.05$	0.055	0.056	0.058	0.056	0.054
	$\alpha = 0.10$	0.107	0.112	0.110	0.107	0.108
				$\delta_i = 1$		
	$\alpha = 0.01$	0.009	0.010	0.008	0.009	0.009
$k = 1$	$\alpha = 0.05$	0.047	0.045	0.045	0.042	0.044
	$\alpha = 0.10$	0.095	0.092	0.095	0.090	0.091
	$\alpha = 0.01$	0.011	0.009	0.008	0.010	0.009
$k = 2$	$\alpha = 0.05$	0.051	0.046	0.045	0.044	0.042
	$\alpha = 0.10$	0.097	0.093	0.090	0.086	0.084
	$\alpha = 0.01$	0.011	0.013	0.011	0.013	0.013
$k = 3$	$\alpha = 0.05$	0.056	0.054	0.055	0.055	0.056
	$\alpha = 0.10$	0.105	0.108	0.108	0.107	0.107

Table 4. Experimental size at nominal level α under S_D (detrending) for (11); DGP: (6) and (7).

	$N =$	10	20	30	40	50
				$\delta_i = 0$		
	$\alpha = 0.01$	0.010	0.010	0.008	0.010	0.010
$k = 1$	$\alpha = 0.05$	0.047	0.047	0.045	0.048	0.044
	$\alpha = 0.10$	0.098	0.095	0.091	0.091	0.087
	$\alpha = 0.01$	0.012	0.012	0.013	0.012	0.012
$k = 2$	$\alpha = 0.05$	0.057	0.057	0.056	0.059	0.057
	$\alpha = 0.10$	0.112	0.108	0.106	0.108	0.111
	$\alpha = 0.01$	0.013	0.008	0.012	0.013	0.010
$k = 3$	$\alpha = 0.05$	0.055	0.050	0.050	0.055	0.049
	$\alpha = 0.10$	0.104	0.099	0.101	0.098	0.099
				$\delta_i = 0.1$		
	$\alpha = 0.01$	0.009	0.009	0.010	0.009	0.010
$k = 1$	$\alpha = 0.05$	0.051	0.050	0.049	0.051	0.048
	$\alpha = 0.10$	0.097	0.103	0.100	0.100	0.096
	$\alpha = 0.01$	0.012	0.013	0.013	0.015	0.014
$k = 2$	$\alpha = 0.05$	0.059	0.062	0.061	0.058	0.063
	$\alpha = 0.10$	0.116	0.117	0.115	0.113	0.117
	$\alpha = 0.01$	0.011	0.012	0.012	0.012	0.013
$k = 3$	$\alpha = 0.05$	0.054	0.052	0.052	0.052	0.055
	$\alpha = 0.10$	0.107	0.104	0.104	0.104	0.107
				$\delta_i = 1$		
	$\alpha = 0.01$	0.011	0.010	0.013	0.011	0.010
$k = 1$	$\alpha = 0.05$	0.052	0.047	0.048	0.050	0.050
	$\alpha = 0.10$	0.104	0.095	0.096	0.098	0.095
	$\alpha = 0.01$	0.015	0.011	0.014	0.014	0.012
$k = 2$	$\alpha = 0.05$	0.062	0.061	0.060	0.062	0.058
	$\alpha = 0.10$	0.119	0.119	0.116	0.119	0.115
	$\alpha = 0.01$	0.013	0.015	0.012	0.014	0.013
$k = 3$	$\alpha = 0.05$	0.053	0.056	0.053	0.053	0.054
	$\alpha = 0.10$	0.110	0.106	0.101	0.112	0.105

We have varied the leading case with the parameterization from (11). First, we allowed for more and stronger trends in the regressors,

$$\mu'_{i,x} = (1, 1, \ldots, 1), \text{ or } \mu'_{i,x} = (1, 2, \ldots, k),$$

with all other parameters fixed. This corrects the mild undersizedness of strategy S_A reported in Table 3 yielding empirical sizes very close to the nominal one. At the same, time power relative to Table 5 is increased, with strategy S_A still dominating S_D. Second, we have increased the magnitude of the random walks, namely $\sigma^2_{i,0} = \sigma^2_{i,1} = \cdots = \sigma^2_{i,k} = 4$, while the other parameters are from (11) and $\delta_i = 0$ (see Table 6). Here, the linear trends are less pronounced, such that S_A results in slightly more conservative tests (compared to the first panel in Table 3), and similarly, power is reduced (compared to the first panel in Table 5). Still, S_A clearly dominates S_D in Table 6. Third, we simulated shorter panels, $T = 100$. This makes both strategies, S_A and S_D, conservative under H_0, which is accompanied by a loss of power.

Table 5. Experimental power at nominal level 5% for (11); DGP: (8) and (7).

$N =$	10	20	30	40	50
		S_A: Theorem 1 for $\delta_i = 0$			
$k = 1$	0.486	0.727	0.859	0.933	0.965
$k = 2$	0.284	0.433	0.559	0.672	0.751
$k = 3$	0.155	0.234	0.288	0.336	0.387
		S_D: Detrended regression for $\delta_i = 0$			
$k = 1$	0.235	0.379	0.497	0.615	0.707
$k = 2$	0.163	0.247	0.331	0.399	0.452
$k = 3$	0.087	0.118	0.133	0.156	0.173
		S_A: Theorem 1 for $\delta_i = 0.1$			
$k = 1$	0.536	0.772	0.904	0.953	0.981
$k = 2$	0.311	0.485	0.622	0.726	0.802
$k = 3$	0.174	0.252	0.319	0.384	0.439
		S_D: Detrended regression for $\delta_i = 0.1$			
$k = 1$	0.262	0.402	0.531	0.636	0.716
$k = 2$	0.170	0.261	0.337	0.417	0.476
$k = 3$	0.090	0.127	0.143	0.168	0.186
		S_A: Theorem 1 for $\delta_i = 1$			
$k = 1$	0.824	0.974	0.997	1.000	1.000
$k = 2$	0.526	0.759	0.890	0.950	0.979
$k = 3$	0.292	0.419	0.553	0.661	0.734
		S_D: Detrended regression for $\delta_i = 1$			
$k = 1$	0.395	0.605	0.757	0.852	0.911
$k = 2$	0.219	0.330	0.433	0.524	0.595
$k = 3$	0.101	0.129	0.145	0.170	0.189

Table 6. Experimental size and power at nominal level 5% for $T = 250$, $\mu'_{i,x} = (1, 0, \ldots, 0)$, $\delta_i = 0$, and $\sigma^2_{i,j} = 4$; DGP: (6) or (8) and (7).

$N =$	10	20	30	40	50
		S_A: size			
$k = 1$	0.043	0.039	0.037	0.036	0.034
$k = 2$	0.043	0.041	0.037	0.034	0.031
$k = 3$	0.050	0.049	0.045	0.045	0.042
		S_A: power			
$k = 1$	0.410	0.622	0.771	0.869	0.920
$k = 2$	0.252	0.383	0.501	0.604	0.683
$k = 3$	0.147	0.205	0.257	0.304	0.364
		S_D: size			
$k = 1$	0.048	0.047	0.049	0.048	0.049
$k = 2$	0.056	0.063	0.061	0.062	0.062
$k = 3$	0.058	0.052	0.053	0.051	0.057
		S_D: power			
$k = 1$	0.236	0.387	0.522	0.622	0.699
$k = 2$	0.178	0.273	0.350	0.437	0.493
$k = 3$	0.102	0.136	0.161	0.192	0.213

4. Conclusions

In time series econometrics, it has been known for a long time that "the deterministic trends in the data affect the limiting distributions of the test statistics *whether or not we detrend the data*" (Hansen [16], p. 103). This has been shown for the residual-based Phillips-Ouliaris (or Engle-Granger) cointegration test by Hansen [16], see also the exposition in Hamilton ([21], p. 596, 597). Analogous results have been given for other cointegration tests by Hassler [30,31], see also the summary by Hassler ([22], Proposition 16.6). In this paper, these findings are carried over to the panel framework, and they are shown to continue to hold for single-equation tests relying on least squares, no matter whether the null hypothesis is absence or presence of cointegration. In a regression involving $m \geq 2$ variables, much of the panel cointegration theory relies on normalization with suitable constants $\bar{\mu}_m$ and $\bar{\sigma}_m$ and letting the panel dimension N go to infinity to obtain a standard normal distribution. The numbers $\bar{\mu}_m$ and $\bar{\sigma}_m$ are tabulated for the case of regressions with intercept only. Different figures $\tilde{\mu}_m$ and $\tilde{\sigma}_m$ are tabulated for regressions with intercept and linear time trend. We show the following: when statistics are computed from regressions with m integrated variables with intercept only, but one of the integrated regressors is dominated by a linear time trend, then normalization with $\tilde{\mu}_{m-1}$ and $\tilde{\sigma}_{m-1}$ is required to achieve asymptotically valid inference under the null hypothesis (Theorem 1). Normalization with $\bar{\mu}_m$ and $\bar{\sigma}_m$, however, which has been the conventional strategy so far, results in a loss of size control under the null hypothesis. In fact, employing $\bar{\mu}_m$ and $\bar{\sigma}_m$ in the presence of linear time trends gives rejection probabilities converging with N to 1 or 0, depending on whether the null hypothesis is no cointegration or cointegration, respectively (see Proposition 1). To avoid such size distortions, one may employ the strategy following Theorem 1, or one may work with detrended regressions. Detrending, however, comes at a price: a regression with intercept only will provide more powerful tests (see e.g., Hamilton [21], p. 598); according to our simulations, power gains of our new strategy over detrending may be considerable and growing with N, and this also holds true if there is a linear trend superimposing the level relation. Our Monte Carlo evidence, however, is limited to the case of testing for the null hypothesis of no cointegration.

Hence, we propose the following empirical strategy if at least one of the integrated regressors is driven by a linear time trend when testing for no cointegration. First, test the null hypothesis of no cointegration with our new strategy S_A from Theorem 1, since it is more powerful than tests relying on detrending. If the null hypothesis of no cointegration is rejected according to Theorem 1, then one may test, in a second step, whether a linear time trend is present, superimposing the level relation between $y_{i,t}$ and $x_{i,t}$. If strategy S_A does not reject the null hypothesis of no cointegration, then one may, of course, try a test building on detrending, although it will tend to be less powerful, since it requires the estimation of N additional parameters.

Acknowledgments: We thank Matei Demetrescu, Christoph Hanck and Joakim Westerlund for helpful comments. Moreover, comments by Katarina Juselius and three anonymous referees that improved the paper are gratefully acknowledged.

Author Contributions: The authors contributed equally to the paper.

Conflicts of Interest: The authors declare no conflict of interest.

Appendix A

Appendix A.1. Proof of Theorem 1

Since group statistics $\bar{G}^{(m)}$ are computed from individual regressions and since panel statistics $\bar{P}^{(m)}$ build on pooled regressions, we suppress the index i and consider the generic case with $\{y_t\}$ and $\{x_t\}$ satisfying Assumption 1. Furthermore, we focus on the stochastic regressors and ignore the constant intercept without loss of generality. We will proceed in four steps.

Step 1: First, note that the regressors may be rotated in such a way that all linear trends are concentrated in one scalar component. To that end, define the k-element vector $\lambda_1 := \mu_x / \sqrt{\mu_x' \mu_x}$ of unit length with

$$\tau_t := \lambda_1' x_t = \sqrt{\mu_x' \mu_x}\, t + \lambda_1' \sum_{j=1}^{t} e_{x,j} \,.$$

At the same time, there exist $k-1$ linearly independent k-element columns collected in the $k \times (k-1)$-matrix Λ_2. Due to the Gram-Schmidt orthogonalization, one may assume that the invertible matrix $\Lambda := (\lambda_1, \Lambda_2)$ is orthogonal: $\Lambda\Lambda' = I_k$. All columns of Λ_2 eliminate the linear trend in x_t:

$$\xi_t := \Lambda_2' x_t = \Lambda_2' \sum_{j=1}^{t} e_{x,j} \,.$$

Hence, ξ_t is a $(k-1)$-vector integrated of order 1 without drift. Now, we are able to write

$$\Lambda' x_t = \begin{pmatrix} \tau_t \\ \xi_t \end{pmatrix} .$$

Step 2: Second, we show that the deterministic term in τ_t dominates the I(1) component, which is clear from

$$T^{-1} \tau_{\lfloor rT \rfloor} = \sqrt{\mu_x' \mu_x} \frac{\lfloor rT \rfloor}{T} + O_p(T^{-0.5}) \Rightarrow \sqrt{\mu_x' \mu_x}\, r , \quad 0 \le r \le 1 \,.$$

More precisely, we can show that empirical moments involving τ_t equal those with $t\sqrt{\mu_x' \mu_x}$ up to $O_p\left(T^{-0.5}\right)$. We have from Park and Phillips ([32], Lemma 2.1) that the row vector

$$\left(\frac{1}{T^2} \sum_{t=1}^{T} \tau_t , \frac{1}{T^3} \sum_{t=1}^{T} \tau_t^2 , \frac{1}{T^{2.5}} \sum_{t=1}^{T} \tau_t \xi_t' , \frac{1}{T^2} \sum_{t=1}^{T} \tau_t \Delta x_{t-j}' \right)$$

equals

$$\sqrt{\mu_x' \mu_x} \left(\frac{1}{T^2} \sum_{t=1}^{T} t , \frac{\sqrt{\mu_x' \mu_x}}{T^3} \sum_{t=1}^{T} t^2 , \frac{1}{T^{2.5}} \sum_{t=1}^{T} t \xi_t' , \frac{1}{T^2} \sum_{t=1}^{T} t \Delta x_{t-j}' \right) + O_p\left(T^{-0.5}\right) ;$$

furthermore, if $\mu_y \neq 0$,

$$\left(\frac{1}{T^3} \sum_{t=1}^{T} \tau_t y_t , \frac{1}{T^2} \sum_{t=1}^{T} \tau_t \Delta y_t \right) = \sqrt{\mu_x' \mu_x} \left(\frac{1}{T^3} \sum_{t=1}^{T} t y_t , \frac{1}{T^2} \sum_{t=1}^{T} t \Delta y_t \right) + O_p\left(T^{-0.5}\right) ,$$

or, if $\mu_y = 0$,

$$\left(\frac{1}{T^{2.5}} \sum_{t=1}^{T} \tau_t y_t , \frac{1}{T^{1.5}} \sum_{t=1}^{T} \tau_t \Delta y_t \right) = \sqrt{\mu_x' \mu_x} \left(\frac{1}{T^{2.5}} \sum_{t=1}^{T} t y_t , \frac{1}{T^{1.5}} \sum_{t=1}^{T} t \Delta y_t \right) + O_p\left(T^{-0.5}\right) .$$

Now, we are equipped to deal with the two cases: residual-based tests from (2) and t-type tests from (3).

Step 3: Consider the least squares regression (without intercept for brevity)

$$y_t = \widehat{\beta}' x_t + \widehat{u}_t$$

with

$$\widehat{\beta} = \left(\sum_{t=1}^{T} x_t x_t'\right)^{-1} \Lambda\Lambda' \sum_{t=1}^{T} x_t y_t = \left(\sum_{t=1}^{T} \Lambda' x_t x_t'\right)^{-1} \sum_{t=1}^{T} \Lambda' x_t y_t$$
$$= \left(\sum_{t=1}^{T} \begin{pmatrix} \tau_t \\ \xi_t \end{pmatrix} x_t'\right)^{-1} \sum_{t=1}^{T} \begin{pmatrix} \tau_t \\ \xi_t \end{pmatrix} y_t .$$

Similarly,

$$\widehat{\beta}'\Lambda = \sum_{t=1}^{T} (\tau_t, \xi_t') \, y_t \left(\sum_{t=1}^{T} \begin{pmatrix} \tau_t \\ \xi_t \end{pmatrix} (\tau_t, \xi_t')\right)^{-1} .$$

Consequently, the empirical residuals are

$$\widehat{u}_t = y_t - \widehat{\beta}'\Lambda\Lambda' x_t = y_t - \sum_{t=1}^{T} (\tau_t, \xi_t') \, y_t \left(\sum_{t=1}^{T} \begin{pmatrix} \tau_t \\ \xi_t \end{pmatrix} (\tau_t, \xi_t')\right)^{-1} \begin{pmatrix} \tau_t \\ \xi_t \end{pmatrix} . \tag{A1}$$

For y_t, we have by assumption

$$y_t = \delta\, t + \beta' x_t + u_t = \delta\, t + \beta'\Lambda\Lambda' x_t + u_t$$
$$= \delta\, t + \beta'\lambda_1 \tau_t + \theta'\xi_t + u_t , \quad \theta := \Lambda_2'\beta .$$

If $\{u_t\}$ is I(1), then the series are not cointegrated. If $\{u_t\}$ is I(0), then there is cointegration, where a linear time trend may superimpose the cointegrating relation ($\delta \neq 0$) or not ($\delta = 0$). In any case, $\{y_t\}$ is composed of the $(k-1)$-vector $\{\xi_t\}$, which is I(1), and a linear time trend asymptotically (since $\delta\, t + \beta'\lambda_1 \tau_t \approx (\delta + \beta'\lambda_1 \sqrt{\mu_x'\mu_x})\, t$ in the sense of Step 2). Therefore, the residuals $\{\widehat{u}_t\}$ behave asymptotically as if they were computed from a regression on $(k-1)$ I(1) regressors and on a linear trend. This establishes Theorem 1 for the case of residual-based tests.

Step 4: Consider the dynamic least squares regression (without intercept and without (lagged) differences as further regressors for brevity):

$$\Delta y_t = \widehat{\gamma} y_{t-1} + \widehat{\theta}' x_{t-1} + \widehat{\varepsilon}_t .$$

In order to investigate error-correction tests relying on the t statistic t_γ, we employ what is sometimes called the Frisch-Waugh-Lovell theorem. In the first stage, regress both Δy_t and y_{t-1} on x_{t-1}, and denote the fitted values as $f_{0,t}$ and $f_{1,t}$, respectively. In the second stage, the regression of $f_{0,t}$ on $f_{1,t}$ produces a slope estimator that is numerically identical to $\widehat{\gamma}$, and so are the residuals, while the t-statistics differ negligibly due to differences in degrees of freedom. As in Step 3, Equation (A1), one can argue that both $f_{0,t}$ and $f_{1,t}$ behave asymptotically, as if they were computed from a regression on $(k-1)$ I(1) regressors and on a linear trend. Hence, because of the Frisch-Waugh-Lovell theorem, t_γ behaves as if x_{t-1} in (3) had been replaced by a linear time trend as regressor plus $(k-1)$ regressors that are I(1). This establishes Theorem 1 for the case of error-correction tests, and the proof is complete. □

Appendix A.2. Proof of Proposition 1

According to Theorem 1, the statistic $\bar{Z}^{(m)}$ requires under $\mu_{i,x} \neq 0$ normalization with $\widetilde{\mu}_{m-1}$ and $\widetilde{\sigma}_{m-1}$, in order to result in a standard normal distribution under H_0. Let $z_{1-\alpha}$ denote a quantile from the standard normal distribution. In the case where the panel tests are left-tailed, the rejection probability of strategy S_I under the null hypothesis becomes approximately for large N (at nominal level α):

$$P\left(\sqrt{N}\,\frac{\bar{Z}^{(m)}-\bar{\mu}_m}{\bar{\sigma}_m}<-z_{1-\alpha}\right)=\Phi\left(\sqrt{N}\,\frac{\bar{\mu}_m-\widetilde{\mu}_{m-1}}{\widetilde{\sigma}_{m-1}}-\frac{\bar{\sigma}_m}{\widetilde{\sigma}_{m-1}}\,z_{1-\alpha}\right). \tag{A2}$$

Analogously for right-tailed tests, the rejection probability of strategy S_I becomes under $\mu_{i,x}\neq 0$ according to Theorem 1 with growing N:

$$P\left(\sqrt{N}\,\frac{\bar{Z}^{(m)}-\bar{\mu}_m}{\bar{\sigma}_m}>z_{1-\alpha}\right)=1-\Phi\left(\sqrt{N}\,\frac{\bar{\mu}_m-\widetilde{\mu}_{m-1}}{\widetilde{\sigma}_{m-1}}+\frac{\bar{\sigma}_m}{\widetilde{\sigma}_{m-1}}\,z_{1-\alpha}\right). \tag{A3}$$

For $N\to\infty$, one gets the limits given in Proposition 1 from (A2) and (A3). □

References

1. Larsson, R.; Lyhagen, J.; Löthgren, M. Likelihood-based cointegration tests in heterogeneous panels. *Econom. J.* **2001**, *4*, 109–142.
2. Groen, J.J.J.; Kleibergen, F. Likelihood-Based Cointegration Analysis in Panels of Vector Error-Correction Models. *J. Bus. Econ. Stat.* **2003**, *21*, 295–318.
3. Breitung, J. A parametric approach to the estimation of cointegration vectors in panel data. *Econom. Rev.* **2005**, *24*, 151–173.
4. Karaman Örsal, D.D.; Droge, B. Panel cointegration testing in the presence of a time trend. *Comput. Stat. Data Anal.* **2014**, *76*, 377–390.
5. Miller, J.I. A Nonlinear IV Likelihood-Based Rank Test for Multivariate Time Series and Long Panels. *J. Time Ser. Econom.* **2010**, *2*, 1–38.
6. Chang, Y.; Nguyen, C.M. Residual Based Tests for Cointegration in Dependent Panels. *J. Econom.* **2012**, *167*, 504–520.
7. Demetrescu, M.; Hanck, C.; Tarcolea, A.I. IV-based cointegration testing in dependent panels with time-varying variance. *J. Time Ser. Anal.* **2014**, *35*, 393–406.
8. Coe, D.T.; Helpman, E. International R&D Spillovers. *Eur. Econ. Rev.* **1995**, *39*, 859–887.
9. Westerlund, J. A panel CUSUM test of the null of cointegration. *Oxf. Bull. Econ. Stat.* **2005**, *67*, 231–262.
10. Hanck, C. Cross-sectional Correlation Robust Tests for Panel Cointegration. *J. Appl. Stat.* **2009**, *36*, 817–833.
11. Hansen, P.; King, A. Health care expenditure and GDP: Panel data unit root test results—Comment. *J. Health Econ.* **1998**, *17*, 377–381.
12. McCoskey, S.K.; Selden, T.M. Health care expenditures and GDP: Panel data unit root test results. *J. Health Econ.* **1998**, *17*, 369–376.
13. Blomqvist, A.G.; Carter, R.A.L. Is Health Care Really a Luxury? *J. Health Econ.* **1997**, *16*, 207–229.
14. Gerdtham, U.-G.; Löthgren, M. On stationarity and cointegration of international health expenditure and GDP. *J. Health Econ.* **2000**, *19*, 461–475.
15. Westerlund, J. Testing for error correction in panel data. *Oxf. Bull. Econ. Stat.* **2007**, *69*, 709–748.
16. Hansen, B.E. Efficient estimation and testing of cointegrating vectors in the presence of deterministic trends. *J. Econom.* **1992**, *53*, 87–121.
17. Juselius, K. *The Cointegrated VAR Model: Methodology and Applications*; Oxford University Press: Oxford, UK, 2006.
18. Pedroni, P. Critical values for cointegration tests in heterogeneous panels with multiple regressors. *Oxf. Bull. Econ. Stat.* **1999**, *61*, 653–670.
19. Pedroni, P. Panel cointegration: Asymptotic and finite sample properties of pooled time series tests with an application to the PPP hypothesis. *Econom. Theory* **2004**, *20*, 597–625.
20. Greene, W.H. *Econometric Analysis*, 7th ed.; Pearson: Upper Saddle River, NJ, USA, 2012.
21. Hamilton, J.D. *Time Series Analysis*; Princeton University Press: Princeton, NJ, USA, 1994.
22. Hassler, U. *Stochastic Processes and Calculus: An Elementary Introduction with Applications*; Springer: Berlin, Germany, 2016.

23. Kao, C. Spurious regression and residual-based tests for cointegration in panel data. *J. Econom.* **1999**, *90*, 1–44.
24. Westerlund, J. New simple tests for panel cointegration. *Econom. Rev.* **2005**, *24*, 297–316.
25. Phillips, P.C.B.; Ouliaris, S. Asymptotic propositionrties of residual based tests for cointegration. *Econometrica* **1990**, *58*, 165–193.
26. Levin, A.; Lin, C.-F.; Chu, C.-S.J. Unit root tests in panel data: Asymptotic and finite-sample properties. *J. Econom.* **2002**, *108*, 1–24.
27. Nabeya, S. Asymptotic moments of some unit root test statistics in the null case. *Econom. Theory* **1999**, *15*, 139–149.
28. Breitung, J. Nonparametric tests for unit roots and cointegration. *J. Econom.* **2002**, *108*, 343–363.
29. Kwiatkowski, D.; Phillips, P.C.B.; Schmidt, P.; Shin, Y. Testing the Null Hypothesis of Stationarity against the Alternative of a Unit Root: How sure are we that economic time series have a unit root? *J. Econom.* **1992**, *54*, 159–178.
30. Hassler, U. Cointegration testing in single error-correction equations in the presence of linear time trends. *Oxf. Bull. Econ. Stat.* **2000**, *62*, 621–632.
31. Hassler, U. The effect of linear time trends on the KPSS test for cointegration. *J. Time Ser. Anal.* **2001**, *22*, 283–292.
32. Park, J.Y.; Phillips, P.C.B. Statistical Inference in regressions with integrated processes: Part 1. *Econom. Theory* **1988**, *4*, 468–497.

econometrics

MDPI

Article

Formula I(1) and I(2): Race Tracks for Likelihood Maximization Algorithms of I(1) and I(2) Cointegrated VAR Models

Jurgen A. Doornik [1], **Rocco Mosconi** [2] **and Paolo Paruolo** [3,*]

[1] Department of Economics and Institute for New Economic Thinking at the Oxford Martin School, University of Oxford, Oxford OX1 3UQ, UK; jurgen.doornik@nuffield.ox.ac.uk
[2] Politecnico di Milano, 20133 Milano, Italy; rocco.mosconi@polimi.it
[3] Joint Research Centre, European Commission, 21027 Ispra (VA), Italy
* Correspondence: paolo.paruolo@ec.europa.eu

Academic Editor: Katarina Juselius
Received: 1 July 2017; Accepted: 15 October 2017; Published: 20 November 2017

Abstract: This paper provides some test cases, called circuits, for the evaluation of Gaussian likelihood maximization algorithms of the cointegrated vector autoregressive model. Both I(1) and I(2) models are considered. The performance of algorithms is compared first in terms of *effectiveness*, defined as the ability to find the overall maximum. The next step is to compare their *efficiency* and *reliability* across experiments. The aim of the paper is to commence a collective learning project by the profession on the actual properties of algorithms for cointegrated vector autoregressive model estimation, in order to improve their quality and, as a consequence, also the reliability of empirical research.

Keywords: maximum likelihood; Monte Carlo; VAR; cointegration; I(1); I(2)

JEL Classification: C32; C51; C63; C87; C99

---

1. Introduction

Since the late 1980s, cointegrated vector autoregressive models (CVAR) have been extensively used to analyze nonstationary macro-economic data with stochastic trends. Estimation of these models often requires numerical optimization, both for stochastic trends integrated of order 1, I(1), and of order 2, I(2). This paper proposes a set of test cases to analyze the properties of the numerical algorithms for likelihood maximization of CVAR models. This is an attempt to start a collective learning project by the profession about the actual properties of algorithms, in order to improve their quality and, as a consequence, the reliability of empirical research using CVAR models.

The statistical analysis of CVAR models for data with I(1) stochastic trends was developed in Johansen (1988, 1991). The I(1) CVAR model is characterized by a reduced rank restriction of the autoregressive impact matrix. Gaussian maximum likelihood estimation (MLE) in this model can be performed by Reduced Rank Regression (RRR, see Anderson 1951), which requires the solution of a generalized eigenvalue problem.

Simple common restrictions on the cointegrating vectors can be estimated explicitly by modifications of RRR, see Johansen and Juselius (1992). However, MLE under more general restrictions, such as equation-by-equation overidentifying restrictions on the cointegration parameters, cannot be reduced to RRR; here several algorithms can be applied to maximize the likelihood. Johansen and Juselius (1994) and Johansen (1995a) provided an algorithm that alternates RRR over each cointegrating vector in turn, keeping the others fixed. They called this a 'switching algorithm', and since then this label has been used for the alternating variables algorithms in the CVAR literature. Boswijk and Doornik (2004) provides an overview.

Switching algorithms have some advantages over quasi-Newton methods: they don't require derivatives, they are easy to implement and each step uses expressions whose numerical properties and accuracy are well known, such as ordinary least squares (OLS), RRR, or generalized least squares (GLS). The downside is that convergence of switching algorithms can be very slow, see Doornik (2017a), and there is a danger of prematurely deciding upon convergence. Doornik (2017a) also showed that adding a line search to switching algorithms can greatly improve their speed and reliability.

The I(2) CVAR is characterized by two reduced rank restrictions, and Gaussian maximum likelihood cannot be reduced to RRR, except in the specific case where it really reduces to an (unrestricted) I(1) model. Initially, estimation was performed by a two-step method, Johansen (1995b). Subsequently, Johansen (1997) proposed a switching algorithm for MLE. Estimation of the I(2) model with restrictions on the cointegration parameters appears harder than in the I(1) case, and it is still under active development, as can be seen below.

While several algorithms exist that estimate the restricted I(1) and I(2) CVAR models, with some of them readily available in software packages, there has been very little research into the effectiveness of these algorithms. No comparative analysis is available either. This paper aims to improve upon this situation; to this effect, it proposes a set of experimental designs that will allow researchers to benefit from the results of alternative algorithms implemented by peers. This should ultimately lead to more effective algorithms, which, in turn, will provide more confidence in the numerical results of empirical analyses.

This paper defines two classes of exercises, called Formula I(1) and I(2), in a playful allusion to Grand Prix car racing championships. Formula I(1) defines a set of precise rules involving I(1) data generation processes (DGP) and models, while Formula I(2) does the same for I(2) DGPs and models. The proposed experiments control for common sources of variability; this improves comparability and efficiency of results. A simple way to control for Monte Carlo variability is to use the same realization of the innovations in the experiments. This is achieved here by sharing a file of innovations and providing instructions on how to build the time series from them.

Econometricians are invited to implement alternative algorithms with respect to the ones employed here, and to test them by running one or more of the exercises proposed in this paper. A companion website https://sites.google.com/view/race-i1 has been created, where researchers interested in checking the performance of their algorithms are invited to follow instruction on how to upload their results, to be compared with constantly-updated benchmarks. Guidelines are illustrated below. The results for all algorithms are by design comparable; moreover, the participation of an additional algorithm may improve the overall confidence in the comparisons, as explained below.

Results from different implementations of algorithms reflect both the properties of the algorithms *sensu stricto* and of their implementation, where one expects different implementations of the same algorithm to lead to different results. Because of this, econometricians are encouraged to participate in the races also with their own implementation of algorithms already entertained by others. This will increase information on the degree of reproducibility of results and on the relative importance of the implementation versus the algorithm *sensu stricto*.[1]

Recent advances in computational technology have fuelled the Reproducible Research movement; the present paper can be seen as a contribution to this movement.[2] The Reproducible Research movement makes use of replication testbeds and Docker containers for replication of results, see e.g., Boettiger (2015). The present project has chosen to keep requirements for researchers at a minimum and it is not demanding the use of these solutions, at least in the current starting configuration.

---

1 In the rest of the paper the word *algorithm* is used to represent the combination of the algorithm *sensu stricto* and its implementation; hence two implementations of the same algorithm are referred to as two algorithms.

2 The reference to the Reproducible Research movement was suggested by one referee; see e.g., the bibliography and links at http://reproducibleresearch.net.

The rest of the paper is organized as follows. Section 2 discusses design and evaluation of algorithms in general terms. Section 3 provides definitions, while Section 4 describes precise measures of algorithmic performance. Section 5 describes the Formula I(1) DGP-model pairs, while Section 6 does so for the Formula I(2) DGP-model pairs. The Formula I(1) races are illustrated in Section 7, the Formula I(2) races are illustrated in Section 8; Section 9 concludes. The Appendix A contains practical implementation instructions.

2. Design and evaluation principles

Each exercise in Formula I(1) and I(2) is built around a DGP-model pair. The chosen DGPs have a simple design, with a few coefficients that govern persistence, dimensionality and adjustment towards equilibrium. Aggregating algorithmic performance across runs of the same single DGP appears reasonable, because one expects the frequency of difficult maximization problems to be a function of the characteristics of the given DGP-model pair.

Two main criteria are used for the evaluation of the output from different algorithms. The first one, called *effectiveness*, regards the ability of an algorithm to find a maximum of the likelihood function. Algorithms are expected either to fail, or to converge to a stationary point. This, with some further inspection, may be established as a local maximum. A comparison of local maxima between methods will provide useful insights.

The second one, conditional on the first, is the *efficiency* of the algorithm to find the maximum, which is closely related to its speed. Effectiveness is considered here to be of paramount importance: it is not much use having an algorithm that runs quickly but fails to find the maximum. Actual speeds can be difficult to compare in heterogenous hardware and software environments: however, measures of efficiency can be informative for an implementation in a fixed environment using different designs.

There are many examples of comparisons of optimization algorithms in the numerical analysis literature. Beiranvand et al. (2017) provides an extensive list, together with a generic discussion of how to benchmark optimization algorithms.[3] In the light of this, only advantages and shortcomings of the present approach with respect to Beiranvand et al. (2017) are discussed here, as well as future extensions that are worth considering.

One important specificity here is the focus on the evaluation of estimation procedures for statistical models. These have numerical optimization at their core, but they are applied to maximize specific likelihoods. In the present setting the exact maximum of the likelihood is not known. Moreover, while the asymptotic properties of the MLE are well understood, these will only be approximate at best in any finite sample.

2.1. *Race Design*

The race design refers to the DGP-model pair, as well as the rules for the implementation of estimators. Because iterative maximization will be used in all cases, algorithms need starting values and decision rules as to when to terminate.

2.1.1. Starting Values

Formula I(1) and I(2) treat the choice of starting value as part of the algorithm. This is the most significant difference with common practice in optimization benchmarking. The starting values may have an important impact on the performance, and, ideally but unfeasibly, one would like to start at the maximum. Optimization benchmarks prescribe specific starting values to create a level playing field for algorithms. This is not done here because implementations may have statistical reasons for

[3] The idea to create public domain test cases based on which programmers may test the performances of their algorithms according to rigorous rules is also not new. For example, the National Institute of Standards and Technology started a website in the late 1990s of the project StRD - Statistical Reference Datasets, see http://www.itl.nist.gov/div898/strd/.

their starting value routine, e.g., there may be a simple estimator that is consistent or an approximation that is reasonable.

Some implementations use a small set of randomized starting values, then pick the best. This approach is general, so could be used by all algorithms. The advantage of the present approach is that one evaluates estimation as it is presented to the user. The drawback is that it will be harder to determine the source of performance differences.[4]

2.1.2. Convergence

The termination decision rule is also left to the algorithm, so it presents a further source of difference between implementations. One expects this to have a small impact: participants in the races should ensure that convergence is tight enough not to change the computed evaluation statistics. If it is set too loose, the algorithm will score worse on reliability. However, setting convergence too tightly will increase the required number of iterations, sometimes substantially if convergence is linear or rounding errors prevent achieving the desired accuracy.

2.1.3. DGP-Model Pair

The chosen DGPs generate I(1) or I(2) processes, as presented in Sections 5 and 6 below; the associated statistical models are (possibly restricted) I(1) or I(2) models, defined in Section 3. Exercises include both cases with correct specification, i.e. when the DGP is contained in the model, as well as cases with mis-specification, i.e., when the DGP is not contained in the model.

Mis-specification is limited here, in the sense that all models still belong to the appropriate model class: an I(1) DGP is always analyzed with an I(1) (sub-)model, and similarly for an I(2) DGP and (sub-)model. Indeed, the sources of mis-specification present here are a subset of the ones faced by econometricians in real applications. The hope is that results for the mis-specification cases covered here can give some lower bounds on the effects of mis-specification for real applications.

Common econometric wisdom says that algorithms tend to be less successful when the model is mis-specified. The present design provides insights as to what extent this is the case in I(1) and I(2) CVAR models, within the limited degree of mis-specification present in these races.

2.1.4. Construction of Test Cases

Different approaches can be used to create test cases:

1. Estimate models on real data

   This is the most realistic setting, because it reflects the complexities of data sets that are used for empirical analyses. On the other hand, it could be hard to study causes of poor performance as there can be many sources such as unmodelled correlations or heteroscedasticities. Aggregating performance over different real datasets may hide heterogeneity in performance due to the different DGPs that have generated the real data.
2. Generate artificial data from models estimated on real data

   This is a semi-realistic setting where it is known from which structure the data are generated. Coefficient matrices of the DGP will normally be dense, with a non-diagonal error variance matrix.
3. Use a purely artificial DGP

   This usually differs from the previous case in that the DGPs are controlled by only a few coefficients that are deemed important. So it is the least realistic case, but offers the possibility to determine the main causes of performance differences.

---

4 A future extension would be to include some experiments that start from prespecified starting values, as well as storing the initial log-likelihood in the results file.

Formula I(1) and I(2) adopt the artificial DGP approach with sparse design as a method to construct test data. The drawback is that it can only cover a limited number of DGPs, which may not reflect all empirically-relevant situations. The present set of designs is no exception to this rule; however, it improves on the current state of play where no agreed common design of experiments has been proposed in this area. A future extension will be to include a set of tests based on real-world data sets.

2.1.5. Generation of Test Data

All experiments are run with errors that are fixed in advance to ensure that every participant generates exactly the same artificial data sets. The sample size is an important design characteristic; test data are provided for up to 1000 observations, but only races that use 100 or 1000 are included here.

In terms of comparability of results for different algorithms, the possibility to fix the innovations, and hence the data in each lap, controls for one known source of Monte Carlo variability when estimating difference in behavior; see Abadir and Paruolo (2009), Paruolo (2002) or Hendry (1984, §4.1) on the use of common random numbers.

The choice of common random numbers permits to find (significant) differences in behavior of algorithms with a smaller number of cases, and hence computer time, than when innovations vary across teams. Moreover, it also allows the possibility to investigate the presence of multiple maxima.

2.2. *Evaluation*

Each estimation, unless it ends in failure, results in a set of coefficient estimates with corresponding log-likelihood. Ideally, all algorithms converge to the same stationary point, which is also the global maximum of the likelihood. This will not always happen: it is not known whether these models have unimodal likelihoods, and there is evidence to the contrary in many experiments considered. Moreover, the global maximum is not known, and this is the target of each estimation. As a consequence, evaluation is largely based on a comparison with the best solution.

2.2.1. Effectiveness

The *overall maximum* is the best function value of all algorithms that have been applied to the same problem. This is the best attempt at finding the global maximum, but remains open to revision. Consensus is informative: the more algorithms agree on the maximum, the more confident one is that the global maximum has been found. Similarly, disagreement may indicate multimodality. This is one of the advantages of pooling the results of different algorithms.

If one algorithm finds a lower log-likelihood than another, this indicates that it either found a different local maximum, converged prematurely, or ended up in a saddle point, or, hopefully not so common, there is a programming error. Differences may be the result of the adopted initial parameter values, or owing to the path that is taken, or to the terminal conditions, or a combination of all the above.

However, algorithms that systematically fail to reach the overall maximum should be considered inferior to the ones that find it. Inability to find the global maximum may have serious implications for inference, leading to over-rejection or under-rejection of the null hypothesis for likelihood ratio (LR) tests, depending on whether the maximization error affects the restricted or the unrestricted model.

2.2.2. Efficiency

Efficiency can be expressed in terms of a measure of the number of operations involved, or a measure of time. Time can be expressed as CPU time or as the total time to complete an estimation. While lapsed time is very useful information for a user of the software, it is difficult to use in the present setting. First, the same algorithm implemented in two different languages (say Ox and Matlab) may have very different timings on identical hardware. Next, this project expects submissions of completed results, where the referee team has no control over the hardware.

Even if the referee team were to rerun the experiments, this would be done on different computers with different (versions of) operating systems. Finally, the level of parallelism and number of cores plays a role: even when the considered algorithms cannot be parallelized, matrix operations inside them may be. When running one thousand replications, one could normally do replications in parallel. This suggests not to use time to measure efficiency.

With time measurements ruled out, one is left with counting some aspects of the algorithm. This could be the number of times the objective function is evaluated, the number of parameter update steps, or some other measure. All these measures have a (loose) connection to clock time. E.g., a quadratically convergent algorithm will require fewer function calls and parameter updates than a linearly convergent algorithm, and usually be much faster as well. However, the actual speed advantage can be undermined if the former requires very costly hessian computations (say).

For the switching algorithms that are most commonly used in CVARs when RRR is not possible, the number of parameter update steps is a better metric to express efficiency. An analysis of all the timings reported in Doornik (2017b) shows that, after allowing for two outlying experiments, the number of updates can largely explain CPU time, while the number of objective function evaluations is insignificant. Both the intercept and the coefficient that maps the update count to CPU time are influenced by CPU type, amount of memory, software environment, etc.

In line with common practice, an iteration is defined as a one parameter update step. This definition also applies to quasi-Newton methods, although, unlike switching algorithms, each iteration then also involves the computation of first derivatives. As a consequence, an iteration could be slower than a switching update step, but in many situations a comparison would still be informative. When comparing efficiency of algorithms, the number of iterations appears to be of more fundamental value than CPU time, and it is certainly useful when comparing the same implementation for different experiments when these have been run on a variety of hardware.

There remains one small caveat: changing compiler can affect the number of iterations. When code generation differences mean that rounding errors accumulate differently, this can impact the convergence decision. This effect to be expected to be small.

Summing up, the remainder of the paper uses number of iterations as a measure of efficiency. An update of the parameter vector is understood to define an iteration, and each team participating to Formula I(1) and I(2) is expected to use the same definition.

3. Definitions and Statistical Models

This section introduces the car racing terminology and defines more precisely the notions of DGP and statistical model.

3.1. Terminology

Analogous to car racing terminology, a *circuit* refers to a specific DGP-model pair, i.e. a DGP coupled with a model specification, characterized by given restrictions on the parameters. Each circuit needs to be completed a certain number of times, i.e. *laps* (replications).

Circuits are grouped in two championships, called *'Formula I(1)'* and *'Formula I(2)'*. The implementation of an algorithm corresponds to a driver with a constructor team, which is called a *team* for simplicity. The definition of an algorithm is taken to include everything that it is required to maximize the likelihood function; in particular it includes the choice of the starting value and of the convergence criterion or termination rule.

In the following there are 96 Formula I(1) circuits and 1456 Formula I(2) circuits. Teams do not have to participate in all circuits. For each circuit, a participating team has to:

(i) reconstruct $N = 1000$ datasets (one for each lap) using the innovations provided and the DGP documented below;
(ii) for each dataset, estimate the specified model(s);
(iii) report the results in a given format, described in the Appendix A.

An econometrician may implement more than one algorithm, so enter multiple teams in the races.

3.2. Definitions

This subsection is devoted to more technical definitions of a DGP, a statistical model and its parametrization. A *DGP* is a completely specified stochastic process that generates the sample data $X_{1:T} := (X_1 : \cdots : X_T)$. Here : is used to indicate horizontal concatenation, with the exception for expressions involving indices, such as $(1 : T)$, which is a shorthand for $(1 : \cdots : T)$. For example X_t i.i.d $N(0, 1)$, $t = 1, \ldots, T$ is a DGP.

The present design of experiments considers a finite number of DGPs; these are grouped into two classes, called the *I(1) DGP class* and the *I(2) DGP class*. Each DGP class is indexed by a set of coefficients; for example X_t i.i.d $N(0, 1)$, $t = 1, \ldots, T$, with $T \in \{100, 1000\}$ is a DGP class.

A parametric *statistical model* is a collection of stochastic processes indexed by a vector of *parameters* φ, which belongs to a *parameter space* Φ, usually an open subset of $\mathbb{R}^m$, where m is the number of parameters. A model is said to be *correctly specified* if its parameter space contains one value of the parameters that characterizes the DGP which has generated the data, and it is mis-specified otherwise. E.g. X_t i.i.d $N(\mu, \sigma^2)$, $t = 1, \ldots, T$, $-\infty < \mu < \infty, 0 \leq \sigma < \infty$ is a parametric statistical model, when X_t is a scalar and $\varphi = (\mu : \sigma^2)'$. The parameter space Φ is given here by $\mathbb{R} \times \mathbb{R}_+$. Note that a parametric statistical model is needed in order to write the likelihood function for the sample data $X_{1:T}$. In the case above, the likelihood is $f(X_{1:T}; \mu, \sigma^2) = \pi^{-T/2}\sigma^{-T} \exp(-\frac{1}{2}\sum_{t=1}^{T}(X_t - \mu)^2/\sigma^2)$.

Consider now one model A for $X_{1:T}$, indexed by the parameter vector φ with parameter space Φ_A. Assume also that model B is the same, except that the parameter vector φ lies in the parameter space Φ_B with $\Phi_A \subset \Phi_B$. The two models differ by the parameter points that are contained in Φ_B but not in Φ_A (i.e. points in the set $\Phi_B \backslash \Phi_A$). If some points in $\Phi_B \backslash \Phi_A$ cannot be obtained as limits of sequences in Φ_A, (i.e., Φ_B does not coincide with the closure of Φ_A) then model A is said to be a *submodel* of model B. For example, model A can be X_t i.i.d $N(\mu, 1)$, $t = 1, \ldots, T$, $\Phi_A := \{\mu : 0 \leq \mu < \infty\}$ while model B can be $\Phi_B := \{\mu : -\infty < \mu < \infty\}$. Here $\Phi_B \backslash \Phi_A = \{\mu : -\infty < \mu < 0\}$ whose points cannot be obtained as limits of sequences in Φ_A. Hence model A is a submodel of model B.

When all the parameter values in $\Phi_B \backslash \Phi_A$ can be obtained as limits of sequences in Φ_A, then model A and B are essentially the same, and no distinction between them is made here. In this case, or in case the mappings between parametrizations are bijective, it is said that A and B provide *equivalent parametrizations* of the same model. As an example, let $\Phi_A := \{\mu : 0 \leq \mu < \infty\}$ as above and let $\Phi_B := \{\mu = \exp \eta : -\infty < \eta < \infty\}$; the two models are essentially the same, and their parametrizations are equivalent. This is because, despite $\mu = 0$ being present only in the μ parametrization, $\mu = 0$ can be obtained as a limit of points in $\mu = \exp \eta$, $\eta \in (-\infty, \infty)$, e.g., by choosing $\eta_i = -i$, $i = 1, 2, 3 \ldots$ Hence in this case the η and μ parametrizations are equivalent, as they essentially describe the same model.

In the present design of experiments all models are (restricted versions of) the I(1) and the I(2) models, defined below. The case of equivalent models in the above sense is relevant for different parametrizations of the I(2) statistical model, see Noack Jensen (2014).

3.3. The Cointegrated VAR

Both the I(1) and I(2) statistical models are sub-models of the Gaussian VAR model with k lags

$$X_t = \sum_{i=1}^{k} A_i X_{t-i} + \mu_0 + \mu_1 t + \varepsilon_t, \qquad \varepsilon_t \text{ i.i.d. } N(0, \Omega), \quad t = k+1, ..., T, \tag{1}$$

where X_t, ε_t, μ_0, μ_1 are $p \times 1$, A_i and Ω are $p \times p$, and Ω is symmetric and positive definite. The presample values $X_1, ..., X_k$ are fixed and given. The (possibly restricted) parameters associated with μ_0, μ_1, A_i, $i = 1, \ldots, k$ are called the mean-parameters and are indicated by θ. The ones associated with Ω are called the variance parameters, and they are here always unrestricted, except for the requirement of Ω to be positive definite. The parameter vector is made of the unrestricted entries in θ and Ω.

The Gaussian loglikelihood (excluding a constant term) is given by:

$$-\frac{T-k}{2}\log\det\Omega - \frac{1}{2}\sum_{t=k+1}^{T}\varepsilon_t'(\theta)\,\Omega^{-1}\varepsilon_t(\theta),$$

where $\varepsilon_t(\theta)$ equal to ε_t in (1) considered as a function of θ. Maximizing the loglikelihood with respect to Ω, one finds $\Omega = \Omega(\theta) := (T-k)^{-1}\sum_{t=k+1}^{T}\varepsilon_t(\theta)\varepsilon_t'(\theta)$, which, when substituted back into the loglikelihood gives $-(T-k)p/2 + \ell(\theta)$ where

$$\ell(\theta) := -\frac{T-k}{2}\log\det\Omega(\theta), \qquad \Omega(\theta) := \frac{1}{T-k}\sum_{t=k+1}^{T}\varepsilon_t(\theta)\,\varepsilon_t'(\theta). \tag{2}$$

The loglikelihood is here defined as $\ell(\theta)$, calculated as in (2).

The I(1) and I(2) models are submodels of (1).

I(1) statistical models The unrestricted I(1) statistical model under consideration is given by:

$$\Delta X_t = \alpha\beta'\begin{pmatrix} X_{t-1} \\ t \end{pmatrix} + \sum_{i=1}^{k-1}\Gamma_i\Delta X_{t-i} + \mu_0 + \varepsilon_t. \tag{3}$$

Here α and $\beta = (\beta^{\star\prime} : \beta_D')'$ are respectively $p \times r$ and $(p+1) \times r$ parameter matrices, $r < p$, with β_D a $1 \times r$ vector. The long-run autoregressive matrix $\Pi = -I + \sum_{i=1}^{k} A_i$ is here restricted to satisfy $\text{rank}(\Pi) \leq r$, because it is expressed as a product $\Pi = \alpha\beta^{\star\prime}$, where α and $\beta^\star$ have r columns. The coefficient μ_1 is restricted as $\mu_1 = \alpha\beta_D'$. The Γ_i matrices are unconstrained. Some Formula I(1) races have restrictions on the columns of α and β.

The I(1) model is indicated as $\mathcal{M}(r)$ in what follows. The likelihood of the I(1) model $\mathcal{M}(r)$ has to be maximized with respect to the parameters α, β, Γ_1, ..., Γ_{k-1}, μ_0 and Ω.

I(2) statistical models The unrestricted I(2) statistical model under consideration is given by:

$$\Delta^2 X_t = \alpha\beta'\begin{pmatrix} X_{t-1} \\ t-1 \end{pmatrix} + (\Gamma : \mu_0)\begin{pmatrix} \Delta X_{t-i} \\ 1 \end{pmatrix} + \sum_{i=1}^{k-2}\Phi_i\Delta^2 X_{t-i} + \varepsilon_t, \tag{4}$$

$$\text{with} \qquad \alpha_\perp'(\Gamma : \mu_0)\beta_\perp = \varphi\eta'. \tag{5}$$

Here $\alpha_\perp$ indicates a basis of the orthogonal complement of the space spanned by the columns of α; similarly for $\beta_\perp$ with respect to β. The I(2) model is a submodel of I(1) model; in fact in (4), as in (3), α and $\beta = (\beta^{\star\prime} : \beta_D')'$ are $p \times r$ and $(p+1) \times r$ parameter matrices, $r < p$, with β_D a $1 \times r$ vector, and μ_1 is restricted as $\mu_1 = \alpha\beta_D'$. In (5), φ is $(p-r) \times s$ and $\eta = (\eta^{\star\prime} : \eta_D')'$ is $(p-r+1) \times s$, $s < p-r$ with η_D a $1 \times s$ vector.[5] The Φ_i parameter matrices are unrestricted.

The I(2) model in (4) and (5) is indicated as $\mathcal{M}(r,s)$ in the following. In the I(2) model there are two rank restrictions, namely $\text{rank}(\alpha\beta') \leq r$ and $\text{rank}(\alpha_\perp'(\Gamma : \mu_0)\beta_\perp) \leq s$. Several different parametrizations exist of the I(2) model $\mathcal{M}(r,s)$, see Johansen (1997), Paruolo and Rahbek (1999),

---

5 One can observe that $\beta_\perp$ can be chosen as

$$\beta_\perp = \begin{pmatrix} \beta_\perp^\star & \bar{\beta}^\star\beta_D' \\ 0 & -1 \end{pmatrix}$$

so that $\alpha_\perp'(\Gamma : \mu_0)\beta_\perp$ can be written as $\alpha_\perp'(\Gamma : \mu_0)\beta_\perp = (\alpha_\perp'\Gamma\beta_\perp^\star : \alpha_\perp'\Gamma\bar{\beta}^\star\beta_D' - \alpha_\perp'\mu_0)$. Using the partition $\eta' = (\eta^{\star\prime} : \eta_D')$, Equation (5) can be written as

$$\alpha_\perp'\Gamma\beta_\perp^\star = \varphi\eta^{\star\prime} \qquad \text{and} \qquad \alpha_\perp'\mu_0 = \alpha_\perp'\Gamma\bar{\beta}^\star\beta_D' + \varphi\eta_D'$$

which is the form of the restrictions (5) used in Rahbek et al. (1999) Equation (2.4) (2.5).

Rahbek et al. (1999), Boswijk (2000), Doornik (2017b), Mosconi and Paruolo (2016, 2017), Boswijk and Paruolo (2017). They all satisfy $\text{rank}(\alpha\beta') \leq r$ and $\text{rank}(\alpha'_\perp(\Gamma : \mu_0)\beta_\perp) \leq s$.[6] Teams can choose their preferred parametrization, but, whichever is adopted, the estimated parameters must be reported in terms of α, β, $(\Gamma : \mu_0)$, Φ_1, ..., Φ_{k-2} and Ω.

Some races have restrictions on columns of α, β or τ, where τ is defined as a $(p+1) \times (r+s)$ matrix that spans the column space of $(\beta : \bar{\beta}_\perp \eta)$, where $\bar{a} := a(a'a)^{-1}$.

4. Performance Evaluation

This section defines a number of indicators later employed to measure the performance of algorithms. As introduced above, θ indicates the parameter vector of mean parameters and Ω the variance covariance matrix of the innovations.

4.1. Elementary Information to Be Reported by Each Team

Each lap is indexed by $i = 1, ..., N$, each circuit by $c = 1, \ldots, C$, and each team (i.e., algorithm) by a. The set of teams participating in the race on circuit c is indicated as $\mathcal{A}_c$; this set contains n_c algorithms. The subscript c indicates that $\mathcal{A}_c$ and n_c depend on c, because a team might not participate in all circuits. The following subsections describe the results that each team a has to report, as well as the calculations that the referee team of the race will make on the basis of it.

For each lap i of circuit c, when team a terminates optimization, it produces the optimized value $\theta_{a,c,i}$ of the parameter vector θ. The team should also set the convergence indicator $S_{a,c,i}$ equal to 1 if the algorithm has satisfied the (self-selected) convergence criterion, and set $S_{a,c,i}$ to 0 if no convergence was achieved. Teams should report the loglikelihood value obtained at the maximum $\ell_{a,c,i} := \ell(\theta_{a,c,i})$ using (2).

In case $S_{a,c,i} = 0$, $\theta_{a,c,i}$ indicates the last value of θ before failure of algorithm a. Algorithm a may not have converged either because $\ell(\theta)$ cannot be evaluated numerically anymore (as e.g., when $\Omega(\theta)$ becomes numerically singular) or because a maximum number of iterations has been reached. In the latter case the final loglikelihood should be reported. In the former case, when the likelihood evaluation failed, the team should report $\ell_{a,c,i} = -\infty$.[7] So, regardless of success or failure in convergence, a loglikelihood is always reported.

For each lap i in circuit c, team a should also report the number of performed iterations $N_{a,c,i}$. This number equals the maximum number of iterations if this is the reason why the algorithm terminated. Choosing smaller or larger maximum numbers of iterations will affect result of each team in an obvious way. Teams are asked to choose their own maximum numbers of iterations.

$N_{a,c,i}$ is assumed here to be inversely proportional to the speed of the algorithm. In practice, the speed of the algorithm depends by the average time spent in each iteration, which is influenced by many factors, such as the hardware and software specifications in the implementation. However, because these additional factors vary among teams, the number $N_{a,c,i}$ is taken to provide an approximate indicator of the slowness of the algorithm.

The choice of starting value of the algorithm a is taken to be an integral part of the definition of the algorithm itself. Starting values cannot be based on the results of other teams. It is recommended that the teams document their algorithm in a way that facilitates replication of their results, including providing the computer code used in the calculations and a description of the choice of initial values.

Reported results from the races should be organised in a file, whose name indicates the circuit, and where each row should contain the following information:

$$(i : \ell^u_{a,c,i} : \ell_{a,c,i} : N_{a,c,i} : S_{a,c,i} : \theta^{R\prime}_{a,c,i}),$$

6 In case of no deterministics, the satisfied inequalities are $\text{rank}(\alpha\beta^{\star\prime}) \leq r$ and $\text{rank}(\alpha'_\perp \Gamma \beta^\star_\perp) \leq s$.

7 Because there is no clear convention on writing $-\infty$, any value of -10^{308} or lower is interpreted as $-\infty$.

where $\ell^u_{a,c,i}$ is the maximum of the loglikelihood of a reference unrestricted model detailed in the Appendix A, and the reported part of the coefficient vector, $\theta^R_{a,c,i}$, is defined as

$$\theta^{R\prime}_{a,c,i} := \left(\mathrm{vec}(\alpha_{a,c,i})' : \mathrm{vec}(\beta_{a,c,i})'\right)$$

for the Formula I(1) circuits. For the Formula I(2) circuits instead:

$$\theta^{R\prime}_{a,c,i} := \left(\mathrm{vec}(\alpha_{a,c,i})' : \mathrm{vec}(\beta_{a,c,i})' : \mathrm{vec}(\Gamma : \mu_0)'_{a,c,i}\right).$$

The reported part of the $\theta_{a,c,i}$ includes the estimated parameters except for the parameters Φ_i of the short term dynamics and the covariance of the innovations Ω. More details on the reporting conventions are given in the Appendix A.

4.2. Indicators of Teams' Performance

After completion of lap i of circuit c by a set of teams $\mathcal{A}_c$, the referee team will compute the overall maximum $\ell^\star_{c,i}$ and deviations $D_{a,c,i}$ from it as:

$$\ell^\star_{c,i} = \max_{\{a\in\mathcal{A}_c:\ S_{a,c,i}=1\}} \ell_{a,c,i}, \qquad D_{a,c,i} = \ell^\star_{c,i} - \ell_{a,c,i}. \tag{6}$$

If all $a \in \mathcal{A}_c$ report failed convergence $S_{a,c,i} = 0$, then $\ell^\star_{c,i}$ will be set equal to $-\infty$ and $D_{a,c,i}$ will be set equal to 0. Observe that $D_{a,c,i} \geq 0$ by construction; $D_{a,c,i}$ is considered small if less than 10^{-7}, moderately small if between 10^{-7} and 10^{-2}, and large if greater than 10^{-2}.[8]

Next define the indicators

$$SC_{a,c,i} := \mathbb{1}(D_{a,c,i} < 10^{-7})S_{a,c,i}, \qquad WC_{a,c,i} := \mathbb{1}(10^{-7} \leq D_{a,c,i} < 10^{-2})S_{a,c,i}$$
$$DC_{a,c,i} := \mathbb{1}(D_{a,c,i} \geq 10^{-2})S_{a,c,i}, \qquad FC_{a,c,i} := 1 - S_{a,c,i},$$

where $\mathbb{1}(\cdot)$ is the indicator function, SC stands for 'strong' convergence, WC stands for 'weak' convergence, DC stands for 'distant' convergence – i.e. convergence to a distant point from the overall maximum – and FC stands for failed convergence. Note that $SC_{a,c,i} + WC_{a,c,i} + DC_{a,c,i} + FC_{a,c,i} = 1$ by construction. When $\ell^\star_{c,i} = -\infty$, note that $SC_{a,c,i} = WC_{a,c,i} = DC_{a,c,i} = S_{a,c,i} = 0$ and $FC_{a,c,i} = 1$.

A summary across laps of the performance of algorithm a in circuit c is given by the quantities

$$SC_{a,c} := 100 \cdot N^{-1} \sum_{i=1}^{N} SC_{a,c,i}, \qquad WC_{a,c} := 100 \cdot N^{-1} \sum_{i=1}^{N} WC_{a,c,i},$$
$$DC_{a,c} := 100 \cdot N^{-1} \sum_{i=1}^{N} DC_{a,c,i}, \qquad FC_{a,c} := 100 \cdot N^{-1} \sum_{i=1}^{N} FC_{a,c,i}.$$

These indicators deliver information on the % of times each algorithm reached strong convergence, weak convergence, convergence to a point which is not the overall maximum, or did not converge.[9]

The set of pairs $\{(\ell^\star_{c,i}, \ell_{a,c,i}) : DC_{a,c,i} = 1\}_{a\in\mathcal{A}_c, i=1:N}$ contain the detailed information on the effects of convergence to a point that is distant from the overall maximum. They are later plotted, together with the distribution of the relevant test statistics. Focusing on the laps where $DC_{a,c,i} = 1$, it is also interesting to calculate the average distance of $\ell_{a,c,i}$ to $\ell^\star_{c,i}$. This is given by

---

8 As all reference values, the present ones of 10^{-2} and 10^{-7} are chosen in an ad-hoc way. In the opinion of the proponents they reflect reasonable values for the differences between loglikelihoods, which can be interpreted approximately as relative differences. Hence a difference of 10^{-2} means roughly that the two likelihoods differ by 1%, while a difference of 10^{-7} means roughly that the two likelihoods differ by 0.1 in a million, in relative terms.

9 One may wish to consider these indicators conditionally on the number of converged cases. To do this, one can replace the division by N in the above formulae for $SC_{a,c}$, $WC_{a,c}$, $DC_{a,c}$ with division by $\sum_{i=1}^{N} S_{a,c,i}$.

$$AD_{a,c} = \sum_{i=1}^{N} D_{a,c,i} \cdot DC_{a,c,i} \left(\sum_{i=1}^{N} DC_{a,c,i} \right)^{-1}.$$

Conditionally on convergence, the average number of iterations is defined as

$$IT_{a,c} := \sum_{i=1}^{N} N_{a,c,i} \cdot S_{a,c,i} \left(\sum_{i=1}^{N} S_{a,c,i} \right)^{-1}.$$

4.3. Summary Analysis of Circuits and Laps

The referee team will compute summary statistics for each circuit. First, in order to identify laps where all algorithms fail, the following DNF indicator is defined:

$$DNF_{c,i} = \prod_{a \in \mathcal{A}_c} (1 - S_{a,c,i}),$$

which equals 1 if all algorithms fail to converge.

In order to harvest information on the number of different maxima reported by the teams, the following indicator is constructed. Let $\ell_{(1),c,i} \geq \ell_{(2),c,i} \geq \cdots \geq \ell_{(m_c),c,i}$ be the ordered log-likelihood values reported by those algorithms $a \in \mathcal{A}_c$ that have reported convergence, i.e., for which $S_{a,c,i} = 1$. This list can be used to define the 'number of reported optima' indicator, NOR, as follows

$$NOR_{c,i} = 1 + \sum_{j=2}^{m_c} \mathbb{1}(\ell_{(j-1),c,i} - \ell_{(j),c,i} > 10^{-2}).$$

Note that for each $j = 2, \ldots, m_c$, the difference $\ell_{(j-1),c,i} - \ell_{(j),c,i} \geq 0$ is the decrement of successive reported log-likelihood values; if this decrement is smaller than a selected numerical threshold, here taken to be 10^{-2}, this means that the two algorithms corresponding to $(j-1)$ and (j) have reported the same log-likelihood in practice. In this case, the counter NOR is not increased. If this difference is greater than the numerical threshold of 10^{-2}, then the two reported log-likelihood are classified as different, and the counter NOR is incremented. Overall, NOR counts the number of maxima found by different algorithms that are separated at least by distance of 10^{-2}. NOR is influenced by the number of participating teams.

Observe that the reported log-likelihood value $\ell_{(j),c,i}$ can correspond to an actual maximum or to any other point judged as stationary by the termination criterion used in each algorithm. No check is made by the referee team to distinguish between these situations; NOR should hence be interpreted as an indicator of *potential presence of multiple maxima*; a proper check of the number of maxima would require a more dedicated analysis.[10]

Especially for a difficult lap i, it is interesting to pool information obtained by different algorithms on convergence to points that are distant from the overall maximum, i.e., when $D_{a,c,i}$ is large. This can be averaged across the set of algorithms $\mathcal{A}_c$ that participate to circuit c in the indicator

$$DD_{c,i} = \sum_{a \in \mathcal{A}_c} D_{a,c,i} DC_{a,c,i} \left(\sum_{a \in \mathcal{A}_c} DC_{a,c,i} \right)^{-1}.$$

The indicators $DD_{c,i}$ and $AD_{a,c}$ are obviously related, and they differ in how they are averaged, either across laps or algorithms.

10 This further analysis is not performed in this paper, but may be considered in later developments of the Formula I(1) and I(2) project.

The DNF and NOR indicators are also aggregated over all laps in a circuit, giving:

$$DNF_c = N^{-1} \textstyle\sum_{i=1}^{N} DNF_{c,i}, \quad NOR_c = N^{-1} \textstyle\sum_{i=1}^{N} NOR_{c,i}.$$

5. Formula I(1) Circuits

This section introduces Formula I(1) circuits, i.e. DGP-model pairs where the DGP produces I(1) variables. The model is the I(1) model $\mathcal{M}(r)$ or a submodel of it. For some circuits the statistical model is correctly specified, whereas for others it is mis-specified, as discussed in Section 3.2.

In the specification of the I(1) and I(2) DGPs, the innovations ε_t are chosen uncorrelated (and independent given normality). This choice is made to represent the simplest possible case; this can be changed in future development of the project.[11]

5.1. I(1) DGPs

The I(1) DGP class for lap i is indexed on the scalars (p, T, ρ_0, ρ_1):

$$\begin{cases} \Delta X_{1,t}^{(i)} = \rho_1 \Delta X_{1,t-1}^{(i)} + \varepsilon_{1,t}^{(i)} \\ X_{2,t}^{(i)} = \rho_0 X_{2,t-1}^{(i)} + \varepsilon_{2,t}^{(i)} \end{cases} \qquad \varepsilon_t^{(i)} = \begin{pmatrix} \varepsilon_{1,t}^{(i)} \\ \varepsilon_{2,t}^{(i)} \end{pmatrix} \sim \text{i.i.d. } N\left(0, I_p\right), \tag{7}$$

for $t = 1 : T$, $i = 1 : N$, $X_t^{(i)} = (X_{1,t}^{(i)\prime} : X_{2,t}^{(i)\prime})'$, $X_0^{(i)} = X_{-1}^{(i)} = 0_p$, where $\varepsilon_{j,t}^{(i)}$ is of dimension $p/2 \times 1$, $j = 1, 2$. Here I_p is the identity matrix of order p. All possible combinations are considered of the following indices and coefficients:

$$p \in \{6, 12\}; \qquad T \in \{100, 1000\}; \qquad \rho_0 \in \{0, 0.9\}; \qquad \rho_1 \in \{0, 0.9\}.$$

Note that in these DGPs,

- the first $p/2$ variables in $X_t^{(i)}$ are either random walks (when $\rho_1 = 0$), or I(1) AR(2) processes whose first difference is persistent (when $\rho_1 = 0.9$). Therefore, ρ_1 is interpreted as 'a near I(2)-ness' coefficient.
- The last $p/2$ variables in $X_t^{(i)}$ are either white noise (when $\rho_0 = 0$), or persistent stationary AR(1) processes (when $\rho_0 = 0.9$). Therefore, ρ_0 is a 'near I(1)-ness' or 'weak mean reversion' coefficient. For simplicity, in the following it is referred to as the 'weak mean reversion' coefficient.

The DGPs can be written as follows, see (3):

$$\Delta X_t = \begin{pmatrix} 0_r \\ (\rho_0 - 1) I_r \end{pmatrix} \begin{pmatrix} 0_r & I_r \end{pmatrix} X_{t-1} + \begin{pmatrix} \rho_1 I_r & 0_r \\ 0_r & 0_r \end{pmatrix} \Delta X_{t-1} + \epsilon_t,$$

where $\mu_0 = \mu_1 = 0$, $r = p/2$, and 0_r is a square block of zeros of dimension r.

To create the Monte Carlo datasets $X_{1:T}^{(i)}$, each team has to use the DGP (7) with relevant values of (p, T, ρ_0, ρ_1), together with the realizations of the ε's as determined by the race organizers. Further details are in the Appendix A.

5.2. I(1) Statistical Models

Using the generated data $X_{1:T}^{(i)}$ as a realization for $X_{1:T}$, the I(1) model $\mathcal{M}(r)$ in (3) has to be estimated on each lap $i = 1, \ldots, N$; as noted above, MLE of the unrestricted I(1) models $\mathcal{M}(r)$ in (3) is

11 In theory, the chosen DGPs can represent a wider class of DGPs, exploiting invariance of some statistical models with respect to invertible transformation of the variables; see e.g., Paruolo (2005). In practice, however, algorithms may be sensitive to scaling.

obtained by RRR. The estimation sample starts at $t = k+1$, so uses $T-k$ observations. Two alternative values for lag length k are used: $k \in \{2,5\}$.

All I(1) circuits use the correct rank $r = p/2$ and are subject to further restrictions on the cointegrating vectors, with or without restrictions on their loadings. To express these restrictions, the following matrix structures are introduced, where an $*$ stands for any value, indicating an unrestricted coefficient:

$$\underset{m\times m}{R_{0,m}} = \begin{pmatrix} * & 0 & \cdots & 0 \\ 0 & \ddots & \ddots & \vdots \\ \vdots & \ddots & \ddots & 0 \\ 0 & \cdots & 0 & * \end{pmatrix}, \quad \underset{m\times m}{R_{1,m}} = \begin{pmatrix} * & 1 & * & * \\ 1 & \ddots & \ddots & * \\ * & \ddots & \ddots & 1 \\ * & * & 1 & * \end{pmatrix}, \quad \underset{m\times m}{R_{2,m}} = \begin{pmatrix} 1 & * & * & * \\ * & \ddots & \ddots & * \\ * & \ddots & \ddots & * \\ * & * & * & 1 \end{pmatrix}. \tag{8}$$

Remark that $R_{0,m}$ sets all elements except the diagonal to zero; $R_{1,m}$ has two bands of unity along the diagonal; $R_{2,m}$ fixes the diagonal to unity, but is otherwise unrestricted. All these matrices are square.

Finally, $U_{m,n}$ stands for an unrestricted $m \times n$ dimensional matrix:

$$\underset{m\times n}{U_{m,n}} = \begin{pmatrix} * & * & \ldots & * \\ * & * & \ldots & * \end{pmatrix}. \tag{9}$$

Restriction I(1)-A Model A has the following overidentifying restrictions on β:

$$\beta' = (R_{0,r} : I_r : U_{r,1}). \tag{10}$$

Specification (10) imposes $r(r-1)$ correctly specified overidentifying restrictions on β.

Restriction I(1)-B Model B has over-identifying restrictions that are mis-specified:

$$\beta' = (R_{1,r} : I_r : U_{r,1}). \tag{11}$$

This imposes $2(r-1)$ overidentifying restrictions on β. These restrictions are mis-specified, in the sense that the DGP is outside the parameters space of the statistical model, see Section 3.

Restriction I(1)-C Model C imposes the following, correctly specified, overidentifying restrictions on α and β:

$$\alpha' = (U_{r,r} : R_{0,r}), \qquad \beta' = (R_{0,r} : R_{2,r} : U_{r,1}). \tag{12}$$

Specification (12) imposes $2r(r-1)$ restrictions on α and β. $r(r-1)$ of them would be enough to obtain just-identification, therefore $r(r-1)$ are over-identifying.

6. Formula I(2) Circuits

This section introduces Formula I(2) circuits, following a similar approach to Formula I(1).

6.1. I(2) DGPs

The I(2) DGP class is indexed by the scalars (p, T, ω, ρ_1); the data $X^{(i)}_{1:T}$ is generated as follows:

$$\begin{cases} \Delta^2 X^{(i)}_{1,t} = \varepsilon^{(i)}_{1,t} \\ \Delta X^{(i)}_{2,t} = \rho_1 \Delta X^{(i)}_{2,t-1} + \varepsilon^{(i)}_{2,t} \\ X^{(i)}_{3,t} = \omega X^{(i)}_{3,t-1} + \Delta X^{(i)}_{1,t-1} + \varepsilon^{(i)}_{3,t} \end{cases} \qquad \varepsilon^{(i)}_t = \begin{pmatrix} \varepsilon^{(i)}_{1,t} \\ \varepsilon^{(i)}_{2,t} \\ \varepsilon^{(i)}_{3,t} \end{pmatrix} \sim \text{i.i.d. } N(0, I_p) \tag{13}$$

where $X_0^{(i)} = X_{-1}^{(i)} = 0_p$, $X_t^{(i)} = (X_{1,t}^{(i)\prime} : X_{2,t}^{(i)\prime} : X_{3,t}^{(i)\prime})'$, $t = 1, ..., T$, $i = 1, ..., N$, and $\varepsilon_{j,t}^{(i)}$ is $p/3 \times 1$. As in the I(1) case, all possible combinations are considered of the following indices and coefficients:

$$p \in \{6, 12\}; \qquad T \in \{100, 1000\}; \qquad \omega \in \{0, 0.9\}; \qquad \rho_1 \in \{0, 0.9\}.$$

The DGPs can be written as follows, see (4):

$$\Delta^2 X_t = \begin{pmatrix} 0_{2r,r} \\ I_r \end{pmatrix} \begin{pmatrix} 0_{r,2r} & (\omega - 1) I_r \end{pmatrix} X_{t-1} + \begin{pmatrix} 0_r & 0_r & 0_r \\ 0_r & (\rho_1 - 1) I_r & 0_r \\ I_r & 0_r & -I_r \end{pmatrix} \Delta X_{t-1} + \epsilon_t,$$

with $\mu_0 = \mu_1 = 0$. Note that in these DGPs,

- $X_{1,t}$ is a pure cumulated random walk, and hence I(2);
- $X_{2,t}$ is I(1), and does not cointegrate with any other variable in X_t. Moreover, $X_{2,t}$ is a pure random walk when $\rho_1 = 0$, and it is I(1) – near I(2) when $\rho_1 = 0.9$; therefore, as in the I(1) case, the parameter ρ_1 is interpreted as a 'near I(2)-ness' coefficient.
- $X_{3,t}$ is the block of variables that reacts to the multi-cointegration relations, which are given by $(\omega - 1) X_{3,t} + \Delta X_{1,t} - \Delta X_{3,t}$. These relations can be read off as the last block in the equilibrium correction formulation in the last display. When $\omega = 0$ one has that the levels $X_{3,t}$ and differences $\Delta X_{1,t}$, $\Delta X_{3,t}$ have the same weight (apart from the sign) in the multi-cointegration relations; when $\omega = 0.9$ the weight of the levels $1 - \omega = 0.1$ is smaller than the ones of the first differences. Hence ω can be interpreted as the 'relative weight of first differences in the multi-cointegrating relation'.

One can see that in this case:

$$\alpha_\perp = \beta_\perp^\star = \begin{pmatrix} I_r & 0 \\ 0 & I_r \\ 0 & 0 \end{pmatrix},$$

so for the I(2) rank condition:

$$\alpha_\perp' \Gamma \beta_\perp^\star = \begin{pmatrix} 0 & 0 \\ 0 & (\rho_1 - 1) I_r \end{pmatrix} = \begin{pmatrix} 0_r \\ (\rho_1 - 1) I_r \end{pmatrix} \begin{pmatrix} 0_r & I_r \end{pmatrix} = \varphi \eta^{\star\prime}.$$

To create the Monte Carlo dataset $X_{1:T}^{(i)}$, each team has to use the DGP (13) with relevant values of (p, T, ω, ρ_1), together with the drawings of ε as determined by the race organisers. Details are in the Appendix A.

6.2. I(2) Statistical Models

Using the generated data $X_{1:T}^{(i)}$ as a realization for $X_{1:T}$, the I(2) model $\mathcal{M}(r, s)$ in (4) has to be estimated on each lap $i = 1, ..., N$. The estimation sample starts at $t = k + 1$, so uses $T - k$ observations. Two alternative values for the lag k are used, namely $k \in \{2, 5\}$.

An I(2) analysis usually starts with a procedure to determine the rank indices r, s. This requires estimating the $\mathcal{M}(r, s)$ model under all combinations of (r, s), and computing all LR test statistics. Usually, a table is produced with r along the rows and $s_2 = p - r - s$ along the columns.

In the I(2) model $\mathcal{M}(r, s)$, the MLE does not reduce to RRR or OLS except when:

(i) $r = 0$, corresponding to an I(1) model for ΔX_t, or
(ii) $p - r - s = 0$, corresponding to I(1) models for X_t, or
(iii) $r = p$, corresponding to an unrestricted VAR for X_t.

All restricted I(2) circuits use the correct rank indices $r = s = p/3$. Restrictions are expressed using the matrix structures (8) and (9). In addition to restrictions on β and α in (4), there are circuits with restrictions on τ, which is a basis of the space spanned by $(\beta : \bar{\beta}_{\perp}\eta)$. Under DGP (13), the correctly specified τ is any matrix of the type

$$\tau = \begin{pmatrix} 0_r & 0_r \\ 0_r & I_r \\ I_r & 0_r \\ 0_{1,r} & 0_{1,r} \end{pmatrix} A$$

with $r = s = p/3$ and A any full rank $(r+s) \times (r+s)$ matrix. Recall that 0_r indicates a square matrix of zeros of dimension r; the $0_{1,r}$ vectors are added in the last row to account from the presence of the trend in I(2) model (4).

Unrestricted I(2) models are estimated for

$$1 \le r \le p-1, \qquad 0 \le s \le p-r-1.$$

The number of models satisfying these inequalities is $p(p-1)/2$. Obviously, some of these models are correctly specified, some are mis-specified.

Restriction I(2)-A Model A is estimated with $r = s = p/3$ under the following overidentifying restrictions on β

$$\beta' = (R_{0,r} : U_{r,r} : I_r : U_{r,1}). \tag{14}$$

This imposes $r\,(r-1)$ overidentifying restrictions on β. These restrictions are correctly specified.

Restriction I(2)-B The following overidentifying restrictions on β are mis-specified:

$$\beta' = (R_{1,r} : U_{r,r} : I_r : U_{r,1}). \tag{15}$$

This imposes $r\,(r-1)$ overidentifying restrictions on β, where $r = s = p/3$.

Restriction I(2)-C Overidentifying restrictions on α and β are used in estimation with $r = s = p/3$:

$$\alpha' = (U_{r,2r} : R_{0,r}), \qquad \beta' = (R_{0,r} : U_{r,r} : R_{2,r} : U_{r,1}). \tag{16}$$

Specification (16) imposes $2r\,(r-1)$ correctly specified restrictions on α and β; $r\,(r-1)$ of them would be enough to just reach identification of α and β, and hence $r\,(r-1)$ restrictions are overidentifying.

Restriction I(2)-D Model D has $r = s = p/3$ and $2r(r-1)$ correctly specified overidentifying restrictions on τ of the type:

$$\tau' = \begin{pmatrix} R_{0,r} & I_r & 0_{r,r} & U_{r,1} \\ R_{0,r} & 0_{r,r} & I_r & U_{r,1} \end{pmatrix}. \tag{17}$$

This imposes $2r\,(r-1)$ overidentifying restrictions on τ.

Restriction I(2)-E The following $2(r-1) + 2\,(s-1)$ mis-specified overidentifying restrictions on τ are imposed in estimation with $r = s = p/3$:

$$\tau' = \begin{pmatrix} R_{1,r} & I_r & 0_{r,r} & U_{r,1} \\ R_{1,r} & 0_{r,r} & I_r & U_{r,1} \end{pmatrix}. \tag{18}$$

7. Test Drive on Formula I(1) Circuits

To illustrate the type of information one can obtain by participating in the Formula I(1) circuits, this Section illustrates a 'test drive' for four algorithms, i.e., teams. The results of these teams also provide a benchmark for other teams willing to participate at a later stage.

Four teams participated in the first Formula I(1) races:

- Team 1: the switching algorithm proposed in Boswijk and Doornik (2004) as implemented in Mosconi and Paruolo (2016) that alternates maximization between β and α. The algorithm is initialized using the unrestricted estimates obtained by RRR. Normalizations are not maintained during optimization, but applied after convergence. The algorithm was implemented in RATS version 9.10.
- Team 2: CATS3 'alpha-beta switching' algorithm as described in Doornik (2017b, §2.2) using the *LBeta* acceleration procedure. CATS3 is an Ox 7 (Doornik (2013)) class for estimation of I(1) and I(2) models, including bootstrapping.
- Team 3: CATS3 'alpha-beta hybrid' algorithm is an enhanced version of alpha-beta switching:

  1. Using standard starting values, as well as twenty randomized starting values, then
  2. alpha-beta switching, followed by
  3. BFGS iteration for a maximum of 200 iterations, followed by
  4. alpha-beta switching.

  This offers some protection against false convergence, because BFGS is based on first derivatives combined with an approximation to the inverse Hessian.

  More important is the randomized search for better starting values as perturbations of the default starting values. Twenty versions of starting values are created this way, and each is followed for ten iterations. Then half are discarded, and they are merged with (almost) identical ones; this is then run for another ten iterations. This is repeated until a single one is left. The iterations used in this start-up process are included in the iteration count.
- Team 4: PcGive algorithm, see Doornik and Hendry (2013, §12.9). This algorithm allows for nonlinear restrictions on α and β, based on switching between the two after a Gauss-Newton warm-up. This is implemented in Ox, Doornik (2013). The iteration count for Team 4 cannot be extracted.

The Formula I(1) circuits are fully described by four features related to the DGP ($p = \{6, 12\}$, $T = \{100, 1000\}, \rho_0 = \{0, 0.9\}, \rho_1 = \{0, 0.9\}$), and two features related to the statistical model: the lag length $k = \{2, 5\}$ and the type of restrictions A, B or C. There are 16 DGPs and 6 model specifications, making a total of 96 circuits.

In the circuits with $T = 1000$, there is not much difference between $k = 2$ and $k = 5$, so the presentation is limited to only one of these values. Combining a long lag length with a small sample size is more problematic. Onatski and Uhlig (2012) consider that situation. They find that the roots of the characteristic polynomial of the VAR tend to a uniform distribution on the unit circle when $\log(T)/k$ and k^3/T tend to zero.

Before analyzing the Formula I(1) races, the tests for cointegration rank are used as 'qualifying races'; this only requires RRR. The qualifying races for Formula I(1) parallel the ones for Formula I(2), reported later. The overall results for the qualifying races show that:

(i) Even when MLE is performed with RRR, inference on the cointegration rank is not easy (not even at $T = 1000$).
(ii) Large VAR dimension, lag length, near-I(2) ness, weak mean reversion are all complicating factors for the use of asymptotic results.

In more detail, Table 1 records the acceptance frequency at 5% significance level of the trace test, using p-values from the Gamma approximation of (Doornik 1998); the null is that the rank is less or equal to r against the alternative of unrestricted rank up to p, where the true rank equals $p/2$. For $T = 1000$ and $p = 6$, the tests behave as expected. When $p = 12$, they tend to favour lower rank values for slow mean-reversion and higher ranks for near-I(2) behaviour.

The results for $T = 100$ are more problematic. When $p = 12$, a lag length of five is excessive relative to the sample size, and leads to overfitting. This is shown in the selection of a too-large rank with frequency close to 1. A lag length of 2 gives opposite results, where a too low rank tends to be selected away from the near-I(2) cases, and a too high rank is chosen in the near-I(2) cases. In the remainder only $k = 2$ is considered, as this already illustrates an interesting range of results.

Table 1. Formula I(1). Acceptance frequencies at 5% significance level of LR test for rank r against rank p. – indicates exactly zero; other entries rounded to two decimal digits. Bold entries correspond to the true rank $p/2$.

k	T	p	ρ_0, ρ_1	$r = 0$	1	2	3	4	5
2	100	6	0.0, 0.0	–	–	0.20	**0.94**	1.00	1.00
2	100	6	0.0, 0.9	–	–	0.01	**0.57**	0.91	0.99
2	100	6	0.9, 0.0	0.81	0.98	1.00	**1.00**	1.00	1.00
2	100	6	0.9, 0.9	0.18	0.52	0.82	**0.94**	0.99	1.00
5	100	6	0.0, 0.0	0.08	0.41	0.81	**0.96**	1.00	1.00
5	100	6	0.0, 0.9	–	0.03	0.19	**0.52**	0.84	0.97
5	100	6	0.9, 0.0	0.22	0.68	0.92	**0.98**	1.00	1.00
5	100	6	0.9, 0.9	–	0.04	0.23	**0.54**	0.82	0.96
2	1000	6	0.0, 0.0	–	–	–	**0.94**	0.99	1.00
2	1000	6	0.0, 0.9	–	–	–	**0.92**	0.99	1.00
2	1000	6	0.9, 0.0	–	–	0.04	**0.95**	1.00	1.00
2	1000	6	0.9, 0.9	–	–	0.02	**0.93**	0.99	1.00
5	1000	6	0.0, 0.0	–	–	–	**0.94**	1.00	1.00
5	1000	6	0.0, 0.9	–	–	–	**0.92**	0.99	1.00
5	1000	6	0.9, 0.0	–	–	0.13	**0.95**	1.00	1.00
5	1000	6	0.9, 0.9	–	–	0.08	**0.93**	0.99	1.00

k	T	p	ρ_0, ρ_1	$r = 0$	1	2	3	4	5	6	7	8	9	10	11
2	100	12	0.0, 0.0	–	–	0.00	0.06	0.31	0.74	**0.94**	0.98	1.00	1.00	1.00	1.00
2	100	12	0.0, 0.9	–	–	–	–	–	–	**0.01**	0.06	0.19	0.40	0.65	0.90
2	100	12	0.9, 0.0	0.11	0.48	0.81	0.94	0.98	1.00	**1.00**	1.00	1.00	1.00	1.00	1.00
2	100	12	0.9, 0.9	–	–	–	–	0.00	0.02	**0.05**	0.13	0.27	0.42	0.62	0.87
5	100	12	0.0, 0.0	–	–	–	–	0.01	0.05	**0.21**	0.47	0.74	0.90	0.97	0.99
5	100	12	0.0, 0.9	–	–	–	–	–	–	–	–	0.00	0.01	0.06	0.39
5	100	12	0.9, 0.0	–	–	–	–	–	–	**0.00**	0.01	0.05	0.21	0.50	0.82
5	100	12	0.9, 0.9	–	–	–	–	–	–	–	–	–	–	–	0.06
2	1000	12	0.0, 0.0	–	–	–	–	–	–	**0.94**	0.99	1.00	1.00	1.00	1.00
2	1000	12	0.0, 0.9	–	–	–	–	–	–	**0.77**	0.97	0.99	1.00	1.00	1.00
2	1000	12	0.9, 0.0	–	–	0.00	0.01	0.16	0.71	**0.98**	1.00	1.00	1.00	1.00	1.00
2	1000	12	0.9, 0.9	–	–	–	0.00	0.02	0.36	**0.88**	0.98	1.00	1.00	1.00	1.00
5	1000	12	0.0, 0.0	–	–	–	–	–	–	**0.94**	0.99	1.00	1.00	1.00	1.00
5	1000	12	0.0, 0.9	–	–	–	–	–	–	**0.72**	0.96	0.99	1.00	1.00	1.00
5	1000	12	0.9, 0.0	–	–	0.01	0.08	0.39	0.84	**0.98**	1.00	1.00	1.00	1.00	1.00
5	1000	12	0.9, 0.9	–	–	–	0.00	0.11	0.51	**0.87**	0.98	1.00	1.00	1.00	1.00

Table 2 presents the Formula I(1) results for the four teams. For each team, the table reports the convergence quality (SC, WC, DC, for strong, weak, and distant convergence) as percentage of laps, followed by the percentage of laps that failed (FC), the average error distance (AD) and the average iteration count for converged laps only (IT). Team 4 does not report the iteration count. The last two columns are averages over all teams and laps. NOR is the indicator of average number of optima reported, where unity means that in all laps all teams have reported the same maximum.

Table 2. Formula I(1). Selected circuits for 1000 laps. $k = 2$ in all cases. '-' means exactly zero, the other figures are percentages rounded to two decimals and multiplied by 100.

			Team 1						Team 2						Team 3						Team 4						All
T	p	ρ_0, ρ_1	SC	WC	DC	FC	AD	IT	SC	WC	DC	FC	AD	IT	SC	WC	DC	FC	AD	IT	SC	WC	DC	FC	AD	IT	NOR
			Restriction I(1)-A (correctly specified)																								
100	6	0.0,0.0	100	-	-	-	-	16	100	-	-	-	-	4	100	-	-	-	-	4	100	-	-	-	-	-	1
100	6	0.0,0.9	100	-	-	-	-	19	100	-	-	-	-	4	100	-	-	-	-	5	100	-	-	-	-	-	1
100	6	0.9,0.0	92	0	3	5	1	77	95	0	5	-	2	15	96	0	4	-	1	35	96	0	3	1	2	-	1.08
100	12	0.0,0.0	100	-	-	0	-	40	100	-	0	-	3	8	100	-	0	-	3	13	100	-	0	-	2	-	1.00
100	12	0.0,0.9	97	-	2	1	2	74	97	-	3	-	2	15	99	-	1	-	2	50	97	0	2	1	4	-	1.03
100	12	0.9,0.0	72	-	13	15	3	263	77	2	21	-	3	61	85	2	13	-	2	115	77	3	14	7	3	-	1.36
1000	6	0.0,0.0	100	-	-	-	-	6	100	-	-	-	-	1	100	-	-	-	-	2	100	-	-	-	-	-	1
1000	6	0.0,0.9	100	-	-	-	-	6	100	-	-	-	-	1	100	-	-	-	-	2	100	-	-	-	-	-	1
1000	6	0.9,0.0	100	-	-	-	-	11	100	-	-	-	-	3	100	-	-	-	-	4	100	-	-	-	-	-	1
1000	12	0.0,0.0	100	-	-	-	-	7	100	-	-	-	-	2	100	-	-	-	-	3	100	-	-	-	-	-	1
1000	12	0.0,0.9	100	-	-	-	-	7	100	-	-	-	-	2	100	-	-	-	-	3	100	-	-	-	-	-	1
1000	12	0.9,0.0	100	-	-	0	-	20	100	-	-	-	-	5	100	-	-	-	-	5	100	-	-	-	-	-	1
			Restriction I(1)-B (mis-specified)																								
100	6	0.0,0.0	82	-	4	14	2	227	91	1	8	-	5	32	96	1	3	-	4	145	74	0	4	22	2	-	1.12
100	6	0.0,0.9	69	-	8	23	4	336	72	1	28	-	10	84	95	1	4	-	5	225	70	-	8	23	3	-	1.36
100	6	0.9,0.0	81	-	5	13	1	350	81	1	18	-	2	33	86	1	13	-	2	110	71	2	9	19	3	-	1.24
100	12	0.0,0.0	14	-	7	79	3	1839	25	5	69	-	5	790	56	3	40	-	3	1456	10	7	13	70	4	-	1.93
100	12	0.0,0.9	2	-	4	95	9	2286	18	8	73	1	8	1428	66	3	31	-	4	2683	3	2	4	91	5	-	1.89
100	12	0.9,0.0	23	0	10	67	2	2034	28	4	68	-	4	589	45	3	52	-	2	977	10	13	19	57	2	-	1.89
1000	6	0.0,0.0	70	-	2	28	7	546	90	2	8	-	51	32	99	0	1	-	39	136	75	3	2	21	3	-	1.10
1000	6	0.0,0.9	68	0	4	28	41	703	69	1	30	-	163	68	96	1	3	-	127	150	77	0	2	21	102	-	1.35
1000	6	0.9,0.0	85	-	4	11	3	191	93	1	6	-	6	20	96	1	4	-	2	117	76	1	3	21	2	-	1.08
1000	12	0.0,0.0	12	-	10	78	48	1974	18	4	78	1	78	1663	62	3	35	-	104	2434	11	1	3	85	80	-	2.08
1000	12	0.0,0.9	3	-	22	76	79	2542	11	3	80	6	110	1801	66	1	32	2	94	4709	6	-	1	93	62	-	2.18
1000	12	0.9,0.0	22	0	9	68	3	1563	25	6	69	-	5	600	48	4	48	-	4	1177	15	7	14	64	4	-	1.95
			Restriction I(1)-C (correctly specified)																								
100	6	0.0,0.0	99	-	0	0	2	17	100	-	0	-	2	8	100	-	0	-	2	73	94	0	3	3	6	-	1.03
100	6	0.0,0.9	99	-	1	0	2	29	99	-	1	-	2	9	99	-	1	-	1	100	92	-	4	4	5	-	1.05
100	6	0.9,0.0	51	0	15	34	1	396	78	2	20	-	1	55	87	2	10	-	1	182	60	1	15	25	1	-	1.38
100	12	0.0,0.0	65	0	21	15	4	268	68	2	30	-	4	70	71	2	27	-	4	202	59	5	9	28	4	-	1.22
100	12	0.0,0.9	49	-	23	28	6	515	59	3	38	-	5	146	68	3	29	-	5	379	43	9	13	35	6	-	1.35
100	12	0.9,0.0	9	-	13	78	5	2068	38	7	54	0	3	452	63	5	32	-	2	826	16	7	17	60	3	-	1.80
1000	6	0.0,0.0	100	-	-	-	-	6	100	-	-	-	-	4	100	-	-	-	-	89	100	-	-	0	-	-	1
1000	6	0.0,0.9	100	-	-	-	-	6	100	-	-	-	-	4	100	-	-	-	-	107	100	-	-	-	-	-	1
1000	6	0.9,0.0	100	-	-	-	-	11	100	-	-	-	-	6	100	-	-	-	-	30	98	-	1	2	12	-	1.01
1000	12	0.0,0.0	100	-	-	-	-	7	100	-	-	-	-	4	100	-	-	-	-	114	98	-	-	2	-	-	1
1000	12	0.0,0.9	100	-	-	-	-	7	100	-	-	-	-	5	100	-	-	-	-	131	98	-	0	2	160	-	1.00
1000	12	0.9,0.0	95	-	4	1	3	20	95	0	5	-	2	10	95	0	5	-	2	55	72	-	9	19	6	-	1.12

Turning attention to some specific circuits, consider I(1)-A, which has valid overidentifying restrictions on β. For a large enough sample, $T = 1000$, all teams finish equally and quickly. This suggests that any estimation problem for $T = 100$ is a small sample issue.

Consider now the circuits with $p = 6$, $\rho_0 = 0.9$, $\rho_1 = 0$, i.e., the third and ninth row of results in Table 2, panel 1. Figure 1 plots three densities: the empirical densities (kernel density estimates) of the likelihood ratio test $LR^{\star}_{c,i} := 2(\ell^u_{c,i} - \ell^{\star}_{c,i})$ for $T = 100, 1000$, where $\ell^u_{c,i}$ is the maximized likelihood under the cointegration rank restriction only, along with the $\chi^2\,(6)$ reference asymptotic distribution. Notice that when $T = 100$ the empirical distribution is very different from the asymptotic one: using the asymptotic 95th percentile of the asymptotic distribution as critical value would lead to severe over-rejection (more than 70%). Finite sample corrections would therefore be very important. Notice that even when $T = 1000$, although the distribution approaches the asymptotic one, the difference is still substantial (the rejection rate is about 10%).

To gain some understanding of the implications of 'distant convergence', for $T = 100$ all laps where any of the teams obtained a distant maximum were pooled, obtaining pairs $\left\{(\ell^{\star}_{c,i}, \ell_{a,c,i}) : DC_{a,c,i} = 1\right\}_{a \in \mathcal{A}_c, i=1:N}$. Figure 1 plots in blue the cdf of the LR test based on the overall maximum, $LR^{\star}_{c,i}$, as the left endpoint of the horizontal lines; the right endpoint represents the LR test based on the distant maximum, i.e., $LR_{a,c,i} = 2(\ell^u_{c,i} - \ell_{a,c,i})$. Considering the $\chi^2(6)$, distant convergence has almost no practical implications, since the inappropriate asymptotic distribution would lead to over-rejection anyway. Conversely, relative to the empirical density, in several cases one would (correctly) accept using $LR^{\star}_{c,i}$, and (wrongly) reject using $LR_{a,c,i}$). Distant convergence has therefore implications for hypothesis testing, at least if one takes finite sample problems into account.

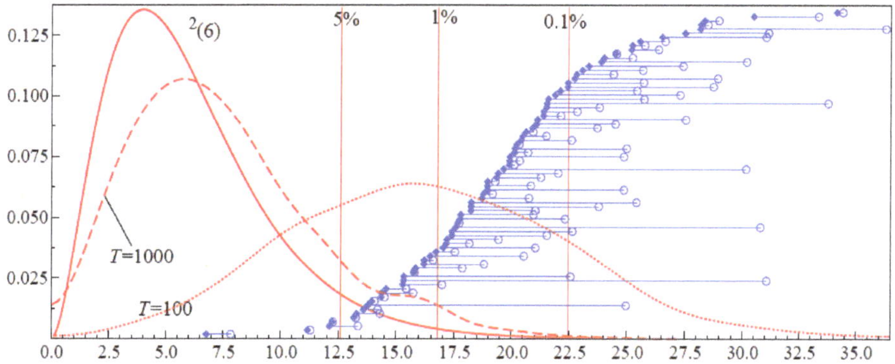

Figure 1. Formula I(1): I(1)-A, $p = 6$, $\rho_0 = 0.9$, $\rho_1 = 0$ circuits. Red: pdfs (on the left scale): kernel-estimate pdfs of $2(\ell^u_{c,i} - \ell^{\star}_{c,i})$ for $T = 100$ and $T = 1000$ based on 1000 laps, along with the asymptotic $\chi^2(6)$. Blue: empirical cdf of $2(\ell^u_{c,i} - \ell^{\star}_{c,i})$ for $T = 100$, considering only laps and algorithms where distant convergence has been reported. The blue filled diamond denotes the LR calculated using the overall maximum $2(\ell^u_{c,i} - \ell^{\star}_{c,i})$, the empty circle the LR calculated using the distant maximum $2(\ell^u_{c,i} - \ell_{a,c,i})$.

Consider now the mis-specified restrictions I(1)-B. Table 2 clearly shows that, whichever the DGP, maximizing the likelihood under mis-specified restrictions induces optimization problems. The number of iterations is, for all teams, much higher than under restrictions I(1)-A, and it does not decrease even when $T = 1000$. Failure to converge (FC) becomes a serious problem for teams 1 and 4, whereas teams 2 and 3 do not suffer this problem, but have a much higher percentage of distant convergence (DC). Whether distant convergence is a nuisance or an advantage in this case is however debatable: since the hypothesis is false, rejecting is correct, and therefore distant convergence increases the power of the test (see below).

Figure 2, in analogy with Figure 1, illustrates the challenging 'weak mean reverting' circuits with $p = 6, \rho_0 = 0.9, \rho_1 = 0$, i.e., the third and ninth row of results in Table 2, panel 3. The asymptotic distribution of the LR test is $\chi^2(4)$, whose 95th percentile is 9.48. Using this as a critical value, $LR^{\star}_{c,i} = 2(\ell^u_{c,i} - \ell^{\star}_{c,i})$ would reject about 70% of the times when $T = 100$, and 100% of the times when $T = 1000$. The power seems reasonably good also in small samples, but one needs to keep in mind that, as illustrated when discussing Figure 1, the asymptotic distribution is very inappropriate here.[12]

Figure 2 also illustrates the impact of distant convergence. Using $LR_{a,c,i} = 2(\ell^u_{c,i} - \ell_{a,c,i})$ instead of $LR^{\star}_{c,i} = 2(\ell^u_{c,i} - \ell^{\star}_{c,i})$ has no practical implication for large samples ($T = 1000$), where the power would be 1 anyway. Conversely, in small samples ($T = 100$) distant convergence has a somewhat beneficial effect on power, increasing the rejection rate. Notice that distant convergence seems to occur more frequently when the null hypothesis is false, like I(1)-B, than when it is true, like I(1)-A; therefore, a tentative optimistic conclusion is that the gain in power due to distant convergence seems to be more relevant than the loss in size.

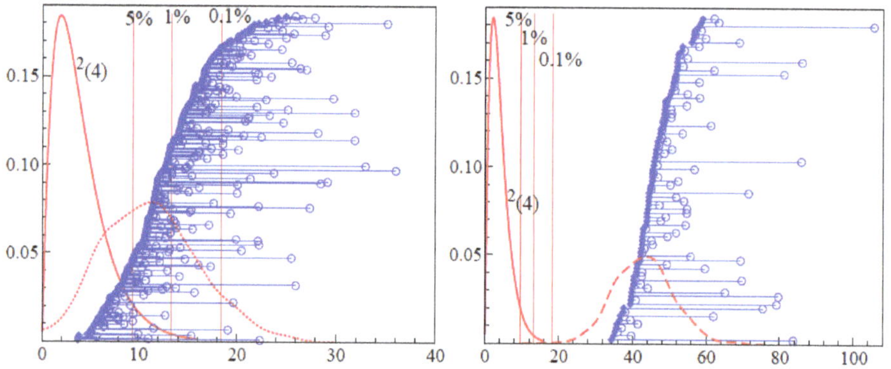

Figure 2. Formula I(1): I(1)-B, $p = 6, \rho_0 = 0.9, \rho_1 = 0$ laps with distant convergence. (**Left**) $T = 100$, (**Right**) $T = 1000$. See caption of Figure 1.

I(1)-C imposes valid over-identifying restrictions on α and β. The first two circuits for I(1)-C are similar to I(1)-A, except that Team 4 has a higher percentage of low and failed convergence. The third circuit shows a more dramatic difference. The effect of the persistent autoregressive effect when $\rho_0 = 0.9$ is to reduce the significance of the α coefficients. As a consequence, some laps yield solutions where some coefficients in α get very large, offset by almost zeros in β. The product Π still looks reasonable, but computation of standard errors of α and β fails (giving huge values), suggesting this may be towards a boundary of the parameter space.

Lap 999 of the third circuit for I(1)-C provides an illustration. Team 1 fails, Teams 2 and 4 have distant convergence. Team 3 has the best results with the following coefficients:

$$\hat{\alpha} = \begin{pmatrix} 0.0369163 & 362.772 & 599.137 \\ -0.00890223 & -17858.0 & -29502.9 \\ 0.0101925 & 11995.8 & 19817.9 \\ -0.0309902 & 0 & 0 \\ 0 & -0.0848045 & 0 \\ 0 & 0 & -0.0545074 \end{pmatrix}, \hat{\beta} = \begin{pmatrix} -4.13543 & 0 & 0 \\ 0 & 1.24557 \cdot 10^{-5} & 0 \\ 0 & 0 & 8.96396 \cdot 10^{-7} \\ 1 & -0.41946 & 0.253898 \\ -6.55434 & 1 & -0.605302 \\ 1.83937 & -1.65209 & 1 \\ 0.664556 & 0.0224937 & -0.013616 \end{pmatrix},$$

[12] Figure 1 shows that, when testing I(1)-A, the asymptotic critical values leads to a 70% rejection rate even if the null hypothesis is true.

where α is numerically close to reduced rank. This model has a loglikelihood that is below the unrestricted I(1) model with rank 2. Because the switching algorithms are really for $\text{rank}(\Pi) \leq r$ rather than $\text{rank}(\Pi) = r$, they occasionally fail or yield unattractive results when α is statistically weakly determined. Team 4 provides more attractive estimates with reasonable standard errors, albeit with a lower loglikelihood.

These characteristics are compatible with several scenarios, including the possibility that in this part of the parameter space the likelihood has a horizontal asymptote. A proper detailed analysis of these and other difficult cases is however beyond the scope of the present paper and it is left for future research.

8. Test Drive on Formula I(2) Circuits

As for Formula I(1), Formula I(2) circuits are illustrated through a test drive for three teams. The following teams participated in the races:

- Team 1: CATS3 'delta switching' algorithm proposed in Doornik (2017b);
- Team 2: CATS3 'triangular switching' algorithm proposed in Doornik (2017b);
- Team 3: CATS3 'tau switching' algorithm proposed in Johansen (1997, §8), implemented as discussed in Doornik (2017b).

As previously illustrated, Formula I(2) is based on 1456 circuits. Although results for all circuits were obtained and stored to serve as benchmark for future comparisons, Formula I(2) circuits and results are too numerous to present in tabular form here; hence only the cases where $p = 6$ and $k = 2$ are shown here.

The first group of circuits are called 'qualifying races', as in Formula I(1). They are designed to:

(i) check the ability of the numerical algorithms to maximize the likelihood of the I(2) model $\mathcal{M}(r,s)$ with no restrictions except for the specification of r and s[13]
(ii) analyze the difficulties of the cointegration ranks tests in spotting the correct r and s in the different DGPs.

Results for task (i) are illustrated in Table 3. For this part of the analysis, only the cases $r = 1, ..., p-1$ and $s = 1, ..., p-r-1$ are considered. This excludes all cases with $r = 0$ and/or $s = p - r$ (i.e., $s_2 = p - r - s = 0$) since in these cases the likelihood of the I(2) model can be maximized exactly by RRR. Preliminary analysis of the results shows that there is relatively little variation for different values of ω and ρ_1. As a consequence, in Table 3 all circuits with the same p, k, T, r, s are analyzed together, irrespective of ω and ρ_1. On the whole, Table 3 shows that the teams perform well. The percentage of 'distant convergence' (DC) is very small, and there are almost no failures. There are a few cases with large 'average distance' (AD), but only when the ranks are smaller than in the DGP.[14] Convergence is quick, usually in about 10 iterations. For $T = 1000$ 'weak convergence' (WC) occurs quite frequently, especially in misspecified (overrestricted) models, and sometimes one observes some large 'average distance' (AD).

[13] This aspect of the qualifying races is specific of Formula I(2), since the qualifying races in Formula I(1) can be reduced to RRR.

[14] In the DGP $r = s = s_2 = p/3 = 2$, and the corresponding row is highlighted in boldface in Table 3. See Noack Jensen (2014) for a discussion of the nesting structure of the I(2) models. As illustrated there, all models listed above $r = s = 2$ are misspecified (i.e., overrestricted), whereas all models listed below $r = s = 2$ are correctly specified, since they nest the DGP. Observe that, for example, $r = 2, s = 2$ is nested in $r = 3, s = 0$.

Table 3. Formula I(2). Qualifying races. Performance for I(2) rank-test table, averaged for different values of ρ_1, ω, with a total of 4000 laps. 0: zero to 2 decimals; '-' means exactly zero, the other figures are percentages rounded to two decimals and multiplied by 100.

r,s,s_2	k	T	p	ρ_0,ρ_1	Team 1						Team 2						Team 3							
					SC	WC	DC	FC	AD	IT	SC	WC	DC	FC	AD	IT	SC	WC	DC	FC	AD	IT	DNF	NOR
1,0,5	2	100	6		99	0	1	–	2	13	99	1	1	0	2	17	99	0	1	–	2	13	–	1.02
1,1,4	2	100	6		100	0	0	–	1	12	100	0	0	–	1	12	99	0	1	–	2	13	–	1.01
1,2,3	2	100	6		100	0	0	–	1	12	100	0	0	–	1	12	99	0	0	–	1	14	–	1.00
1,3,2	2	100	6		100	0	–	–	–	9	100	0	–	–	–	8	100	0	–	–	–	11	–	1
1,4,1	2	100	6		100	0	0	–	0	8	100	–	0	–	0	6	100	–	–	0	–	9	–	1.00
2,0,4	2	100	6		100	0	0	–	1	9	100	–	0	0	1	10	99	–	1	–	1	9	–	1.01
2,1,3	2	100	6		100	–	0	–	0	11	100	–	0	–	1	10	100	0	0	–	1	11	–	1.01
2,2,2	**2**	**100**	**6**		**100**	–	**0**	–	0	**6**	**100**	–	**0**	–	**0**	**5**	**100**	**0**	**0**	–	**0**	**8**	–	**1.00**
2,3,1	2	100	6		100	–	0	–	0	5	100	–	0	–	0	4	100	–	–	–	–	6	–	1.00
3,0,3	2	100	6		99	1	0	–	0	12	98	2	0	0	0	15	99	1	0	–	1	12	–	1.00
3,1,2	2	100	6		100	0	0	–	0	10	100	0	0	–	0	11	100	0	0	–	0	10	–	1.00
3,2,1	2	100	6		100	–	0	–	0	8	99	1	0	–	0	16	100	0	0	–	0	8	–	1.00
4,0,2	2	100	6		100	0	0	–	0	9	99	1	0	0	0	18	99	0	0	–	1	10	–	1.00
4,1,1	2	100	6		100	0	0	–	0	9	96	4	0	–	0	22	100	0	0	–	0	8	–	1.00
5,0,1	2	100	6		100	0	0	–	0	6	97	3	0	–	0	18	100	–	0	–	1	7	–	1.00
1,0,5	2	1000	6		78	22	1	–	21	13	46	54	1	–	16	21	78	21	1	–	23	14	–	1.01
1,1,4	2	1000	6		80	20	–	–	–	8	74	26	0	–	0	10	78	22	–	–	–	10	–	1.00
1,2,3	2	1000	6		83	17	–	–	–	8	77	23	–	–	–	9	79	21	–	–	–	11	–	1
1,3,2	2	1000	6		88	12	–	–	–	5	86	15	–	–	–	4	79	21	–	–	–	9	–	1
1,4,1	2	1000	6		87	13	–	–	–	4	87	13	–	–	–	4	77	23	–	–	–	6	–	1
2,0,4	2	1000	6		99	1	0	–	20	3	98	1	0	–	16	3	99	0	1	–	26	3	–	1.01
2,1,3	2	1000	6		96	4	0	–	1	5	92	8	0	–	1	6	95	5	0	–	3	6	–	1.00
2,2,2	**2**	**1000**	**6**		**100**	–	–	–	–	**1**	**100**	–	–	–	–	**1**	**100**	–	–	–	–	**1**	–	**1**
2,3,1	2	1000	6		100	0	–	–	–	1	100	0	–	–	–	1	100	0	–	–	–	1	–	1
3,0,3	2	1000	6		81	19	0	–	0	10	62	38	0	–	0	16	80	19	0	–	0	10	–	1.00
3,1,2	2	1000	6		91	8	1	–	1	11	91	8	1	–	1	13	99	1	0	–	1	7	–	1.01
3,2,1	2	1000	6		97	3	0	–	0	8	67	33	0	–	0	18	100	0	0	–	0	5	–	1.00
4,0,2	2	1000	6		97	3	0	–	0	9	74	26	0	0	0	26	97	2	0	–	1	10	–	1.01
4,1,1	2	1000	6		98	2	0	–	0	8	48	52	0	0	0	33	100	0	0	–	0	6	–	1.01
5,0,1	2	1000	6		100	0	–	–	–	6	48	52	0	0	0	29	99	0	0	–	0	6	–	1.00

On the whole, likelihood maximization is reasonably accurate, for each circuit and lap; one can then proceed to find the maximum of the maximized likelihoods reported by the three teams. On this basis, the likelihood ratio tests for the cointegration ranks r and s were computed on the overall maximum. As done in Table 1 for the I(1) case, Table 4 records the acceptance frequency at 5% significance level of the LR cointegration test, using p-values from the Gamma approximation of (Doornik 1998); the null is that rank $(\alpha\beta') \leq r$ and rank $(\alpha'_{\perp}(\Gamma : \mu_0)\beta_{\perp}) \leq s$ against the alternative of unrestricted VAR.

Table 4. Formula I(2). Qualifying race. I(2) rank-test table, $p = 6, k = 2, r = 1$. Acceptance frequencies at 5% significance level of LR test for ranks (r, s) against the unrestricted VAR, with $p = 6$, $k = 2$ and $s_2 = p - r - s$. Bold entries correspond to the true ranks $r = s = s_2 = p/3 = 2$. Cases with $r = 0$ and $r = 1$ have been omitted for readability, since the acceptance rate is always zero or very close to zero.

T	ρ_0, ρ_1	$r = 2$					$r = 3$				$r = 4$			$r = 5$	
		$s_2 = 4$	3	2	1	0	$s_2 = 3$	2	1	0	$s_2 = 2$	1	0	$s_2 = 1$	0
100	0.0, 0.0	0.00	0.01	**0.87**	0.69	0.34	0.88	0.97	0.94	0.74	0.98	0.99	0.92	0.99	0.99
100	0.0, 0.9	0.91	0.87	**0.65**	0.32	0.07	0.98	0.93	0.73	0.34	0.98	0.93	0.69	0.98	0.93
100	0.9, 0.0	0.01	0.25	**0.50**	0.28	0.06	0.52	0.76	0.66	0.33	0.83	0.87	0.64	0.92	0.91
100	0.9, 0.9	0.58	0.46	**0.25**	0.07	0.01	0.74	0.62	0.32	0.09	0.82	0.67	0.34	0.87	0.72
1000	0.0, 0.0	0.00	0.00	**0.94**	0.85	0.48	0.94	0.99	0.98	0.83	0.99	1.00	0.95	1.00	1.00
1000	0.0, 0.9	0.00	0.12	**0.93**	0.77	0.40	0.94	0.99	0.97	0.78	0.99	1.00	0.94	1.00	0.99
1000	0.9, 0.0	0.00	0.00	**0.92**	0.77	0.39	0.90	0.98	0.97	0.77	0.99	0.99	0.93	1.00	0.99
1000	0.9, 0.9	0.00	0.07	**0.88**	0.70	0.33	0.91	0.98	0.95	0.71	0.99	0.99	0.91	1.00	0.98

For this aspect of the analysis, all cases $r = 0, ..., p - 1$ and $s = 1, ..., p - r$ are considered. However, Table 4 does not report $r = 0$, since the acceptance rate is exactly zero for all values of s in that case. Also the case $r = 1$ is not reported, because the acceptance rate is always zero for $T = 1000$ and very close to zero for $T = 100$ (less than 0.02, except for $\omega = \rho_1 = 0.9$, where it is 0.06). The model corresponding to the DGP, i.e., $r = s = s_2 = p/3 = 2$, has been highlighted in boldface.

Note that r is almost never underestimated even when $T = 100$, irrespective of the value of ω. This seems to be a major difference with respect to Formula I(1), where r is frequently underestimated when ρ_0 is 0.9. It is important to remark that the interpretation of ρ_0 in Formula I(1) different from the interpretation of ω in Formula I(2), although they both affect the magnitude of the coefficients in Π. In fact ρ_0 may be interpreted as 'weak mean reversion', whereas ω has no implication for the speed of adjustment, but it is rather related to the relative weight of levels and differences in the polynomial cointegration relations; this might be the reason why for $\omega = 0.9$ there is no to underestimation of r.[15] It is, however, surprising that when $\omega = 0.9$ (so that the weight of the levels is reduced to $1 - \omega = 0.1$) one tends to overestimate r, rejecting $r = 2$ in favour of $r = 3$ or even $r = 4$.

The impact of the 'near I(2)' parameter ρ_1 is linked to the form of the DGP in (13): when $\rho_1 = 0.9$ the variables in $\Delta X_{2,t}$ are stationary but slowly mean reverting, so that $X_{2,t}$ is almost I(2). Not surprisingly then, when $\rho_1 = 0.9$ the tests tend to underestimate s (i.e., overestimate $s_2 = p - r - s$) at least when $T = 100$, so that very frequently $r = 2, s = 0$ is selected. When $T = 1000$ the power vs $s = 0$ goes to 1, but one would still select $r = 2, s = 1$ about 10% of the times.

The results on the Formula I(2) circuits with restrictions on the cointegration parameters (in addition to the restrictions on the ranks) are illustrated in Table 5. The cases I(2)-A, I(2)-B and I(2)-C involve only the matrix Π; more specifically, as in Formula I(1), models I(2)-A involve correctly

[15] Formula I(2) circuits may be extended in the future introducing another coefficient in analogy with ρ_0 of Formula I(1). This would amount at replacing the third equation in (13) with

$$\Delta^2 X^{(i)}_{3,t} = (\rho_0 - 1)((\omega - 1)X^{(i)}_{3,t-1} + \Delta X^{(i)}_{1,t-1} - \Delta X^{(i)}_{3,t-1}) + \varepsilon^{(i)}_{3,t}.$$

specified restrictions on β, models I(2)-B contain misspecified restrictions on β, while models I(2)-C contain correctly specified restriction on α and β. All three algorithms seem to perform quite well in maximizing the likelihood of the I(2) model under restrictions on Π only, with Triangular-hybrid beating the others. In particular, under the correctly specified restrictions A and C the likelihood is easily and quickly maximized (especially when $T = 1000$), with almost no case of distant convergence.

Conversely, the misspecified restrictions in model I(2)-B require more iterations and, for the first two teams, induce distant convergence quite frequently. However, as observed when discussing Formula I(1) results, it is important to keep in mind that distant convergence is indeed a problem when the restriction is correctly specified since it leads to over-rejection, whereas for misspecified restrictions it can be seen as beneficial, since it increases the power of the test.

More generally, the analysis of restrictions A, B, C, seems to suggest that estimation of restricted α and β is easier in the I(2) case with respect to the I(1) case. Note however that the comparison is not completely fair, since most of the difficulties in the I(1) case are found when $\rho_0 = 0.9$ (weak mean reversion), and this coefficient does not appear in the current Formula I(2) design.

Consider finally the restrictions I(2)-D and I(2)-E, reported in the last two panels of Table 5. Remember that I(2)-D is a correctly specified model with restrictions on τ, while I(2)-E is a misspecified model with restrictions on τ. Table 5 shows serious difficulties in maximizing the likelihood under restrictions on τ; in both cases (i.e., whether the hypothesis is true or false), the number of iterations is much higher than under restrictions A, B and C and it does not decrease even when $T = 1000$. Failure to converge (FC) becomes a serious problem for triangular switching (and to some extent delta switching), and there is an high percentage of distant convergence (DC) for all three algorithms; Triangular hybrid performs better, having a smaller average distance (AD). Notice that for model I(2)-D (where the null hypothesis is true) distant convergence is more problematic since it leads to over-rejection.

To analyze this problem, as done in Formula I(1), Figure 3 illustrates the impact of distant convergence. It is apparent from the figure that over-rejection is substantial here. Since the 5% critical value of the asymptotic χ^2 (4) distribution is 9.49, the analysis clearly shows several cases where one would (correctly) accept using the overall maximum, and (wrongly) reject using the distant maximum. The striking difference with respect to Formula I(1) is that here the over-rejection due to distant convergence remains even when $T = 1000$.

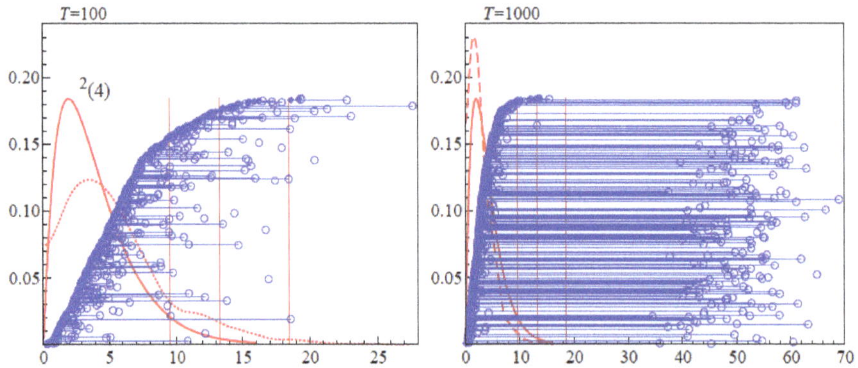

Figure 3. Formula I(2): I(2)-D, $p = 6$, $\omega = 0.9$, $\rho_1 = 0$ laps with distant convergence. (**Left**) $T = 100$, (**Right**) $T = 1000$. Three extreme outliers for $T = 1000$ have been removed for readability. See caption of Figure 1 for more details.

Table 5. Formula I(2). Performance for restrictions I(2)-A, ..., I(2)-E, for 1000 laps. '-' means exactly zero, the other figures are percentages rounded to two decimals and multiplied by 100. Empty cells mean that the team did not take part in the race.

Res	k	T	p	ρ_0, ρ_1	Team 1						Team 2						Team 3						DNF	NOR
					SC	WC	DC	FC	AD	IT	SC	WC	DC	FC	AD	IT	SC	WC	DC	FC	AD	IT		
A	2	100	6	0.0,0.0	100	-	-	-	-	3	100	-	-	-	-	3	100	-	-	-	-	40	-	1
A	2	100	6	0.0,0.9	100	-	-	-	-	5	100	-	-	-	-	5	100	-	-	-	-	49	-	1
A	2	100	6	0.9,0.0	100	-	0	-	2	11	100	-	0	-	2	14	100	-	-	-	-	71	-	1.00
A	2	100	6	0.9,0.9	99	-	1	-	1	14	99	-	1	0	1	17	100	0	-	-	-	75	-	1.01
A	2	1000	6	all	100	-	-	-	-	1	100	-	-	-	-	1	100	-	-	-	-	32	-	1
B	2	100	6	0.0,0.0	73	0	27	-	3	40	69	1	30	0	3	128	98	1	1	-	1	184	-	1.33
B	2	100	6	0.0,0.9	79	1	20	-	3	27	76	2	22	-	3	78	98	2	0	-	6	158	-	1.23
B	2	100	6	0.9,0.0	95	0	5	-	2	19	93	1	6	1	2	35	99	1	0	-	1	134	-	1.06
B	2	100	6	0.9,0.9	96	0	3	-	2	19	95	1	4	0	2	39	99	1	0	-	1	117	-	1.04
B	2	1000	6	0.0,0.0	71	3	26	0	4	100	67	6	27	1	3	184	89	5	6	-	2	252	-	1.41
B	2	1000	6	0.0,0.9	71	3	26	-	3	50	70	3	28	-	4	105	95	2	2	-	0	182	-	1.37
B	2	1000	6	0.9,0.0	74	2	24	-	10	56	71	2	26	1	10	135	97	2	1	-	3	195	-	1.30
B	2	1000	6	0.9,0.9	73	1	26	-	10	33	73	1	27	0	10	85	99	1	-	-	-	160	-	1.28
C	2	100	6	0.0,0.0							100	-	-	-	-	4	100	-	-	-	-	35	-	1
C	2	100	6	0.0,0.9							100	-	-	-	-	7	100	-	-	-	-	39	-	1
C	2	100	6	0.9,0.0							100	-	0	-	2	11	100	-	-	-	-	35	-	1.00
C	2	100	6	0.9,0.9							99	0	1	-	2	11	100	-	0	-	0	32	-	1.01
C	2	1000	6	all							100	-	-	-	-	1	100	-	-	-	-	30	-	1
D	2	100	6	0.0,0.0	74	4	12	10	8	212	61	1	4	34	12	136	90	4	6	0	0	416	-	1.21
D	2	100	6	0.0,0.9	77	4	17	2	19	163	59	2	14	26	14	210	73	8	19	0	6	514	-	1.43
D	2	100	6	0.9,0.0	76	5	12	7	1	174	72	1	3	24	1	134	90	4	5	0	0	390	-	1.17
D	2	100	6	0.9,0.9	72	4	21	3	1	141	59	3	13	25	1	189	79	9	12	-	1	433	-	1.38
D	2	1000	6	0.0,0.0	41	14	9	37	414	263	35	19	4	42	543	296	66	8	17	8	0	708	0.03	1.26
D	2	1000	6	0.0,0.9	66	8	18	7	25	253	48	4	17	32	30	318	63	8	26	3	5	683	0.00	1.54
D	2	1000	6	0.9,0.0	35	22	3	41	31	241	40	29	3	28	12	279	85	7	5	2	0	568	0.01	1.09
D	2	1000	6	0.9,0.9	67	8	18	7	14	230	49	5	15	31	14	258	79	6	14	0	1	522	-	1.44
E	2	100	6	0.0,0.0	46	3	42	10	2	193	36	2	38	24	3	284	79	3	15	3	1	427	0.01	1.76
E	2	100	6	0.0,0.9	61	2	35	2	4	116	57	2	27	14	4	156	85	4	9	2	1	302	0.00	1.59
E	2	100	6	0.9,0.0	75	4	15	6	2	147	64	2	12	22	2	159	84	6	9	1	1	409	0.00	1.27
E	2	100	6	0.9,0.9	73	3	22	1	2	102	61	3	22	14	2	169	81	6	13	-	1	374	-	1.44
E	2	1000	6	0.0,0.0	38	6	35	21	27	358	27	8	39	26	12	450	49	8	39	4	5	665	0.01	1.91
E	2	1000	6	0.0,0.9	49	4	41	7	7	247	33	4	47	16	6	353	52	4	41	3	3	511	0.01	2.11
E	2	1000	6	0.9,0.0	36	7	44	14	13	310	22	6	50	23	13	337	69	5	23	4	5	640	0.00	1.99
E	2	1000	6	0.9,0.9	58	3	37	2	10	130	44	5	43	9	10	235	69	5	26	1	6	374	0.00	1.84

As the final aspect of Formula I(2), consider the misspecified restrictions on τ in model I(2)-E. Figure 4 shows that distant convergence has no practical implication for large samples ($T = 1000$), where the power would be 1 anyway. Conversely, in small samples ($T = 100$) distant convergence slightly increases the rejection rate, which would be quite high in any case.

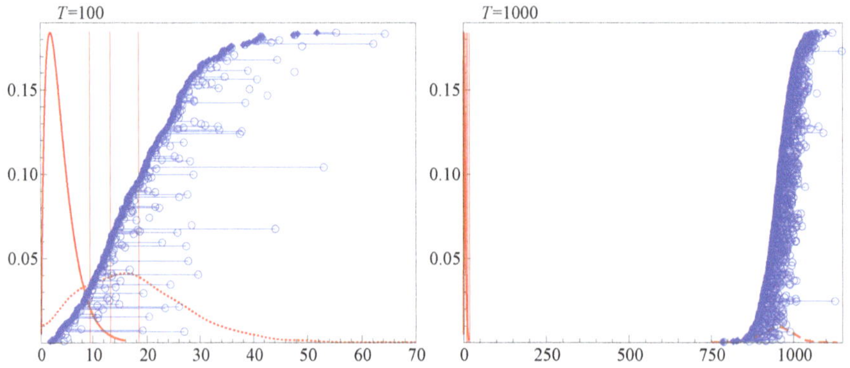

Figure 4. Formula I(2): I(2)-E, $p = 6$, $\omega = 0.9$, $\rho_1 = 0$ laps with distant convergence. (**Left**) $T = 100$, (**Right**) $T = 1000$. See caption of Figure 1 for more details.

Overall, in the setting of Formula I(2), maximizing the likelihood under correctly specified restrictions on α and β seems fast and accurate. Conversely, when correctly specified restrictions on τ are introduced, finding the overall maximum of the likelihood is not easy. Since β is one of the components of τ, one might guess that the problems arise from the complementary directions with respect to β within τ; the issue deserves further exploration.

As in the I(1) case, maximizing the likelihood under misspecified restrictions is difficult; however, the consequence of this difficulty are benign, because they appear to increase the power of the test for the current design of the Formula I(2) races.

9. Conclusions

The test run of the championships shows that there is room for improving algorithms. It demonstrates the strength of this 'collective learning' experiment, where other researchers may try and propose new algorithm to improve on the existing ones. All algorithms win in the end, since each team learns where and how to improve the algorithm design.

Other circuits may be added in the future, as algorithms improve. Races with a similar spirit can be set up in other adjacent fields, like fractional cointegration; the same principles may in fact be applied to any other model classes where maximizing the likelihood needs numerical optimization.

Acknowledgments: Financial support from the Robertson Foundation (Award 9907422) and the Institute for New Economic Thinking (Grant 20029822) is gratefully acknowledged by the first author and from the Italian Ministry of Education, University and Research (MIUR) PRIN Research Project 2010–2011, prot. 2010J3LZEN, 'Forecasting economic and financial time series' by the second author. The authors thank two anonymous referees for useful comments on the first version of the paper.

Author Contributions: The authors contributed equally to the paper.

Conflicts of Interest: The authors declare no conflict of interest.

Appendix A. Practical Requirements for Submission

To facilitate submission and automated processing of results, some conventions are established that submissions to the project must adopt.

Appendix A.1. Innovations

A file containing 12 000 i.i.d. $N(0,1)$ time series of length 1000 is provided (`ERRORS.CSV`) in the companion website. The series are organized column-wise and labelled `eps00001` to `eps12000`. In other words, this file contains the $1000 \times 12\,000$ matrix E. The p-dimensional vector $\varepsilon_t^{(i)}$, $t = 1, ..., T$, is obtained as the transpose of the t-th row of the submatrix $E(1 : T, [i-1]p + 1 : ip)$, assuming indexation starts at element $(1,1)$.

Table A1 provides the first five generated observations for lap 1 of the I(1) and I(2) DGP with $p = 6, \rho_0 = \rho_1 = \omega = 0.9$.

Table A1. The first five observations of the generated data for I(1) and I(2) DGPs with $p = 6, \rho_0 = \rho_1 = \omega = 0.9$. Ten significant digits given; computation uses double precision.

t			**Formula I(1)** $X_t^{(1)\prime}$			
1	0.2548828200	−2.009603960	0.5542620800	0.7913726500	−0.5458015100	−1.349741980
2	0.7806863280	−6.446826254	0.1020649020	−1.468146855	−1.017498239	−2.539647722
3	−0.3490545448	−9.526135279	−0.08454244820	−1.010888930	0.04508386490	−0.3954565398
4	−0.4230090503	−11.98920553	−0.6228956034	−2.179696857	−1.063624342	−1.528447976
5	−0.09820491529	−14.61563411	−1.559382683	−1.481900221	0.05204249257	−0.4856795382
t			**Formula I(2)** $X_t^{(1)\prime}$			
1	0.2548828200	−2.009603960	0.5542620800	0.7913726500	−0.5458015100	−1.349741980
2	0.8061746100	−6.647786650	0.1020649020	−0.6767742050	−0.7626154190	−4.549251682
3	−0.2454976300	−10.37177830	−0.08454244820	−1.687663135	0.8257701929	−6.842282794
4	−0.3543575900	−13.78746208	−0.6228956034	−3.867359991	−1.412678886	−11.05458325
5	−0.07185436000	−17.61281121	−1.559382683	−5.349260212	−0.3709665578	−12.47488507

Appendix A.2. Report File Naming

For each circuit, a team needs to upload an output file on the companion website with either `txt` or `csv` extension. The former is a text file where numbers are separated by a space, while the latter is a csv spreadsheet file using a comma as separator (and without column headers). In all cases there will be one lap per line in the output file.

The output file should be named `FIxDGPyyyMODzzz.csv` (or `FIxDGPyyyMODzzz.txt`), where:

x 1 for Formula I(1), 2 for Formula I(2);
yyy three digits DGP index n, as defined in Table A2;

Table A2. Definition of the DGP index n.

		DGP index $n := 8i_T + 4i_p + 2i_0 + i_1 + 1$	
$i_T = 0$	$T = 100$	$i_0 = 0$	$\rho_0 = 0$ for Formula I(1) or $\omega = 0$ for Formula I(2)
$i_T = 1$	$T = 1000$	$i_0 = 1$	$\rho_0 = 0.9$ for Formula I(1) or $\omega = 0.9$ for Formula I(2)
$i_p = 0$	$p = 6$	$i_1 = 0$	$\rho_1 = 0$
$i_p = 1$	$p = 12$	$i_1 = 1$	$\rho_1 = 0.9$

zzz three digits model index m, as defined in Table A3;

Table A3. Definition of the model index m.

Model index $m := 2i_r + i_k + 1$	
$i_r = 0$	Restriction I(1)-A or I(2)-A
$i_r = 1$	Restriction I(1)-B or I(2)-B
$i_r = 2$	Restriction I(1)-C or I(2)-C
$i_r = 3$	Restriction I(2)-D
$i_r = 4$	Restriction I(2)-E
$i_r = 4 + r + (r + s - 1)(r + s)/2$	$\mathcal{M}(r, s)$ with ordering as in Table A4
$i_k = 0$	$k = 2$
$i_k = 1$	$k = 5$

The ordering of the unrestricted I(2) estimates corresponds to the column vectorization of the upper diagonal of the relevant part of a ranks test table. For instance, in case $p = 6$ the ordering of models is the one in Table A4.

Table A4. Ordering of the models $\mathcal{M}(r, s)$ for case $p = 6$. Entries in the table correspond to the numbering of models, where $s_2 = p - r - s$. The ordering is similar for the case $p = 12$.

$r \backslash s_2$	**5**	**4**	**3**	**2**	**1**
1	1	2	4	7	11
2		3	5	8	12
3			6	9	13
4				10	14
5					15

As an example, results for the Formula I(2) circuit with $n = 13$ ($i_T = 1$, $i_p = 1$, $i_0 = 0$ and $i_1 = 0$) and $m = 6$ ($i_r = 2$, $i_k = 1$), should be stored in a file named `FI2DGP013MOD006.csv` (or `FI2DGP013MOD006.txt`).

Appendix A.3. Report File Content

Formula I(1) files have N lines with $4 + 2(p + 1)r$ numbers, whereas Formula I(2) files have N lines, each with $4 + 2(p + 1)r + p(p + 1)$ numbers. Each line contains the following information:

$$(i : \ell^{u}_{a,c,i} : \ell_{a,c,i} : N_{a,c,i} : S_{a,c,i} : \theta^{R\prime}_{a,c,i}),$$

where:

1. i is the lap number, $i = 1, ..., 1000$;
2. $\ell^{u}_{a,c,i}$ is the unrestricted loglikelihood, reported with at least 8 significant digits:
   - Formula I(1): loglikelihood of the unrestricted I(1) model;
   - Formula I(2) $i_r > 4$: loglikelihood of the VAR;
   - Formula I(2) $i_r \leq 4$: loglikelihood of the unrestricted I(2) model.
3. $\ell_{a,c,i}$ as defined in (2) with at least 8 significant digits;
4. $N_{a,c,i}$, the iteration count;
5. $S_{a,c,i}$ is the integer convergence indicator, 1 for convergence, 0 for no convergence;
6. $\theta^{R\prime}_{a,c,i}$ is part of the coefficient vector, which is for Formula I(1):

$$\theta^{R\prime}_{a,c,i} = \left(\mathrm{vec}(\alpha_{a,c,i})' : \mathrm{vec}(\beta_{a,c,i})'\right).$$

For the Formula I(2) circuits use instead:

$$\theta^{R\prime}_{a,c,i} = \left(\mathrm{vec}(\alpha_{a,c,i})' : \mathrm{vec}(\beta_{a,c,i})' : \mathrm{vec}(\Gamma : \mu_0)'_{a,c,i}\right).$$

Coefficients must be reported exactly in the given order, providing at least 8 significant digits (but 15 digits is recommended). No particular normalization is required.

If the algorithm failed because likelihood evaluation failed (e.g., singular Ω), then $\ell_{a,c,i} = -\infty$ should be reported. The data is processed with Ox, so `.NaN` and `.Inf` are allowed. Because there is no clear convention on writing $-\infty$, any value of -10^{308} or lower is interpreted as $-\infty$.

Table A5 provides the start of the first three lines of three selected output files.

Table A5. Three examples of output files. Beginning of first three lines given.

		FI1DGP001MOD001.csv		
1,	84.7587177451401,	82.2423190842343,	3,	1,-0.187577914295476, ...
2,	30.1177483889851,	28.6953188342152,	5,	1,0.299447436254108, ...
3,	64.5916602781794,	59.9799720330047,	4,	1,-0.0746786280148741, ...
		FI1DGP001MOD001.txt		
1	84.75871775	82.24231908	10	1 -1.8757787e-001 1.6004096e-002 ...
2	30.11774839	28.69531883	20	1 2.9944720e-001 -5.8528461e-002 ...
3	64.59166028	59.97997203	16	1 -7.4678444e-002 -1.5937408e-001 ...
		FI2DGP001MOD001.csv		
1,	76.4430824288192,	76.2400219176979,	10,	1,0.0844284641160844, ...
2,	27.5347594941493,	26.6849814069451,	19,	1,0.0711585542069055, ...
3,	48.709883495749,	48.2827756129209,	24,	1,0.12242477122602, ...

References

Abadir, Karim M., and Paolo Paruolo. 2009. On efficient simulations in dynamic models. In *The Methodology and Practice of Econometrics: A Festschrift in Honour of David F. Hendry*. Edited by Jennifer Castle and Neil Shephard. Oxford: University Press, pp. 270–301.

Anderson, Theodore Wilbur. 1951. Estimating linear restrictions on regression coefficients for multivariate normal distributions. *The Annals of Mathematical Statistics* 22: 327–51. Correction in Annals of Statistics 8, 1980: 1400.

Beiranvand, Vahid, Warren Hare, and Yves Lucet. 2017. Best practices for comparing optimization algorithms. *Optimization and Engineering* 18: 1–34.

Boettiger, Carl. 2015. An introduction to docker for reproducible research. *ACM SIGOPS Operating Systems Review* 49: 71–79.

Boswijk, H. Peter. 2000. Mixed normality and ancillarity in I(2) systems. *Econometric Theory* 16: 878–904.

Boswijk, H. Peter, and Jurgen A. Doornik. 2004. Identifying, estimating and testing restricted cointegrated systems: An overview. *Statistica Neerlandica* 58: 440–65.

Boswijk, H. Peter, and Paolo Paruolo. 2017. Likelihood ratio tests of restrictions on common trends loading matrices in I(2) VAR systems. *Econometrics* 5: 28.

Doornik, Jurgen A. 1998. Approximations to the asymptotic distribution of cointegration tests. *Journal of Economic Surveys* 12: 573–93. Reprinted in Michael McAleer and Les Oxley. 1999. *Practical Issues in Cointegration Analysis*. Oxford: Blackwell Publishers.

Doornik, Jurgen A. 2013. *Object-Oriented Matrix Programming Using Ox*, 7th ed. London: Timberlake Consultants Press.

Doornik, Jurgen A. 2017a. *Accelerated Estimation of Switching Algorithms: The Cointegrated VAR Model and Other Applications*. Working Paper 2017-W05. Oxford: Nuffield College.

Doornik, Jurgen A. 2017b. Maximum likelihood estimation of the I(2) model under linear restrictions. *Econometrics* 5: 19.

Doornik, Jurgen A., and David F. Hendry. 2013. *Modelling Dynamic Systems Using PcGive: Volume II*, 5th ed. London: Timberlake Consultants Press.

Hendry, David F. 1984. Monte Carlo experimentation in econometrics. In *Handbook of Econometrics*. Edited by Zvi Griliches and Michael D. Intriligator. New York: North-Holland, vol. 2, pp. 937–76.

Johansen, Søren. 1988. Statistical Analysis of Cointegration Vectors. *Journal of Economic Dynamics and Control* 12: 231–54.

Johansen, Søren. 1991. Estimation and Hypothesis Testing of Cointegration Vectors in Gaussian Vector Autoregressive Models. *Econometrica* 59: 1551–80.
Johansen, Søren. 1995a. Identifying restrictions of linear equations with applications to simultaneous equations and cointegration. *Journal of Econometrics* 69: 111–32.
Johansen, Søren. 1995b. A statistical analysis of cointegration for I(2) variables. *Econometric Theory* 11: 25–59.
Johansen, Søren. 1997. A likelihood analysis of the I(2) model. *Scandinavian Journal of Statistics* 24: 433–62.
Johansen, Søren, and Katarina Juselius. 1992. Testing structural hypotheses in a multivariate cointegration analysis of the PPP and the UIP for UK. *Journal of Econometrics* 53: 211–44.
Johansen, Søren, and Katarina Juselius. 1994. Identification of the long-run and short-run structure: an application of the ISLM model. *Journal of Econometrics* 63: 7–36.
Mosconi, Rocco, and Paolo Paruolo. 2016. *Cointegration and Error Correction in I(2) Vector Autoregressive Models: Identification, Estimation and Testing*. Mimeo: Politecnico di Milano.
Mosconi, Rocco, and Paolo Paruolo. 2017. Identification conditions in simultaneous systems of cointegrating equations with integrated variables of higher order. *Journal of Econometrics* 198: 271–76.
Noack Jensen, Anders. 2014. Some Mathematical and Computational Results for Vector Error Correction Models. Chapter 1: The Nesting Structure of the Cointegrated Vector Autoregressive Model. Ph.D. Thesis, University of Copenhagen, Department of Economics, Copenhagen.
Onatski, Alexei, and Harald Uhlig. 2012. Unit roots in white noise. *Econometric Theory* 28: 485–508.
Paruolo, Paolo. 2002. On Monte Carlo estimation of relative power. *Econometrics Journal* 5: 65–75.
Paruolo, Paolo. 2005. *Design of Vector Autoregressive Processes for Invariant Statistics*. WP 2005-6. Insubria: University of Insubria, Department of Economics.
Paruolo, Paolo, and Anders Rahbek. 1999. Weak exogeneity in I(2) VAR systems. *Journal of Econometrics* 93: 281–308.
Rahbek, Anders C., Hans Christian Kongsted, and Clara Jørgensen. 1999. Trend-Stationarity in the I(2) Cointegration Model. *Journal of Econometrics* 90: 265–289.

MDPI
St. Alban-Anlage 66
4052 Basel, Switzerland
Tel. +41 61 683 77 34
Fax +41 61 302 89 18
http://www.mdpi.com

Econometrics Editorial Office
E-mail: econometrics@mdpi.com
http://www.mdpi.com/journal/econometrics

www.ingramcontent.com/pod-product-compliance
Lightning Source LLC
Chambersburg PA
CBHW051844210326
41597CB00033B/5768
* 9 7 8 3 0 3 8 4 2 9 5 5 5 *